OFFICIAL REPORT

OF THE

TWENTY- EIGHTH INTERNATIONAL

CHRISTIAN ENDEAVOR CONVENTION

HELD IN THE 71st REGIMENT ARMORY

AND MANY CHURCHES

NEW YORK CITY, N. Y.

JULY 6 - 11, 1921.

First Fruits Press
Wilmore, Kentucky
c2015

First Fruits Press
The Academic Open Press of Asbury Theological Seminary
204 N. Lexington Ave., Wilmore, KY 40390
859-858-2236
first.fruits@asburyseminary.edu
asbury.to/firstfruits

The Story of the New York Convention

The Official Report
of
The Sixth World's and
Twenty-eighth International
Christian Endeavor Convention

Held in the 71st Regiment Armory
and Many Churches

New York City
N. Y.

July 6 to 11, 1921

United Society of Christian Endeavor   Boston, Mass.

THE ABBOTT PRESS, NEW YORK

CONTENTS

ILLUSTRATIONS

WORDS OF APPRECIATION

IN compiling the official report of the Sixth World's and Twenty-Eighth International Christian Endeavor Convention, the compiler is not unmindful of the fact that this report would not have been possible were it not for the splendid assistance rendered by the Editor and Assistant Editors of *The Christian Endeavor World*. Also we are not unmindful of the splendid co-operation we enjoyed on the part of the *New York Evening Post*, the Christian Endeavor field secretaries, and many of those who participated in helping to make this one of the greatest conventions in the history of world-wide Christian Endeavor.

With many simultaneous meetings in different places it is a physical impossibility to get a report of each meeting as full and concise as we would like it to be. However, we feel that the report here rendered gives a true statement of the many meetings held during this wonderful Convention.

Believing that this report will stimulate the work of Christian Endeavor both at home and abroad and that it will in many instances prove a lasting memento of a wonderful occasion, and with a spirit of thankfulness for the opportunity to participate. for all of which we are deeply thankful, this report is respectfully submitted.

A. J. SHARTLE,

Treasurer and Publication Manager.
United Society of Christian Endeavor,

Boston, Mass.

July 6-11, 1921.

6

NEW YORK
1892-1921

By A. J. Shartle.

WE have been to the New York 1921 Convention at least 16,000 strong. We had a great and glorious time in spite of "unusual" weather tempered with humidity sufficient to wilt the enthusiasm, ardor and spirit of any similar number of just humans, but Christian Endeavorers stood the test. We returned home in a spirit that will assure the success of Christian Endeavor Foursquare. Then we began to think things over. How about New York in 1892? We took from the library a report of the 1892 New York Convention and refreshed our memory.

We were now back twenty-nine years looking things over. We noted, comparatively speaking, that then, the thousands gathered in Madison Square Garden for the opening session Thursday afternoon, July 7, 1892, while in 1921 similar thousands gathered in the 71st Regiment Armory at the opening session July 6. They complained of the heat in 1892, and we were equal to the occasion in 1921. New York City in 1892 was slow to recognize the advancing hosts of delegates with fluttering Christian Endeavor badges as a factor above the ordinary, and inquired, "What is this?" were informed, woke up and co-operated magnificently. In 1921 they asked similar questions, only added after seeing some of the delegations in uniform. "Are these firemen?" Again they were informed, woke up, and gave us (newspapers and all) a reception and a brand of co-operation only capable of the largest city in America.

In 1892 the Ohio delegation sang:

> "Ohio,
> We won't go
> To the World's Fair,
> If open on Sunday,
> Or liquor's sold there;
> Ohio."

In 1921 they sang, "We're from Ohio."

In 1892 John Willis Baer, then General Secretary of the United Society, was ill and unable to attend; in 1921 Dr. William Shaw, our former General Secretary and Dr. Daniel A. Poling, Associate President, because of accidents were unable to attend. In 1892 Dr. Clark presided with a gavel made of granite from

7

the cornerstone and black walnut from the original pews of Williston Church; in 1921 he used the same gavel. In 1892 Rev. Charles F. Deems, D.D., pastor of the Church of the Strangers, New York, made the address of welcome, and everybody was happy; in 1921 Commissioner of Immigration, Frederick Wallis, made the address of welcome, and everybody was hilariously happy. In 1892 President Gates of Amherst College responded to the address of welcome; in 1921 General Secretary Gates responded to everybody's welcome. Some of the speakers told good stories in 1892; we noted that some were resurrected in 1921. In 1892 statements were made by friendly critics that Christian Endeavor would soon "die out." After twenty-nine years we still have the same kind of friends predicting our "passing on." Just to illustrate how it is done, I note that in 1892 General Secretary Baer reported 21,080 societies, and this eleven years after the organization of the first society. On July 6, 1921, twenty-nine years later, Secretary Gates reported 80,000 societies, an average increase of 2,029 societies per year for twenty-nine years—and thus we "pass on."

In 1892 they discussed the liquor traffic and its elimination; today we rejoice in the fact that we helped to settle it. In 1892 Rev. H. W. Sherwood brought greetings from New York State; in 1921 Carlton M. Sherwood, Field Secretary, performed a similar act. It was just fine to have the Hon. John Wanamaker at the 1892 Convention and enjoy his remarkable addresses on timely subjects. However, it was an event worth while to have him with us at New York 1921, and enjoy his matchless Christian Endeavor spirit. They introduced the Quiet Hour, the first Junior Rally, and the first Denominational Rallies in 1892, and the success through all these years, and especially the 1921 Convention has proved how wise their decision was.

New York 1892 was a wonderful convention; New York 1921 was a marvellous convention; we point with enthusiasm to both. Both are a lasting credit to Greater New York. Long may it live, and always will Christian Endeavor live because it is born of God.

Officers
United Society of Christian Endeavor

DANIEL A. POLING, LIT D., LL.D.
Associate President

EDWARD P. GATES
General Secretary

ALVIN J. SHARTLE
Treasurer and Publication Manager

REV. FRANCIS E. CLARK, D.D., LL.D.
President

RODERICK A. WALKER
Manager Western Office

REV. STANLEY B. VANDERSALL
Superintendent Alumni Department

REV. ROBERT P. ANDERSON
Editorial Secretary

Chapter I

ANNUAL MEETING OF THE UNITED SOCIETY OF CHRISTIAN ENDEAVOR

THE Annual Meeting of the United Society of Christian Endeavor was held in the New England Room of the Prince George Hotel, New York City, Wednesday, July 6 at 3.00 P. M., President Francis E. Clark presiding. The minutes of the previous meeting were read and approved.

Annual reports were presented by Dr. Clark, A. J. Shartle, Stanley B. Vandersall, Chaplain Ramsden, C. F. Evans, and W. Roy Breg. These reports were accepted and approved.

The following were elected officers and trustees of the United Society of Christian Endeavor:

Officers

President	Rev. Francis E. Clark
Associate President	Daniel A. Poling
Vice-President	Howard B. Grose
Clerk	H. N. Lathrop
Treasurer	A. J. Shartle
Auditor	J. J. Arakelyan

Denominational Trustees
(For four years)

Rev. J. Stanley Durkee, D.D.	Rev. J. T. McCrory, D.D.
Rt. Rev. Samuel Fallows, D.D.	Rev. Rufus W. Miller, D.D.
Bishop J. S. Flipper	Rev. H. F. Shupe, D.D.
Rev. J. H. Garrison, LL.D.	Rev. Egbert W. Smith, D. D.
Prof. James Lewis Howe, Ph.D.	Dr. Elmer Johnson
Rev. Albert W. Jefferson	Rev. H. R. Allen
Bishop L. W. Kyles, D.D.	Rev. James G. Ryder
Rev. Ira Landrith, D.D., LL.D.	Rev. P. O. Ortt

Trustees-at-Large

Rev. R. P. Anderson	A. J. Shartle
Charles H. Jones	Stanley B. Vandersall
Daniel A. Poling	Charles G. Stewart
Edward P. Gates	Clarence Hamilton
	Amos R. Wells

MINUTES OF THE MEETING OF THE BOARD
OF TRUSTEES

The Annual Meeting of the Board of Trustees of the United Society of Christian Endeavor was held in the New England Room of the Prince George Hotel, New York City, Wednesday, July 6, 1921, at 4.00 P. M., President Francis E. Clark in the chair.

The minutes of the last meeting were read and approved.

The following officers, secretaries and superintendents were unanimously elected by ballot:

Officers

General Secretary............EDWARD P. GATES
Publication Manager..........A. J. SHARTLE
Editorial Secretary...........REV. ROBERT P. ANDERSON
Extension Secretary..........REV. IRA LANDRITH, D.D., LL.D.
Southern Secretary...........CHARLES F. EVANS
Southwestern Secretary........W. ROY BREG

Superintendents

Alumni ....REV. STANLEY B. VANDERSALL
Intermediate ....PAUL C. BROWN
Citizenship ....DANIEL A. POLING
Army and Navy.............REV. S. C. RAMSDEN

The following were unanimously elected to serve as an

Executive Committee

Rev. F. E. Clark, D.D., LL.D.	Asa Burgess
Daniel A. Poling	J. J. Arakelyan
A. J. Shartle	Rev. James L. Hill
William Shaw	Rev. Howard B. Grose
Amos R. Wells	Charles H. Jones
Rev. Robert P. Anderson	Rev. F. M. Sheldon
Edward P. Gates	H. N. Lathrop
Stanley B. Vandersall	Clarence Hamilton

It was unanimously voted that the president be requested to express the profound sympathy of the Board of Trustees to Doctor Poling and Doctor Shaw.

Dr. Ira Landrith, Dr. James Lewis Howe, and Dr. Howard B. Grose were appointed by the president as a committee on resolutions.

It was unanimously voted that thanks be extended for the entertainment of the trustees during the Convention.

It was voted to adjourn until five minutes past twelve, Thursday noon, July 7.

Thursday, July 7, 1921

The adjourned meeting of the Board of Trustees was held at 12.05 P. M. in Room 7 of the Seventy-first Regiment Armory. President Francis E. Clark in the chair.

It was unanimously voted to approve the Foursquare Campaign proposed by Dr. Clark for the next two years.

At this point representatives from cities desiring to entertain the 1923 Convention were introduced. Speakers appeared from Des Moines, Iowa, and Portland, Oregon.

An informal vote was taken by ballot on the selection of the next convention city, and it was

VOTED, That the votes should be sealed and opened at the next meeting of the Board. The meeting then adjourned to meet Friday afternoon, July 8, at 4.00 P. M.

Friday, July 8, 1921

The adjourned meeting of the Board of Trustees met in Room 7 of the Seventy-first Regiment Armory at 4.00 P. M. The informal ballot on the selection of the next convention city was opened and counted. It was then unanimously

VOTED, That the 29th International Christian Endeavor Convention be held in Des Moines, Iowa, in 1923.

VOTED, That Dr. Hiram Foulkes, A. E. Cory, Rufus Miller, Fred. L. Ball, A. J. Shartle and E. P. Gates be appointed a committee to secure additional funds for the work of the United Society of Christian Endeavor, with full power to act.

The meeting then adjourned.

E. P. GATES,
General Secretary.

CHAPTER II.

A MEMORABLE OPENING MEETING

71st Regiment Armory, Wednesday Evening, July 6

HAVE you ever been to New York? We have. In fact, we attended the great Christian Endeavor Convention in the 71st Regiment Armory, July 6-11, and what a wonderful time we had. We sat up on the platform the first evening with some other folks that we knew and some that we didn't know, and it was simply wonderful, magnificent! As we looked out over the sea of expectant faces radiant with the spirit of the occasion, we could not help but feel that it was good to be present. That incomparable audience presented a harmony of color, an abundance of enthusiasm, and a spirit of devotion to a cause that will never die, and that can only be found in a great convention like that of the Christian Endeavor. Really, Christian Endeavor had arrived in New York.

It was the opening evening of the Convention and the 71st Regiment Armory was a busy place. It was hello time, hand-shaking time, time to renew old acquaintanceships and form new friendships. Everybody was joyous; everybody was happy; and well supplied with a superabundance of good fellowship. And so they came together thousands strong from the four quarters of this old world, determined to catch every message delivered that it might be carried back home to the less fortunate, there to create new hope, new desire, and new determination to give their best to a noble cause; and so, when Dr. Clark opened the first public session of the Convention. And what a colorful multitude it was! A great red splotch in the body of the hall marked the Iowa delegation, men and women, in bright red blouses and white caps. The Dixie group showed up well with their striking red fezes with the Christian Endeavor monogram and the word "Dixie" in white. Farther over in the hall were a host of Pennsylvanians with red and white caps. Massachusetts had a large crowd in shining red and white, surely far more colorful than ever Pilgrims dressed. And so with delegation after delegation, the blue and white and the yellow and white showing up here and there in competition with the more vigorous red.

Seldom has Christian Endeavor had a better Convention hall; a hall of splendid acoustics, compact, airy, and adapted in every particular for such a gathering as this.

12

THE NEW YORK CONVENTION COMMITTEE

The fronts of the spacious galleries were beautifully draped with red and white bunting, with groups of United States flags, and also, most appropriately, with the flags of many nations.

Behind the platform, above, were beautifully draped United States flags, in the centre of which was a huge Christian Endeavor monogram lighted with alternate blue and white electric bulbs.

At the back of the hall were the literature tables, and at each side were three stalls of the All Nations' Bazaar.

The cheering and the singing of the various delegations subsided as Homer Rodeheaver, song-leader, broke in with his trombone, and, securing quiet, led the great host in a brief prayer for blessing, followed by a rousing song service which began with the familiar "Faith of Our Fathers." And what singing! The great volume of it rose like a mighty flood of sound and turned back its echo from the draped roof far above us.

The arrangements were perfect in every way, as they could not fail to be with such a committee faithful and tirelessly at work. Every committee, be it said with all emphasis, covered itself with deathless glory.

The choir of seven hundred voices, trained under the magnetic leadership of Fred Victor, chairman of the music committee, responded magnificently to every call made upon it; and this throughout the entire Convention.

It was a fitting motto Dr. Clark gave to the Convention in the words of Paul, which the great gathering repeated with one voice, *"We make it our aim, whether present or absent, to be well pleasing unto Him."* Dr. Floyd W. Tomkins, of Philadelphia, led in simple, earnest prayer.

Dr. Clark introduced the officers of the United Society and the editors of *The Christian Endeavor World*. Commissioner Frederick A. Wallis, chairman of the Convention Committee, received a magnificent ovation when Dr. Clark presented him. And not less was the ovation given Miss Julia Arthur when the Commissioner introduced her to recite "The Battle-Hymn of the Republic." The Commissioner said:

I am sure this Convention is to be full of wonderful surprises of God's grace and mercy. It is my privilege to introduce to you one who on account of her beautiful Christian spirit, her great and wonderful dramatic art, her power as a platform speaker, and the wonderful service that she rendered to this government during the war has won her place in the hearts of the American people. She will now recite the "Battle-Hymn of the Republic," and I now refer to Miss Julia Arthur.

How the pictures painted by those lines flashed before every mind as the thrilling voice of the speaker flung out the patriotic message! The whole soul of the speaker was in voice and gesture in this and in the encore, "Hats off! the Flag is passing by." What could Mr. Rodeheaver do but break into "The

Star-spangled Banner," the overflowing auditorium and galleries singing with its whole heart?

Commissioner Wallis introduced Mayor John F. Hylan, of New York City, who gave the address of welcome for the city. In presenting him, Mr. Wallis said:

> The welcome of the Convention in this great city would not be complete without the spoken word of the mayor of this city. The mayor of this city is a Christian gentleman, and he is known for his rugged and immovable honesty; and, if I were speaking to a great political meeting, I would say this, that, if the present mayor of this city should again run for that office, he would sweep the city more completely than he did the first time. It gives me great honor to present to this great Convention the Honorable John F. Hylan, mayor of Greater New York.

He paid a beautiful tribute to Christian Endeavor as an organization which is seeking to perpetuate the stability of Christian civilization. He touched upon the interdenominational and inter-racial character of the movement; and upon the fact that Christian Endeavor aims at liberating our people from material purposes engendered by the World War. He threw the city wide open to the Endeavorers, a friendly city, a city of wonders, the greatest city in the world. Mayor Hylan showed his interest by staying through to the very end of the meeting, when the hands of the clock were pointing to eleven. He spoke as follows:

Chorus, Ladies, and Gentlemen:

I am very glad as mayor to meet so large a gathering of delegates to the Christian Endeavor Convention, coming as you do not only from every State of the Union, but from almost every country of the globe, representative of every color and every race. I bid you all most hearty welcome to this city. In the turmoil and bustle of our active and sometimes self-centred existence we are apt to overlook, or fail to show adequate appreciation of, the potent agencies so quietly, but no less effectively, performing valuable service in the formation of the American character. In this record we must acknowledge the great value of such instrumentalities as the church and organizations which by seeking to make our people better citizens are helping to ensure the stability and perpetuity of our national structure.

It is particularly pleasing to know that the Christian Endeavor Convention is interdenominational in its spiritual advancement, and in its Christian fellowship all are free. We are reminded that there is but one sun in the heavens above, and its life-giving rays extend to the people of all the earth. This is the spirit of equality, the true American spirit, which has permeated our national structure from the very founding of the republic. We are all children of the same heavenly Father.

I believe one of the principal aims of your Convention is to emphasize the religious and spiritual side of our national life. This is fitting and opportune. America has been characterized as a materialistic nation, and New York as the center of materialism. This is an impeachment not sustained by facts. While it may be true in the center of the world's population there are some more interested in making financial gains than in the finer things of life, the mass of people are neither self-centered nor selfish. As a result, we have a city unparalleled in growth and grandeur. From time to time self-seeking and sordid people through newspapers they control attempt to besmirch the fair name of our city, and it is for people to recognize the character of these facts, that they may not be falsely misled. Every thinking citizen knows there is a steady movement for improvement. The death rate of this city is fifty per cent. lower than at the time of the organization of the board of health, and we have a public school system second to none. The new departments are helping to make up for past neglect, and the task we have encountered has been the greatest undertaken by any municipality. New York in its cleanliness and morality as a great city challenges the appreciation and admiration of all, both from abroad and from large cities in the United States. There are people who are determined to discredit those in the public service who are honestly endeavoring to do their duty in working for their city's welfare, and I ask you as visitors to observe conditions in every quarter of the city, and compare with the stories circulated for political purposes. New York is admittedly the healthiest, most intellectual, and richest city in the world, a city you may come to with your families in perfect security.

It is a pleasure as mayor of this great city to welcome the Christian Endeavor Convention to the largest, busiest, and pleasantest city in the world, this city having the best hotels, the greatest variety of wholesome entertainment, incomparable parks, and to make your stay in this world's metropolis both interesting and agreeable.

Dr. Finis Idleman brought a greeting from the churches of the city. He said:

Welcome from the Churches of New York

Members of the Sixth World's Endeavor Convention:

It is both a solemn joy and a high and exalted privilege to bring the greetings and welcome of the churches of New York City to your convention. It is both an inspiration and a challenge. You have been in this city but a few hours, and I dare say it has revealed to you something of its magic. The teeming millions of this great city come from every flag. Within this city are 150,000 Poles, 195,000 Germans, 210,000 Irishmen, 495,000 Russians, 1,700,000 Jews, or 2,000,000 born upon foreign soil; and here you are tonight to help us with this herculean task. Within this city are 750 Jewish synagogues and 1,000 Protestant churches. Our task would seem almost hopeless, and our powers inadequate, so that you can easily understand what your presence in this city means to us. Here your heart will be challenged. The church of God must be equipped and you must be equipped for the leadership, the refining, purifying, and heartening of the metropolitan areas of the great American life. Wishing this Convention the high fulfilment of its exalted purpose, and in the name of the churches of New York I bid you most sincere and cordial welcome.

Commissioner Wallis's welcome in the name of the Convention Committee was a splendidly eloquent and witty effort. The Commissioner, however, hardly needed to put welcome into words, for its welcome was evident in labors abundant. "Our New York, your New York; our avenues, your avenues; our homes, your homes. Our subways suggest the depth of our welcome; our sky-scrapers, the height of our welcome; Wall Street, the wealth of it; Broadway, the longest street in the world, the length and the brightness of it; the seas, the wideness of it; a welcome as far-flung as from Hell Gate to the Golden Gate in the West." This was the spirit of New York's wonderful welcome, and every Endeavorer felt it. He said in part:

I think this committee can best express its welcome by what you see on all sides, and what shall be revealed to you as this great Convention progresses. The very rafters in this great auditorium cry out to you their welcome; the flags wave you welcome; the sky smiles you welcome; the choir sings you welcome; and in these decorations all of the harmony and blending of colors emphasize the consummation and fruition of the committee who labored for your reception. Our New York is your New York; our avenues, your avenues; our homes and churches, your homes and churches; our convention, your cenvention; what is ours is yours; what is ours is Christ's, and what is Christ's is God's. I think this city welcomes you because it loves the pure, the sweet, the lovely, the ambitious, and the Christ-like.

Our subways suggest the depth of our welcome; our skyscrapers, the height of our welcome; Wall Street, the wealth of our welcome; and Broadway, the longest street in the world, suggests the length and brightness of our welcome; the sea that surrounds us suggests the wideness of our welcome.

"There's a wideness in God's mercy
Like the wideness of the sea."

There is a warmth in New York's welcome that extends to all seas, and to the great number who come to us from lands beyond the seas we would extend an especial welcome, a world-wide welcome, which extends from New York's Hell Gate to California's Golden Gate.

I wish all Endeavorers might see New York's Hell Gate. It is easily within the limits of this great city, not very far from this Convention, and it is safe for you to go; and there you will see the greatest single arch in the world, spanning Hell Gate. It was built by the ingenuity of man, and over it pass the commerce and traffic of the world. That is a great engineering achievement; but. Endeavorers, there is a greater bridge than that, a greater span than that. Christian Endeavor spans from here to there over that great impassable gulf which has been fixed, and over which no one can ever return. Nineteen millions of Christian Endeavorers, fifteen millions of gradutes, and four millions of present-day Endeavorers have staked their lives and their all on the blessed assurance, the sweet confidence and redeeming love, of God, who has spanned that great gulf in Jesus Christ our Lord; and our great boast to the world today is that not a single trusting soul in all of Christendom who has ever gone on that great span has ever risked passing over that great chasm and been disappointed. It always leads unto the Eternal City. That, I say, is our great boast today.

Here we are in the great city of New York, coming from all parts of the world, all States. We selfishly want what you can bring to New York in the freshness of your youth, the vigor of your thought, the ambition and aspirations of the youth of a nation. New York wants more of the warm life-blood of youthful enthusiasm and energy that is in this Convention, sweeping out over this great city, sweeping through the avenues of trade through the homes and churches, giving new life and vigor and new food to this great imperial city by the sea; for as goes New York, so goes the rest of our country, so goes the city, so goes the town.

A Portion of the Audience on the Opening Evening

I know there are great elements at work, great destroying elements in our cities. It is so in our cities, all cities of the nation, where Bolshevists, I. W. W.'s, and anarchists are fanning the fire of discontent. It is in our cities that these festering influences are at work among the immigrants, these influences that would trample the law underfoot, and where the hold-up man laughs at conceded authority. I say that it is in our cities that the criminal classes are being recruited, and it is in our cities that crime reaps its greatest harvest.

Absolutely the day has come when Christian men and women must exercise and exert their power in the civic life of the community. The day has passed when we leave all these things to the politicians. Every man living under this flag, even the immigrant coming to Ellis Island, is a part of this great government, and you cannot shift the responsibility to the shoulders of some one else. If we stay away from the polls on voting-days, we are as guilty as the Congressman who stays away from Congress when some important measure is pending before that body. I am mighty glad that the mayor of this city has drawn the line, has spoken of the material advancement and the spiritual advancement.

Dr. Clark, I believe the day has come when our vision must be with the eye of the soul. We talk about material prosperity, and I believe if the boys lying today in Flanders fields could speak, and if the crippled and blind boys were asked, they would point to the invisible thing, and say, "See to it that neither things within nor things without this government be allowed to endanger or destroy the fabric of our constitution, or tear down the pillars of our great institutions."

Christian Endeavorers, raise high your ideals, which are our heritage. The city, the town, the country, must have the fearless and undivided support of the Christian people; and so as my last word of welcome, because we love you, because of what you bring to us now, we welcome you.

A response to these welcomes was made by Rev. Edgar E. Strother, general secretary of the China Christian Endeavor Union, who is from Missouri and was welcomed with a song from an amazingly large delegation from his home State. He brought the greetings of 1,200 societies, with 60,000 members scattered through all the provinces of China. "Christian Endeavor," he said, "meets the greatest need of China, which is Jesus Christ." He further said:

It is a great privilege to bring to you the greetings of your Chinese fellow Endeavorers, from the 1,200 Christian Endeavor societies of all the provinces of China, containing 60,000 members. They send to you through us their hearty greetings.

We are glad to say that there are great possibilities for the extension of Christian Endeavor in China, as well as in India, and all other mission lands throughout the world. At this great Convention we should indeed fix our attention on the world-wide field of Christian Endeavor. Christian Endeavor meets the greatest need of China. This need of China is Jesus Christ and a strong, virile Christian church, a self-propagating church in China; and Christian Endeavor just meets this need as scarcely any other movement can do, because Christian Endeavor puts emphasis first of all upon the spiritual realities, upon the spiritual side of things; first things first, their motto "Trusting in the Lord Jesus Christ for strength, we promise him we will do whatever He would have us do." This is just what the Christian church in China needs.

This is not all that Christian Endeavor does; it discovers and trains leaders for the church. It has done it here in America and in other lands, and in China it discovers gifts that would never be known but for the opportunity presented by Christian Endeavor which brings them out. It also enlists the rank and file of the church into Christian service. It is not enough to live a Christian life, but every member must be evangelistic, a worker for Christ. I trust this may be the greatest of all Conventions, this fortieth anniversary of Christian Endeavor, and that it may be the means of sending back the delegates to their societies with a wider world-wide vision of Christian Endeavor; that they may go back to their societies and tell of the great possibilities for extending Christian Endeavor in the lands beyond the seas, for the extension of this great movement within the church, the motto of which has always been, "For Christ and the Church."

A second response was made by Rev. John Fleming, of Scotland, a representative of the great Presbyterian bodies there. His response was:

Dr. Clark and Dear Friends:

One feels almost overwhelmed to address an audience like this; and, if I did not have memories like this of other great Christian Endeavor conventions, I should feel more out of it than I do. However, I cannot go back so far as Mr. Foster who attended the New York Convention of 1892, but I was present and spoke at the Montreal Convention in 1893. I think there were at least ten thousand present on that occasion. I was a very active Christian Endeavorer for at least twelve years, and had something to do with the extension and building up of the movement in Scotland and England. During all this time I was as a comrade in arms with Mr. Pollock. You will hear from him later if not tonight. I feel that it is necessary that we be together at a Christian Endeavor convention because people sometimes mistake one for the other, but after he speaks you will see the difference.

Although I am no longer in the ranks of Christian Endeavor, there is one principle not in the pledge, but I think it is a cardinal principle bound to come to the front as the years roll on. Christian Endeavor is not only interdenominational, but it is also international. Dr. Clark, I am sure, will agree with me in this, that one of the notes of this Convention is the spirit of international Christianity. As I am called upon to respond to the greetings of this Convention to those across the seas, I want to take all Europe. I want to speak in behalf of poor, bleeding, distracted Europe. I ask your prayers and sympathy for Europe, torn by hatred and violence, the scene of much confusion, disorder, and suspicion. Europe needs Christ. The Christian Endeavorers of the future need to go as crusaders, not necessarily to leave this land, but we need the crusade of the spirit, not as in olden days, but to take their stand for disarmament; and any effort put forth by your government towards that great end will meet with the enthusiasm and support of Endeavorers from all over the world. That is my plea tonight for the spread and preaching of international Christianity. I believe God has raised up this movement for this moment. As I look over this great audience, and know the great influence you have exerted, and the greater influence during the later years, my heart beats with greater hope that you may bring this world of blood and tears, and all humanity to Jesus Christ. I thank you in the name of those who have sent me to attend this Convention.

Mr. Hiram N. Lathrop, clerk of the United Society, read this message from Dr. William Shaw:

> With a heart full of gratitude for the privilege of nearly two-score years of service in Christian Endeavor and rejoicing in the divine blessing that has rested upon our movement through all the years—and never more manifestly than today—I send affectionate greetings to the Sixth World's Christian Endeavor Convention and all whom it represents. I congratulate the Endeavorers on the splendid record of successful service made by my successor as general secretary, E. P. Gates. My message to those who come forward to fill our places as we drop out is, "*Carry on.*" The principles embodied in Christian Endeavor were never more needed by the world than today. Accept them; exemplify them; propagate them; that Christ may be glorified, His church strengthened, and His kingdom of righteousness, peace, and good will established among men.

The Convention indorsed a message read by Rev. David James Burrell, of the Marble Collegiate Church (the great church where for a year Dr. Poling has preached every Sunday evening), to be sent to Dr. Poling. The telegram follows:

> To you and yours the trustees and Convention unitedly send love and sympathy. We are praying for you and expecting a speedy recovery. Do your best, and all blessings attend you.

Dr. Floyd W. Tomkins read this message to Dr. Shaw:

> To William Shaw, our friend and brother, long time our inspiration in Christian Endeavor, the New York Convention sends loving greetings, with earnest prayers to God for his speedy recovery. May the dear Master be very near to bless and comfort.

After the Convention had voted these telegrams, Dr. James L. Hill offered a fervent prayer for the recovery of these two dear friends and leaders.

General Secretary Gates was welcomed by a large delegation from the District of Columbia, where formerly he made his home. His report was made in a striking way. The vital facts he presented on a huge canvas. The message of the canvas was:

> *9,263 new societies organized since July 1, 1919. More members in more societies in more denominations in more nations than ever before.*

The next speaker was Roger W. Babson, of Wellesley Hills, Mass., a man who is foremost in the business life of America. He paid a warm testimony to Christian Endeavor. "All that I am and all that I own," he said, "I owe to a little Christian Endeavor society in Gloucester, Mass., of which I was once a member. I owe more to this society than I do to any college, or any banking institution, or any business organization with which I have ever been connected." He said:

> My first connection with the church was through a little Christian Endeavor society in my home town in Gloucester, Mass. That was when I was a very small boy, but I still remember distinctly the principles I learned there. While in some minor respects the Christian Endeavor organization has changed, its fundamental principles are exactly the same as they were then; and I make the pre-

diction that the boys and girls who live a thousand years from now will find Christian Endeavor standing for the same things. They are based on the teachings of Jesus Christ, and people are finding that the way of living which Jesus taught makes people the happiest, the healthiest, and most prosperous. Yes, I mean it—the most prosperous.

Any man or woman who has tried the life of a true Christian knows that it is the happiest. Any physician will agree that the rules laid down in the Bible are the best prescription ever written for keeping well. Now people are beginning to realize that the Bible is the greatest book on practical economics. It is about this third phase that I want to talk.

When you see a boy or girl who is truly living up to his membership in the Christian Endeavor society, you know, first, that he is honest; second, that he is industrious; third, that he is religious and is seeking the things which count in the sight of God. I tell you there is a combination that can't be beaten. If a young man has average ability and these three qualifications, it's a safe bet that he will make a success.

Let the majority of the young men and women in any country become imbued with these principles of Christian Endeavor, and the success of that country is assured. The future safety and prosperity of the United States will not be determined by the men in Washington; it will not be determined by our great banks or our mines, factories, farms, or forests. The future safety of the United States lies in the hands of your organization and the other institutions which are working on the same principle as you.

Honesty Is Business Safeguard

On a recent visit to Chicago I was taken by the president of one of the largest banks to see his new safe-deposit vaults. He described these—as bank presidents will—as the largest and most marvellous vaults in the city. He expatiated on the heavy steel doors and the various electrical and mechanical contrivances which protect the stocks and bonds deposited in the institution.

While I was at the bank, a person came in to rent a box. He made the arrangements for the box, and a box was handed to him. In it he deposited some stocks and bonds which he took from his pocket. Then the clerk who had charge of the vaults went to a rack on the wall, and took out a key and gave it to the man who had rented the box. The man put the box into one of the little steel compartments, shut the door, and turned the key. He then went away, feeling perfectly secure on account of those steel doors and various mechanical and electrical contrivances existing to protect his wealth.

I did not wish to give him a sleepless night; so I said nothing; but I couldn't help thinking how easy it would have been for that poorly paid, humpbacked clerk to make a duplicate of that key before he delivered it to the renter of that box. With such a duplicate the clerk could have made that man penniless within a few minutes after he had left the building. The great steel doors and the electrical and mechanical contrivances would have been absolutely valueless.

My point is that the real security which that great bank in Chicago had to offer its clientele lay not in the massive stone columns in front of its structure; nor in the heavy steel doors; nor the electrical and mechanical contrivances. The real strength of that institution rested in the honesty, the absolute integrity, of its clerks.

And, when you think of it, there is really no value at all in the pieces of paper which one so carefully locks up in these safe-deposit boxes. There is no value at all in the bank book which we so carefully cherish. There is no value at all in those deeds and mortgages upon which we depend so completely. The value rests, first, on the integrity of the lawyers, clerks, and stenographers who draw up the papers; second, on the integrity of the officers who sign the documents; third, on the integrity of the courts and judges which would enable us to enforce our claims; and, finally, on the integrity of the community which would determine whether or not the orders of the court will be executed.

These things, which we look upon as of great value—the stocks, bonds, bank books, deeds, mortgages, insurance policies, etc., are merely symbols. While fifty-one per cent. of the people have their eyes on the goal of integrity, these investments are secure; but with fifty-one per cent. of them headed in the wrong direction these investments are valueless. The first fundamental of prosperity is integrity. Without it there is no civilization, there is no safety. Mind you, also, that this applies just as much to the man who is working for wages as to the capitalist and every owner of property.

Integrity, however, is very much broader than the above illustration would indicate. Integrity applies to many more things than to money. Integrity requires the seeking after, as well as the dispensing of, truth. It was this desire for truth which founded our educational institutions, our sciences, and our arts. All the great professions, from medicine to engineering, rest upon this spirit of integrity. Only as they so rest can they prosper or even survive.

Now do you see the point of contact between the work of Christian Endeavor and the development of the country's business? Did you ever think of it in just this way before? Every member of the Christian Endeavor Society here who is true to his vows and abides by what he learns at your gospel meetings contributes to the stability, safety, and the prosperity of the business of the world.

Principles Will Increase Production

There are other sides to this question. Protection is only one part of the problem. Being honest is only one of the requisites to business success, for honesty by itself will never make two blades of grass grow where one grew before. It will never make clothes, or grow food, or build houses. We must have initiative, we must have production and service. Does the work of Christian Endeavor have any bearing on these things?

Some time ago I dropped in at one of the regular gospel services of a little mission over in the East Side. Among the many testimonies given was one by a Swedish servant girl. In her broken English she told what being a Christian meant to her. Said she: "Before I found Jesus I used to hate my work. I hated to sweep and to wash dishes and make beds. I just did it because I had to earn a living; but now I am a Christian. I like my work. I am happy. When I am sweeping, I just think; 'I'm doing this for Jesus. It will make Him glad for me to do the best work I can, and so I sweep in all the corners and under things that I used to skip, because Jesus will know and will feel bad if I don't." That little servant girl had found the secret.

About three years ago I was travelling in South America. When going from Sao Paulo up across the table-lands to Rio Janeiro, I passed through a little poverty-stricken Indian village. It was some 3,000 feet above sea-level; but it was located at the foot of a great water-power. This water-power, I was told, could easily develop from 10,000 to 15,000 horsepower for twelve months of the year. At the base of this waterfall lived these poverty-stricken Indians, ploughing their ground with broken sticks, bringing their corn two hundred miles on their backs from the seacoast, and grinding it by hand between two stones. Yet, with a little faith and vision they could have developed that water-power, even though in a most primitive manner, and with irrigation could have made that poverty-stricken valley a veritable Garden of Eden. They simply lacked faith. 'They lacked vision. . They were unwilling, or unable, to look ahead to do something for the next generation and trust to the Lord for the results.

I met the head man of the village, and said to him, "Why is it that you don't do something to develop this power?"

"Why, if we started to develop this thing," he answered, "by the time we got it done we would be dead."

Indians had lived there for the last two hundred years, lacking the vision. No one in that community had the foresight or vision to think or see beyond the end of his day. It was lack of faith which stood between them and prosperity.

Religion Makes Communities

Religion is not only the vital force which protects our community, but it is the vital force which makes our communities. The power of our spiritual forces has not yet been tapped. Our grandchildren will look back upon us and wonder why we neglected our trust and our opportunity, just as we look back on those poor Indians in Brazil who ploughed with crooked sticks, grinding their corn between stones and hauling it on their backs two hundred miles from the sea-board.

Faith and vision do not come from the wealth of a nation. It is the faith and vision which produce the wealth. The wealth of a country does not depend on its raw materials. Raw materials are to a certain extent essential and to a great extent valuable; but the nations which today are richest in raw materials are the poorest in wealth. Even when considering one country, the United States, the principle holds true.

The coal and iron and copper have been here in this country for thousands of years, but only within the last fifty years have they been used. Water-powers exist even today absolutely unharnessed. Look the whole world over, and there has been no increase in raw materials. There existed one thousand years ago more raw materials than we have today, but we then lacked men with a vision and the faith to take that coal out of the ground, to harness the water-powers, to build the railroads, and to do other things worth while.

If all you Christian Endeavorers will live up to the fundamental principles of your pledges, if you will get a firm hold on that faith in and companionship with God, you will develop a greater producing force than all the steam or water powers in the world.

Right Living Prevents Panics

Here is a picture of the course of United States business over the past seventeen years. The large black areas on the adjoining chart are formed by combining and plotting current figures on new buildings, crops, clearings, immigration, total foreign trade, money, failures. commodity prices, railroad earnings, stock prices, and politics in order to give a composite view of business in the United States. (When Interstate Commerce reports of earnings of all United States railroads became available January, 1909, this record was substituted in place of the earnings of ten representative roads which had been used previous to that time. Revised scales for monetary figures were also introduced in August, 1912.)

The line X Y represents the country's net gain or growth, based on the economic theory that action and reaction are equal when the two factors of time and intensity are multiplied to form an area. the sums of the areas above and below said line X Y must, over sufficiently long periods of time, be equal, provided enough subjects are included, properly weighed and combined. An area of prosperity is always followed by an area of depression; an area of depression in turn is always followed by an area of prosperity. The areas, however, need not have the same shape.

It will be seen that each area is divided into halves by a narrow white line. This is to emphasize the fact that the first halves of areas below the X Y line are really reactions from the extravagance, inefficiency, and corruption which existed during the latter half of the preceding prosperity area. Contrariwise, the first halves of areas above the X Y line are really reactions from the economy, industry, and righteousness developed during the hard times just preceding.

At the present time we are in a period of business depression, as the chart illustrates. People are out of work, it is much harder to get a job. The papers are filled with reports of bankruptcies and distress throughout the business world. A year or two ago conditions were just the opposite. There were jobs enough for everybody; factories were running overtime; and people said that the country was prosperous.

What is the difference? There is just as much raw material available as before; there are just as many people to work; there is just as much money in the country. Why should we have this condition in business, or why should we have had any of the ten or more panics and depressions that have occurred in the last century —the panics of 1907, 1893, 1884, 1872, etc.? There is one fundamental reason. We are not living close enough to God to stand continuous prosperity. The causes of bad times are found in the periods of good times just preceding them.

These prosperity periods are invariably characterized by a wave of wanton extravagance, unwise and dishonest promotions, and a general tendency on the part of people to try to get more than they give. The spirit of service gives way to the spirit of getting. The workman insists on more pay, but loafs on the job; the manufacturer, merchant, and jobber are tempted by opportunities to squeeze exorbitant profits. Interest in religion and the teachings of Jesus gives way to the race for money. You feel it in Christian Endeavor, and it shows in the membership of the churches. People take their troubles to the Lord, but they run to the devil with their happiness.

Our business depressions are only the natural result of living and acting contrary to the fundamental laws of God. If the majority of the people in the world should suddenly turn about and live the way Christ taught us to live, we should never have the spasms of hard times and boom times. Business would develop steadily, evenly, and in the long run far more rapidly than it does now.

Again I say the causes of our business depressions are spiritual, and the only means by which they can be remedied and prevented are spiritual means. This power of faith which you talk about once a week in your gospel meetings is the greatest power of the universe. The principles of Christian Endeavor are sound enough to bear the structure of civilization. Handle them with reverence and respect when you discuss them in your meetings. Understand that they are practical, powerful things, not simply theories. Take them seriously, for you can no more afford to play with them than you can to play with electricity.

This, Christian Endeavorers, is my message to you. What I have told you is not simply an idea conceived in the preparation of this talk. It is the result of years spent in studying business life. It is the conclusion reached after talking with hundreds of successful men. Take it and use it!

Mrs. Francis E. Clark was called to the front, and the audience saluted her with the most cordial enthusiasm, as it later saluted Dr. Clark himself when he rose to deliver his great program-and-policy speech. In an impromptu introduction he told of a desire of years' standing to retire from the burdens of the presidency of Christian Endeavor. The trustees refused to let him go, and Dr. Clark told the great audience that he could only accept re-election if the Endeavorers would support him by supporting the world-wide work of Christian Endeavor. At this point, Treasurer Shartle made an inspired appeal to the audience. He stated Dr. Clark's position, and told of his self-sacrifice during all these years that Christianity might be promoted. It was an impelling presentation and in response the entire audience rose in pledge to give Dr. Clark their support in prayer and in material gifts, that Christian Endeavor may not languish in the earth.

Touched to the heart, Dr. Clark stirred the multitude by his answer to their promise, *"I accept your election, backed as it is by your promise of support."* He said:

CHRISTIAN ENDEAVOR FOURSQUARE

Annual Message of Francis E. Clark, President of the United Society of Christian Endeavor and of the World's Christian Endeavor Union, at the Sixth World's Convention of Christian Endeavor, July 6, 1921.

Forty years of Christian Endeavor history are behind us. Their scroll is rolled up and laid aside. We cannot alter it. But we do thank God for it. We may well be humbly grateful for these years of His right hand. We may well draw courage and inspiration from the story of these two-score years.

A growth from one society to far more than a hundred thousand, though some that did run well for a time have fallen by the way. A multiplication of the original fifty-seven members by more than three hundred thousand, until the number of our past and present comrades reaches eighteen millions. A distribution of our society from one little corner of the United States to every continent and every nation between the two poles. Surely this is another miracle of the loaves and fishes. This is a mighty underscoring of the age-old truth, "Not by might, nor by power, but by my Spirit, saith the Lord."

I will not dwell upon the past. A society that relies upon former glories is already decrepit and decadent. As one has truly said, "The fortieth mile-stone will become a millstone unless we leave it behind us." Mile-stones are inspiring things to leave behind. They mark progress. They allow us to say, "The best is yet to be."

There are two ways of using a mile-stone. We may read it as forty miles back to our starting-point, or forty miles forward to our destination. How shall we mark this mile-stone? Not by the inscription, "Forty years back to Williston," but, "Forty years forward to a larger, intenser loyalty to Christ and His church." I propose, with the advice and consent of my colleagues, the trustees, and of the denominational leaders of Christian Endeavor, that we wage *A Foursquare Christian Endeavor Campaign* for the next two years.

The Christian Endeavor movement lies foursquare, however we view it. Like the New Jerusalem, which the Revelator describes, it has four sides. Our movement has four great divisions, four great principles, four great spheres of activity, four great methods of expressing our loyalty to Christ and the church of Christ.

The four divisions of our society are the *Junior, Intermediate, Senior* and *Alumni*.

The four great principles are *outspoken loyalty to Jesus Christ, constant service for Christ, constant loyalty to Christ's church, constant fellowship with Christ's people*.

Our four great spheres of action are the *Church*, the *Home*, the *Community*, the *World*.

Our four great methods are *Expression* by prayer and testimony, *Service* through our committees, *Fellowship* through our unions, *Personal Stewardship* of our money, time, strength and ability.

What, then, may a Foursquare Campaign accomplish?

First. Such a campaign will make clear to ourselves and the world the constituency of Christian Endeavor. This is made up of children (the Juniors), youth (the Intermediates), older young people (the Seniors), graduates (the Alumni).

Second. It will define the Principles we have to establish.

Third. It will make plain the Field we have to cultivate.

Fourth. It will indicate the Tools and Weapons we have to use.

It is not a complicated program that I would suggest. It simply strives to show *whom* we endeavor with, *what* we endeavor for, *where* we expend our endeavors, and *with what* instruments we endeavor to do our work for the Master. I think I may claim that this is a comprehensive, sane, symmetrical program. It is not one-sided or lopsided. It will not make cranks or faddists. If carried out, it will develop all the Christian muscles—hearts to feel, brains to think, hands to work, feet to run on the Master's errands.

Let us examine briefly each side of our proposed program.

I.

The *first* is our *Membership*. We neglect any one class of our members at our peril. The Juniors—of course we must win the boys and girls. The Intermediates—they constitute the age of conversion, of decision, the age of the deepest and most lasting impressions. The Seniors—they constitute the very backbone of our movement. Our united outstanding work for the Master in church, and community cannot exist without them. Without them our *unions* will die.

Our Alumni—they are our connecting link between older and younger, between the church in its wide activities and its influence and the children of the church, who need the church as the church needs them. Our Alumni *Fellowships* connect us with our fellow Alumni and Alumnae in all the nations, and help support our world-wide work. Our Alumni *Councils* in the local church may prove most helpful for the guidance and encouragement of the young people by their elders.

If we should emphasize any one division more than another during the next two years, it should be the *Senior* societies. In earlier days this section of Christian Endeavor was overemphasized compared with the others. In later years it has been underemphasized. Many of our societies that call themselves Senior are really Intermediates, with two or three Seniors who are members by a kind of sufferance. One remedy for this is to better standardize or grade our movement.

Let us remember that each of these divisions has a genuine and natural significance and importance. The Intermediates, while they must lead their own meetings, man their own committees, largely plan their own program, at the same time need the guidance and encouragement of a wise superintendent. An Intermediate society that runs wild, especially along social lines, though with no bad intent, may be a disgrace to the church and the cause at large.

We need beginners; we need learners; we need older and more expert workers; we need graduates. In short, we need all the four grades of Christian Endeavor. There is a place for all in our organization, and a wise standardization, though it may not always be possible, will avoid many difficulties and prevent many failures.

Let these four names always mean something definite: *Juniors*, as a rule—the children from seven to fourteen; *Intermediates*—the high-school age, from fourteen to seventeen inclusive; *Seniors*, eighteen and over—eighteen—plus what you please; *Alumni*, all graduates and older friends who are interested in our work. We are all working together for the same great ends, but we can work far more effectively if we are thus divided into groups of the same approximate age. It will not always be practicable, and we must adapt ourselves to our circumstances; but it is the ideal toward which we should strive.

If your society is composed of teen-age young people, *call* it Intermediate; have a wise superintendent appointed; and then form a Senior society separately. However small it may be at first, the inevitable march of the years will soon graduate the *Juniors* into the *Intermediates* of today, into the *Seniors* of tomorrow. It may be best to have a different set of topics to mark still further the advance from adolescence to maturity.

So much for one side of our foursquare movement.

II.

The second side of our quadrangle relates to our Principles. Every one of these is important. They are all involved in our covenant pledge.

The first principle is *outspoken loyalty to Jesus Christ*. That means our prayer meeting, of course. "I will attend and take some part in every meeting." If we drop the participation by all, we drop our *distinctive prayer meeting idea* which differentiates Christian Endeavor from other young people's meetings, and have no right to call ourselves by the name "Christian Endeavor." Do not often substitute a lecture, a sermon, a debate, a secular forum, for the voluntary participation of all by prayer and testimony. Such meetings should be exceptional if held at all.

Our second principle is *constant service for Christ*, a principle that must never be overshadowed. Every one of our committees shouts out this principle, if you will but listen.

Our third principle is *constant loyalty to Christ's church*, another essential. "I will support my own church in every way," says our pledge. No society can be a hundred-per-cent. Christian Endeavor that does not put this foremost in its program.

Our fourth principle is *constant fellowship with Christ's people*. This means our unions—*local, county, State, national, world's unions*. This principle binds four millions of us who belong to a hundred denominations, who live in five continents, and who speak a hundred languages, in bonds which even death will not break, for the fellowship of Jesus' followers will endure throughout eternity.

Make much of the social fellowship of your own local society, fellow Endeavorers, and make it a kind of sociability of which our Lord would not be ashamed. I should like to see a League of Endeavorers set themselves against *indecent dress, sensuous promiscuous dancing, sensual and suggestive moving pictures*, all of which are destroying the modesty and eating out the souls of millions of young people. Let not Christian Endeavor be tainted by practices that lead to conformity with the world, the flesh and the devil.

III.

Third. The third side of our Foursquare Campaign relates to our four Spheres of Action.

Our first sphere is the *Church*. Christian Endeavor is in and of and for the church, the denomination, and the particular local church, to which any society belongs. Christian Endeavor is no orphan, no foundling, but the legitimate child of the church, loyal and true to the backbone. It was born in a church to do the work of the church, to bring young people into the church, and to train them for the church, in closest co-operation with the Sunday School and other agencies of the church. Our outside efforts are conditioned upon our relation to the church and derive their strength from it.

Our second sphere of action is the *Home*. There are other relations besides the church which we cannot and would not forget. The Home is one of the chief among them. We are all children or parents or brothers and sisters. We belong to Homes. Why should not *Family Christian Endeavor* be a vital part of our program for the years to come? Many of us may establish or help sustain family prayers, at least breakfast-table prayers, even in these busy days. The decline of family religion is a terrible menace to the Christianity of the future. The men and women of generations yet unborn, O Endeavorers, will have reason to bless you if you stem the tide of worldliness in the home and establish there an altar to our God.

Our third sphere of action is the *Community* and the *State*. They, too, are within the wide boundaries of our influence. We cannot escape our relation to the community and the nation. Christian Endeavor must be patriotic but not partisan. It must take its stand against the desecration of the Sabbath and of every high and holy thing. It must stand for temperance and purity, and against beastly, nauseating prize fights. In other words, it must stand everywhere and always for *Christian citizenship*.

Our fourth sphere of action is the *World*. We are citizens of the world. We are in it if not of it. We cannot help ourselves. We would not if we could. The very world-wideness of our organization emphasizes our duty. It is a glorious privilege to belong to an organization that has an influence in every continent. No religious organization has a battle-line farther flung than ours. It extends from beyond the Arctic circle to the Antarctic. The sun never sets upon Christian Endeavor. This means our duty to stand for *world peace* and *world fellowship* and *world evangelization*. Who are our neighbors in Christian Endeavor? British and French, Germans and Slavs, Magyars and Finns, Scandinavians and Russians, Hindoos and Mongols, Chinese and Japanese. Australians and New Zealanders, Africans and the dwellers in the remotest islands of the seas and the uttermost parts of the earth. "Neighbors," did I say? Yea, more than neighbors, *brothers* with the same pledge, *"I will strive to do whatever He would like to have me do."*

The following is a muster roll of the countries in which Christian Endeavor is found: Africa, Argentina, Armenia, Australia, Austria, Azores, Barbadoes, Belgium, Bermuda, Bolivia, Bohemia, Brazil, British Guiana, Bulgaria, Burma, Canada, Canal Zone, Cape Colony, Caroline Islands, Ceylon, Chile, China, Colombia, Congoland, Costa Rica, Cuba, Denmark, Ecuador, Egypt, Ellice Islands, Esthonia, Fiji Islands, Finland, Formosa, France, Germany, Gibraltar, Gilbert Islands, Great Britain, and Ireland, Greece, Grenada, West Indies, Guatemala, Haiti, Hawaii, Holland, Hungary, Iceland, India, Italy, Jamaica, Japan, Jugo-Slavia, Korea, Labrador, Laos, Lapland, Latvia, Lithuania, Loyalty Islands, Madagascar, Madeira Islands, Marshall Islands, Mauritius, Mexico, Natal, Norway, Newfoundland, New Zealand, Orange River, Palestine, Panama, Persia, Peru, Philippine Islands, Poland, Porto Rico, Portugal, Russia, Samoa, Siam, Soudan, Spain, Sweden, Switzerland, Syria, Tasmania, Tokelau Islands, Transvaal, Trinidad, Turkey, United States, Upper Hebrides, Uruguay, Venezuela. There may be a few others which we have not listed. Do you miss any?

IV.

Fourth, our *Methods*. The fourth side of our Foursquare Campaign relates to our methods, our plans, our tools, we might call them. I need not dwell upon them. You know them as thoroughly as I do. Naturally, they, too, fall under four heads. Our *meetings*, our *committees*, our *unions*, our *personal stewardship*. They are but the practical working out of the principles I have before named. "Constant loyalty to Christ" as Lord and Master finds expression in our *meetings*. "Constant service for Him" finds expression in our *committees*. "Constant fellowship with His people" is expressed by our social gatherings and our unions. "Constant personal loyalty to His church and His cause throughout the world" is expressed by giving our money, time and strength to His cause. Let me dwell for a moment on the last point. Comprehensively, the word for it is *personal stewardship*.

We are stewards of our money, of our time, of our influence, of our powers, and all, all are for Christ and His church. Endeavorers, make much of this thought in the biennium for which we are planning. "*Personal*" and "*Stewardship*" are mighty words. When united they express a tremendous thought. When fully understood they would mean for the cause of Jesus Christ a revolution in many lives.

Not stewardship in a general, impersonal, theoretical way, but stewardship that leads to real sacrifice of *money, time* and *strength*. If every Christian did no more than *tithe* his money, his time, his influence, his powers, this old world would not long remain two-thirds pagan and nine-tenths indifferent to Christianity. Many of us should give far more than a tenth of our money, time and strength.

Especially let us remember that we are *stewards of souls;* stewards of our influence over young people who are not professors of religion. God has brought hundreds of thousands of these young people within the radius of Christian Endeavor through our associate membership and other ways. Are we striving to lead them to decide definitely for Christ? Do we have every year Decision Days? Do we face our associate members and others with the question, "Am I on the Lord's side?" Failure to do this is, I fear, one of the weak points of Christian Endeavor, as it is of the whole church today.

As stewards of souls I would suggest an *evangelistic committee* in every society, unless the lookout committee is doing this work. We should have *unfailing Decision Days* in Christian Endeavor Week, and at other times when appropriate. I recently attended such a service when twenty-eight earnest young people of the high-school age for the first time stood together to say, "*I will strive to do whatever He would like to have me do.*" They were evidently waiting for just this opportunity to declare themselves. Thus best can we get our future stalwart recruits. I commend this to you most earnestly.

Why not also have an *evangelistic committee in every union*, with a special program of service each year, under wise and sane leadership? What more appropriate time for such a program to lead up to life-time decisions than the Lenten season, when many minds are turned to the suffering, dying, risen Lord?

In a Fellowship of Stewards we might enlist not only Life-Work Recruits and Tenth Legioners and evangelistic workers, but all who would solemnly promise to give systematically a proportion (a decent proportion, I mean) of their money, time, influence and effort to God's cause. Each one must decide for himself what proportion of his life he can thus distinctly give. But let our motto be, "It is required in stewards that a man be found faithful," and our slogan, "Never say 'No' to God."

Thus by our Foursquare Campaign, if we enter into it, all the fundamental questions of Christian Endeavor will be answered. *Who belong?* Children, youth, young men and women, older friends. *Why do we belong?* To give testimony, to serve, to be loyal, to be brotherly. *Where do we serve?* In the *church*, the *home*, the *community*, the *nation*, the *world*. *How do we serve?* In our *meetings*, in our *committees*, in our *unions*, by our *personal stewardship*.

You have often in the past asked me to suggest a definite program and watchword for the biennium ahead, to set goals for us to aim at, that we may feel that we are striving together with the same targets in sight. I hesitate to do this, and will accept any better suggestion you may put forth.

Our goals should be plain, simple, but *never low or easy*. The athlete must *strain* his muscles; the scholar must burn the midnight oil; the would-be millionaire must be *doubly diligent* in business; the ideal Christian, too, must be *doubly vigilant*. These are the goals I would suggest.

Our Society Goals for 1921-23

Let our first goal be the better grading of our societies, so that wherever possible there shall be *Junior, Intermediate, Senior societies,* and *Alumni Councils.*

Let our second goal be closer and more vital relations with pastor, church and denomination, promoted by the pastor's active membership, wherever possible, by the pastor's closing five minutes in the prayer meeting; by the pastor's use of committees and members who shall be at his beck and call for any service; by an *Alumni Council* in every church, composed of Endeavor graduates and older friends. Let this closer relationship also be promoted by increased emphasis on *attendance on church services;* by *co-operation in denominational and local church plans* which our pledge demands; including denominational history and doctrines; by *leadership-training classes;* and by efforts to obtain *recruits for life-work or part-time Christian service.* Our Efficiency Chart will admirably record our efforts to reach these goals.

Let our third goal be more emphasis upon religion in the *home.* Let us magnify Christian standards within the *home;* let us embody Christian principles in our conduct and service within the *home;* let us through *Bible study, prayer, the family altar, etc.,* help make the *home* an agency of constructive Christian training.

Fourth and last, but not least, let our goal be to place more emphasis on *personal stewardship,* remembering that "stewardship" is a word of very wide import, and relates to our duties, to our community and our country, as well as to God. Here are two searching questions that stewardship involves:

Is your society faithful to the four ages which it may influence?

Is it faithful to our principles of *testimony, proportionate giving, service, church loyalty, Christian citizenship* and *Christian fellowship?*

There is a significant verse in one of the epistles of Peter in which he speaks of the disciples as "stewards of the *manifold* grace of God." That is just what a Christian Endeavor society is. It is a steward of *manifold* grace. It is not a one-sided or a one-track society. It has everything to do for the Master that it can do. "I will strive to do *whatever* He would like to have me do," says our pledge. O Endeavorers, He has made you stewards of *manifold* graces, of a *multitude* of boys and girls and men and women, of a *multitude* of services for your Lord, stewards in your *church,* in your *home,* your *community,* your *world—all for Jesus Christ, Jesus Christ for all.* Let that be the dominant thought of our Foursquare Campaign for the two years to come.

"It is required in stewards that a man be found faithful."
"Never say 'No' to God."

This great meeting, one of the best opening sessions of all of our International Conventions, was brought to a fitting close by singing, "Blest be the tie that binds," and the benediction pronounced by Dr. Ira Landrith.

CHAPTER III.

QUIET HOUR SERVICES

MARBLE COLLEGIATE CHURCH

Dr. Burrell's Quiet Hours

PERCY FOSTER introduced the four sessions of Dr. David James Burrell's Quiet Hours with his inimitable song services. They were spiritual, prayerful, joyous.

There were bits of fun here and there, and in them all was the sovereign and sweet spirit of song. One of their most notable features was their rich variety, ready with innumerable devices to hold the attention of the Endeavorers and bring out their very best.

The main auditorium of Dr. Burrell's beautiful church on Fifth Avenue, one of the chief historic churches of the city, was filled with the Endeavorers at eight each morning, eager to hear the honored and famous pastor of the church, who has been Dutch Reformed trustee of the United Society for many years, and who in his ripe age is still at the best of his mental and spiritual powers.

The theme of his Quiet Hour talks was in harmony with the Uniform International Sunday School lessons, taking up the early life of Saul of Tarsus, and culminating in his shining conversion and entrance upon his unparalleled life-work. It would not have been Dr. Burrell if these talks had not been thoroughly Biblical, substantial in their hold on history and on fundamental truth, and at the same time picturesque and vivid in their crowding details. They were warm and human, full of spirit and interest, and never let go until they had gripped the hearts and consciences of the Endeavorers, leading them to holier and braver issues. It was a great privilege for the Endeavorers to hear this man of God during those four Quiet Hours.

BRICK PRESBYTERIAN CHURCH

Dr. Foulkes's Quiet Hours

In the Brick Presbyterian Church, where a memorial tablet to a former pastor recalled also a beloved Christian Endeavor trustee, Dr. Maltbie D. Babcock, a trustee, Dr. William Hiram Foulkes, led three deeply spiritual services on "The Uplifted Cross," "Burning and Shining Lights," and "The Fourth Dimen-

30

sion." Mr. Rodeheaver's leadership of the praise service furnished true preparation for what followed.

Dr. Foulkes turned the thought of those present to what Christ must have seen from the cross. Never in the 1,921 intervening years, it was said, has He looked upon a world so much like that as may be seen today. We ought to see the world as Christ saw it, one in infinite need of Him. We must stretch out our hands as He stretched out His. That is, we must get upon our cross; we must be crucified with Him. I like to name the left hand of Jesus on the cross, the hand nearest His heart, "Come," and the right hand, the hand of majesty, "Go." The only kind of social service that I believe in is the social service of the bleeding feet nailed to the cross, and in that I believe with all my heart.

We must have our hearts broken as He did. The only proper Christian attitude toward sin is that of grief. If Christ is truly uplifted in your life, He is going to draw all unto Himself.

CHAPEL, MARBLE COLLEGIATE CHURCH

Intermediate Quiet Hours

It was not a large crowd of Intermediates which came out to the first Quiet Hour service for teen-age Endeavorers on Thursday morning, not nearly so great a crowd as ought to have come, judging by the beauty, the gripping power, and the importance of the meeting.

Paul Brown was the interesting leader, and Stanley Fellows, of New York City, led the singing and put into it the sweetness and the fragrance of worship. No preparation of the heart could have been better than these few moments of singing prayers of aspiration. As they were sung they brought the young people into the very presence of the Eternal.

The speaker for these Intermediate young people's Quiet Hours was Dr. E. L. Reiner, of Chicago, who showed by the simplicity of his instruction, and its splendid helpfulness, that he understands not only the message of the gospel, but how to apply that message to the needs of youth.

Dr. Reiner's topic was, "I am the Way, the Truth, and the Life," and one morning hour was devoted to each of these words, and another to Jesus as the Light. The message was delivered with winsome power, morning by morning. The minds of young people are confused by the raucous voices of the day, and they are turning perplexed faces seeking for light. The speaker made plain the beautiful simplicity of the gospel.

The world has lost its sense of direction and needs to be turned back to Christ, the way. Jesus is the way, the straight way, not the mystic or crooked way, and He is the short way that all may tread.

He is the Truth as well, the truth about God and man, the Life that enables us to walk in the way of truth, and the Light that shows us what to believe and what to do.

These worshipful hours surely helped to clear up difficulties and direct the fresh ardor of youth to Christ, Saviour, Lord, and King. Dr. Reiner's discourse each morning follows:

I. John 14:6—Jesus the Way

He said, "I am the way."

1. THE WORD "WAY"

The word way in this passage is a proper noun, inasmuch as it was the first name the Christians gave their religion.

The prophets of Jehovah spoke of a great highway.

The early disciples, when they realized their growth into an organized body spoke of this organized force as the way.

It is noticeable that the early church did not define its faith in terms of ritual or creed, but said they were "of the way."

The way is not a series of gyrations, a tortuous experience through some abnormal theological propositions.

The way is not a scholastic creed which the few can understand and follow.

The way is not a conjecture of some cult.

The way is a well-planned journey from earth to heaven.

The way is a narrow way in contrast with the broad deserts of sin and worldliness in which the traveller is readily lost.

2. WHAT IT MEANS TO BE IN THE WAY

Jesus gave it its full definition when He said, "I am the Way."

The world is lost. It has strayed from the heart of its Father, God. It seems to be groping along to find the road back. Jesus is the way, the definite article signifying that He is the only way.

The world needs to find its sense of direction. Christ is the only open highway back to the Father's heart, to heaven.

A little girl standing in the shadow of our church building was crying as though her heart would break. She was lost. Looking into her face and recognizing her as one of the children of our street, we took her by the hand, led her to the corner of the street, about ten feet from where she stood crying, and, pointing to her house, said, "Is that your house?" Without a word she dried her tears, and ran swiftly towards her home.

She was lost. She had lost the sense of direction. From where she stood she could see the way which was familiar to her. A knowing and guiding hand soon had her back home.

Jesus has done this for a lost world. He is not merely the way-shower, but He is the way.

3. SOME THOUGHTS BY "THE WAY"

The world has some misconceptions about the way.

Some say Jesus is the way-shower. Now, a wooden sign or guide-post may be a way-shower; but it does not go the way, and it is not itself the way.

Jesus said, "I am the way."

Jesus is not "in the way." We use this term in the sense of God's having arbitrarily placed Jesus between man and his joys.

Jesus is not something to be surmounted by terrific climbing and struggle before reaching eternal security.

Jesus is the way because He is the shortest and most natural approach to God, our Father.

Jesus is the way because He is the only claimant to be the truth and the light. His claim is true. He illumines the journey with His presence.

Jesus, then, is not the way-shower to a better way, nor a revelation of a way, but He is the way.

The way suggests a journey.

The resting places on the journey to heaven are Prayer, Pardon, Peace and Prosperity.

Some one says: "Being in the way suggests action. Jesus,. the way, went about doing good"; and those who follow in the way will do something for 1. Those who walk in it with them; 2. Those who are near its edges; 3. Those who stumble and wander about.

CONCLUSION

Life's Journey

A gentleman once sailing the Pacific Ocean asked of the captain, "Where are we at this moment?" He spread out a large chart, on which there were three lines, which stood for three possible courses. "This one," he said, "is the nearest to the Philippines; the central one is the course my owners demand that I take; but this third one is the course I myself prefer to take. At this moment, however, we are at this point"; and he marked the point on a little speck in the central course, the course his owners had challenged him to take. We can liken this to the voyage of life. The Lord is our captain. There are three courses:

1. One the devil wants us to take;
2. One we ourselves like to choose;
3. One our captain challenges us to take.

If we should mark the point where we are at this particular moment, where should we have to make it?

Could we put the point in the course to which He challenges us just where He would mark it?

Or must we mark some other course?

Remember Jacob at Bethel, with the sense of the presence of God and heaven and his strong resolves? But, when he got out into a foreign country, from his scheming ways to get his gains and the entanglements to which his Jacob nature led him, he got himself into trouble. Then God appeared to him and said, "Get back to Bethel."

And in the journey back God met him, and they wrestled together until his self-dependence was broken and he fell over, and leaned on God. Then he went forth a new man—a prince with God, and with power.

Dr. David James Burrell says under the title "The Way That Seemeth Right":

The only safe plan for the pilgrim is to ask the Lord. To your knees, therefore, O traveller! Will God answer? "If any of you lack wisdom, let him ask of God, that giveth to all men liberally, and upbraideth not; and it shall be given him." "Thine ears shall hear a word . . . . saying, This is the way; walk ye in it." The voice is behind you; the Speaker is unseen; but if so disposed you can surely hear Him.

We are admonished by the divine Guide, who speaks through the inspired Guide-book, and in answer to prayer, that there is only one right way. The Latins had a proverb, "All ways lead to Rome," and there are those who imagine that in like manner all roads lead to heaven. But the Scriptures teach otherwise. "There is a way which seemeth right unto a man, but the end thereof are the ways of death." A man's destination is not altered by the fact that the wrong way seemeth right to him. His sincerity has nothing to do with it.

The right way is the old way. Here went righteous Abel, and Enoch, and Abraham, and all the gray fathers. These red footprints

are those of the noble army of martyrs, who "climbed the steep ascent
of heaven through peril, toil and pain." This is the road traversed by
our fathers and mothers, who believed in "the old-time religion"; and
there is none better for us. The progress of the centuries has opened
up no shorter or better route.

II. John 14-6—Jesus the Truth
He said, "I am the truth"

1. THE WORD "TRUTH"

Yesterday we saw the proper use of capital letters. Today we shall
look at their improper use.

Our criticism is towards the various isms, cults, and "thoughts," of
this day because they misuse capitals.

Take, for instance, the word "truth." Spelled without any capital
it is an easily definable term, and everybody understands it. It means
"conformity to fact," "accuracy of statement," "exact correspondence
of affirmation with existing conditions." Yes, it does mean that a
spade is a spade and that other things go by their real names.

So, as soon as the capital letter is added to "truth" it means something else.

When these good people talk to you about Truth, they do not
necessarily mean truth. The term as thus employed has no necessary
relation to the facts.

It becomes a technical term used as the title of a system of meta-
physical speculation.

To say, "There is no matter," or "There is no sin," is not truth;
but under a system of nomenclature it can easily take to itself the name
of Truth.

To say that a person fatally sick was healed miraculously may not
be truth; but, though he may not have been very sick before nor very
well now, his alleged cure can quite easily conform itself to Truth
thus defined. That is to say, Truth is no longer an accurate statement
of a condition of factuality, but it is something supposed to be good
for the backache. It is something that can be put up in platitudinous
pellets and taken like little liver pills.

As thus defined, Truth may be so unlike truth as to be a flat contradiction of it. But it may be just as good for hysteria and some
other troubles as if Truth was truth. We have high regard for truth,
but we accept it with some misgivings.

Any person who undertakes to find out the truth of things undertakes a large contract, for there is a problem at the heart of everything.

The road leading to the Egyptian oracles was lined with sphinxes,
by which the truthseeker was to understand that he was to look for
mysteries all along life's way.

For instance, the whole problem of sin is a big one. God says,
"All have sinned." Man says, "I do not believe it." Yet the fall of
man is indicated in our lives every day. We lie to ourselves and others
about our sins. Lying is the twist which "the fall" has given to our lives.

Hear the truth. He said unto them, "He that is without sin among
you, let him first cast a stone at her."

Accept the truth, "If we confess our sins, He is faithful and just
to forgive us our sins and to cleanse us from all unrighteousness."

This is the twist which the fall has given our natures.

Nineteen hundred years ago there was a memorable trial. Jesus,
the central figure of the group in the judgment-hall, was accused of
blasphemy in that, being a man, he called himself God.

Around the victim stood a motley crowd.

Roman soldiers, great, big, hard-hearted fellows, inured to all kinds
of cruelty.

The Sanhedrin.

A crowd of Jewish hoodlums clamoring for His blood.

The Roman governor sits in state, for he it is who will decide the victim's fate.

Pilate, you say that you crushed truth?

Remember, "Truth crushed to earth will rise again."

Jesus said, "Destroy this temple, and in three days it will be raised." It came to pass as He said.

Modern man, how much of your knowledge is truth? How much do you really know?

A grain of sand is a sphinx.

A human being is a mystery.

A soul's destiny is a riddle.

Truth in speech. "Work out a problem in mental arithmetic to see what discount to make before accepting judgment."

"On three things stands the world," said Simon the Just, "on law, on worship, and on charity." Yes; cut it down to one—truth.

Jerusalem, according to the Talmud, was destroyed because the instruction of the young was neglected—truth.

2. WHAT IT MEANS TO BE IN THE TRUTH

The simplest lessons we learn in childhood are the profoundest in human experiences.

The mother teaches a child to tell the truth.

Pontius Pilate asked Jesus, "What is truth?" The question was flippant and mocking; he did not wait for an answer.

What is truth? The first and simplest definition in the dictionary is, "Conformity of thought with fact."

Train ourselves.

Train others to place objects and events in their true perspectives and to tell forth what they have seen, simply, directly and accurately, that is, truthfully.

There is an immense amount of lying in the world; there is also a lot of thinner stuff called "faulty observation" and "inaccurate definition," growing not out of the lack of mental training, but out of the lack of moral perception.

Ask yourself:

1. What are the facts?
2. What did you see?
3. What did you hear?

Visit a court of justice, and you will convince yourself that there is none too much truth in the world. Justice is blindfolded as to one eye only.

3. SOME THOUGHTS ABOUT TRUTH

It is not only knowing a fact and mentally conforming to the fact with certain mental reservations, but truth is conformity of our conduct with the facts of truth in our possession.

Pilate, wait a moment; do not go out so hastily. What is truth? I give you no formal definition.

This man who stands before you at the bar, bruised, friendless and alone; with priests and howling mob against Him, crying for His blood, He is innocent. That is truth; you know it.

Of course, if you release Him, and say His position is true (He is the truth), you endanger your position as procurator, and incur the hostility of the priests.

Pilate, Jesus of Nazareth is not merely telling the truth, He is the truth.

All the truth you need in answer to your question is standing before you in this person. Crucify Him, and you crucify truth, and the truth will rise up against you in that great day. More than that: it will hand your name down to eternal infamy in the creeds that men repeat in the liturgies of the ages.

What is truth, Pilate? The truth is personal.

Every one that is of the truth cometh to the Father by Him.

CONCLUSION

Jesus was the incarnation of truth.   We are unwilling to trust a liar.

Jesus did the truth. He did not say, "Do as I say and not do as I do." He said, "Follow Me" in thought, in word, and in deed.

III. John 14:6.—Jesus the Life

He said, "I am the\life"

1. THE WORD "LIFE"

A way is easily pointed out.

The truth is more difficult of definition.

But life, who can define it?

One of the most baffling questions is, What is life? No one is able to give a definition.

It is unlike any other force in the universe. In itself it exerts no pressure; it gives no chemical reaction.

It is not directly convertible into any other force.

Yet it is the mightiest of all forces in the universe.

It may well be the force into which all other forces are ultimately to be resolved.

Most definitions attempt to define it only in terms of that which is conceived of as its opposite, namely, death.

But now comes a strange declaration of modern science, that life and death are not complete antitheses.

Professor Edward A. Schafer in a recent address before the British Association for the Advancement of Science denies that life and death are terms directly antithetic. "Death," he says, "is the final phase of life."

Death cannot be affirmed of a merely lifeless thing. We can only say of a thing that it is dead after it has once been alive, so that life and death, if what he tells us is true, are not complete antitheses.

Rather, life and death stand together. The soul that sinneth it shall die.

We do not know how life begins; we do not know how living things are related to things that never have lived.

We do not know how life relates itself to material forms that in themselves are lifeless, but grow animate when the matter is quickened by the spark of life.

The seed and the clod by chemical analysis are not wholly unlike each other; but one of them left to itself will remain forever as it is until it is acted upon from without, and the other has power to transform matter into marvellous and growing forms. The seed must "die" before it can "live."

It is characteristic of the system of truth which Jesus taught that He was never content to call it a mere creed or declaration of fact. He came into the world that it "might have life and have it more abundantly." He came to reveal a God who "is not a God of the dead, but of the living." He came to set forth a relationship to God which is in its very essential life. He used the words "eternal life," meaning not simply duration of moral quality, completeness, totality, but an endless experience of bliss. In God we live. He is our life.

Jesus was in accord with the last word of science in what He said about spiritual death. "He never predicated the death of a thing that never had been alive." That which is dead is a thing to which God imparted the marvellous glories of life.

Mere matter can never die. It is not dead. In its own way and sphere it is alive.

There is not a particle of matter in the universe but thrills with all the forces which exist in the sphere of natural law. There is not dead matter, for the life of God is in it; but life in its larger sense, God's own imparted life, belongs to things and beings that are higher. God breathed His own breath into man, and he lived, not with the mere life of gravitation and chemical force, not with the life of animal passion—these were there; but with the life which God imparted in that creative breath was the life which is life indeed.

2. WHAT IT MEANS TO HAVE LIFE
Three Aspects of Life

a. *Physical.*
1. Is it simply to exist, eat and sleep?
2. Is it simply to work, shop or office? Pursue common tasks?
3. Is it simply to return, then home again? Eat and sleep more?
4. Is it simply to return to the familiar treadmill?

Finally—pulse flutters ominously, doctor is called in, crape on the door, hearse rumbling through streets, new stone in graveyard, "Rest in peace." (Dr. Burrell.)
Is this life? Is this all?
This is the lowest conception of life, merely physical.

b. *Intellectual.*
The intellectual conception of life is higher.
A splendid thing to cultivate the mind; "knowledge is power."
But is even that worth while if that be all?
Wisest man in his time in France Voltaire, whose friends were fond of calling him the encyclopaedia.
He was an encyclopaedia bound in pigskin, for in many respects he was the most vicious of men.

c. *Spiritual.*
This is life eternal, to know God and Jesus Christ, whom He hath sent.
St. Augustine said we came from God and we shall ever be home-sick until we return to Him.
We are alienated from God by sin.
The problem of all problems is, How shall I regain my lost estate and live the life that will please God?
John 1:4; John 8:12; John 11:25; Rom. 8:6; Heb. 3:6.
Give Me thine heart. The heart is a tremendous force. "Not many men think of sending their hearts to school for culture." The brain counts for a great deal more today than real culture. The brain will win applause; genuine goodness is often overlooked.
I believe that in heaven the highest places will be given to the gentle lovers of earth with "hearts."
Intellect without soul is more cunning in arts of devilishness.
Often the greatest intellectuality is consistent with the greatest vulgarity.
It is by this sin that almost every one of the leading characters in Shakespeare's dramas is dragged down. Note, please, Richard the Third, Cardinal Wolsey, Lord and Lady Macbeth, Edmund in "King Lear," Iago in "Othello." The Iago is intellectual enough to see that virtue is a fig-leaf in his day; that love is a lust of blood; and that the quintessence of wisdom consists in "putting money in one's purse."
Intellect is not enough; the heart must go with it to save it.
In the eighteenth century, two great men left their impress upon the world, Goethe and Wesley.
Intellectually Goethe was like a great mountain towering above all; Wesley was strong in his intellect, stronger in his heart.
If you weigh these two men by their influence, Goethe cannot be compared to Wesley. Germany became rationalistic, heady; and this was the cause of her defeat by the Allies. England was saved from a somewhat similar fate by Wesley; the greatest Christian colonizer of the world. Goethe represents culture; Wesley represents culture and heart.

3. SOME THOUGHTS ABOUT LIFE

There are forms of life that are merely a living death.
A writer says: In Palestine the writer saw a leper standing in the middle of the road. The disease had eaten out his eyes and left great

ulcerous caverns; the ends of his fingers were gone, and he lifted their white stumps above him; and in his terrible leprous voice he cried, "I live; I live." It was one of the saddest words ever uttered. There are forms of life that are only another name for death.

There are forms of sin which eat the soul and life to a mocking caricature of what God meant it to be.

Rom. 12:18; 2 Cor. 5:15; Gal. 2:20; Heb. 13:18; 1 Peter 2:24.

Our earthly life—show its imperfection.

Ours is a world where gold is mixed with the dross; brass mixed with clay; goodness mixed with weakness.

The finest column in the edifice, has a blemish; there is not a statue from a Michelangelo without sand-specks and chisel-slips in the marble.

John Calvin had an intellect like unto a two-edged sword; yet his juvenile irritations lost him power and prestige.

Luther was a "despondent," and lived often under sombre skies.

Milton, listening to the sevenfold Hallelujah Chorus and writing his "Paradise Lost," could not tolerate the frivolity of his daughters, and was unduly harsh with the silly girls.

Even Washington and Lincoln, men of common sense and sanity, sometimes slipped a cog and spoiled the rhythm.

IV. John 8:12—Jesus the Light

He said, "I am the light"

1. THE WORD "LIGHT"

"Just the opposite of darkness," said a girl. A colored preacher took for his text Isa. 60:1, 2, "Arise, shine; for thy light is come, and the glory of the Lord is risen upon thee. . . . For, behold the darkness shall cover the earth, and gross darkness the people; but the Lord shall arise upon thee, and his glory shall be seen upon thee."

In explaining "gross darkness" he said, "Mah, deah friends, you all know what dahkness is, what a dahk night is, so dahk that you kain't see yoh finger befoh you. Well, you all know what a gross in numerals is, twelve dozen, 144. Well, if you take one ub de dahkest nights you eber remembah, and multiply hit by gross, you will hab some idea ob gross dahkness."

The sun, the great central body of the solar system, is our light. In appearance it is as a great shining globe. Astronomical measurements show that the sun has a diameter more than one hundred times the diameter of the earth, and therefore more than a million times its volume.

Its small apparent diameter is due to its distance, ninety-three million miles.

All light in this world is borrowed light.

Without light there would be no life; light is essential to life.

2. WHAT IT MEANS TO BE IN THE LIGHT

"God is light." The godly are in the light.

Exod. 10:22. "Moses stretched forth his hand toward heaven, and there was a thick darkness in all the land. They saw not one another, neither rose any from his place; but all the children of Israel had light in their dwellings."

It is not the same thing to walk in darkness and to walk in the light.

So it is not the same thing to be in the church and out of it any more than it is the same thing to live for Christ and to live for the pleasure of this world.

"Come out from among them, and be ye separate."

Jesus said, "Ye cannot serve God and mammon."

It is a monstrous perversion of the Christian ideal to go to church on Sunday and then live in the realm of base appetite on Monday.

Your studies, your play, your work, all must be shot through with the rays of gospel light. Look before you act. Let your actions be those of the illumined ones.

Jesus said, "The light of the body is the eye; if therefore thine eye be single, thy whole body shall be full of light. But if thine eye be evil, thy whole body shall be full of darkness. If, therefore, the light that is in thee be darkness, how great is that darkness?"

3. SOME THOUGHTS ABOUT LIGHT
Jesus said, "I am the light"

a. Light is active.

It moves with greater rapidity than any other element. It travels at the rate of 186,000 miles a second. In comparison to light, wireless telegraphy is a feeble, palsied, rheumatic old man.

"Ye are my witnesses."

Men are in darkness; let us be active in showing them the light.

Satan is the prince of darkness.

Christ is the Prince of light.

Let me ask, "Are the children of darkness more active than the children of light?"

b. Light is clean.

It can go into the foulest place without contamination.

Marble can be blackened; air can be tainted; and water can be polluted, but light is the same always. Christ, knowing of His departure from this world, said to his disciples, "Ye are the light." Hence, if we live in Christ, in the light, we can labor for God in the foulest cesspools of moral decay and remain clean.

A lily growing at the mouth of the pit of a coal mine kept its pristine whiteness though black coal dust was all around.

c. Light is immutable.

It is the most reliable of all elements. Dependable. Terrestrial things are unstable. Decay is written everywhere. Change is the order of every earthly thing. Climate changes; soil changes; atmosphere changes; things of the animal, vegetable, and mineral kingdoms change; but light is ever the same. "Jesus Christ (the light) is the same yesterday and today and forever."

Are you dependable?

Moody said some Christians, like weather, are changing their religious views with every breath of trouble, sorrow, or adversity.

d. Light dispels darkness.

The world about us in darkness. The people need light. Jesus Christ brought light into the world. We are now "the light"; so our mission is to send out the light. Three kinds of darkness need light.

The darkness of ignorance

This is true in the intellectual as well as in the spiritual realm. The spiritual darkness is most appalling. Some of it is innocent; people do not know of the light. Most of it is wilful. A man can stand in the blaze of the noonday sun and shut it out with his little finger. So little sins may disclose the glorious light of Christ.

The darkness of indifference

All about us there are poor, benighted souls with no thought of the light; they live in realms of darkness. We must turn on light of the Word until we have aroused them from their lethargy.

The darkness of iniquity

There are still others about us who are steeped in vice and sin. They are in such abysmal darkness that we must turn on the searchlight of God's Holy Spirit until they realize what they are missing by remaining in darkness. None but Jesus can convince such.

CHAPTER IV.

THURSDAY MORNING MEETING

ARMORY, JULY 7

A. J. Shartle, Presiding

IT was superfluous to put Rodeheaver down for an address on "How to Lead Singing," for all his work during the Convention was a perfect illustration of the right way to do it.

He was jolly and put every one in a good humor. He was earnest, and ever ready to add a word of prayer or of exhortation when it was appropriate. He was full of resource. Did the men seem to drag? He had them all on their feet, and the Convention seemed all men; then we had a male chorus: "The Little Brown Church in the Wildwood," or some other song rolled out as only some thousands of men could do it. He was ready for any emergency, with his prompt trombone and his clarion voice.

Our honored Lutheran trustee, Dr. Heilman, of Baltimore, offered the opening prayer in the Armory on Thursday morning, and was followed by a stirring address by Dr. A. E. Cory, of the Disciples' Missionary Society. He said:

"CHRISTIAN ENDEAVOR AND CHRISTIAN UNITY"

How tired we are of hearing of the war and the results of the war! How weary we are of all things pertaining to war! But remember, young people, today, that they are dead; they have paid the price; and, though we are weary and forgetful, they are there today on the battlefields making our obligations more real and more assured. How tired we are of hearing of the discontent and of the indifference of the world today! I think every time that I hear a man start on world conditions I shut my mind and even my heart, but we cannot ignore the condition of the world. The moral effect of the war will not be erased for fifty years. We have been put back half a century. I heard Dr. Jefferson say that "diplomacy has been the greatest failure the world has ever seen. The diplomacy of the world might have been in the hands of idiots and gorillas, as they could not have left more than ten million dead on the roads of France."

We cannot ignore this obligation of America. We boast, as I have heard it in this Convention, "America is a Christian nation." A Japanese diplomat in Japan a few months ago said, "America is a so-called Christian nation." Already men out yonder are questioning our right to the name of "Christian nation." What are the facts today, friends? Jews, Catholics, and Protestants are less than half of the population of America. The religious force in America is not half of America's population. While we of the church have been seeking our own, the great forces of non-religion have captured America.

40

What is the need of the world today? I speak not as a preacher. What is the need of America, the world, today? That need can be described in one word. The world needs the religion of Jesus Christ, the one great commanding need of the world. In order that you may not think this partisan sentiment, let me bring a statement from the document of the Prime Minister of Great Britain pleading that the British Empire shall stand by the eternal verities of religion. Here is a sentence or two: "In the recognition of the fact of the fatherhood of God and the divine purpose of the world, in the essentials of Christianity, we have found the only foundation for reconstruction and harmonious life for all men." I want you to bear in mind that these men call the British Empire and the world to the recognition of religion. It is time for us to pause, and, whatever we are politically, all of America has been silenced by words of our President that "faith in God only can save us in this hour." Secretary Davis of the Department of Labor, when asked what would save America, replied, "Only the church of Jesus Christ."

That cultured ambassador from China, who is not a Christian, said, "Let no Chinese or any one else say to you that you must not send missionaries; send them quickly, and the best you have, for the religion of Christ is the hope of China." So with these thoughts in mind we are compelled to say that religion is the greatest need of the world in this hour.

But how can that be expressed? Let us be very frank with ourselves. Can the church in its present divided state solve the world problem? No; for centuries we have labored at it. America was Christian numerically; but today we see the numbers slip beyond us, and the United States is no longer Christian numerically. The present divided state of the church is against the will of Jesus Christ. It is against the will and teachings of the Scriptures, and it is absolutely against the spirit of the age. A leader of finance said the other day that "no inharmonious group can solve any problem commercial or otherwise, particularly religious." So we may come here and pray and sing together, but we need unity of Christ to meet the oncoming hosts of Satan.

This union must of necessity be slow. Here is what I wish to say to you as a group of young people; there must be a group in the church of Jesus Christ who will commit themselves to the consciousness of unity. Numerically you are practically one-fifth of the Christian force of America, or perhaps a slight fraction less. If from the beginning all of us had been committed to this great consciousness of unity, what an effect might have been brought about in the world today! One of the New York papers said, "The only hope we can see upon the horizon for the necessary union of the churches of Jesus Christ is this grouping of young people with no prejudices, only a desire to serve." When a New York daily, which does not stand for religion, comes out editorially and says a thing like that, we must pause, and not be willing to go on with our prejudices and in our own groove. Again, we know that we are not committed to an easy task. We know the best interests of the divided church will reach out to hold the young people for themselves. They did it in the past. They will do it again, but you and I have a different background and obligations. The hour has come when we must be willing to go forward and commit ourselves in the local church, State, nation, and in the world to this absolute program of unity. It must come in acquaintanceship. We have said how we love it, but went to different churches in spite of it.

The next important step is co-operation in the important tasks, the really essential tasks, before the church of Jesus Christ. This hour will come, the great hour when we shall save the world, and I appeal to you as young people; first of all it must be like-minded people. The essentials of Christianity must be emphasized. You are the ones who are non-partisan in your belief in the whole gospel of Jesus Christ. No difficulties daunt you. While you reverence the past, you are not ancestor-worshippers. You are willing for the sake of Christ to lose your identity in the whole.

What we need now today is not more resolutions, but more action together for the saving of the world. The doctrine of Christ has been preached, but now the world wants service. Do you realize there is no difference in creed, no theological battle, around the Sermon on the Mount, no theological division? What the world wants today is the practice of the Sermon on the Mount. Some of us do not like to take it, as it is too personal. What we want to do at this time is to bring our own lives up to the ideals of that mountain sermon, go out and put it into practice for the world and Christ.

I come but to outline with all brevity some of the tasks that await Christian union and co-operation. I believe the church ought to speak, and must speak with a united voice upon the moral and political issues of the time. I believe the church must not be silent; when it is, it is an injustice. I believe in the church, the whole church of Jesus Christ. I think that, if the Protestant Church had had a voice, a united voice, that the exhibition over here in New Jersey last Saturday would have been utterly impossible. I come today as no fanatic on the question of the prize-fight. I recognize no organization. One man said, "We have now made the prize-fight so respectable that even the reformers cannot object." It is foolish to talk about arresting Dempsey for this fight; we all need to be arrested in our downward course. .This is not a question of law; it is a question of morals. You know the local problems of your community better than those of us removed from them. You know what they are. You know your individual church cannot save your community alone. If the church cannot save the community, it cannot save itself. You must get to the point where the church must either save itself and the community or be lost entirely.

I want you to remember certain great principles. First, in the greatest hour of tragedy the world has ever known, these millions of young men were called (they wouldn't have me, as I had no fighting qualities). It was young men they wanted. What happened when the war was over? They demobilized, and the young voices have been silenced as never before. What we need now is mobilized young life, and where can we overnight find mobilized young life as we have it here, four million, and fourteen million more who have been Endeavorers? We call upon you to bring unity to Christianity, to voice it in the world. This is not only your opportunity, but this is your responsibility. You are the sportsmen of the world. I defy any man to make Dempsey the sportsman of the world. These men are not the men to say what the sports of today shall be. You can make the sports of the day, make golf and ball and all, respectable.

A united church alone can cleanse, can save, can disarm, the world. A united church alone can settle the disputes between capital and labor, and fix the real thought of the world. What a banner we have for Christ and the church! Not many churches, but we must instead bring about the fulfilment of His prayer and make it truly "Christ and His Church."

Mr. Shartle, in introducing Mr. S. D. Gordon, said that there was no one whom Endeavorers had more learned to love during recent years than this apostle of the Quiet Hour.

In his characteristic calm and sweet way Mr. Gordon spoke on his striking theme, "There's Some One at Your Side You

Can't See," He pictured the Bethany home saddened by the death of the brother Lazarus, and the wonderful difference which the presence of Jesus made. In language poetic and sympathetic the speaker told the marvellous story of the great resurrection miracle. This is the Master. No one ever loved as He loves. And He, this great Lover, is now standing by your side. Some folks know us but do not love us. The knowing bothers the loving. But Jesus knows us better than any one else knows us, yet loves us more than any one else loves us. He showed His love for us by dying for us. That dear Saviour has come down from the cross, and is here by your side. There is one more here than the statistics will show.

Mr. Gordon painted the picture of the risen Christ, as He came back to His sorrowing disciples, and promised that He would be with them all the days, even to the end of the world. He is keeping that promise, right here in this meeting. If He thought good He would open our eyes, and we should all see Him and instantly recognize Him. Let us all reach out our hands, and get in touch with Him. The address in full follows.

"THERE'S SOME ONE AT YOUR SIDE YOU CAN'T SEE."

Jesus was a man without a home. He used to live in the home with His Father, but left His old home to live with us. He made His home here on the hill in a little village at the eastern end of a sea in the middle of the earth. But they didn't like His preaching there; it didn't suit their way of living, and they wouldn't change. They didn't like His preaching in the home; they wouldn't change their way of living to fit His preaching; and He couldn't change His preaching down to the level of their living; so there was trouble right away. One day things came to a break, and they forced Him to leave His old home in Nazareth; and Jesus for at least two years had no home.

Down in Bethany in the southland He had a very simple home with three young people, Mary, Martha, and Lazarus. They loved Him; He loved them. Then came that sorrow to the home. The sky had been blue, but now it is black. Their cheeks had been round with laughter, but now they were white and wet; one was taken out and carried away. They came back, and tried to forget; but there was the empty chair, the unused room; and they would catch themselves looking up to see him come in, and they would try to forget; but all the time their hearts were saying,

"O, for the touch of a vanished hand
And the sound of a voice that is still!"

But neither touch nor sound came. Then Jesus came, and Jesus' presence changed everything. The sky was black, but now blue, birds singing, the sun is out, all laughing again; for here comes their brother Lazarus on his own feet, in his own clothes. Jesus' presence brought this change.

I want to bring you the message that changed things in the Bethany home. The Master is here, and is talking with thee. There is somebody at your side you can't see, but He is there. Suppose you had been in Bethany, had been a stranger visiting these kinsfolk of yours; and you say to these people, to Mary, Who is your friend? Who is the Master? Mary's eyes are full of tears, and she begins to smile out of her eyes through the tears; and I suppose that must have made a rainbow, because light shining on drops of water makes a rainbow, you know. It is one use of tears that we sometimes miss. Mary smiles, and says: "I will tell you who He is. One day up north of us this simple scene took place; a dry, dusty country road, a village nestling on both sides, a crowd of people coming out of the village, some men carrying a burden, the body of a young man, a woman just beyond, alone, in distress plainly, a crowd behind her, they come along slowly, another crowd. coming from the other way, Jesus leading the other crowd. As they come, He motions the men to lay the burden down, and He takes\ one cold hand of the man; and life came to the young man. He sat up, looked at his mother." Can you see her eyes? She can hardly keep them in her head. Then the finest touch of the whole story; Jesus gave him back to his mother.

Have you noticed how Luke tells that story? It is one of Luke's physician's stories. Luke does not say that when Jesus saw *him*, but when He saw *her*, alone in life, and Jesus couldn't stand that; for her sake He touched him, and brought him back, and then gave him back. Will you listen with your hearts? He is the lovingest-hearted man the old world ever knew, the biggest heart, the softest heart, the womanliest heart. Could I say more? Yes, at least the superlative of the words "woman" and "mother"; and Jesus was and is the motherliest-hearted man the world knew, and no one loves as He did. No one loves as He does. This is the Master, and He is here. There's somebody at your side you can't see, but He is there.

I think if you had been talking with Mary, I know what you would have said. I have heard people say it in China and on the Continent, "Tell us more about Jesus; talk about Him." I thought I could hear Mary say: "One evening, over the hills here in the city where we do our shopping, there went a lawyer down a side street to talk with the Master; and he said, 'I believe you are the teacher.' And Christ said to this lawyer, 'Dear sir, what you need is not a teacher person, not something more for your head, but your need is a new inside.'" I said He loves as nobody else loves, and He knows as nobody else knows. Some people know us and don't love us; the knowing bothers the loving; and some folks love us because they don't know us. But listen, softly; Jesus knows you better than you do. He loves as nobody else loves. That's the Master, and He is here. There's somebody by your side you can't see, but He is there.

Then a few months later did you see the wall near the city? A crowd there, three men above the crowd; fastened up to the middle one, that is the Man. Look at Him a moment, thirty-three years of age, pure, life as sweet to Him as to you and me; and ten times He held the crowd off, and they couldn't touch Him. This time He allowed them to take Him, and I shall not allow myself to say in a moment why Jesus died. All the theories together don't tell much of His story, but that cross tells a double story in black and red, one in black and one in red. The story of black is a story of sin, sin scattered abroad; sin drove the nails, your sin and mine, that is the color. Then, the story in red is the story of love, His love for us that drove Him to the cross. I know this. He said that thing, the dying, had to be done, and for us. The simple message is this: the Master who knows, and who loves, and who died—the Master is here. There's somebody by your side you can't see. There is one more here than the statistics will show. He is there by your side as surely as you are sitting by His side.

You remember the evening of the resurrection-day in Jerusalem. Come down a side street; upstairs are the people sitting around the room, men and women; they are the closest of friends of Jesus, and these people are saying, "If this thing spreads in town." They are talking this man over. One man says, "The Master has risen." The woman over says, "Risen? what do you mean?" That man says, "I saw Him; I touched Him." Can you hear them wondering and questioning?

And then all at once, who is this in the center of the room? There was nobody there a moment ago, but there is somebody there now. It looks like Jesus. Nobody ever saw His face and forgot, or sees and forgets. How I wish the old church might see His face today! It might change a thing or two. But they are frightened, and their faces go white, and they say, "We are seeing things; it has been a hard day on our nerves." But you can see their eager eyes searching between sandal-straps on His feet. There are the ugly holes. Then He spoke as nobody ever heard Jesus speak and forget, or hears and forgets. If the old church might hear His voice today, it might change a thing or two. But what He said was almost unaccountably simple, "My friends, have you something to eat?" They got broiled fish and a barley loaf. They sat around Him, talking and nudging each other. That is the finest evidence of the resurrection produced thus far. It leaves all theoretical libraries invaluable. How did He come in? Don't ask me.

There is one big reason behind the forty days of the burden of sympathy, "Lo, I am with thee all the day," bright days, shiny days, showery days, convention days, armistice days, all the days the Master in here. There's somebody by your side you can't see, but He is there, and I am very sure of this; you would know an unseen hand on your arm; and, if you sat very still, you would hear a quiet inner voice talking: "I know you; I know your name; I know your life; I have been thinking about you"; and then He softens His voice, and says: "I died for you. I am after you; I need you." The Master is here, and He is talking with us. I don't know just where He is. It may be in the middle aisle; it may be over here. One thing I am sure of, as a man grows older, he becomes less positive about many things. If He would open our eyes, you would see Him right here. You'd know him as quick as a flash, that face that combined all the fineness of the finest woman's face and the strength of the strongest man's face, torn with thorns. He is talking; and, if we bow in prayer, we might each reach out a hand and touch Him, and get in touch; and then coming to New York would be the best thing you have ever done. You will go back hand in hand and heart to heart.

One night at the end of a lecture John Gough found a man waiting for him, a young man with him. Mr. Gough talked with the son. Mr. Gough in his kindly way drew out the young man's thought that the Bible was not true. Usually you scratch a sceptic and find a sinner. But this was an exception. Mr. Gough said, "Why not pray?" To whom would he pray, questioned the young man, there was no God, he thought. Mr. Gough said, "You believe in love, your mother's love for you?" This was the young man's tender spot.

He went to his bedroom that night, and kneeled, and prayed very earnestly, "O love." Instantly, ever so softly, the word he knew by heart seemed spoken in his heart, "God is love." There came an impulse, and he obeyed it; and he said, "O God"; and again quick as a flash, very quietly as though the words were spoken out of his mouth, "God is love; He gave His only begotten Son." The third time the impulse came; again he obeyed it, and said, "O Christ." Then something happened. Outwardly everything was as it was, but inside there was peace. A score of questions remained unanswered, but he was in touch at heart with the Man who died. That settled all things for him. O, that we might keep in touch with the One at our side!

CHAPTER V.

BOOKS AND POCKETBOOKS

ARMORY, THURSDAY AFTERNOON, JULY 7

Rev. R. P. Anderson, Presiding

"MY name is Percy Foster; I don't care what yours is so long as you sing," was the way in which the leader of the praise service Thursday afternoon won the good humor of the audience that quickly became an effective chorus. After two or three hymns "The Little Brown Church in the Wildwood," started without announcement, kept growing in volume. Under the leader's skilful direction it was soon heard as it might sound to one gradually nearing the singers. This swung into "Rock of Ages." Then followed "I come to the garden alone," and on reaching the cnorus the men whistled the melody as an accompaniment to the soft singing of the words.

The presiding officer at the session was Editorial Secretary Robert P. Anderson. He introduced as especially qualified to treat the theme of "The Endeavorer and His Reading" the Christian Endeavor editor and poet, Dr. Amos R. Wells, whose address appears in the chapter of addresses.

As a man who knows the Bible Dr. Floyd W. Tomkins was called to discuss "The Endeavorer and His Bible." In the first place, he said, every Endeavorer should have his own Bible. He should use it freely. Do not be afraid to mark your Bible, and do not be afraid to put into it anything that marks your religious life.

A minister divided the Bible's contents into two P's and four D's, persons and places, dates, doings, doctrines and duties. There are three characteristic elements, history, poetry and prophecy. Christians should know where to find any book of the Bible. There are some ministers even that do not know how to turn to the minor prophets readily.

Read your Bible; read it through; and read it through again continuously as you would read another book, only remembering that it is God's book. We should be so familiar with it as to be able to quote it readily.

Use the Bible as a means of spiritual growth. It is the inspired word of God. To me there is only one religion in the world, and that is the Christian.

46

Some get spiritual dyspepsia through not meditating enough and applying it. Go to the Bible in all the experiences of life. A Scripture calendar is an excellent thing to have. When I was a minister in New York, one day everything went wrong. I said, "What shall I do?" I looked at my calendar, and the text for the day was, "Whatsoever he saith unto you, do it." I grabbed my hat, went to see several persons that I knew wanted to see me; and, when I came back, everything was clear.

Be sure that every promise in the Bible is given to be fulfilled. Hold fast to them; study them; use them; and you will find in them that which will reveal them to you more and more every day.

Books as the Endeavorer's tools were presented by A. J. Shartle, the publication-manager of the United Society. Construction, instruction, and inspiration he emphasized as the three essentials for a Christian Endeavor society. He rapidly and with clever comments mentioned some of the most useful books put forth by the United Society, holding up posters giving the titles. Especial attention was called to some of the publications just from the press, like the new "Junior Manual," by Mr. Anderson; Dr. Wells's poems; Mrs. Clark's "Bible Autobiographies"; Mrs. Wood's "On the Highway"; "Religious Vocations," by Frank Lowe, Jr.; and "Successful Socials," by Mrs. E. P. Gates.

The Endeavorer and various books had furnished themes for the preceding speakers. An important addition to the list, the pocketbook, was earnestly treated by Rev. W. A. Mactaggart. He approached the subject with the more readiness because it had to do with the Endeavorer, not with the business man. First were reviewed the principles shown in the financial campaign conducted at Corinth according to Paul's directions, a campaign universal, systematic, successful. The same principles applied in Ephesus, in Jerusalem, at Rome. It was a victorious campaign because it rested on the victory that Christ had won over death. That was the bond of fellowship that moved the disciples to contribute for the help of brethren in need. "Inasmuch as ye did it unto one of My brethren" was the inspiration of the giving. But philanthropy is only temporary. Armenia and China need more than a collection; they need the gospel and the cross.

A few years ago a group of high-school girls raised eighty dollars that a Korean girl might be kept in school. She was later persecuted and imprisoned for her patriotism. In prison she took the opportunity to give the gospel. Punished for it, she used the time allowed for the women in the prison to comb their hair, and, when their loosened hair hid their lips, she spoke to her companions of the Saviour. When she left the prison, every woman had been won to Christ. After her release she went with other women from house to house giving the message. All in consequence of an investment of eighty dollars.

Let us all join the Tenth Legion. We could sweep the world for Christ with the sum thus gained. But be just as conscientious in the administration of the nine-tenths as in that of the one-tenth.

Another Quiet Talk from S. D. Gordon was a treat for which the immense audience gladly tarried, though the afternoon was about as hot as is made. His subject, "Peter Johnson's New Fishing Experiences," piqued the curiosity of the Endeavorers.

Peter Johnson was of course Simon Peter, the son of John or Jonas. He would be called Mr. Johnson today, or perhaps Bishop Johnson. He was in trouble, for he had denied his Master. He made a suggestion, for he was good at making suggestions. He said, "I'm going fishing." It is good to get off by one's self when in trouble, and think it all out. The other disciples said, "We'll go along." It is easy to lead men, if you are in earnest about anything.

Thus, in quaint language, and with picturesque and practical hints scattered all through, Mr. Gordon told the story of the great catch of fish on the Sea of Galilee, the fire on the shore, and Christ's kind words to His disconsolate disciple after the meal.

It was a sweet, warm, friendly talk, poetic all the way through, the words of a Christian philosopher and saint. S. D. Gordon has thousands of friends among Christian Endeavorers, who love him for his big brain, his big heart, and best of all for his great love of his Saviour.

Note.—For the addresses in full by Dr. Amos R. Wells, Dr. Floyd W. Tomkins, A. J. Shartle, Dr. W. A. Mactaggart, and S. D. Gordon, see chapter of addresses

---

CHAPTER VI.

STATE CONVENTIONS

PENNSYLVANIA STATE CONVENTION, COLLEGIATE CHURCH OF
ST. NICHOLAS

Thursday Afternoon, July 7

MORE than a thousand delegates to the World's Convention from Pennsylvania crowded into the Collegiate Reformed Church of St. Nicholas to hold their inter-convention State rally. Mr. Stanley Fellows, of New York, one of the Convention song-leaders, conducted a spirited song service. Mr. Bert E. Rudolph, president of the Pennsylvania union, presided at the meeting.

The State union's general secretary, Mr. Haines A. Reichel, reported the following facts regarding the preceding two-year period from September, 1919, to July 1921:

Eight county unions were organized: 125 Senior societies were organized; 1,665 Senior, 230 Intermediate, and 657 Junior societies were recorded, a grand total of 2,552 societies. Nine new county Alumni Fellowships have been formed, making a total of thirteen, and purity and Alumni departments have been organized.

Of mission-study classes 215 were reported, the enrolment being 2,250 while the total gifts from Pennsylvania societies to missions in the two-year period is $75,000; 2,988 Quiet Hour Comrades have been enrolled in these two years.

The State has been divided into eight districts, the counties in these districts being grouped around certain cities, and the districts being named after their central cities, Franklin, Pittsburg, Altoona, Williamsport, Harrisburg, Scranton, Allentown and Philadelphia. The district secretary is the key-man between the district and State headquarters. The State union is planning for a series of eight district county-officers' conferences in the early fall to map out a program for the coming year. This is a new and much needed feature in Pennsylvania.

State officers and department superintendents also presented their programs and policies for the coming year, linking them up with the new world-wide program of "Christian Endeavor Foursquare."

Mr. Clarence C. Hamilton, of Boston, thrilled and inspired the delegates by an energetic presentation of the topic, "Putting over the Program." He said 'if Pennsylvania is the biggest Christian Endeavor union in all the world she ought to be the biggest in every respect, accomplishments, enthusiasm, and

49

finances.   He pointed to numerically smaller States such as Kansas, which in the past year has outstripped many States; to Michigan for her new program, with an assistant secretary included; and to West Virginia with less than four hundred societies and more than $4,000 budget.   Pennsylvania with her 1,665 Senior societies only raised and spent a little more than $4,500 from July, 1920, to July, 1921, everything included.

Mr. Charles C. Culp, World's Convention chairman for Pennsylvania, through whose efforts the biggest State delegation came to New York, called to the platform the chairmen of the counties in the State which have done the best to raise their quotas of delegates to New York.   Counties reaching their quotas were Somerset, Fulton and Lehigh; Cumberland County secured 86.6 per cent., although it had been organized as a union only thirty days prior to the World's Convention.   Each of the first three received $15 in cash for having exceeded its quota.

Dr. Floyd W. Tomkins, Pennsylvania's beloved spiritual leader, conducted a very helpful consecration service looking forward to the successful completion of our plans for the coming year.

The Convention by vote approved the executive committee's indorsement of the Near-East Relief, and pledged co-operation to put over this worthy project.

Mr. Marc Edmund Jones, executive secretary of the New York Committee, presented the final message to the Convention in an instructive talk pointing out some faults in Christian Endeavor societies and recommending some wise remedies.

New York State Convention, Marble Collegiate Church

Thursday Afternoon, July 7

One of the important events of the World's Christian Endeavor Convention, was the gathering of the New York State delegates for the Thirtieth Empire State Convention, in the Marble Collegiate Church, Twenty-ninth Street and Fifth Avenue. Thursday afternoon.   Hundreds of Endeavor delegates from all parts of this State filled the auditorium.   Homer Rodeheaver, who has a warm spot in the hearts of New York State Endeavorers from his many campaigns in this State with Billy Sunday, led the opening song service, and in appreciation of those present in the singing, Mr. Rodeheaver and Miss Fairbanks of Albany sang "In the Garden" to the delight of the audience.

Dr. George H. Scofield of Highland, State Intermediate superintendent, led the devotional service.   In the absence of Dr. Francis E. Clark, the founder of the movement, who was unable to be present, the Endeavorers joined in silent prayer for him and his great work.

Edward P. Gates, general secretary of the United Society of Christian Endeavor, brought to the Convention the greetings of the United Society and of the World's Union. Mr. Gates paid a high tribute to the Empire State for the work accomplished during the past year. He went so far as to say that no State in the Union had made more rapid strides, nor accomplished more in real results in this year.

Carlton M. Sherwood, general secretary of the New York State Union, then spoke briefly on "Prophecy: The Future Reflected from the Past." Mr. Sherwood reviewed some of the high spots of his activities during the past year—the 30,000 miles travelled in field work up and down the State, the fifty-five counties visited for conventions, conferences, rallies and executive gatherings, and the great amount of printed matter sent out.

Dr. Ira Landrith of Nashville, Tenn., extension secretary of the World's Christian Endeavor Union, gave the delegates a spirited talk on "The Challenge of the Present Opportunity." Dr. Landrith closed his address with an impressive appeal to the delegates to stand behind their State Union work to the limit in self-forgetting service and sacrifice. The response of those assembled was gratifying and showed itself in the nearly $3,000 pledged from individuals present for the carrying on of the increased program of work in the State Christian Endeavor Union for the coming year.

In the absence of Dr. Daniel A. Poling, the closing message of the convention was brought to the Convention by Dr. Clarence A. Barbour of Rochester, president of Rochester Theological Seminary. Dr. Barbour is a past president of the State Union, and spoke with enthusiasm and assurance of the great progress of the work in this territory in the days past.

These officers of the State Union for the coming year were elected: President, William H. Brown, Rochester; first vice-president, William A. Boyd, Ithaca; recording secretary, C. Fayette Lawrence, Katonah; Junior superintendent, Mrs. Grace Worden Brewster, Syracuse; Intermediate superintendent, the Rev. George H. Scofield, Highland; treasurer, H. Earle Howe, Syracuse.

Carlton M. Sherwood of Buffalo continues as the general secretary of the State Union, with the office headquarters and executive work in that city.

The trustees at large elected are: Hon. Frederick A. Wallis of New York; Fred C. Collins, Syracuse; Harry A. Kinports, New York; John R. Clements, Binghamton; the Rev. F. P. Hunter, Middletown, and Edwin P. Howard, Rochester.

In appreciation of his faithful and efficient services, the retiring president, Fred C. Collins of Syracuse, was elected as the State vice-president of the World's Christian Endeavor Union.

BANQUETS AND BANQUETS

HELD IN MANY PLACES, JULY 6-11

The Junior Banquet

A FINE company of one hundred and fifty Junior superintendents met in the Adams Memorial Church for their banquet on Thursday evening. Miss F. Lucy Hollings, chairman of the Junior World's Convention Committee, was in charge, aided by Mr. Harry Galloway, Miss Agnes E. Baker, and the other members of her efficient and devoted committee.

It is because of this committee's work that the splendid number of 1,600 Juniors were registered as Convention delegates. Juniors do not travel far, and it is natural that only 150 of these should be out-of-town delegates, mainly from the neighboring States of New Jersey and Connecticut. Most of this notable record is therefore to be credited to metropolitan Juniors, and we congratulate them on their splendid showing.

This Junior banquet, in good "eats," delightful companionship, and bright addresses, was in every way a success.

The Intermediates' Banquet

The Y. W. C. A. Hall was crowded with more than 250 hearty diners at the Intermediate banquet on July 7. In all Christian Endeavor there is absolutely nothing that can compare with Intermediate Endeavor for its youthful spirit, for its boundless enthusiasm, and for the freshness of its red-hot ardor. All that is best and noblest in Intermediate Christian Endeavor was in evidence at this meeting.

Representatives were present from all parts of the country, showing that Intermediate Endeavor has already taken root in practically every State.

The leader of the banquet and toastmaster was Paul Brown, the national Intermediate superintendent. As his right hand sat his mother, who received a great welcome from the young people.

Commissioner Wallis, who declared himself a "dynamic Intermediate," was made an Intermediate life-member by acclaim. In a stirring speech he told of the need of influencing the child and the youth in the building of the church and of America.

The Missionary Tea

A unique and picturesque feature of the Convention was the missionary tea on Thursday afternoon. At the close of the afternoon session sightseeing automobiles were in readiness to take small groups of delegates to Chinatown, where Dr. Lee To, in charge of the Morning Star Mission, directed the arrangements. Badges proclaimed many a friendly looking Celestial along the crowded sidewalks as a member of the Christian Endeavor reception committee. The event called out a large unofficial reception committee of different nationalities, young and old swarming in the street and at the windows commanding a view. Oriental music from Chinese orchestras floated from open windows.

Five Chinese restaurants opened their doors to receive the guests, and showed most courteous hospitality. The proprietor of one showed by his face and bearing the sincerity of his words when he spoke of it as "a happy day." After the generous meal had been served the delegates gathered again in the street, which soon echoed with the strains of "Since Jesus came into my heart" and "Brighten the corner where you are" and cheers for Chinatown. The progress of the departing delegates was marked by their songs as they made their way along the streets, and many of those living along the Bowery were drawn to hear and to gaze.

The company of visiting Endeavorers made their way to an assembly-hall in the neighborhood, a hall in which, they were reminded, had been held some of the greatest Russian gatherings during the war. It is in the foreign section of New York. In London 96 per cent. of the population is of native birth; in some blocks in New York 97 per cent. and more is of foreign birth. The city could furnish foreigners enough to make sixteen Jerusalems. America, it was said, is what the immigrant has made it.

In such surroundings, the meeting-place of a Chinese Sunday School, the Chinese welcome to the visitors put in the forefront the unity of the East and the West through Jesus Christ and the love that He has awakened.

Some exercises by Chinese children were among the most interesting parts of the rally. A group of them sang sweetly "God loves the little Chinese children."

CHAPTER VIII.

FRATERNAL MEETING

ARMORY, THURSDAY EVENING, JULY 7

Rev. Francis E. Clark, Presiding

THE session on the second evening of the Convention was quite as crowded as was the hall on the first night. The song-leader was Percy S. Foster, the inimitable, who made the great crowd not only sing but shake hands with nearest neighbors. Evidently the delegates who had come to New York came for business, for in spite of heat and the many outside attractions the sessions were not only well attended forenoon, afternoon and evening, but the many side rooms connected with the hall were constantly utilized.

There are always surprises—pleasant surprises—at our Conventions. The first at this meeting was a gramophone session when the audience heard the voice of Dr. Poling with startling clarity and distinctness. Secretary Gates, Mr. Shartle and Dr. Clark have all made records, although these were not given in the meeting.

This was the evening for fraternal messages. Five young people's organizations sent representatives with hearty greetings to the Convention.

Dr. George J. Fisher spoke for the Boy Scouts, co-workers with us, equally interested in the youth of the land. Both Christian Endeavor and Boy Scouts believe that if social service is to be done it must be done by voluntary workers, and the greatest need of the boys of America is wise, consecrated, adult leadership; and this leadership must come, as it is now coming, from the church.

Secretary Frank L. Brown, of the World's Sunday School Union, spoke eloquently for the Sunday School with its 30,000,-000 members and its great teaching staff. He brought a message from the Hon. John Wanamaker, who spoke of Christian Endeavor as a mighty factor in the educational program of the church.

The Y. W. C. A.'s representative was Mrs. Robert E. Speer. Her message was a vigorous and beautiful plea that the new generation may think in fresh terms of Jesus Christ, who is the same yesterday, today, and forever, that we may grow nearer to Him and understand Him better, so that the young people of the world may make of the future what. He would have them make.

For the Y. M. C. A., Secretary Cooper, of the Washington, D. C., organization, who is also a member of the Christian Endeavor Alumni and who is in constant touch with Christian Endeavor activities, gave us an eloquent message.

The ideals of Christian Endeavor and the "Y" are identical, as Mr. Cooper pointed out, and the two bodies unite in advancing them.

It was truly an inspiration that made Dr. Clark ask all the men in the audience to rise. The splendid showing was a conclusive answer to those who charge that the young men are deserting the church.

Mrs. Selden Bacon spoke for the Girl Scouts, who stand, like Christian Endeavor, for voluntary organization. In the old days young people *had* to do their duty or suffer. Today Girl Scouts and Endeavorers are in the work because they want to be in it, not because others make them. The Girl Scouts, from their motto alone, are one with Endeavor. That motto is, "Help everybody all over the world wherever you can."

One of the missionary statesmen of the world is Dr. Samuel Zwemer, who speaks out of long experience and knowledge of the needs of the Mohammedan world. His address on "The Call of the Kingdom" was a masterly effort, passionate, eloquent, and packed full of good things. He began with a comparison of our great Christian Endeavor Convention with the immense conventions of Mohemmedans in Mecca in desert Arabia, conventions twenty times the size of ours. What a magnificent influence the faith of the Moslem exerts! That faith has stood against all attacks of Christianity, and constitutes the greatest problem of the Oriental world. What is the power of this non-Christian religion, so immense in its statistical dimensions? The map of the world contains great sections whose population is numbered in teeming millions which today are utterly unevangelized.

Mohammedanism is a usurper. All other non-Christian religions antedate Christ, but Christianity had a six-hundred-year start of Mohammedanism, which has pushed Christ out of lands where once His gospel was known. Dr. Zwemer suggested in a series of heart-moving questions the baffling nature of the problem of the East.

Mohammedanism is also a political problem. Of 200,000,000 Mohammedans in the world only 13,000,000 are politically free, so that the great majority of the Moslem world lives under foreign flags.

The problem is also a social problem. The Mohammedan world is 96 per cent. illiterate, and of every thousand women only three can read and write. And illiteracy is always accompanied by superstition and infant mortality. Add to this the threefold curse of Mohammedanism, polygamy, concubinage, and slavery.

The Christian remedy is to let in the light. The children especially need it, and this call for service is the clarion call of the Kingdom. It is a call for consecration and for volunteers who will dedicate themselves to service.

The problem is a religious as well as a social one. Between the Moslem religion and ours there yawns a chasm which is deep as hell, a chasm which is thirteen centuries wide. Dr. Zwemer gave the audience a glimpse of the missionary's difficulties as he collides with the deep-rooted convictions of the Moslem world. It was a revelation to many to know that the devout Mohammedan speaks of Mohammed in the same terms as Paul speaks of Jesus, and clothes him with the same high glories as those with which we Christians clothe Jesus Christ.

What is the outcome to be? It is a call to service. The dark, dark Moslem world is a tremendous challenge to Christians today, a challenge to the youth of the world to invest life in some part of the vast Moslem field. Once before Jesus won the Near East, not by the sword, but by sacrifice, and so alone can it be won again.

Another beautiful surprise was a speech by one of Oregon's representatives who in the name of Oregon Endeavorers presented to Dr. Clark a splendid bouquet of roses, which to the delight of the audience he turned over to Mrs. Clark.

Dr. Clark read this telegram from the Governor of Maine:

"On behalf of the people of Maine I extend to you my congratulations upon the wonderful organization that you founded. Maine and Portland are proud to have been the home of the first Christian Endeavor society, and your four million members form an army of Christian soldiers who can be relied upon to fight for everything that makes for better citizenship.

"PERCIVAL P. BAXTER,
"*Governor of Maine.*"

The last speaker was Rev. John Pollock, of Belfast, Ireland, president of the European Christian Endeavor Union, whose subject was "Christian Endeavor in the World Crisis." Mr. Pollock is no stranger to American Endeavorers, having been several times in this country. His canny Scotch wit put him at once in sympathy with the audience, and his reference to the Irish question immediately made people sit up in expectation. Christian Endeavor, he said, has done something to alleviate the differences that exist in Ireland, and there is some evidence to show that Christian Endeavor is not wholly unknown or unappreciated in the Roman Catholic Church in Ireland.

His address sparkled with dry wit and made many sly digs at some of the misunderstandings of the relation of the races—

A Fine Group from Connecticut

The Colorado Delegation

English, Scottish, Irish and Welsh—which constitute the United Kingdom. He made it clear that Great Britain will never permit Ireland to achieve independence, but will grant to Ireland, within the empire, the fullest possible measure of self-government. Endeavorers can pray for Ireland and hasten the day of peace.

Christian Endeavor is one of the unifying forces in the continent of Europe today. In Germany Christian Endeavor has done more than any other organization to sweeten the national sentiment toward the Allies. In Germany Christian Endeavor made during the war greater progress than in any other country. It has more field-secretaries than before the war,—ten in all,—and it has a printing-press to carry on its work. In Germany Christian Endeavor is doing great things to restore peace. "Christian Endeavor," said Mr. Pollock, "has raised my estimation of the German Christian character. There is a Christian Germany and an unchristian Germany, just as there is a Christian and an unchristian America. The time is coming when we shall love and honor one another as we have done before. Once, years ago," said the speaker, "while I was addressing a great Christian Endeavor convention in Berlin, the German flag and the Union Jack were unfurled above me; *and I hope to have the same experience again,* for I have been officially invited to address an Endeavor audience in Bremen in October. Let me close with this Spanish proverb: 'The sword makes the war; the heart, and the heart alone, can make peace.'"

It was a great evening, gloriously worth while, an evening of inspiration and high hope.

NOTE.—For greetings and addresses in full see chapter of addresses.

CHAPTER IX.

DENOMINATIONAL RALLIES

IN MANY PLACES, NEW YORK CITY, JULY 8

FRIDAY morning was largely given up to the rallies of the Endeavorers of the different denominations. A few of the denominations, chancing to have churches near the Armory, held their rallies in those churches, but most of them were assigned to various rooms of the Armory, or different corners of the great Armory Auditorium.

The editors visited as many rallies as they could, and found them all splendidly attended, enthusiastic, and hugely enjoying a wonderful series of practical and forward-looking addresses. The following reports have been received. All were arranged for.

Rally of the Christian Church

The denominational rally of the Christian Church was the largest, the most enthusiastic, and was pronounced the best, ever held by them at any World's or International Convention.

Five brief addresses were enjoyed by those present. These were "Christian Endeavor Deepening the Devotional Life," Rev. Ralph G. English, Albany, N. Y.; "Christian Endeavor and the Evangelistic Program," Rev. J. F. Morgan, Norfolk, Va.; "Christian Endeavor Aiding in Christianizing the Intellectual Life," Rev. F. E. Rockwell, Albany, Mo.; "Christian Endeavor and the Great Commission," Miss Frieda Kirkendall; "Christian Endeavor and Stewardship of Self and Substance," Rev. A. E. Kemp, D.D., Troy, O.

The addresses were all of a high order, glowing with enthusiasm, burning with earnestness, intensely practical, forward looking.

The rally closed by the singing of the Christian Endeavor Forward Movement Crusade rally song composed by Rev. A. B. Kendall, D.D., secretary of the Christian Endeavor Board of the Christian Church, and repeating the Mizpah benediction.

Rally of the African Methodist Episcopal and African Methodist Episcopal Zion

The denominational meeting under the auspices of the Allen Christian Endeavor Society of the African Methodist Episcopal Church and the Varick Christian Endeavor Society of the

African Methodist Episcopal Zion Church was largely attended and most inspiring from beginning to end.

Rev. S. S. Morris, general secretary of the African Methodist Episcopal Church, presided, assisted by Professor Aaron Brown, general secretary of the African Methodist Episcopal Zion Church.

The praise service was conducted by Rev. C. B. Lawyer, of Massachusetts, and Rev. A. F. B. Hory, of South Carolina.

An address of welcome was given by Mrs. F. E. Hebbons, of New York City, and the response was made by Dr. Pharr, of Florida.

The Foursquare Program of Christian Endeavor was interpreted in the light of each denomination by the general secretaries Brown and Morris, and approved by the Endeavorers. Emphasis was placed on the twenty-five-per-cent. net increase in membership; better attention paid to Intermediate and Junior work, a movement in the interest of foreign missions, a program of religious education and Alumni Fellowship, wide-awake district and city unions.

An address on "Our Obligation to Africa" was made by Bishop W. H. Heard, of Philadelphia, while Dr. F. M. Jacobs, of New York, spoke on "The Challenge to the Youth."

The meeting was brought to a fitting close with a service of consecration effectively conducted by Dr. M. E. Davis and Dr. G. C. Taylor, of Virginia.

The Primitive Methodist Rally

Rev. J. Proude, pastor of the First Primitive Methodist Church of Brooklyn, presided.

There were delegates from Maryland, North Carolina, Iowa, Pennsylvania and near-by States, fifty-five in all.

Splendid reports were given of the work done in each section, and some splendid methods were explained.

While much has been done on financial lines by several sections, the spiritual part of the work was stressed, and good results have been obtained. It was a very helpful conference to all present.

The Lutheran Rally

Lutherans from all parts of the country assembled in Room 4 of the Armory, until the capacity of the room was exhausted. The meeting was called to order by Rev. P. A. Heilman, D.D., pastor of St. Paul's Lutheran Church of Baltimore. Miss Clara Dohme, secretary for the past two years, was re-elected secretary. Rev. P. A. Heilman, a United Society trustee, was elected president for the coming two years. After a brief song service and the repeating of the Nineteenth Psalm in concert, short, happy remarks were made by various Lutherans on the work being done by the different societies throughout the country. Special stress was laid on the Quiet Hour and the tithing system, and it was declared that the financial difficulties of the churches would all be solved if the Lord's people would give the Lord His own.

Emphasis was laid upon the memorizing of portions of the Word of God daily, that our minds and hearts may be filled with it. The Lutheran Church places the Word of God first and above everything else, and anything out of harmony with the Word has no place in the Lutheran creed.

Foreign missionary giving was also insisted upon in the meeting. Some of the Lutheran societies support their own missionary in the foreign field, others a catechist or student, all making foreign missions the leading cause. A few of the societies reported young men for the ministry, and one reported a foreign missionary. A liberal offering was taken for the foreign work of the Christian Endeavor society, and was turned over to the treasurer, Mr. A. J. Shartle.

The following two resolutions were heartily adopted by a rising vote:

"WHEREAS, The Dempsey-Carpentier fight held last week in Jersey City was an exhibition of brutality and disregard of law, and contrary to all that is uplifting,

"*Therefore be it Resolved*, That we, the delegates of the Lutheran Christian Endeavor societies here assembled in Convention in New York City, do hereby most earnestly protest against the same, and call upon all citizens to do all in their power to advance the cause of civic righteousness.

"*Second*, That, because of the growing disregard of the Sabbath, we urge all our members to do all they can to preserve this divine institution."

After singing "Blest be the tie that binds," the meeting adjourned to meet two years hence. It was a most enthusiastic meeting, notwithstanding the intense heat.

The Congregational Rally

Congregationalists to the number of about eight hundred responded enthusiastically to the denomination's rally in the Auditorium of the Armory on Friday morning.

Rev. George Reid Andrews, New York secretary of the Congregational Education Society, presided.

He explained in particular the Pilgrim Federation of the Congregational Church, laying particular stress on the fact that it is not another organization, but a plan to organize the young people of the denomination to carry out the Congregational program. He urged all of those present to communicate with him or the Education office at Boston for details of organization, that all may work together more effectively.

Rev. Alden H. Clark, recruiting secretary of the American Board and a former missionary to India, presented the opportunities offered by the American Board for foreign service. He stated that at the present time the Board needs 19 doctors, 15 nurses, 6 agriculturists, 39 educators, 42 ordained men, 10 women social and evangelistic workers, and urged those present to consider the great call to Christian service.

Rev. William S. Beard, promotion secretary of the Congregational Home Missionary Society, presented the cause of the home field, laying particular stress upon the fact that Christian Endeavor stands for service.

The leaders were particularly gratified with the large attendance and the spirit of enthusiasm that prevailed.

The Brethren Rally

The watchword, "Forward to the goal!"
The motto, "We can and we will!"
The pressing need, "Trained leadership."

After an introductory message by the leader of the rally, Rev. G. C. Carpenter, Rev. Earl Riddle, of Louisville, O., gave a stirring inspirational message, just the kind to be expected from a live-wire Endeavor pastor and county-union officer.

A round-table discussion of Endeavor problems and possibilities followed, in which twelve of the delegates present took part.

Plans were made to pass along the Convention inspiration in the largest measure possible to all Brethren Endeavorers, this to be accomplished through conferences and through the weekly message in the church paper, *The Brethren Evangelist*.

The Presbyterian Rally

The Presbyterian, U. S. A., conference in the Brick Presbyterian Church Friday morning *was* a conference, not a song-singing, speech-making rally. Rev. William Ralph Hall, denominational director of Young People's Work, announced that a letter had come to his desk from a group of young people in a church where a new Christian Endeavor society had just been started. These folks asked, "What should be the relationships of our new society to the agencies of our own denomination, and what can you do for us to help us achieve success?"

Mr. Hall said that upon learning that several of the members were to be in New York for the World's Convention he had written that he would arrange for representatives of the Presbyterian Boards to which they were directly related to meet them at the Convention and answer all their questions and give them helpful advice. So they were on hand at the conference, and so were the national denominational leaders.

While the large number of Presbyterian delegates from all over the country listened with interest and made many entries in their note-books, the new society was instructed and coached by Miss Ann T. Reid, candidate secretary of the Board of

Foreign Missions; Miss M. Josephine Petrie, young people's
secretary of the Woman's Board of Home Missions; Mrs. W. T.
Larimer, general secretary, Women's Department, Board of
Missions for Freedmen; and Frank D. Getty, associate director
of Young People's Work, Board of Publication and Sabbath-
School Work. Then Walter D. Howell, one of the pioneer State
field secretaries in Christian Endeavor and now general field-
representative of the Sabbath-School Board, rose from among
the delegates and urged Presbyterian Endeavorers to a simultaneous and balanced loyalty to their own denomination and to
Christian Endeavor. The conference was closed with prayer by
Dr. Ira Landrith.

The Baptist Rally

This rally was held at the Madison Avenue Baptist Church,
with Dr. M. M. McGorrill, director of Young People's Work
for the American Baptist Publication Society, presiding. Stanley
B. Hazzard, of the Baptist Mission Society of New York City,
gave the introductory speech on denominational co-operation.
He asked for co-operation in training and service. Miss Jessie D.
White, candidate secretary of the Women's Baptist Home Mission Society, spoke on the possibilities for life service in home
mission work. Dr. Joseph Robbins, of the Baptist Foreign Missionary Society, spoke of the challenge of the foreign field for
young people. W. J. Sly, of the Baptist Publication Society,
described the work for new Americans, pleading for increased
activity with and for new Americans. Dr. Chalmers, educational
secretary for the Baptist Publication Society, spoke on the
denominational fellowship and co-operation. He said that, no
matter under what name our societies may be organized, we
are interested in the forward march of Christ's kingdom through
the church of God.

A fellowship luncheon was held in the parlors of the church.
It was an inspirational affair enjoyed by all. Immediately after
the luncheon a stirring address was given by Rev. C. Wallace
Petty, pastor of the Mt. Morris Baptist Church of New York
City. His subject dealt with the lack of leadership at the present
time and the wonderful possibilities that await the younger
generation to succeed where the generation of today has failed.
Where is the co-operation that was heralded so loudly at the
time of the World War? Where is the consecration of life?
Today men are hungry for something that is big and noble. It
is our business to lead onward and upward.

The United Brethren Rally

The United Brethren denominational conference was attended
by more than fifty delegates from twelve States from Nebraska
to New York, and included three State secretaries: R. L.
Lanning, of Missouri; C. E. Hetzler, of West Virginia; La Verne

Spafford, of Michigan; and R. F. Robson, president of the Des Moines union.

Rev. H. F. Shupe, editor of *The Watchword* and trustee of the United Society, presided. Rev. Mr. Van Saum, of East Freedom, Penn., was elected secretary.

After a brief message from Secretary O. T. Deever the delegates in an informal way introduced themselves, and told briefly about the good things being done by their home societies and the best things they were getting out of the New York Convention. Forty-four persons participated in the meeting in true Christian Endeavor style, with characteristic United Brethren freedom and fervor.

Pennsylvania furnished the largest number of delegates, and Des Moines, Ia., was the city represented by the largest delegation, five.

Methodist Protestant Rally

A really enthusiastic denominational rally was held by the Methodist Protestants. Dr. A. G. Dixon, of Baltimore, general secretary of the denominational board of Young People's Work, presided.

Many officers of the conference young people's unions, secretaries, and leaders were introduced. Among those speaking was Rev. E. A. Sexsmith, of Baltimore, and president of the general board of Young People's Work. He stressed two particular points. First, the young life of every church constitutes a challenge to the church. Second, the church of Christ throws out a challenge to every young life.

Mrs. H. W. Maier, of Columbus, O., superintendent of children's work, spoke on Junior and Intermediate work. She said the child life of our church is our challenge. Every boy and girl is an opportunity. Hers was a stirring address in behalf of the boys and girls.

Mr. Carroll M. Wright, of Baltimore, spoke on "Building up Christian Endeavor in Our Denomination," expressing the belief that present-day Christian Endeavorers do not know Christian Endeavor as some of the older ones once knew it.

Lawrence C. Little, of Chattanooga, Tenn., All-South field secretary, spoke optimistically of the spread of Christian Endeavor among the Southern Methodist Protestants.

Rev. L. W. Gerringer, president of the North Carolina Conference Young People's Union, spoke of the increased interest in Christian Endeavor among North Carolina Methodist Protestants. The members of societies in that denominational union has increased from ten societies five years ago to seventy-seven at present.

Rev. Mr. Slater, president of the Eastern Conference union, spoke briefly of the work of his conference.

Dr. Dixon stated that years ago the Methodist Protestants adopted Christian Endeavor as the organization for their young people, and know of no better organization for them, and Christian Endeavor may depend on the Methodist Protestant Church in years to come.

The Mennonite Rally

In the absence of Brother N. B. Grubb the meeting was conducted by Rev. R. F. Sandes, of the Zion Mennonite Church of Souderton, Penn. The meeting was opened with a song, after which Rev. Mr. Sandes spoke on the principles of the Mennonite Church. In spite of the fact that there are sixteen branches of Mennonites with a membership of 110,000, only nine were represented in this rally, an extremely small portion considering the other denominations present. The Sermon on the Mount has been exemplified in all our services, no matter what the denomination.

The rally passed a resolution to adopt and stand loyal to the Foursquare Program of Christian Endeavor as suggested by Dr. Francis E. Clark, for the next two years.

Rev. Mr. Sandes being obliged to leave, Dr. Daniel Sandes, of Perkasie Mennonite Church, took charge, and spoke on the life of the Christian as not being a hard life, but an easy one when one lives with Christ, because we walk in the light. "Let your light so shine."

Miss Heistand, of the First Mennonite Church of Philadelphia, sang "In the Garden." The different ones present made remarks about what they had gained from the Convention. Miss Heistand sang another solo, and the rally closed with the Lord's Prayer.

United Evangelical Rally

The United Evangelical rally, in charge of the general secretary, Rev. W. E. Peffley, according to the testimonies of those present was by far the largest and most enthusiastic rally of the denomination held in connection with the general Convention. Representatives were present from all but two of the ten participating conferences, and from the Evangelical Association. A large percentage of the delegation was made up of pastors who gave hearty indorsement to the young people's work, and encouraged the workers with their counsel. Greetings were brought from the conferences by the respective representatives and from the Evangelical Association delegation. The meeting was characterized by its inspirational value as manifested by the spirited song service under the direction of Rev. H. R. Wilkes, Baltimore, Md., and by the fervent prayers. Many

A Group of United Society Officers and Trustees

delegates took part in the discussion of such topics as "How do you conduct your prayer meetings?" "What is your society doing for missions?" "How do you assist the church in evangelism?" E. S. Shilling, Harrisburg, Penn., offered helpful suggestions for a campaign of publicity. Resolutions expressing sympathy and the assurance of the prayers of the Keystone League of Christian Endeavor and the church were sent to Dr. D. A. Poling, who is a member of the United Evangelical Church. Dr. Clark's "Foursquare Christian Endeavor" Program was heartily indorsed.

Rally of the Reformed Church in the United States

"The banner of the Reformation." Under its folds eighty-three delegates to the Sixth World's Christian Endeavor Convention gathered in the room assigned at the Armory for the denominational gathering of the Reformed Church in the United States. A small group compared to others, yet encouragingly large considering that almost none of the delegates came from New York City. Eight States were represented.

Encouraging, too, was the enthusiasm with which the new "Song of Service" rang through the great building, and the program was as carefully planned as if for the entire Convention. A devotional service led by Dr. Hauser, educational superintendent, was followed by an address which challenged the young people to a new Reformation, beginning in the heart and extending even to the ends of the earth.

"Reformed What?" was the question answered by Dr. Rufus W. Miller, secretary of the Publication and Sunday School Board.

In "What Shall We do With Today?" Miss Catherine A. Miller, secretary of Young People's Work, outlined the immediate opportunities for service; and the crowning message, "The Young People's Opportunity in Japan," by Rev. Alfred Ankeney, of Aomori, Japan, resulted in an immediate recruit for the foreign field, as well as new interest on the part of all the delegates.

The rally closed, as it began, with the "Song of Service," and the young people went out to eight different States to live true to the theme of the song:

> "Free church of a free nation!
> On high forever hold
> The banner of the Reformation,
> Crimson, black and gold!
> For by the crimson blood, we know,
> The darksome night of sin
> Turns to the gold of morning glow
> When Christ's love enters in."

Disciples' Rally

One of the difficulties with the Disciples' rally in the Armory was to accommodate the crowd that came. They filled the seats and flowed out through the door into the corridor.

Neal K. McGowan presided and spoke on "The Present Status of Christian Endeavor Among the Disciples." The open forum discussion that followed brought many to their feet with both inspiring reports of work done and suggestions for enlargement.

There was enthusiastic unanimity among those present as to the necessity for the employment of a young people's secretary for the denomination. A resolution to this effect was passed and ordered sent to the proper authorities. Several pointed out that the opportunity has never been greater to line up the young folks in a forward movement and bind them firmly to the church through Christian Endeavor. All that is needed is leadership, and a young people's secretary, it was said, would greatly help both church and young people.

Rally of the Presbyterian Church in the United States

The chairman of this rally was Lieutenant Duncan B. Curry.

The matter of closer co-operation between the Christian Endeavor Society and the Foreign Mission Committee at Nashville was fully discussed, with a view particularly to securing more helps for the Junior and Intermediate societies.

Dr. Kirkpatrick, of Atlanta, presented the goals of the Home Mission Committee, urging all societies to seek to reach these goals. In regard to the goal set for the offering to home mission work it was suggested that the committee present to the Endeavorers a definite amount which they are asked to raise.

Dr. Hopper gave a brief sketch of Beechwood Seminary, telling of the splendid work being done there.

A letter from Dr. Sweets was read, stating the work he would like to have Endeavorers do for his committee.

Upon the motion of Dr. Kirkpatrick, a committee was appointed by the chair to put the wishes of this conference regarding the relation of Christian Endeavor to the different Assembly's committees in the form of a recommendation, this recommendation to be sent to the several committees. The committee appointed is composed of Dr. Kirkpatrick, chairman, Dr. Howe and Miss Williams.

Rally of the Reformed Church in America

About one hundred and fifty young people met in the Marble Collegiate Church. Rev. Abram Duryee, the educational secretary, presided.

After a brief period of worship, Rev. Dr. Thomas H. Mackenzie, president of the General Synod, brought greetings to the Endeavorers. He said, "God calls us as a part of the church of Christ to efficient service for the upbuilding of the Kingdom." Mr. Duryee explained briefly the young people's program.

As a most acceptable surprise Dr. Samuel M. Zwemer, of Cairo, Egypt, and a son of the Reformed Church, was introduced, and spoke on "The Cross of Christ at the Crossroads of the World." He said, "I am owned by the Reformed Church and loaned to the United Presbyterian Church." He showed how mission work in Egypt was like bringing white lilies out of mud. Dr. Zwemer had the privilege of preaching to the Mohammedans in the famous and beautiful Mosque of Saint Sophia in Constantinople, using for his text a passage from the Koran.

Rev. F. S. Wilson, president of the Board of Publication and Bible School Work, showed that the chief part of the young people's work is evangelistic. Miss Frances E. Davis, secretary for young women's work, spoke of the need for mission study, and outlined methods. Dr. John A. Ingham, general secretary of the Progress Campaign, urged the young people "to be loyal, to know the history and work of the church, and to do."

At the noon hour a reception was tendered the delegates at the Reformed Church Building. One of the interesting features of the occasion was the presence of four young women who will go to the foreign field this fall: Miss Bessie Bruce, to China; the Misses Ruth and Rachel Jackson, to Arabia; and Miss Edith Teets, to Japan. S. D. Gordon lifted a prayer for God's blessing upon these workers so soon to go forth.

United Presbyterian Rally

United Presbyterian Endeavorers, representing California, Wisconsin, Colorado, Pennsylvania, New Jersey, Rhode Island, Massachusetts, the District of Columbia, and New York, had a splendid session of inspiration and good fellowship over in Section I of the Armory on Friday morning.

Through some oversight no leader or program had been provided, and Miss Alice S. Fyfe, the only New York City United Presbyterian representative, member of the Second Church, New York, James P. Lytle, pastor, acted as chairman, extended a welcome on behalf of New York United Presbyterians, and then conducted a roll-call meeting, calling on each one present in turn to tell what city or State he was from and something of the progress of Christian Endeavor and young people's work in the denomination in his section of the country. Much of instruction and interest came out of this informal discussion, and it seemed to be the expressed opinion that a still larger percentage of United Presbyterian churches ought to introduce Christian Endeavor societies instead of Christian Union societies, the chief reason being the wider fellowship with the young people of other denominations afforded the young people in Christian Endeavor societies through union gatherings, etc., which could not be secured in the more widely scattered denominational conferences with their infrequent meetings.

Space will not permit telling of all the practical work reported as being conducted by United Presbyterian Christian Endeavor societies. The following will serve as samples of the reports given by the various representatives:

Miss McFadden of Santa Ana, Cal., reported three societies in their church, Senior, Intermediate and Junior, all "live" societies. She also spoke of the work being done in the Italian district of Santa Ana by the Christian Endeavor societies, stating that their Senior society furnished a number of the workers.

Mr. Earle Miller of the Germantown, Philadelphia, United Presbyterian Christian Endeavor societies said they were proud of an Intermediate society of thirty-five members, also that their society is starting alien work along the lines of a Y. M. C. A. hut in South Philadelphia, and that their young people are responding to this practical bit of good citizenship in a remarkable way.

Mr. C. D. Tanguy, of Greenville, Penn., reported that of Mercer County's seven delegates to the Convention, three were from the Greenville United Presbyterian Society, Mr. C. D. Tanguy, Roy McGeary and Mark Mabon.

Rev. S. P. Barackman, of the First United Presbyterian Church of West New York, took up the closing minutes of the conference, speaking in a general way of the many perplexing problems of the day, the delegates all joining in the discussion, item by item, under his leadership with the conclusion that only the principles that Christ taught, lived by us every day, will ever solve these problems.

The thought expressed as the conference closed was "It has been good for us to be here."

CHAPTER X.

ALUMNI DEMONSTRATION

ARMORY, FRIDAY MORNING, JULY 8

Rev. Stanley B. Vandersall, Presiding

FRIDAY morning was as hot as ever. and as humid as ever, but nothing could daunt the zeal of the Endeavorers. and a glorious audience faced the speakers in the Armory.

Alumni Superintendent Vandersall presided, and Dr. William Patterson. of Toronto, made the opening prayer.

"The Social Task of the Church" was the great theme of Rev. George W. Richards, D.D., professor of church history in the Reformed Church Seminary of Lancaster, Penn. The way in which the church sets about this task depends on its attitude toward the kingdom of God, and as a historian Professor Richards traced the variations in this attitude through the ages, —expecting the immediate establishment of the Kingdom on earth, or seeing its equivalent in the institutions of the church, or expecting to see the Kingdom in the next life. It is only in the last two generations that we have caught a glimpse of the social embodiment of the kingdom of God. Now we do not neglect personal evangelism, but add to it the ideal of a transformed society. Our conception of religion used to be a circle, with personal salvation in the centre. Now it is an ellipse with two foci. the individual and society. This is a great undertaking. If it is a great task to evangelize the world, it is surely a task equally vast to Christianize society. We must Christianize the social conscience. Then in the name of Jesus we will start movements for social health, such as the establishment of public playgrounds. We will seek political righteousness everywhere. We must have a Christlike industrial order, which is perhaps the most difficult of all. We do not believe in dictation, either of labor or of capital. What we want is a co-operative democracy. All this is not in the power of man, but it is in the power of our Lord, who will work it out through us.

The Massachusetts delegation then put on an Alumni demonstration in three scenes. They were grouped on the stage in half-circles of chairs, and they presented the Alumni idea and methods in the most natural way,' with questions and answers. Some of them brought out the usual perplexities and objections regarding the Alumni. and others answered these queries.

69

The names given to the various "performers" on the program were comical transformations of the names of well-known Endeavorers: Mrs. Lira Andrith, Clark E. Francis, Mrs. Wells Ramos, Miss Nan P. Oling, Miss Lillian Shaw, Mr. S. H. Artle, Rev. R. Panderson, Mr. Edward Peagates. There were also Mr. Balded, Miss Ida Vision, Mr. Gainwell, and many others.

The opening scene was the prayer meeting room of a church, where an Alumni Council was formed. The second scene was a church parlor, and gave us a glimpse of an Alumni Council's activities. The third scene was a church dining-hall with the banquet tables in place, the toastmaster conducting affairs immediately after the meal. This last scene demonstrated real Alumni fellowship, and the many accomplishments of Christian Endeavor Alumni.

The scenes were changed with lightning-like rapidity. There were lots of bright hits, and there was a heap of good sense and of practical methods. To name the stars would be to name the entire cast. The Successful Union (its president is Mr. Newkamp Payne). is certainly a union to belong to, not to speak of Promotion Union, whose president was visiting the Successful Union.

This bright play was written by Superintendent Vandersall, and any union wishing to present it to its Endeavorers may obtain a copy from him.

Note —For address in full by Rev. George W. Richards, D.D., see "Chapter of Addresses."

CHAPTER XI.

AN AFTERNOON WITH THE JUNIORS

ARMORY, FRIDAY AFTERNOON, JULY 8.

Ira Landrith, D.D., LL.D., Presiding

"I AM substituting for Dan Poling; nobody can take his place," said Dr. Landrith in opening the session Friday afternoon. "The greatest Christian Endeavor address I ever heard was by Dr. Barbour," he continued as he introduced the first speaker, Dr. Clarence A. Barbour, the president of Rochester Theological Seminary.

Dr. Barbour announced two texts. The one was the title that the Pilgrims brought to great territory that it took generations to settle. The second was Kipling's phrase, "Go and look behind the ranges; something lost behind the ranges, lost and waiting for you." These two texts on the process of achievement apply to many phases of life.

As to the intellectual life, there is no way of gaining intellectual power save by treading the path between the parallels toward the farther sea. Margot Asquith tells of asking a tramp how those of his class decided in what direction to start out each morning. "Why, lady, that's easy," was the answer. "Every morning we starts out with the wind at our back." A lot of people determine which way they go on the same principle.

The truth applies to knowledge of the Bible. Our Bible is just as big as that part of it which we have actually entered. It is a great mistake to think of the Bible as one great plain instead of a vast continent diversified with mountain ranges.

Some think world peace is to be gained by merely signing a document. The process of elimination of the poison of militarism will take as long as the process of inoculation.

Marvellous advances in medicine and surgery have taken place within a single lifetime; do you suppose God is not going to lead us into as great discoveries in other realms, including that of religious truth? We may have the old-time religion, but God is leading us into new ways of stating it.

As another of the four Christian Endeavor Alumni speaking at the session Mr. Winslow Russell, the vice-president of the Phoenix Life Insurance Company, followed President Barbour. As Dr. Barbour had spoken on "The Endeavorer in Action," Mr. Russell treated "The Endeavorer in Business," or, as he

71

preferred to spell it, "busyness." A composite photograph of a thousand faces has given a result startlingly like the artists' portraits of Christ. The resemblance is more striking, probably, than would have been noted if the same experiment had been made a hundred years ago. A composite sketch of business conditions would perhaps mark a like advance.

Just before the great war an American entertained by Kaiser Wilhelm asked whether it might not be possible that within a hundred years there would be no more emperors, czars or kings. The German emperor thought it might be so. The American asked what in that case would be the form of government surviving, and what nation would be the leader. The Kaiser was not sure about the first answer, but said, "I believe that the nation which first gives up alcohol will rule the world." Prohibition is an illustration of what vitalized Christian Endeavor can accomplish.

"Do unto others as though you were the other" is a motto that if followed would work a transformation in moral, business and religious life in this century. With work and tolerance and faith we could carry out a revolution that would revitalize this whole nation of ours.

No one in Christian Endeavor ranks would be a more suitable speaker for the topic, "The Endeavorer in Public Life," than the Hon. Frederick A. Wallis, former police commissioner of New York City, and now United States Immigration Commissioner at Ellis Island, a most important post. Mr. Wallis has enlarged and adorned every office he has held, as Dr. Landrith said in introducing him. He did not talk directly about his subject, but about our present-day immigration problem, which he is doing so much to solve, and thereby is giving a glorious illustration of Christian Endeavor in public life.

Success with the immigrant depends upon human sympathy, and that is just what Wallis is putting into his job. If the immigrant is properly handled during his first few days, he is sent far on his way toward fine American citizenship, with no limit to his possibilities. The speaker told about the present Secretary of Labor, who came to New York as a poor immigrant's child, and only a few days ago he was inspecting Ellis Island as the head of the great department of government to which that immigration station belongs.

Commissioner Wallis urged one greatly needed reform, that all would-be immigrants should be inspected before they cross the Atlantic, rather than suffer the tragedy of being sent back in so large numbers as unfit for American citizenship.

He spoke with great eloquence about the attempt of foreign anarchists to get entrance into this country; but we have no room in all America for these foes of organized government.

He advocated very earnestly that the immigrant should be allocated to the parts of the country where they are needed and

Some of the Participants in the Junior Pageant

Sectional View of the Citizenship Demonstration, Central Park

where they can prosper. instead of crowding into the already congested regions.

The address was full of vivid facts, many of them startling; it was a great object-lesson in American patriotism, and the Endeavorers will never forget it.

The president of the New York City union, Dr. A. Ray Petty, pastor of the Judson Memorial Church, introduced to speak on "The Challenge of the Teen Age," began by reading a message from Mrs. Poling conveying Dr. Poling's love to the Endeavorers. Dr. Petty said that when touring through Oregon in an automobile he constantly saw signs saying, "Under Construction." and beneath it, "Dangerous, but Passable." We ought to put up the sign in regard to those of the teen age "Under Construction."

The first challenge of the teen age to the church of Christ is "Wake up." There is to be a demand for better leadership than in the past. What is the church going to do in regard to industrial problems, immigration, prohibition, the peace problem?

Another challenge of the teen age is for an interpretation of religion that meets the special need of the boy or the girl. He or she wants a hero that shall call for the best that he or she can give.

Another challenge is to give the boys and girls a constructive program of action in the kingdom of God instead of constantly saying, "Don't, don't, don't." If we can enlist their lives in service for others, we can arouse their enthusiasm.

These teen-age young people can make sacrifices. A girl was struck by a truck. When she reached the hospital, the surgeon dared not operate without transfusion of blood. He was told that a boy wanted to see him, saying that he was the girl's brother. The operation of transferring blood from one to the other was performed and the boy was told to rest awhile. He seemed uneasy, lifted himself, and said, "Well, doc, when do I croak?" The boy had thought that he was giving his life when he offered his blood for his sister, but never asked a question.

At this point the older Endeavorers yielded the platform and the front part of the hall to the Juniors, who had marched from their World Convention in the Marble Collegiate Church to have the Junior Demonstration in the Armory. Under the leadership of Mr. John Peters they sang spiritedly. Along the front of the platform a line of Juniors in appropriate costumes ranged themselves holding the flags of various nations to which those in the body of the hall gave their salute. Vigorous cheers for Dr. Clark, Mr. Wallis and Dr. Poling followed.

> "Two, four, six, eight,
> Whom do we appreciate?
> Mrs. Clark, Mrs. Clark, Mrs. Clark,"

was the greeting that met Mrs. Clark as she was brought to the platform to give a welcome to the Juniors.

She then welcomed them because they were Juniors with life before them and because they were Junior Christian Endeavorers, who are to do a great work.

The response to the welcome was given by Miss F. Lucy Hollings, who appealed to the older ones representing churches still without Junior societies to consider their opportunities. Miss Hollings was not allowed to leave the platform without an expression of the Juniors' appreciation in the form of hearty cheers and a gift of flowers.

Mr. Harry Galloway explained that Junior C. E. means "Coming Endeavorers." In answer to a statement in a recent number of a New York paper that three-fourths of the boys and girls in the city know very little about the Ten Commandments he called on the company to repeat them, which was done without the slightest hesitation without any rehearsal or knowledge that the test was coming. On a table were ten blue lighted candles and before them two golden ones representing Christ's summary of the law. The children told how the two golden laws fully covered the ten blue laws, Christ's laws never being really blue laws, but gold. Mr. Galloway's friends in Philadelphia, his earlier home, at this time presented him with flowers in expression of their lasting interest in him and his work.

A bright pageant, "America's Garden," was the next number on the program. Mother Earth called for Summer, who responded. Nine boys dressed as farmers in overalls and straw hats sang of sowing, going through the motions of scattering seed. Then Summer called for the flowers, and a troop of girls in costumes of many gay colors came and ranged themselves across the platform. Then a company of little girls representing the birds appeared. A group whose decorations suggested butterflies danced forward and took their stand before the others. Then to the accompaniment of "America the Beautiful" came a representative of Columbia and with her the impersonations of Christian Endeavor and the Sunday School. Juniors standing for different States came forward one by one and told the religious needs of the children of those States, and pleaded for them. Some girls bearing palms and representing truth, love, self-sacrifice, and other forces bringing strength and help came forward to tell what they could do for the land. The audience showed unmistakably their appreciation of the beautiful pageant and those that had had charge of directing it.

Ten metropolitan Junior societies and several others had attained a registration of one hundred per cent. in the Convention, and to each was presented a shield in recognition of their merit, the presentation being made by Commissioner Wallis.

Note.—For addresses of Dr. Barbour, Winslow Russell, Mr. Wallis and Dr. A. Ray Petty, see chapter of addresses.

CHAPTER XII.

———

ALUMNI BANQUET

HOTEL MAJESTIC, FRIDAY EVENING, JULY 8

Rev. Francis E. Clark, D.D., LL.D., Presiding

A REALLY brilliant gathering, and a happy one, this first national, or rather international, Alumni Banquet, when about 1,140 Alumni sat down to table at the Hotel Majestic, in a great holly-and-flag-decorated dining-hall. The Alumni have not lost the art of yelling, and all through dinner groups vied with one another in demonstrating their vocal efficiency. Mr. Percy Foster kept everybody interested by leading in some snappy songs, and the banquetters amused themselves by hilariously singing such classic melodies as "Jingle Bells" to the accompaniment of the table glassware. There may have been merry parties in this dining-room before, but this for clean and joyous fun beat everything. Age was banished for one night. The good spirits of Christian Endeavor was in glorious and noisy evidence, and were more than welcome.

A new Alumni song by Charles S. Brown had been written for this banquet, and Percy Foster proceeded to teach it to the gathering. The first stanza of this Alumni song reads:

"C. E. Alumni! C. E. Alumni!
Trusting in my Lord for strength and skill,
Seeking grace and power to know His will,
I have promised Him, and will strive to do
What will please Him best all life's journey through.

Dr. Clark was toastmaster, and a witty one at that, and indeed the audience was well prepared to laugh by all the jokes and laughter that had gone before. The weather made a good subject, and Dr. Clark told an apt story of one who was running for the Presidency of the United States. He was on his way to attend a meeting, but was hindered by a washout on the railroad. He wired: "Can't come. Washout on the line." The reply was flashed back, "Buy another shirt and come anyhow!" Most of those present had wash out on the line, Dr. Clark confessedly among them.

W. N. Ells, president of the New York City Alumni, was the first speaker, and his pleasant duty was to welcome the

75

guests. He referred to Spain's old motto, "Ne Plus Ultra," "Nothing Beyond," which when the new world was discovered was changed to "Plus Ultra," "Something Beyond." This must be true of the Alumni.

Rev. John Pollock, of Belfast, Ireland, in the regalia of his British office, was made splendidly welcome, and responded with ready and scintillating wit. The Alumni movement he characterized as the best device ever devised for preventing the Y. P. S. C. E. from becoming an O. P. S. C. E. Mr. Pollock received an encore, and he scored off the audience when it continued to cheer by asking, "Do you love me?" "Yes," came the reply. "Then you'll excuse me," he said, and sat down amid a thunder of applause.

Mr. Winslow Russell, of Hartford, Conn., was next on the list. One said to him, he remarked, "that the working people want to get nearer the heart of the employer, and that the Christian Endeavor Alumni should make their efforts practical and seek to get a little nearer to some one in his or her community and help each his load to bear."

One of the first Alumni is Fred L. Ball, of Cleveland, O., and also one of the most earnest Alumni workers. It is only six years ago since Fellowship No. 1 was formed in Cleveland, and today this group has an annual pledge of $2,500. These Alumni have found inspiration in Christian Endeavor, and they are now giving inspiration in practical help to others. Mr. Ball urged a large and worthy program for the Alumni which will mean big things for Christian Endeavor the world over.

Mr. Ball introduced Daniel A. Johnson, treasurer of the Cleveland Alumni, called the Daniel A. Poling Foundation, who presented to the Alumni department in the name of Cleveland's Alumni a check for $1,000 for the work.

Mr. and Mrs. Ball generously offered to provide three silver loving cups to be competed for by the Alumni of the country, the cups to be presented to the winners at the next International Convention in Des Moines.

One of the best beloved of Alumni speakers is Mrs. Francis E. Clark. She told a good story to the delight of every one. "Grandpa," said a little fellow, "were you in the ark?" "No, of course not." "Well, grandpa, if you weren't in the ark, *why weren't you drowned?*"

Mrs. Clark then called on two members of the Christian Endeavor school of 1881,—Mrs. Sayward and Mrs. Plummer, —charter members of the first society, to make at least a bow to the audience.

Dr. Clarence A. Barbour, of Rochester, spoke suggestively and helpfully on the necessity and the beauty of good will, which, indeed, was the dominant note of the banquet; and not of this banquet only, but of the whole Christian Endeavor

THE ALUMNI BANQUET

At the Hotel Majestic, New York City, N. Y. Friday evening, July 8

movement. Youth has good will, and youth will find ways to show it.

A Boston pastor, Dr. Vaughan Dabney, was the next speaker. With the title of Vice-President Coolidge's book, "Have Faith in Massachusetts," as his text he urged all to have faith in Christian Endeavor as capable of specializing in the impossible and doing what no one thinks can be done.

Percy Foster, song-leader, and president of the Washington, D. C., Alumni, told of the Washington Alumni's invitation to President Harding's secretary, Mr. Christian, to attend an Alumni luncheon and accept an honorary membership in the Alumni Fellowship. Mr. Christian accepted, and when a member of the committee called to take him to luncheon, Will Hays, Postmaster-General of the United States, happened to be present, and he was invited to come along and become an Alumnus too. He hopped into a taxi and came along and became a member. It is interesting to know that at one time Mr. Hays was secretary of a Christian Endeavor union. So now the President of the United States, his private secretary, and the Postmaster-General are members of our Christian Endeavor Alumni organization. Not only that; Mr. Foster told of receiving a day or two ago from Hon. Charles E. Hughes, Secretary of State, a check for $10 to go to the funds of the Christian Endeavor Alumni Fellowship.

The speech of the evening was made by Dr. Ira Landrith, a talk that sparkled all through, yet a talk in places tender, sympathetic, and generous. How he drove home the statement that if Christian Endeavor had gone as far and had been as influential in the old world—and it might have been that if there had been money enough to push it—there would have been no World War, for you cannot get up a world war when the young people of the world are permeated with a spirit of good will. He characterized Christian Endeavor as the most potent influence in the religious life of America. It was Christian Endeavor that made Ellis Island, through Commissioner Wallis, the Golden Gate to the New Jerusalem.

Ira Landrith is nothing if not original and eloquent, and he waxed eloquent on two things for which Christian Endeavor has stood throughout its history—prohibition and woman suffrage. The *men* gave the women the mop after the men had cleaned house, and the saloon will never come back because the women will use the mop and keep the house clean.

"Christian Endeavor," he said, "has reached the parting of the ways. The opportunities in all the world are boundless. but Christian Endeavor cannot go forward unless Endeavorers provide the means."

He read a telegram from Mrs. Poling: "Dan's condition a little brighter this morning. He is especially praying for financial success tonight. Tell Ira (Landrith) he is praying for him.

Say Christian Endeavor is just entering into fields of unparalleled opportunity; she must have, she will have, and she will begin to receive tonight modest but absolutely necessary funds to enable her to accept her high commission. *Accept our pledge for one hundred dollars."*

Already gifts of $1,300 have just been given to the cause by the men in the Boston office. Dr. and Mrs. Poling's gift made it $1,400. And Dr. Landrith made it $1,500.

Envelopes were passed around and pledges amounting to $3,900 were collected before the meeting closed.

CHAPTER XIII.

THE OPPORTUNITY MEETING

ARMORY, FRIDAY EVENING, JULY 8

Edward P. Gates, Presiding

HOMER RODEHEAVER gave us a great praise service on Friday evening. He began it in a jolly way with a series of popular airs which he played on his useful trombone, thus quieting the pandemonium of State yells and songs which the Endeavorers were practicing all over the auditorium. Dixie as usual went best. He sang a solo magnificently. He had the boys whistle an accompaniment to a song, and then for a change the girls, who proved just as good whistlers as the boys.

The big Alumni banquet made no impression on the Armory crowd, but the big auditorium was crowded as ever. Considering the overpowering heat, the great attendance was nothing short of wonderful.

Secretary Gates was very happy in his management of this meeting, and made a hit with his sing-song announcements, arousing attention, putting every one in good humor, and at the same time carrying his message to the farthest corner of the auditorium as he could in no other way.

Bishop Fallows, of Chicago, who conducted the devotional exercises, is a long-time trustee of the United Society and a warm advocate of Christian Endeavor. In harmony with the thought of the evening, he spoke of "the unity and loyalty of the American household," which is of far more importance to our nation than the tariff or the budget. All peoples on earth are represented largely in our country, but they proved themselves during the World War to be true and loyal Americans. Christian Endeavorers can do much to unify our heterogeneous population. They can do much to help America to bear the white man's burden. This message of Bishop Fallows was strong and eloquent, and full of characteristic fire.

Gates' introduction of Dr. Landrith was brief but all-sufficient, "Every Endeavorer in America knows and loves Ira Landrith."

"We have recognized more miracles in America during the past few months," said Dr. Landrith in starting out, "than your Master and mine ever accomplished. I believe Him when He

79

said that this very thing should come to pass. The church can do what it will when it wills to do what it can.

"I believe that the three greatest events in human history since the birth of Christ have occurred in 1919, 1920 and 1921. In 1919 we made the world democratic and self-determining— that is, the United States cast the final ballot after Canada had licked the Kaiser. A democratic world will not long tolerate any kind of organized iniquity, and the abolition of the saloon in America in 1920 means a saloonless world. We men cleaned house before we gave you women the mop, and if you can't keep the house clean, shut up with all your claims to be good housekeepers. Then in 1921 we gave the women the right to protect their children and their homes at the polls.

"God put it into the heart of Francis Clark to found our idealistic society that in this time of great beginnings our nation should have an army of four million clean young souls to fight these new battles, as it had an army of four million to beat the Kaiser. Did you ever stop to thank God that, in the most dangerous segregation of sex this country ever knew, every tenth young man of our great armies had been trained in Christian Endeavor and every fifth man had been trained in some young people's society?

"Christian Endeavor came at a time when the church was living in a corner. When we came to New York twenty-nine years ago Christianity got into the newspapers, front page, double-column heading, top of column."

These are only hints of Landrith's rapid-fire fun and good sense and sparkling eloquence. He gripped every last person in the audience, and excelled even his own unique record as Christian Endeavor orator.

He did an especially remarkable thing. He swung the close of his address into an appeal for money to promote Christian Endeavor all over the world, and he remained just as popular as ever, and even more popular. The money has not yet been counted, but we know that it was a generous sum.

Dr. Landrith left the hall to speak at the Alumni banquet amid the uproarious applause of the audience, the delegation from his own Texas singing enthusiastically after him "The eyes of Texas are upon you."

While we were waiting for an expected speaker from the Alumni banquet—a speaker who was sick and could not come —Rodeheaver showed his amazing versatility. He gave a beautiful concert of Negro melodies all by himself, and ended by reciting beautifully Paul Dunbar's "When Malindy Sings."

Secretary Gates closed the meeting with more of his unique announcements, ending with two of especial interest.

In the first place, he told us that the Convention registration already exceeded by fifty per cent. all Conventions since we

A Section of the Parade

Some Intermediates at the Convention

have adopted the plan of paid registrations, being nearly 16,000, with more coming all the time. This is especially remarkable when the hard times are considered, and the high railroad and hotel rates.

In the second place, he told us that our next Convention, in 1923, is to be held in Des Moines, Ia. This announcement was greeted with immense applause, and the red-jacketed Iowa crowd were on their feet in an instant, giving us with heartiness a very beautiful welcome song.

Portland, Ore., was the strong rival of Des Moines in this matter, and its invitation was so attractive, and so finely presented and backed up, that the minds of the trustees were perplexed and divided. But the invitation of Des Moines was not only attractive and finely presented and backed up, but it came first by several years. If Portland continues to want the Convention, it will doubtless get it next time, unless the situation changes.

And now three cheers for our next Convention city, one of the finest cities, in one of the finest States, with one of the finest Christian Endeavor crowds in all the world! There is no reason why Des Moines, '23, should not surpass even New York, '21!

CHAPTER XIV.

INTERMEDIATE RALLY

MARBLE COLLEGIATE CHURCH, SATURDAY MORNING, JULY 9

Miss Alice S. Fyfe, Presiding

AFTER the praise service that opened the Intermediate rally the leader called the names of different States; and, as the delegates rose in response, they were greeted by the applause of the rest. The visitors were welcomed by Mr. Schofield, New York's State Intermediate superintendent, who reviewed some of the "Intermediate Opportunities." A girl once confessed to her priest that her friend Tim had kissed her as they were walking the evening before. "Only once, my daughter?" asked the priest. "Well, father, I'm confessing, not boasting." If we look at the record of the past year, we may feel that it is not a time for confessing, but that there may even be ground for boasting.

Great opportunities come through the size and scope of Christian Endeavor and through its fellowships. But the greatest opportunities are those coming from the very task of Christian Endeavor to line up the boys and girls for definite religious service. We are not simply a social or literary organization.

There is a great opportunity in the Intermediate society as a training school. Training fleas was done long ago, but the training of boys and girls is a modern affair.

Another great opportunity is that for testimony, not simply in the meeting, but in the life. An invitation to a meeting has borne fruit in a life given to the foreign field.

A third opportunity is that for consecrated service, serving our Lord Jesus Christ by serving those right about us.

A great Mohammedan leader received a message demanding surrender of his forces to an enemy. He bade one of his followers plunge a dagger into his own side; another, to leap into a river; a third, to throw himself from a precipice. All obeyed at once without a question. Then the leader told the envoy to report to the enemy that sent him that all soldiers were of that kind, and would not surrender. The Intermediates have the Leader of all leaders, Jesus Christ; the challenge to them is for loyalty to Him.

Mr. Paul Brown, the beloved national Intermediate superintendent, prefaced his address by asking how many of those present were actually Intermediates. A show of hands proved that a large proportion of the audience were such. He then told why he believes in Intermediates.

He believes in them because, when they take hold of anything, they do so earnestly. When they say, "Yes" to the Lord Jesus Christ, they are glad to make that "Yes" not only of the lips, but a reality of the life.

There is a big task, and no one can accomplish it better than the Intermediates. The leaders can do nothing more than furnish advice. There are approximately twenty-six million young people, very largely of the Intermediate age, in this country who are yet to be won for the church and Sunday School. This calls for great efficiency on the part of the Intermediates to meet the situation. They can reach many of those outside with the religion of Jesus Christ by the power of friendship shot through and through by His spirit.

A special reason for loving Intermediate Endeavor is that it goes for the boys and girls at just the age when they need it most.

It is a great thing to be an Intermediate Christian Endeavorer in these days if you are emphasizing the word "Christian" and are seeing first of all the Lord Jesus Christ, and if the society is not self-centred, a clique of friends forgetting others.

Christian Endeavor that commands enthusiasm is the kind that makes no apology, but is really pressing on to the deepest things, the prayer life that means talking to Christ in a true conversational relationship, and the service that challenges young people.

The conference on Intermediate work that followed the addresses dwelt on the value of the prayer service with the leader before a meeting, the cultivation of the spirit of prayer in a society by activity on the part of the natural leaders among the Intermediates, and ways of gaining and holding boys or girls when there is disproportion in its membership.

———

CHAPTER XV.

THE CHRISTIAN ENDEAVOR PARADE

(Citizenship Demonstration)

Saturday Morning, July 9

BEYOND question, the event of the entire Convention that most impressed itself upon the delegates, not to say New York City, was the parade up Fifth Avenue at noon on Saturday. It was a big affair, even for the world's biggest city. The pace was fast, the lines were broad, about twenty persons in each, and they were closely packed together, yet the parade took fifty minutes to pass one point.

The delegations formed on the side streets running into lower Fifth Avenue, from Eighteenth to Twenty-third. They filled those streets with compact masses of happy young folks, cheering and singing and waving their banners.

The procession started with remarkable promptness, considering its great size.

First came a fine escort of New York police, followed by a band, and then the automobile in which rode Dr. and Mrs. Clark and William Jennings Bryan.

Then, marching on foot and headed by Commissioner Wallis, came the United Society trustees and officers and the members of the New York Convention Committee.

Following them, a float appropriately showing a gilded figure, "Liberty Enlightening the World," the famous statue which appeared on the Convention posters. Behind it on the float were Endeavorers admirably dressed to represent immigrants from various lands. This float bore the Convention motto, "Let your light so shine that men may see your good works, and glorify your Father in heaven."

Following this float, an indescribable marching glory of bright young faces, lovely girls in charmingly modest attire, and splendid young men of the very best of the nation.

We took photographs until our camera struck for higher wages. We took notes until pencil refused to scribble. We moved backward and forward over the long line, freely asking questions and trying, but in vain, to grasp the full spectacle.

FREDERICK A. WALLIS
Chairman of the New York Convention Committee, marching at the head
of the Christian Endeavor procession up Fifth Avenue

At the head of the marching host was the band from Colorado, brilliant with banners. Colorado won this honor by being the first State to complete its quota of Convention registrations, which it did gloriously, and thirty per cent. more.

The Colorado Endeavorers, with those from Texas, Oklahoma and Arizona, made a beautiful showing with white garments and white sunshades, each marked with the name of its State in red. Roy Breg had good reason to be proud of the showing of the Southwestern Federation. Dr. Landrith, in the Trustee division, marched gayly under a Texas sunshade. When this big delegation sang, in the pauses of the band music, they swung their sunshades back and forth in time to the music, producing a striking effect.

Kansas furnished a delegation with bright yellow-petalled sunshades with black centres—sunflowers, of course; and they carried a large banner, "Watch Kansas grow." Another banner read, "We exceeded all our goals."

The fine District of Columbia crowd bore Christian Endeavor banners and wore little caps of red and white stripes, the Christian Endeavor colors. These caps, so popular today among the boys, were adopted by numerous companies of Endeavorers, and added much to the brilliancy of the parade.

The splendid Dixie contingent—only a handful came from south of Mason and Dixon's line to the first New York Convention— wore perhaps the most striking costume of all, the leading feature of which was a bright red fez bearing the word "Dixie." We noted especially the fine companies from Louisiana and Virginia and Kentucky; but it is unfair to particularize where all the States did well.

Pennsylvania was a regiment divided into county companies. All wore red and white caps. A big banner informed us that "The Next Largest Convention Will Be the Pennsylvania Convention of 1922 at Reading."

Rhode Island carried a big white and blue sign, an anchor flag, and other devices.

West Virginia delegates wore a unique headgear of paper representing a mountain peak crowned with the Christian Endeavor monogram. Each cap bore the legend, "C. E. on Top among West Virginia Hills."

Illinois sent a large company of Endeavorers who marched under the punning banner, "C. E. Noise from Illinois." They were led by a girl cornetist.

Maine Endeavorers bore a banner letting the world know that Christian Endeavor was born in their State.

Oregon Endeavorers, carrying white sunshades, made clear by a banner that Portland, the City of Roses, wants the 1925 Convention.

California Endeavorers were a lovely sight with their purple and yellow banner, and their purple sashes and hatbands.

No delegation presented a nattier appearance than that of Massachusetts, in bright red jackets, and white trousers or skirts. The same bright uniform directed attention to the vigorous Iowa delegation, marching in three full divisions, and exultantly displaying the announcement that the next Christian Endeavor Convention will be held in Des Moines.

Maryland's black and orange caps showed Lord Baltimore's colors to great advantage.

The largest company of Connecticut Endeavorers carried novel pennants consisting of big sausage balloons, some blue, some yellow, and some red, truly a bright display. One of their banners was justifiably proud of the fact that the first local Christian Endeavor union was formed in New Haven. Another reminded us of the Christian Endeavor slogan, "A Saloonless Nation by 1920," and added, "We Helped."

Indiana wore red caps. A capital delegation came from Winnipeg, Manitoba. Missouri had a big purple banner and announced "St. Louis, Best Attendance." Minnesota carried a long banner which was supported by a row of Endeavorers. We noted especially the gallant bands of Nebraska and Michigan delegates.

The New York delegation, being the Convention hosts, closed the procession. And what an army they were! It seemed as if the beautiful marching companies would never cease to pass. They marched by counties. We noted especially the fine delegations from Oneida County, Dutchess County, Livingston County. Orange County, Onondaga County, Queens County, and Staten Island. Rochester wore wonderful blue and yellow paper robes. Albany carried a long chain of national flags. Binghamton, the Broom City, bore brooms. The Yonkers union had a float. The Westchester Juniors made a lovely showing. Troy and Buffalo were fine.

New York City marched thousands strong, and we cannot begin to list even their most striking components. The Broadway Tabernacle society exalted the Bible in their banner. Calvary Baptist Endeavorers carried Paul's words to Timothy, "Study to show thyself approved unto God," etc. The North Presbyterians had the sweetest of the floats, a flower-bedecked car marked "America's Garden," with forty-eight flower-faced Junior girls, one for each State. The Marble Collegiate Endeavorers, the Endeavorers of the Washington Heights District, of the North Baptist Church, of the DeWitt Memorial, of the Anderson Memorial, deserve especial mention. The Brooklyn union made a splendid showing, notable for its fine body of men. New York City had among its marchers some spirited Negro societies. One company carried a banner, "Better Lives for Better Service." One bore a long chain of flags. "A Spanish Christian Endeavor Society" attracted much attention. So did the Business Women's Council of the Billy Sunday

Campaign, with their white dresses, yellow sashes, and blue caps. The boy band of the Ottilie Asylum led a great host of Intermediates, the Intermediate union of New York City. The green flag of the Intermediates was conspicuous here, and many groups carried it alternating with the national flag. We noted especially the Varick Intermediates, the Westchester County Intermediates, and a large company of Girl Scouts.

Bringing up the rear of this great procession came an enormous map of China, a big yellow affair carried by Rev. George H. Hubbard, who introduced Christian Endeavor into China many years ago, and Rev. O. Braskamp, of Shantung.

A wonderful series of floats showing the principal scenes of Bunyan's Pilgrim's Progress was interspersed among the delegations on the march, the various characters being finely portrayed by New York Endeavorers in remarkably effective costumes. Seven bands, among them the New York Police Band and the band of the Seventy-first Regiment, whose armory we were using, furnished inspiring music, and all of these served us without charge.

This is the marching army that swung along Fifth Avenue from the Washington Arch all the way past the great stores and famous hotels, the churches where men like John Hall and Jowett, Van Dyke and Maltbie D. Babcock, have preached, past Dr. Burrell's church and Poling's, past the Public Library and the palatial homes of New York millionaires like the Vanderbilts, and then swung into Central Park, winding around the broad and beautiful parkways until we came to the Sheep Meadow.

The Sheep Meadow is a great field, well up in Central Park. In the middle of this field the speakers' stand was constructed. We have seen many charming scenes in Christian Endeavor, but none more beautiful and exhilarating than when the marching host came pouring into that green field with their flood of bright color, their brilliant banners, their ringing music, and their joyful faces. They marched around the field in a wide circle, and then closed up around the speakers' stand. The march that will never be forgotten in our Christian Endeavor history was over.

The speakers' stand was large, but it was instantly crowded. Rodeheaver was to the front at once with his trombone, leading us in "Come, we that love the Lord," then "Brighten the corner"—which brightened all the big meadow.

He told about overhearing a comment from one of the sidewalk throng that watched us all the way along the parade: "Don't these folks carry any dry banners?" with the significant answer: "They don't need any. Just look at them!"

Dr. Landrith presided. "There is but one voice," he said, "that any one would hear asking a blessing on this occasion," and he called on Dr. Clark. Our president's opening words were: "I understand that this is called the Sheep Meadow. We are all sheep of the great Shepherd. Let us pray to this Good Shepherd of the sheep."

Mr. Bryan asked that "I'll Go Where You Want Me to Go, Dear Lord," should be sung, and it was. This honored statesman has requested in his will that this song shall be sung at his funeral.

Said Dr. Landrith, referring to the liquor men's parade up Fifth Avenue on the Fourth of July, a parade of old sots and young ninnies still thirsty for their booze, said with emphasis: "This parade is not a competitor of anybody. It is conceived in no spirit of opposition to anybody else's parade, nor is it intended to excel any other. Prohibition in America is settled forever, and that discussion is ended. But this parade will at least impress this city with the character of the folks that did dry up America."

Rev. David G. Latshaw, D.D., chairman of the parade committee, and Captain William R. Fearn, its marshal, were introduced and received loud applause.

Judge John A. Leach, the First Deputy Police Commissioner of New York, was introduced, and was received with the "Ellis Island yell" which Commissioner Wallis made popular,—a yell of the ordinary Wild West variety broken up into scores of little yells by patting the mouth: "It is a wonderful thing," said Judge Leach, "to see such a throng of Christian young people. It bodes well for our city, and for the future of our country, when, in the midst of the heat of a hot summer, so many thousands of young folks will walk for several miles, and listen to speeches which, so far as I am concerned, do not amount to much anyhow."

A message was read from Mrs. Poling, "For two nights in his delirium Dan has been marching with that parade." The telegram ended with an encouraging word regarding Poling's condition, for which all hearts were deeply grateful.

Next we had a word of greeting from the man without whose kindly co-operation the meeting in Central Park would have been impossible, Park Commissioner Gallatin. "This great mass of color," he said, "is very beautiful. I hope that your actions will be as beautiful as your appearance. We could not ask more than that."

Then Commissioner Wallis made one of his happy and forcible addresses. He began: "Commissioner Gallatin hopes you are as good as you look. The fact is, you are good-looking because you are good inside."

He went on to say: "I believe that the great hope of America is not only in young America, but in the young people who are coming from other lands to become young Americans. They look on their fathers' country as something foreign. They want to dress like American children, speak the English language, play with American children. They will be American if we

Bryan Speaking at Central Park

let them alone." Then he told the story of the little Italian boy whose father brought him into court as incorrigible, and who said, when the judge asked him why he didn't mind his father, "Judge, I'm not going to let any foreigner whip me."

Eighty-three per cent. of immigration to America passes through Ellis Island and through Commissioner Wallis' hands, so that it means much for him to say: "Those gates at Ellis Island swing outward as well as inward. We are extending to the immigrant a reception in keeping with the dignity and honor of this nation; but those gates which swing inward with such cordial hospitality to all that value American ideals swing impressively and eternally outward for all that would destroy the institutions of our great American government."

The last speaker of the Central Park meeting was one always greeted by a Christian Endeavor audience with respect, admiration and affection, the Hon. William Jennings Bryan, former Secretary of State, one of our nation's noblest orators and truest Christian gentlemen. Dr. Landrith introduced him as from Florida, alluding to the fact that Mr. Bryan has recently made his summer home there his legal residence; whereupon Bryan promptly put on the Dixie fez which the Southern delegates had given him.

The address was characteristically witty and wise. It follows:

Members of the Christian Endeavor Society: I know of no higher honor that can come to any American citizen than to be deemed worthy of a place on the program of the Christian Endeavor Society in its national gathering. I want to express my fervent appreciation of the compliment thus paid me.

The thought that came to me as I watched this parade is this, that it does not make much difference what we may say here, but the impression made by the presence of these delegates is a more eloquent speech than can come from any tongue.

It has been said that this parade is not intended to be contrasted with the parade that this city witnessed on the Fourth of July. You did not march in rivalry to those advocates of the saloon; but if those people who carried empty bottles in that parade had come here, they would have found the people who emptied the bottles they carried. They had cans with cotton sticking out of them to imitate foam. I am glad the Southland has been able to furnish a product so much better than beer-foam.

That parade represented the sunset; and whatever glow there was, was the glow of a closing day. This parade of yours represents the dawn, a dawn that grows brighter every minute. Isn't it far happier to join the crowd that shall continue to increase, than to be numbered among those that are dying and will soon disappear?

My friends, I have not time to say all that I should like to say. They have given me also an evening hour on your program, and that will not be long enough. But I understand that this meeting is encroaching on the hours assigned to recreation, and I know too well the hold of recreation on young folks to delay you long. I fear that some of you will apply to me a story that Adlai Stevenson once told me about Joe Blackburn. Joe always made a speech when he got a chance. When he ran for Congress the first time, he heard that there was to be a hanging in his district. Those were the days when executions were in public. A crowd gathered, and Blackburn attended that he might electioneer. The sheriff recognized him and invited him to take a seat on the scaffold. Discovering that five minutes remained before the time when the hanging might legally take place, he told the prisoner that he might address the crowd for five minutes. But the prisoner said that he had nothing to say; whereupon Blackburn remarked, "If the prisoner does not want to use the time, I should be glad to occupy it." So he spoke for a few minutes, asking the people to vote for him for Congressman. But the prisoner at length interrupted him and addressed the sheriff, "If it is the same to you, I wish you would go on with the hanging now, and let him talk after I get through." I am afraid some one of you will come up to this platform and say that you would like to have your recreation now, and let me speak after you have gone.

I am asked to speak on Peace and Patriotism. Patriotism requires peace. I am interested in having this great Christian Endeavor Society do the greatest possible work. I want to speak of the basis upon which a human being can rightfully collect money from society. Every one of us draws daily from the sum of human toil. We must pay for what we get; and if we do not, we are sponging on the world for a living.

How much money can one rightfully collect from society? No more than he honestly earns. I want to astonish you. I want to get an estimate of what one man can actually earn, giving to society an equivalent in return for what society gives to him. A hundred thousand dollars? A million dollars? Ten million dollars? That would be at the rate of $300,000 a year for a working life of a third of a century. Can a man really earn one hundred million dollars? Five hundred million dollars? I believe that it is possible for one man to do work worth to society five hundred million dollars, or at the rate of fifteen millions a year for a working life. I believe that it is possible to render services so great as to earn sums as vast as this.

I am not willing to fix a maximum to what a single man can earn.

I should like to suggest the names of a few persons who have earned more than five hundred million dollars. I will name only dead men, for we are liable to differ in regard to living men. I will name Thomas Jefferson and Abraham Lincoln. Each of these men, I know you will agree, could honestly have collected five hundred million dollars in return for their services to the world. You see that I am fair, and name one Republican with one Democrat. I will not name other statesmen, for I am not going to hunt around for a Republican to match every Democrat that I might bring before you.

But who can put an estimate on the value of the services of the men who enabled us to utilize the power of steam, who brought down the lightning from the cloud to light our homes and carry our traffic over the land and waft our messages around the globe? Who can estimate the value of the work of the inventor of the gasoline engine which made possible the automobile and the flying machine, and heaven only knows how much more may come from it? There are seventeen millions of automobiles now, and every one of them was made since I began to run for President. Indeed, for four years after that time, when my Democratic friends met me at the station as I came to address them, they conveyed me to the halls in Republican automobiles borrowed for the occasion.

How much we owe to the inventor of the machine for making ice, whose statue has been placed in our national Hall of Fame in Washington! For no two weeks of my life have I revered the maker of the ice machine more than the last two weeks in New York.

What is it worth to the world to have the sewing machine? or the men who discovered how to prevent typhoid fever and yellow fever? I served in the Spanish War and saw twenty-seven men of my regiment die of typhoid fever. Not one soldier of all our millions that reached France died of typhoid fever. What has it been worth to the world already to have a remedy for that fever?

What value shall we set on the services of Raikes, who established our Sunday Schools? Less than a century ago George Williams founded the Young Men's Christian Association, which now numbers a million members. We have with us on this platform today a man who forty years ago gathered a few young folks around him and founded the Christian Endeavor Society. Now he is the commander of an army larger than the one we raised to serve in the World War. How shall we estimate such services as these? Or what value shall we place on the work of Frances E. Willard, whose statue the State of Illinois placed in the national Hall of Fame at Washington? How can we measure her fame?

Never, in a single case, did the persons I have named collect the full amount they earned. Those who have collected five hundred millions of dollars have been so busy collecting it that they have not had time to earn it, and those who have earned five hundred millions of dollars have been so busy earning it that they have not had time to collect it. What is injustice? It is this, that a few are able to collect more than they earn, and therefore those that earn the greatest sums are not able to collect them. Happy is our brother here who has lived to see the greatness of the cause that he has established. But not even Francis E. Clark has any conception of the value of his services to the world. It is a great thing by the use of the telephone to speak to people ten miles away, but it is a far greater thing to start some great movement that will touch the hearts of people thousands of years hence. When we stand before the judgment bar of God, and the righteous shall shine like the sun in the kingdom of their Father, a multitude will come up and pay their respects to the man who showed them what a Christian life should be.

And now for the second part of my topic. It requires no mandamus from any court to compel me to speak on peace. I rejoice today in the prospects of peace. We have a President who is a Christian, who believes in God, and the Son of God, and the Bible. He has delivered in the presence of our dead soldiers a speech which, if he can carry it out, will live alongside the address of Lincoln at Gettysburg. He said, "It shall never occur again." If he can accomplish that prophecy, he will have written his name among the immortals.

I am cheered by some indications of the coming of permanent peace. The Senate, by the vote of 74 to none, asked the President to call an international conference on the reduction of armaments. The House of Representatives, 303 to 4, concurred in the Senate resolution in favor of disarmament. I believe that this conference will be called. I believe that it will result in an agreement among the leading nations with navies, and that the rest of the world will soon join them, and that war will be put where Lincoln wanted to put slavery, in the process of ultimate extinction.

I believe that we shall find an agreement possible; I believe it probable. But we must not overlook one fact. At Washington we have influences at work trying to prevent disarmament. They tried to prevent the Borah resolution. If these influences are powerful in Washington, they may be still more potent in the capitals across the sea. We must not promise any one that we will not do anything unless we can get international agreement. If the agreement fails, decide then what you will do. I, for my part, have already decided what I will do. There are only two alternatives: one is a continuance of war with bankruptcy of the world; the other is the disarmament of the world. God forbid that I should say that if the militarists and navalists and manufacturers of war material should control the governments over the ocean, they should therefore control our nation. We must not forget that ours is the most permanent government. The governing bodies of the nations across the sea can be changed at any time by a vote of lack of confidence. If the delegates they send to the disarmament conference are such, or their instructions are such, that we cannot get an agreement, and if we continue to agitate for disarmament, we shall be the leaders of the greatest movement that history has recorded; we shall allow mankind to stand up straight again and begin a new life, with peace forever established, a peace built upon confidence and co-operation. The only light of the future is the light that shines from the cross of Jesus Christ. The only hope of the world is brotherhood. They have tried to win peace by force, and it has ended in the bloodiest war the world has ever known. The only hope for a lasting peace is in the brotherhood taught by Him whose coming was foretold when He was described as the Prince of Peace, by Him at whose coming the angels sang of "Peace on earth, good will to men."

I count it an honor to be the guest of this great society with the names of "Christian" and "Endeavor." There can be no Christianity without endeavor, as all endeavor without Christianity behind it fails to secure the highest things that are within the possibility of man. Stand ready, Endeavorers, to preach Christianity by the great endeavor to make our nation, if that is necessary, lead the world by giving it a noble example. "Disarmament by agreement if possible, by example if necessary"—this is the slogan I would suggest to you.

CHAPTER XVI.

___

ARMORY, SATURDAY, JULY 9

THE SATURDAY EVENING MEETING

Rev. Francis E. Clark, D.D., LL.D., Presiding

"HOW many of you have ever been in a Billy Sunday campaign anywhere?" asked Homer Rodeheaver in the praise service Saturday evening. Those that did not hold up their hands must have felt lonesome. "He wanted me to give his love to every one of you," added Mr. Rodeheaver, telling how much the evangelist appreciated what Dr. Clark and the Endeavorers have been to him in his work throughout the country.

Mr. Fred A. Victor was introduced to the audience at this service in recognition of their debt to him as chairman of the Convention music committee and the organizer of the excellent Convention chorus.

"To develop an evangelism with teeth in it" is a task of this generation according to Bishop Lynwood Westinghouse Kyles, who represents the African Methodist Episcopal Zion Church on the board of trustees of the United Society. In the devotional service led by him he made prominent Christian Endeavor as an evangelistic power.

Dr. Clark read the following messages from President Harding and Vice-President Coolidge, which were received with great demonstrations of enthusiasm:

THE WHITE HOUSE.

DEAR DR. CLARK,—I am very sorry indeed that it is impossible for me to accept your gratifying invitation to meet with the World's Convention of Christian Endeavor societies in New York in early July. Much as I should like to do so, I find demands of public business entirely precluding my making engagements at this time or for a considerable period in future.

I am sure you will understand my circumstances and will not doubt my very genuine interest in behalf of the splendid work of your organizations. They represent precisely the sort of inspiring purpose that the world so greatly needs in these times, and it would be a very real pleasure to me to add my own word of personal commendation and encouragement, were it possible.

Most sincerely yours,

WARREN G. HARDING.

MY DEAR DR. CLARK,—It had been my hope to be able to attend the Christian Endeavor Convention at New York, but my official duties require my constant attention at Washington.

I can think of no organization more likely to prove a permanent public benefit than the Christian Endeavor Society. These are days when we need to re-enforce our ideals. We need to define and defend them day by day and strive without ceasing to make them the realities of every-day life. There is no surer method of accomplishing this than through the recognition of our common brotherhood which comes from mutual co-operation for the same purpose. Your organization represents an effort to put religion into practice When men look about the world today, they will not be able to find any other remedy for our present condition or any other motive strong enough to promise any solution.

Respectfully yours,

CALVIN COOLIDGE.

Greetings were also read from Mrs. Grace Hooper Hoar, formerly the national Junior superintendent; the National Council of Congregational Churches; Dr. William Shaw; Rev. Charles M. Sheldon, D.D.; Rev. J. G. Holdcroft, missionary to Korea; Rev. Thomas Phillips, pastor of Bloomsbury Baptist Church of London; the Dutch Christian Endeavor Union of South Africa; the German Christian Endeavor Union; Dr. Sauvin, the secretary of the European Christian Endeavor Union; Rev. James Kelly, for the British union; Mr. Bush, president of the Australasian union; and the Esthonian Union of Christian Endeavor.

Chairman Frederick A. Wallis, of the Convention Committee, stated that he had personally called on President Harding, the Secretary of the Navy, and the Postmaster-General, who gave assurance of their purpose to attend the Convention. Soon after, the Secretary of the Navy sent word that official duties would prevent his attendance. This was followed by this message, which had just been received:

It is with keen regret that because of unexpected developments I am not permitted to address your meeting. The spirit of true Christianity properly observed and thoroughly disseminated is the balance-wheel of our modern civilization. No single question compares with it in its power for molding the destiny of our country and the welfare of our future generations. Your organization is carrying on this work in a most commendable manner, and is deserving of the fullest measure of support and encouragement at this time when the country is so disturbed by the influences that are bound to creep in after the terrible war we have just experienced. Your efforts are of inestimable value in keeping the thought of the country directed to clean and wholesome channels, and in helping to overcome the unfest and defection that are so prevalent at a time like this. You have my heartiest good wishes, and I would indeed be happy, were it possible, to tell you so in person.

EDWIN DENBY.

Chairman Wallis then read the following extracts from a letter from his "official boss at Washington," the Secretary of Labor:

It would give me the greatest pleasure to witness your proceedings and to see the great troops of Christian workers assembled at your history-making Convention. Not to be able to be with you gives me keen regret. This is no empty phrase, because my life is filled with grateful recollections of the Christian Endeavor society and the influence for good it exercised on me. I owe to the organization endless happy associations, a constant call to Christian duty, and an everlasting inspiration to service.

It calls to service in the Master's cause, and it makes that call, not as a summons to a stern duty, but to a friendly communion of good, clean souls. It has the right idea. It makes the service of the Master not only a holy thing, but a happy privilege. It makes for friendship with Jesus through friendship with His happy, earnest, self-giving children.

Never in all the years I have known it has the Christian Endeavor Society lived beneath its name. Always it has been what its name implies, a society for Christian endeavor. The good it has accomplished is beyond compute. Its people are the best bone and fibre of our citizenship.

May the society, with the guidance and blessing of the Master, go on its way of well-doing to a larger usefulness, to a greater influence for good, to a still higher esteem in the hearts of our people.

JAMES J. DAVIS.

Hon. William J. Bryan, who was to give the address of the session, had an appointment also to speak at an evangelistic meeting at Tent Evangel, and before his arrival Dr. Clark asked the audience whether they would like to have Mr. Bryan made an honorary Alumnus of the society, a suggestion that called out a united "Ay."

Great cheering announced Mr. Bryan's entrance. In telling him of the action just taken in regard to making him an Alumnus of the society, Dr. Clark referred to the Christian Endeavor members of the Cabinet. President Harding and his secretary, Mr. Christian, and Postmaster-General Hays are Alumni; Secretary Davis was an early Endeavorer; and later in the evening it was announced that Secretary of State Hughes has applied for membership in the Christian Endeavor Alumni Association of the District of Columbia. Dr. Clark gave to Mr. Bryan the right hand of fellowship as an Alumnus, and Treasurer Shartle pinned a Christian Endeavor badge on his coat. In introducing Mr. Bryan to speak Dr. Clark referred to an evening paper that, thinking of the procession of the afternoon as a "dry" demonstration, stated that a few scattering people had been at Central Park to hear Mr. Bryan; and his attention was called to the "few scattering people" then waiting to hear from him the powerful address entitled "Building on the Rock." He said:

My few and scattered friends, I feel greatly honored to be made an honorary Alumnus of this great organization. I think not even your revered president has a larger estimate of the power and opportunity and responsibility of the Christian Endeavor Society. And it is because I have that conception of what you can do, and ought to do, and will do that I have been looking forward with pleasant anticipations to this day ever since Dr. Clark was good enough to honor me with an invitation. I so arranged my dates that I could be here. I travelled all night to reach New York, and I travel all night tonight to get back to my appointments tomorrow. But, my friends, it would be worth coming thousands of miles instead of hundreds to catch the inspiration of this day. And tonight I want to speak on a subject that I hope you will regard as worthy of this occasion.

A few years ago in re-reading the concluding verses of the last chapter of Matthew I was surprised to find, because it had not impressed me before, that the little word "all" was used four times by the Saviour in a very brief space, and this was His last talk with His followers. It was after His crucifixion and after His resurrection. It was His final word. He said that all power in heaven and in earth had been given into His hands, not some power, but all power. He sent His followers out to make disciples of all nations, not of some nations, but of all nations. He told them to teach all the things that He had commanded them, not some of the things, but all of the things. And He concluded with that wonderful promise, "Lo, I am with you always, even unto the end of the world." Is there any other organization with such a commission back of it? Here is a gospel intended for every human being. Here is a code of morals that is to endure for all time. Here is a philosophy of life that fits into every human need. And back of these is all power in heaven and in earth.

My friends, the measure of responsibility is opportunity multiplied by power, and if it be true that God has put into the hands of His church a solution for every problem that can vex a human heart or perplex a world, if it be true that He has not only put into the hands of the church a solution, but the only solution, then how will you measure the responsibility of the church as it confronts the infinite opportunities of today? How shall we be true to these responsibilities? If you will take the Sermon on the Mount, that moral code of Christ that had nothing like it before it was spoken, and there has been nothing like it since, that code of morals that rises above all the teachings of all history before and after, that wonderful sermon which, if there were nothing else, would raise Christ above the level of man and answer forever the question that is put by those who inquire whether He was man or God, how will you account for that code? Coming from a young man reared in a carpenter shop, with no opportunity to know the wisdom of sages past except as it was found in the Old Testament, and no opportunity to confer with sages living, I believe that that one sermon bears within itself the proof of Christ's divinity. And you will find that as He finished He used this idea, the thought that I have chosen as the basis of my remarks tonight. Let me read; although it covers several verses, I want you to take it as it is recorded in the Bible. Beginning with the twenty-fourth verse and ending with the twenty-ninth verse of the seventh chapter of Matthew, I read: "Therefore whosoever heareth these sayings of mine, and doeth them, I will liken him unto a wise man, which built his house upon a rock; and the rain descended, and the floods came, and the winds blew, and beat upon that house; and it fell not, for it was founded upon a rock. And every one that heareth these sayings of mine, and doeth them not, shall be likened unto a foolish man, which built his house upon the sand; and the rain descended, and the floods came, and the winds blew, and beat upon that house; and it fell, and great was the fall of it. And it came to pass, when Jesus had ended these sayings, the people were astonished at his doctrine; for he taught them as one having authority, and not as the scribes."

You will notice, my friends, that it is not in fair weather, but in storm, that we have the test of a house's foundation. When all is pleasant, when there is not a cloud in the sky, the sand may safely be built upon; but, when the storms come, and the rains descend, and the winds blow, only the house that is built upon the rock will endure; and so we are dealing with the gospel that teaches us how to be strong in time of storm; and tonight I ask your attention for just a little while while I speak of the rock foundation, the Rock of Ages on which the Christian can stand if he will.

Our Bible gives us a rock foundation.

In the first place, it teaches us that there is a God. I believe that that is the greatest thought that ever entered a human mind or heart, that there is a God. If the mainspring of a watch is broken, it is no longer a time-keeper. If the case is a handsome one, it may be carried as an ornament, and the parts though broken may have a small market value; but it is not a watch in the sense in which that term is used. I believe there is in every human life that which corresponds to the mainspring of a watch, that without which the life cannot be what it ought to be; and this that corresponds to the mainspring of a watch is belief in God. If one does not believe in God, he may be an ornament in some kinds of society, and he may have a certain market value; but I do not believe it is possible for him to measure up to the infinite possibilities that God has placed before His creatures.

On this belief in God rest certain things that are fundamental. Unless one believes in God he cannot have a consciousness of God's presence in his life; he cannot have a sense of responsibility to God for every thought and word and deed. My friends, I think the most potent influence that acts upon a human life is that sense of responsibility for every thought and word and deed. Do you think that it is the criminal law, or a sheriff in each county, or an occasional policeman— do you think that these are the things that give us security of life and property? By no means. For every man made honest by law a hundred are made honest by conscience. For every man kept in the strait and narrow way by fear of prison walls a multitude are kept righteous by those invisible walls that conscience rears about us, walls that are stronger than the walls of stone. My friends, law is but the crystallization of conscience, and this conscience must be roused before a law can be passed; and in so far as the Christian Endeavor Society helps to awaken a nation's conscience and stir a nation to an understanding of what is wrong it stands back of the law, and comes before the law, and is the cause of that upon which the law must finally rest and that which gives force and vitality to the law. So, when we are dealing with the consciences of men and women, we are dealing with the great motive power of all the world; and there is nothing more consoling than the consciousness of God's presence in the life.

Tolstoy has said that religion is the relation that man fixes between himself and God, and he declares that morality is but the outward manifestation of this inward relation. If it be true that morality is but the expression of religion, then religion is the most practical thing in the world. And Tolstoy administers, I think, the severest rebuke to what he calls the cultured crowd. He says there are some who regard religion as superstition, who say that it is good enough for the ignorant to hold them in check and restrain them; but who believe that man can outgrow the necessity for religion when he reaches a certain limit of intellectual development; and then he administers this rebuke: He says that every one who has experienced religious feeling knows that it does not rest on a vague fear of the unseen forces of nature, but it does rest on man's consciousness of his finiteness and of his sinfulness; and then he adds with that force and directness in which few have surpassed him—he adds, "And that consciousness man can never outgrow." I know of nothing more sweet, nothing more consoling, nothing more strengthening, than the belief that there is a power that is infinite, so that, when we reach the limitations of our strength, we do not despair, we feel that there is One whose arm is all-powerful. In our weakness we look to God for strength, and in our sinfulness we look for one who is sinless. I know not how man can meet the duties of this life if he does not believe in God.

My father did not leave me a great amount of money. When I was a boy, I thought he was rich. He owned about six hundred acres of land; we lived in a nice house; and the thing that worried me when I was a boy, as I thought about my father's wealth, was whether I could find any girl that would marry me for love, or whether some one would marry me for my money. By the time I was ready to get married I found that we had only about three thousand dollars apiece.

and I feel quite sure that the one who finally accepted me did not take me for my riches.

But, while my father did not leave me much money, he gave me something that I think was worth more to me than any amount of money that a father ever left a boy. He taught me to believe in God. He taught me to believe that God stood back of every righteous cause with an arm strong enough to bring victory to His side. He taught me to believe that there is nothing omnipotent but truth. He told me that I could afford to be in the minority, but that I could not afford to be wrong on any subject. He told me that, if I should be in the minority on any subject and was right, I should some day be in the majority; but he taught me to believe that, if I was in the majority and wrong, I should some day be in the minority. I think that teaching of my father was worth more to me than money, and I believe that the Bible speaks the truth when it says that one with God shall chase a thousand and two put ten thousand to flight. I can understand now better than I could when I first read it how a few righteous men might have saved a wicked city. I know now that no wicked city can be saved except by the righteous who live in it, and I know there is no wickedness that the righteous cannot drive from a city if they believe in God and take their stand without stopping to count how many. Those who fight for the right travel with their faces to the dawn, and the sky grows brighter hour by hour. If you fight for the right, you never know what things will come to justify you that you did not think of.

Let me give you an illustration. It took seventeen years to secure an income-tax, and I doubt if anybody who fought for an income-tax had any conception of the uses that would be made of it when it came. They fought for it because they believed it just, because they thought it would more equitably distribute the burdens of the government, and it would adjust those burdens to the strength of the backs of the people. That was the thought that inspired them as they worked. But, my friends, we had no more secured an income-tax than we found it was just in time to meet the last argument made in favor of the liquor traffic. Do you remember where they finally made their stand? After they had been beaten on every other proposition they said, "How can you run your government without our money?" and they would tell us impudently that we had to have the saloon because we collected hundreds of millions of dollars from intoxicating liquors and from licenses. But just about as they got behind that barrier we could look the scoundrels in the face and say that never again would an American boy be auctioned off to the saloon for money enough to run our government.

We have great faith in co-operation. Co-operation is a mighty machine in the physical world. They have sought in vain for what they call perpetual motion. They will get perpetual motion whenever they can find a machine that will generate more power than is required to start it and to keep it running. That is all that is necessary. Whenever somebody will invent a machine that will multiply energy and produce more units of power than are required to start it going and keep it going, we shall have perpetual motion. But lots of people have found their way into the insane asylum as they searched for that machine. It has not yet been found; but society has a machine that multiplies energy, and that machine is called co-operation. You have four millions of members in this great organization. Can they do four million times as much as they could do acting separately? O my friends, they can do forty million times as much. They can do four hundred million times as much. They can do what the individual never would think of undertaking.

To illustrate. Suppose all the people on God's footstool, estimated at a billion and a half, had marched single file across the Isthmus of Panama before they commenced digging that canal. It never would have occurred to any one of them that he could dig it alone; but it took only forty thousand men organized together to do that greatest engineering feat in history.

But, my friends, there is one danger that comes with co-operation, and that is that it may extinguish or discourage individual initiative. You must not forget that co-operation does not begin great causes; it concludes great causes. But every great cause started with one, and in the loneliness of that one vision begins the righteous cause. And, my friends, the best evidence that we have on earth that man was made in the image of God and is not a descendant of the lower animals—the best evidence is found in the fact that throughout the ages man when he has heard the voice of truth has stood erect and been ready to die that he might preach that truth to the world. That is the evidence that man was made in the image of God. We may share physical courage with the brutes about us, but we share moral courage with God only. And, when that truth is first discovered, it is ridiculed, it is denounced; but the force that is back of every truth is as constantly at work and as irresistible as the forces of nature that assure us seedtime and harvest. If a voice once proclaims the truth, that truth can never be recalled. They may burn at the stake the man who spoke it; they may boil him in oil; they may drown him in the ocean; but they cannot drown the truth. That voice goes on. It echoes and it echoes until that echo drowns out all other sounds. Some one has said that you may build your capitals until they reach the skies; but, if they rest on injustice, the pulse of a woman will beat them down. You cannot believe it unless you believe in God, and nothing but faith in God will enable a man to do his duty as a man and take the consequences.

Belief in God comes first. On it rest these other things. Next to that consciousness of God's presence, next, my friends, to that sense of responsibility to God for what we do, comes prayer. You can't pray unless you believe in God. You must not only believe in God, but you must believe that He is near enough to hear and willing to answer. You cannot believe in a general God and pray to Him. It must be a personal God, a God who knows you, a God who loves you, and a God who will hear you and will help you when you need His aid. Sometimes we hear people say who do not believe in prayer—they do not pray themselves, but they say it may do men some good even if it is not answered. But, my friends, the man who believes prayer is not answered won't pray, so that back of prayer must be a faith in God.

And then third comes belief in immortality. Unless we believe in God we shall not believe in a world beyond. If there be no God, then the grave ends all. Have you thought what it would mean to take from life the restraint that comes from belief in God? I was reading the other day the story of Ivan the Terrible. When his son came back from college, the dissolute father said, "Son, is there a life beyond?" and the son said, "No, father." He said, "Are you sure that death ends all?" "Sure, father." "Then," said the father, "we can do as we please."

Have you thought what it would mean to take from the human race belief that in a world beyond they would be held accountable for the deeds done here? I say to you that we cannot compute in any way, by language or by figures, what it means to us to look forward to a life beyond the grave. It encourages us when we come to die, for we feel that it is just a change to a life beyond. It is a comfort when those about us die to believe that death is but a narrow star-like stripe between the companionship of yesterday and the reunion of tomorrow.

And, my friends, belief in God is that which gives us hope of immortality. Every thing that God has made proclaims that there is a life beyond. If the Father deigns to touch with divine power the cold and buried heart of the acorn and make it burst forth from its prison cell, will He leave neglected in the earth the soul of man made in the image of his Creator? If He stoops to give to the rose-bush the sweet assurance of another springtime, will He withhold the words of hope from the sons of men when the frosts of winter come? Will the imperial spirit of man suffer annihilation when it has paid a brief visit like a royal guest to this tenement of clay? No, I am as sure that I shall live again as that I live today.

In Cairo I secured a few grains of wheat that had slumbered for three thousand years in an Egyptian tomb, and this thought came into my mind: If one of them had been planted on the Nile the day after it matured, and all its descendants had been planted and replanted, the progeny of that one grain of wheat would have been sufficient to feed the teeming millions of today. There is something in it that gives it power to rebuild a new body so much like the old that you cannot tell one from the other. And, if that grain of wheat can pass unimpaired through three thousand resurrections, I shall not doubt that my spirit has power to clothe itself with new existence when this frame of mine shall crumble into dust. But we could not believe in that future life if we did not believe that there is a God back of the world, above the world, in whose hand the destiny of this world is.

Without a belief in God we could not believe in human brotherhood. We trace our kinship with our brother through the common Father of us all. And I believe that brotherhood is the hope of the world. I see no chance for the history of the world to be written otherwise than in characters of blood unless men can be brought together in that universal brotherhood. And it is that belief in brotherhood that offers us the promise of solution of all great problems that today annoy and disturb us. Take the industrial question. How are we going to bring employers and employees together in harmonious co-operation if not by Christ's plan? The church believes in God, and it believes that the same God who made one made the other. The church believes in Christ, and it believes that the Christ who died for one died for the other. The church believes in a universal brotherhood, and believes that when it comes it must include the man who works for wages and the man who pays wages. I know of nothing else except this gospel of brotherhood taught by Him who spake as never man spake, I know of nothing but that that can fill the world with willing workers and satisfied employers toiling together, giving to society the maximum of the powers that they both possess. Brotherhood, I believe, rests therefore on a belief in God.

I need not tell you that the Bible rests for its authority on a belief in God. If there be no God, there can be no word of God. Neither is it necessary to emphasize the fact that belief in Christ rests upon belief in God. If there be no Father, there can be no Son.

And so, my friends, here are six great essential things upon which character is built, upon which society rests, upon which our hope must stand, and they all rest upon belief in God. These are parts of that solid rock upon which our church stands. These are a part of the Rock of Ages on which the Christian Endeavor Society is built, and I rejoice that those who have been at its head have preached a spiritual belief to those that have marched under the banner of this great organization.

Now, my friends, I believe that everything that attacks belief in God is an enemy to the church and, because the church is a factor in civilization, is an enemy to civilization; and I want just for a moment here to lay before you one matter that has been on my heart. And that is the effect of the doctrine that has respectable authority back of it that is shaking the faith of boys and girls in the Bible. And that is the doctrine that man instead of being created by the Almighty with a purpose and according to a plan is nothing but a development from the lower animals. There are many who believe that that doctrine must be accepted. The fact that you can find no authority for it in the Bible ought to be sufficient to make a Christian hesitate before he accepts it. Take the word of God from the first verse of Genesis to the last of Revelation, there is not a sentence or a syllable that can be invoked to support the idea that man has in him the blood of the brute.

But, my friends, is it possible to support that doctrine by testimony outside the Bible? I have been studying the subject some eighteen years. I began to investigate it when I found its chilling influence upon young men in college. I went back then and reviewed the doctrine of Darwin, and I reached the conclusion that, if Darwin was right, Christianity was wrong; that, if man had reached his present position by a cruel law under which the strong kill off the weak, then, if there is any logic that can bind the human mind, we must turn backward to the brute if we dare to substitute the law of love for the law of hate. I believe that logic is irresistible; and, as I believe that the law of love and not hatred is supreme, I repudiate the brute doctrine.

My friends, you may search the universe, and you will find not one single fact that supports the idea that man is an improved ape or monkey or any other form of brute. Darwin's doctrine was—and it was but a guess—Darwin's doctrine was that everything that we now see is the result of change, slow, imperceptible change. His doctrine was that about two hundred millions of years ago a few germs of life appeared upon the planet, one or a few germs, and that everything that we now see is the result of the development from resident forces, not forces outside. Darwin permitted God to act two hundred millions of years ago; but some go farther and put the last act of the Almighty, if He ever acted at all, billions of years ago.

Within a year one of your New York papers, the *Times*, published the substance of a sermon delivered in London. The papers said it had caused a great sensation. Canon Barnes, of Westminster Abbey, had interpreted evolution. He said that the universe was filled with stuff; that is where he begins; and out of stuff came atoms or electrons, and out of the electrons came matter; and out of matter came life, and out of life came mind, and out of mind came soul. He said there was a time when there was neither matter nor life nor soul nor mind, but now we have them all, a part of God's plan. But God had been shut out of His own universe for billions of years. Who will estimate the time that has elapsed since electrons came out of stuff and formed matter?

When I was in college, they did not go back any farther than the nebular hypothesis. Men could stand it to have God that far away. And that hypothesis was that matter was divided into particles infinitely fine, and each particle was separated from every other particle by distances infinitely great; and then, having guessed that matter was there, though they could not explain it, and that force was there, though they could not define it, they said that force working on matter created a world. They have gone farther now and discovered that 1,740 electrons make an atom, so that now God has not been allowed to have anything to do with His universe since 1,740 electrons formed a chorus and sung, "We'll be an atom by and by."

What do you think, my friends, is the effect of that sort of doctrine on the Christian? You raise your boy to believe in God and prayer. You teach him the Bible, that he is precious in God's sight, that the Father is more willing to give good gifts to His children than earthly parents are; and then you send him to school where they teach Darwinism, and a professor whom he is taught to respect takes a book six hundred pages thick, and tries to convince your boy that the Bible is not true, but that he is the descendant of the animal below. And for days that professor will call his attention to points in which he resembled the brute. You notice, Darwin says, you notice the point of the ear; that is like an ape's ear. You can wiggle your ears like a horse. And after spending days at that Darwin takes your mind, and tries to convince you that your mind is the mind of a brute. He tells you that you have not anything in your brain that cannot be found in miniature in the beasts of the field. And he then turns to your moral nature, and he tells you that you have developed along brute lines, and that even the more moral qualities are the outgrowth of the brute.

There you find it, first, second, third, fourth, fifth, sixth, never a mention of God, never a suggestion of religion; and, when your child finishes that book, if he believes his teacher and believes Darwin, he believes that your Bible is a story-book; he believes that Christ is but a man, that His ancestor on His mother's side was a brute, and most of them believe that His ancestor on His father's side also was but a brute. That is the conclusion they come to.

I have talked with mothers who have been distressed when their daughters came home. They went from Sunday School to college, but they never went back from college to Sunday School. I have talked with fathers whose boys have started out with a belief in God and have come home from college without chart or compass for life's sea. In this very State I was speaking a few nights ago and giving some illustrations that have come under my own observation; and a young man said: "I know the son of a Baptist minister who started to prepare for the ministry. He went to Brown University, and within two years' time he was an atheist and gave up his purpose to enter the ministry." A young man in Pennsylvania told me his brother was in Yale under a professor who had the reputation of making every student in his class an atheist.

On the fifteenth day of last April I spoke in South Carolina. When I was through, a young man twenty-two years old came up to me, and said, "Two teachers in a Christian college made an atheist out of me with that doctrine of Darwin." He prayed that night for the first time in years; and on the fourteenth day of June he wrote: "You asked me to let you know when I was ready to recant. I am ready. I recant. I see how false it is." And, when I met him the other day, he was on the way to visit a Methodist preacher to join the Methodist Church and take up Christian work.

A few years ago I visited Ann Arbor, Mich., and while I was speaking to the students on religion that night, a professor of philosophy was speaking in another hall; and I learned from an Episcopal clergyman who heard him, and whom I met at the train as we were leaving town, that this professor told his audience that Christianity was a state of mind and that there were only two books in the Bible that had any literary merit.

In Madison, Wis., a Methodist minister gave me this incident: A Catholic girl came out of a class much disturbed, and said: "My professor has just said that the Bible is a collection of myths. I do not like to doubt my teacher, but I have been taught to believe that the Bible is the word of God. What should I believe?" Within three months I visited Madison again. I spoke to 1,950 people, nearly all students, but among others was the president of the university. I called attention to that professor. He was not disturbed by that. All he said was—and he said it in an interview in the paper next day—he said Mr. Bryan was making a great mistake in trying to link the faith of students to discarded scientific theories. He said my speech was of the kind that the fathers and grandfathers of the students used to listen to. Now, when taxes are getting too heavy, I think we could save at least one president's salary if we did not hire a man to speak contemptuously of the religion of the fathers and mothers of this generation.

Speaking on this subject before the United Brethren a few weeks ago, I gave some of these illustrations. When I was through, a Congressman from Pennsylvania came up to me, and said: "My daughter has just come back from Wellesley; and she said, 'Father, I used to believe those Bible stories.' I said, 'What do you mean?' 'Why, the Bible stories; I used to think they were true.' 'Do you mean to, say that you don't believe the Bible?' 'Why, nobody believes those stories now.' "

That was the return from Wellesley, and I have found four young ladies from Wellesley by whom reports have been made. One from Evanston, Ill., was the daughter of a preacher. She handed in a paper in which she wrote down answers according to the book, and then wrote, "I do not believe in it." The professor sent for her, and asked her about it, and said, "Your father is a minister, isn't he?" "Yes." "Where did he get this theological training?" "Princeton." "O yes, Princeton is away behind the times."

We have some theological seminaries in which they are now teaching that the first three chapters of Genesis are not true, and the next thing after they convince a student that the first three chapters of Genesis are not true they tear out the first chapter of Matthew, and give us a Christ not born of the Holy Ghost and the Virgin Mary.

In western New York there was a young preacher just ordained who did not believe in the virgin birth, and could say no. more than that Christ was a good man.

My friends, within two weeks a Baptist preacher in New York has told me of a meeting that they had in western New York where one of these men who had become saturated with higher criticism complained that the parents taught the children at home doctrines that they had to give up when they went to school; and his theory was to quit teaching at home.

They have a man named James H. Leuba as professor of psychology in Bryn Mawr, who, having taught for a session that there is no God, put it to vote in the class; and the majority voted that there is no God. That same man Leuba has written a book on belief in God and immortality in which he attempts to prove that these beliefs are dying out. He takes a book of scientists with fifty-five hundred names in it. He says it contains the names of practically all the prominent scientists. He sent them a questionnaire, and collected their answers; and these show that more than half of them do not believe in a personal God or personal immortality. He made inquiries of the students of nine representative colleges; and the answers show that only about 15 per cent. of the freshmen have given up their belief in God or immortality, about 30 per cent. of the juniors have; and, when they come to graduate, between 40 and 45 per cent. of the men, not so large a per cent. of the women, have discarded the cardinal principles of the Christian faith. Christians, are you prepared to trade purity of heart for training of the intellect and have your child come back from college with a swelled head and a shrivelled heart?

There was a man by the name of George John Romanes. He was sometimes called the successor of Darwin. He was born in Canada, and then lived in England, where he received his education. You will find a description of him in the "Encyclopaedia Britannica" and the "Encyclopaedia Americana." He was weaned from his faith by evolution; and I may add that, when you confront these people with the absurdities of Darwin, they will tell you that very few accept Darwin's theories now. That is very true, but without any explanation these people tell you that the theory is established although they cannot explain it, although it has nothing to support it. Now, this man Romanes wrote a book in which he denied the existence of God. He used these words: "I am not ashamed to confess that with this virtual negation of God the universe to me has lost its soul of loveliness"; "and when at times I think, as think at times I must, of the appalling contrast between the hallowed glory of that creed which once was mine and the lonely mystery of existence as now I find it, at such times I shall ever feel it impossible to avoid the sharpest pang of which my nature is susceptible." He wandered for twenty-five years, and he said he was not able to bring himself to the simplest form of prayer. After a time he found his way back to God, and then he gave expression to his new-found conviction that faith is more than reason; and he quoted those wonderful words of Bourdillon:

> "The night has a thousand eyes,
> And the day but one;
> Yet the light of a whole world dies
> With the setting sun.
>
> "The mind has a thousand eyes,
> And the heart but one;
> Yet the light of a whole life dies
> When love is done."

Darwinism gives you no plan in life; Darwinism spends its time trying to find resemblances between yourselves and the brutes.

My friends, I believe that the time has come for the Christian Church to understand the ravages that infidelity and agnosticism and atheism are making in our schools. They took a census in one university, and they found that only twenty-five per cent. of the boys and girls who went from Christian schools and Sunday Schools to that university ever returned to those Sunday Schools and churches. The mortality is too great. We cannot afford to lose three-fourths of our children in the effort to educate them.

I have reached two conclusions. One is that no Christian college should permit a person to teach who is not a Christian and a believer in the Bible. A bishop of the Southern Methodist Church who is officially connected with a great Christian university told me he received an application from a man who wanted a chair of science, one of the chairs that had become vacant; and after describing his qualifications he said, "I think I ought to tell you that I am not a Christian, and never will be; but I am tolerant toward Christians." It seems to me that, if a man is going to teach in a Christian college, and draw a salary from Christians, he ought at least to be tolerant toward Christians. But why should a Christian college have to explain why it had to find a man not a Christian to teach anything?

I believe the time has come for the Christian people of this country who pay taxes to say that 'no man who draws his pay from the public treasury shall attack the Bible and destroy the faith. If we are to have neutrality of religion, let it be a real neutrality and not a sham neutrality. Before the war they were teaching Nietzsche's theology in colleges where the Bible was not taught. He denies God, overthrows every standard of Christianity, says democracy is the refuge of the weak and Christianity is the belief of the degenerate, that pity is unmanly, that sympathy has no place in the heart, and that war is not only good but desirable, and that hatred is good because it leads to war. He holds up Napoleon as the great man of his century because he made war respectable. I believe that Nietzsche took Darwinism and made it the foundation of the bloodiest war that this world has yet known, and that they are applying Darwinism to industry, and are setting up the doctrine of efficiency, every one for himself, and the devil take the hindmost. They are dragging our industrial world down into a conflict with the spirit of brotherhood eliminated from the hearts of men.

That, my friends, is what I believe it is leading to, and that is why I value the opportunity presented by such an opportunity as this to tell you the things that are on my heart. You are worshippers of a miracle-performing God, and I appeal to you to help bring the world back to a belief in God, not to acquiescence in a theory that there may be a God, but to such a belief as is expressed in the commandments of the Saviour when He condensed them into one, "Thou shalt love the Lord thy God with all thy heart and with all thy soul and with all thy mind and with all thy strength"; and, when we have given to God all our love, when He dominates every thought and impulse and energy of life, then we are prepared to understand and obey the second commandment, "Thou shalt love thy neighbor as thyself." The first is the belief in God, and so I appeal to you with your mighty membership, help to carry the world back to a real belief in God; and then, with the Bible as our authoritative guide and with Christ as not only example but Saviour, the world can enter on an era brighter than ever before, with peace in every human heart and peace among the nations resting upon love and brotherhood and co-operation. I thank you for your attention.

"Faith of our fathers" was the well-chosen closing hymn.

CHAPTER XVII.

WORLD WIDE CHRISTIAN ENDEAVOR

ARMORY, SUNDAY AFTERNOON, JULY 10

Mr. Hiram N. Lathrop, Presiding

IN opening the Sunday afternoon meeting in the Armory Dr. Clark read a message from Brazil: "He is our peace, who hath made both one," the motto inscribed on the statue of Christ placed on the Andes on the boundary between Argentina and Chile.

Mr. Hiram N. Lathrop, clerk of the United Society, presided over the session brightly. "When you want a thing well done, get a woman to do it," he said in introducing Mrs. May Pashley Harris, who directed the Missionary Pageant.

This pageant was beautifully impressive. To the singing of "Onward, Christian Soldiers" a young girl representing Christian Endeavor, clad in white and bearing a large silver cross, came down the central aisle to the platform. She was followed by "Service," another girl dressed in yellow; "Love," a girl dressed in violet; and "Loyalty," a girl dressed in blue. These took their places, Christian Endeavor in the centre, upon the choir steps, Service in front of her lower down, and Love and Loyalty on either side. Then the Sowers entered, as the choir sang "Bringing in the Sheaves,"—girls attired likewise in yellow, violet, and blue, who marched forward making motions as if sowing grain, and grouped themselves in three lovely tableaux around Service, Love, and Loyalty.

The girls in yellow, grouped around Service, were Juniors, each of whom took hold of a bright ribbon of yellow held by Service, and all marched forward along lines radiating from Service, symbolizing the outreach of Christian Endeavor activities. Then entered "the Sons of Earth," a long line of young folks costumed to represent the different nations whose banners they bore—and numbers of them were evidently the actual representatives of those nations. As the choir sang " Rejoice, rejoice, Jehovah reigns," these "Sons of Earth" marched within the radiating lines of Service, until they were held by them.

Then the choir struck up "Blest be the tie that binds," when the Love maidens, joining hands across the stage, pressed backward upon the central group, uniting them all in one by "the bonds of love."

One more change as the choir sang "True-hearted, whole-hearted, faithful and loyal," in true-blue Loyalty girls coming to the centre facing the cross and falling on their knees in devotion. They rose at the second stanza, and the entire audience joined in the third stanza, thus bringing the pageant to a close. The children sat on the floor, making a charming and significant background for the remainder of the program. It was a simple pageant, made unforgettable by the sweet faces of the girls, the beauty of the colors and costumes, and the wonderful meaning of it all.

Dr. Clark—and no one else could have done it so well—next took charge of one of the most interesting periods of the Convention, the "Greetings from Other Lands."

First came greetings from the Christian Endeavorers of Burma, brought us by Mr. San Ba, a Burmese student here in the United States, and a Christian Endeavorer. He told us that "there are hundreds of Endeavorers in Burma, and the Endeavor movement has meant a lot to the people there and has been a source of strength to the church. "Whatever spirit of initiative I have," said he, "I owe largely to the training I received in Christian Endeavor work in one of the mission schools of Burma. I began as a staggering and stammering associate Endeavorer, and worked my way through the different positions in the society. The Endeavorers of Burma are one with you in spirit and purpose. I wish to thank Dr. Clark and all those who are responsible for the origin and spread of this movement. We Christians in Burma are still weak; we look to you for leadership."

Mr. San Ba spoke easily and in admirable English, and was a fine example of Christian Endeavor. Dr. Clark told of the two hundred Burmese Endeavorers who attended the World's Convention at Agra, India, traveling 1,500 miles and paying their own expenses and the expenses of twenty of their missionaries.

We turned next to China, and Dr. Clark introduced Rev George H. Hubbard, who introduced Christian Endeavor into China in 1884, before there was a single society in Great Britain. The Strothers, our secretaries in China, are workers of wonderful devotion and self-sacrifice, of which Dr. Clark spoke in introducing Mr. Strother, who brought the greetings of the 1,200 societies and 60,000 Endeavorers of that great republic. "Since Mr. Hubbard started that first society in Foochow," said Mr. Strother, "Christian Endeavor has spread into every corner of China. Now there are societies in every province and practically every mission. I have hundreds of testimonies from the missionaries of every denomination saying that Christian Endeavor societies give them the best chances for evangelistic work."

Mr. Strother then presented to Dr. Clark for the Christian Endeavor Museum in the Headquarters Building in Boston two very beautiful and interesting banners. One, which was held up by a Korean Endeavorer, came from Korean Endeavorers of Shanghai. A charmingly colored map of Korea occupied the centre of the banner. "Christian Endeavor" in the Korean language ran across the top, with the Christian Endeavor and the Korean flags painted beneath. "The Koreans," said Mr. Strother, "are under restraint now and are not able to have Christian Endeavor societies as they would wish; they ask for your prayers."

The other was a Chinese banner, charmingly designed by the Chinese secretary of Christian Endeavor. Down the banner were five stripes of the five colors of the Chinese national flag. Over them was painted the map of China bearing the C. E. monogram and encircled with a garland, since China is the Land of Flowers. Across the top are the Chinese characters for Christian Endeavor, and across the bottom is the Great Commission in Chinese.

Still another representative of Chinese Christian Endeavor was the well-known and honored missionary, Miss Emily Hartwell, one of the original Endeavorers in China, leader of the Christian Endeavor work there for many years. She also presented to the Museum a beautiful Chinese banner, which was held up by two fascinating Chinese children. It was a gift from the 1,500 Chinese Juniors belonging to the Junior Christian Endeavor Union of Foochow. This banner carries in Chinese the characters for Foochow city and suburbs. The meeting at which this banner was presented was entirely conducted by Chinese Juniors, and the presiding officer was a Junior boy.

Miss Hartwell made a very earnest and strong plea for the suppression of the traffic in morphia, so much of it carried on under the American flag. Morphia is ruining China. It is as much worse than opium as opium is worse than cider. It is made out of opium raised in India and other places. Much of it is manufactured in New York and Philadelphia, and some of it in London. It is distributed in China through the Japanese and other foreign post-offices over which the Chinese have no control. Much of it is smuggled back into our country to ruin thousands here. Let us remember the tens of thousands of widows and orphans in China, made such by the morphia manufactured under the American flag. Let us send petitions to our Government and try to influence other governments to stop this awful business.

Canada was finely represented by Lieutenant W. Steenson, of Winnipeg, secretary of the Manitoba union. In eloquent periods he pictured the extent and prosperous growth of Canada. "The church of Christ," said the speaker, "is confronted by many problems. We need not expect God to work a miracle to solve them, unless we first have done our best to solve them ourselves. The Christian Endeavorers are striving to do their part."

Calling upon Mrs. F. H. Gates to speak for India, Dr. Clark said that she has "held up the banner of Christian Endeavor higher than perhaps any other missionary in that vast land."

Mrs. Gates gave us a wonderful five minutes' talk, bringing the greetings of the 60,000 Endeavorers of India and Ceylon. She declared that "the terrible diseases which invade India are only a symbol of the pestilential moral influences surrounding the young people of India." But Christian Endeavor rises from this foulness like pure lilies from the mud.

Mrs. Gates specified some particulars in which Indian Endeavor societies are ahead of ours. Front seats there are never vacant. Their meetings never have pauses. Every one is ready to give his testimony or pray his simple, earnest prayer to God.

Telling of the beautiful Hindoo custom of placing garlands of flowers around the necks of those they would honor, Mrs. Gates said that when she left India the fourteen Christian Endeavor societies of Sholapur placed on her neck and in her hands twenty-eight beautiful garlands. The Sunbeam Society of the girls' school of Sholapur, wishing to give her something that would last, presented to her a long chain of beads interspersed with circles of brass. This she gave to Dr. Clark, throwing it around his neck.

"I never felt better decorated in my life," exclaimed Dr. Clark. "Now I can rival Mr. Pollock," referring to the beautiful golden presidential chain worn by the European president according to British custom.

Mr. Polhemus Lyon was introduced by Dr. Clark as "a most generous and devoted layman who lived for many years in Cape Town, South Africa, and was largely the stay and support of Christian Endeavor there." Though the speaker had only recently come from the hospital and was very weak, he spoke clearly and eloquently.

"Fellow citizens of the world," he said, "I bring to you the official greetings, transmitted to me, of the South African union, of which I was a member for twenty years. Christian Endeavor was imported into South Africa by American women who went down there to teach in the large boarding-schools. The girls, as they graduated from these schools, started Christian Endeavor in their homes. But there was no cohesion in the work until Dr. Clark came to us in 1897 and inaugurated our union, with Andrew Murray as its first president. In 1898 we held our first convention, and the Endeavorers were carried to Cape Town in a train bearing along the side a big Christian Endeavor banner—the first train in Africa that ever was solely designated for a religious convention. The papers had much to say about it.

"The Christian Endeavorers of South Africa want to work for Christ and the church, and build up the kingdom of God here on earth, which is their reasonable service. One of our serious problems is the rapid growth of Mohammedanism among the colored people, and we Endeavorers are doing what we can to meet this vast peril."

Rev. Bohumil Prochasna brought the greeting of Czechoslovakia and Poland. He said: "About the time when Columbus was reaching the shores of this country the Bohemian people lost their freedom. Through the ruin of Austria, Slovakia received back again its freedom and independence, a nation risen from the grave. For this we are thankful, first to God, and then to America and her allies. About one million persons in Slovakia have left the Roman Catholic Church. Great crowds gather wherever the truth is preached. No one other country affords so great an opportunity for the spreading of the gospel. The Christian Endeavor societies can do a great piece of work by sending us a man who can encourage the societies we have and help us organize new ones. We should be very happy if the next World's Christian Endeavor Convention could be held in Prague. May God awaken in us the spirit of our great leader and martyr, John Huss, so that the whole nation may become one great Christian Endeavor society."

Lady Anne Azgapetian spoke for Armenia, "the country of woe," as Dr. Clark called it. She came forward robed in black, and made a most pathetic and powerful plea on behalf of her people, who have suffered so terribly of recent years at the hands of the barbarous Turks, and who now, after they have aroused the hatred of the Turks by joining the Allies and giving a quarter of a million soldiers to their armies, are now deserted by the Allies and threatened with extinction. The Turks declare that every mosque or minaret destroyed in the World War shall be rebuilt with Armenian skulls. She begged that our nation would intervene, and the audience was eager to adopt on the spot a strong resolution to be sent to the President, but the matter was referred to the resolutions committee.

Rev. W. T. Marsh represented the Endeavorers of Australia, and spoke brightly and vigorously in spite of his advanced years. He said that Australia was very ready to adopt Yankee notions. Christian Endeavor was one of these. Prohibition is another, and "by the grace of God we are going to have it in Australia." Mr. Marsh pleaded for a recognition on the part of all Christians of the "power and teaching and consecration of the Holy Ghost." He ended by comparing the Endeavorers of Australia to their unique animal, the kangaroo: "They do not run nor walk, they jump."

The last of these messages was from Finland, the country that has suffered so much through so many years. The message was pleasingly presented by Miss Esther Kokkinen, secretary of the Massachusetts Finnish Christian Endeavor Union. She told us that her country had adopted prohibition years before the United States, women have had the vote there since 1906, and the country has only four-tenths of one per cent. of illiteracy. "The Finnish societies in New England wanted me to say that we are one with you, as all Christian Endeavorers are one in Christ."

That great-brained and big-hearted Christian business man, Fred B. Smith, gave the address of the afternoon on "Christianity the Hope of the World.' He is himself an old-time Endeavorer, and told how the preceding part of the meeting had brought up some of the fairest memories of his lifetime. "I am very glad," he said, "to stand on the platform of this wonderful Convention and testify to the wonder and marvel of the leading of God in this Christian Endeavor society. I was a charter member of the first society organized in South Dakota, and had the privilege of serving as its president. I think that the first time I gave a testimony to Jesus Christ was in a Christian Endeavor society. I owe very much of all I am to those early years of training and experience as an Endeavorer.

"I am also glad to be here in this Convention, which I presume is the most solemn in the whole history of Christian Endeavor." Mr. Smith spoke of a large number of popular and able writers who insist that civilization is tottering to its fall, but all of them are reckoning without God. All around the world men are looking to America as the material hope of Christianity. There have been times when one nation, such as Rome, has made all the world fear it; there has never before been a time when one nation has been looked to as the world's hope.

"Two voices are calling this nation. One says, 'Our duty in this hour is to look out for our own, to make ourselves secure while the going is good.' This is the voice of paganism, it is antichristian. Thank God there is another voice calling America to service, to sacrifice, to pour out herself for the good of the world. Within the next two years our country must take her stand with one of these ideals. Let every society of Christian Endeavor establish some kind of forum in which the second doctrine shall be advocated as the spirit of America."

When Mr. Smith spoke out his definite insistence that the United States should "take her place somewhere in some kind of organization of the world to work for peace" the entire audience rose spontaneously to signify its eager assent. The speaker voted for President Harding, working hard for his election, having had repeated assurances that the President would labor for the enduring peace of the world. "Now," said Mr. Smith, "I want him to know that I am not among those that voted a protest against the League of Nations." Not insisting on any form of the association of nations, yet the speaker did insist that some form is essential or the war will have been fought to no purpose. In his heart he believed that it is the President's purpose to range this country in the international association for peace, and he believes this purpose to be shared by the members of his Cabinet, certainly by Secretaries Hughes, Hoover, and Hays. All that troubles them is how to get rid of the "bitter-enders."

Mr. Smith's address was full of intimate revelations of the views of prominent men, was broad and statesmanlike, and led out his audience into the largest fields of thought. He summed it up in a slogan which he offered us, "A warless world and a universal brotherhood."

Mr. Foster closed the meeting with one stanza of "The Battle-Hymn of the Republic," having us change one line to "Let us live to *keep* men free." Then Dr. Landrith offered a most inspiring prayer, including the sentence, "We may not know *what* is the hope of the world, but we know who is the hope of the world," and including also the significant phrase, "America first—for the peace of the world."

Note.—For address by Mr. Smith in full, and greetings from foreign lands, see chapter of addresses.

THE ALL NATIONS BAZAAR
An interesting place during the Convention

A CANADIAN DELEGATION

CHAPTER XVIII.

FOR CHRIST AND THE CHURCH

ARMORY, SUNDAY EVENING, JULY 10

Rev. Francis E. Clark, D.D., LL.D., Presiding

IT was a wonderfully inspiring audience that greeted the speakers on this memorable evening in the Armory. Every seat was filled and many were standing. The praise and song service had brought the vast audience into a spirit of receptiveness. It was an opportune time for timely things. Dr. Clark introduced Dr. Egbert W. Smith, D.D., as the first speaker.

"There is one thing that no good Christian Endeavorer wants to be, and that is a failure." That was Dr. Egbert W. Smith's beginning in discussing "The Secret of Successful Endeavor."

THE WORLD FOR CHRIST

There is one thing that no good Christian Endeavorer wants to be, and that is a failure. There is one thing every one of us is aiming at, and that is to make good in that great and solemn, joyful business of improving society so that the world may be happier for our ambition. What is the secret, Christian Endeavorers? Is it money, social position, brains, genius? A multitude have had all of these, while other multitudes have had none of them, but succeeded. The secret of achievement, what is it? Read the Bible. God has summed up the whole Old Testament in Hebrews 11. In that chapter God puts that writer on an inspired mountain-top to look back and report how deeds have been accomplished; and there the inspired writer looks back over the centuries, and he reports that every deed has been wrought by faith.

In the New Testament we find our Saviour confirms this. According to your brains? No. According to your education? No. "According to your faith be it unto you." You remember how the afflicted father said, "If You can do anything, have compassion on us," and the Lord replied, "If thou hast faith, all things are possible to him who has faith. If ye have faith as a grain of mustard-seed, ye shall be able to remove mountains, and nothing shall be impossible unto you." If the Bible teaches anything, it is that the master word of achievement is faith. What is this faith? When we take the whole Bible and put together everything God has told us in history, precept, and parable, we are led to something like this definition: Faith is courage to go forward in the path of duty and service, doing our best with what we have, and trusting God to back our best with His almighty power.

What is the most fatal word for its size in the English language? If. You will say, I would do great things for the kingdom of God on earth "if" I had more friends, education. money, health, better surroundings, something different in the future.

113

Always "if," "if." How many careers have been shrouded and coffined in this little word! God said to Moses, "Go down and deliver my message to Israel." Moses replied with a string of "ifs" as long as your arm, and replied, "If I was a great man, but I am a nobody." I think that is cowardice masquerading under modesty. If I had sufficient knowledge, if I had the necessary gifts; I haven't eloquence; I stammer. Then the last one, "I would be glad to do it if there were any chance of success." As these "ifs" came pouring out of Moses' lips, God wanted him to look at what he had. God said, "What is it in thine hand?" It was simply a stick cut on the Arabian hillside to defend his sheep, and it was in his hand all the time that the ten plagues were brought on Egypt; it brought water out of the rock in the wilderness, and opened the Red Sea. We who would follow the Christian life must have faith and courage to go forward in the path of duty and service, doing our best with what we have, and trusting God to back our best with His almighty power. I want to tell you this, that Jesus was teaching this lesson on every page. Jesus said to the man with the withered hand, "Stretch forth thine hand"; and suppose he had replied; "Lord, to stretch forth my hand two things are necessary, will power and muscle power; and the latter is impossible." If he had said that, he would have carried his withered hand to the grave. He said, "I have no muscle power; but I can exert my will, and do my best, and trust You to back up my best with Your almighty power." So out went his hand, and it was restored whole.

Ten lepers cried, "Have mercy on us." Jesus said, "Show yourselves to the priests." According to Jewish law, before they could join society they must get certificates of cure. Suppose one had said: "To get my certificate of cure two things are necessary. I must go to the priest, and I must have a clean skin to show him. But I have no clean skin. What would be the use of going? What they did say was: "To get a certificate of cure two things are necessary. I have no clean skin; but I can do my part, and I can trust You for the rest"; and now what is the record? As they went, they were cleansed.

There were five thousand men besides women and children. Jesus said, "Give them to eat." One said, "If we had seventy-five dollars' worth of food, then we could not give any one but a little."

Jesus said, "How much have you?"

They replied, "Five loaves and two small fishes." Jesus gave a little to each of the apostles, and said, "With what I have given you go and feed these thousands"; and, doing their best with what Jesus had given them, I see them going; and presently the whole are filled, and twelve baskets full taken up.

I hear you say, "If my opportunities could be multiplied like those loaves and fishes." According to the Bible your powers and opportunities will be multiplied in just that way. "Unto every one that hath shall be given, and he shall have abundance; and from him that hath not shall be taken even that which he hath." Do you know, my friends, that that expression closes the parable of the talents, also the parable of the pounds? It is Christ's own explanation of both parables.

One man comes to Jesus with two talents. The Saviour says, "Do your best with what you have"; and his two talents soon grew into four talents. Another comes and says, "I want to do a ten-talent work in the world, but I have only five talents"; and Christ says, "Do your best, and they will become ten talents."

A young man comes to Jesus; he is a very common-looking fellow, and says, "Master, I want to do a ten-pound work in this work for you, but I have only one pound." Did Jesus discourage him? No. Did Jesus say, "A one-pound man can never do a ten-pound work"? I don't believe Jesus ever discouraged any one in ambition. He said, "Do your best with one little pound, and see what follows. To every one that hath, that uses what he has, shall be given an abundance; but from him that will not use what he has, shall be taken even that which he has."

Many years ago I read the life of Moody, and I remember one sentence that is worth its weight in gold to every Christian Endeavorer in this house. When Moody was converted, one of his friends said, "Now, Moody, you can serve God in other ways, but you should not try to talk, because you make foolish blunders every time you open your mouth." Suppose Moody had done that; what a loss the world would have sustained! Moody said, "I know I make many mistakes, but I am doing the best I can with what I have." My friends, libraries have been written to explain the secret of Dwight L. Moody. I tell you right there is the secret of Moody and every man or woman who has turned one pound into ten, or ten into one hundred. Some people speak contemptuously of youthful enthusiasm. History shows that nearly every great forward movement began as enthusiasm in the breast of some young man or woman. The secret of every great life is given in the words of William Carey: "Expect great things from God, and attempt great things for God." Where does the pathway of great things begin? At the gateway of sunset. The beginning of every great life, the pathway, starts right at your feet in your youth, followed to the uttermost of the powers and opportunities God has put into your hands, and from that point it goes on and up in every upward power. This is your vision and joy. Why do not more of us tread that ascending path? I will tell you the reason. Because we focus both eyes on poor little opportunities, one little pound. We see the great needs in church and state. We hear God calling for leaders in every community, but we have both eyes fastened on our poor little one pound. What we should look at is that we have the promise of Almighty God, Isa. 41:10, 12. "Fear thou not, for I am with thee; be not dismayed, for I am thy God. I will strengthen thee; yea, I will help thee, yea, I will uphold thee with the right hand of my righteousness, for I, the Lord God will hold thy right hand, saying unto thee, Fear not, I will help thee." What right has the disciple of an almighty Saviour to say anything but "I can; I can"? Some one says there has been advertised the American Can Company. I do not know what kind of cans. I know every Christian Endeavorer should belong to the can company. Paul belonged to that company. "I can do all things." How did he become a member? "Through Christ which strengtheneth me."

Let me close with a picture for the encouragement of every Christian Endeavorer. We are told of the poor widow woman with a son who got heavily in debt, and in accordance with Oriental custom the creditor comes to take her two boys to be his slaves. I see her going towards the prophet's house. She walks along hurriedly. Her head is full of "ifs." "If I had a thousand dollars; if I had many friends." The first thing the prophet says to her is, "Tell me, what hast thou in the house?" The poor woman had been thinking of what she lacked. She said, "Nothing at all but one little pot of oil."

The prophet had all he wanted. He said: "It is all right now; we have something to start with. Get all the empty vessels you can." She brought back all she could find. She pours the oil into a great many oil-cans, and she pours and pours until they are all full. She was richer than she ever dreamed of being. The minute she began to pour out, God kept pouring in. When she stopped pouring out, God stopped pouring in. This is the way God supplies great needs of little vessels, and the answer is, "By faith, by faith."

"I believe," said Dr. Clark in introducing the next speaker, "that if the question were put to the young people of America whom they would rather hear, in this continent or across the seas, they would say, 'Robert E. Speer.'" The audience emphatically expressed their agreement.

Dr. Speer began his address on "Many Members but One Body" by telling how when Chief Justice Taft was governor of the Philippine Islands he made an address while on a visit to the United States in which he referred to the Filipinos as his brothers. When the report reached the Philippines, a certain element of the American population there expressed its feeling in a song two lines of which were,

> "He may be a brother of William H. Taft,
> But he ain't no brother of mine."

That song embodies one of the oldest and the newest problems with which mankind has had to deal, the problem of the right relationship of race to race. It is the oldest and the most difficult problem of all ages. The great movements of history have been the racial movements. The great wars have been the racial wars. The great problems of our own day are the racial problems.

It can be truly said that our one great issue and that of almost every other nation in the world is the race issue. What is its right solution? What are the meaning and the use and end of race? How are diverse races to think and act towards one another?

One answer is that there is now, and is always to be, a continuing racial conflict, that the chasms between races cannot be bridged, and that across these chasms there must always be discord and misunderstanding and war. Between Asia and Europe, so Mr. Meredith Townsend argued in his writings, there is a gulf fixed that will never close. The yellow and the white races must accept the fact of their mutual intellectual isolation and unending alienation.

A second answer is that races exist not to struggle with one another, but to let one another wholly alone; that each race has its own rights, and should not be invaded or interfered with by other races. Prof. Giuseppe Sergi of Rome maintained this view at the Universal Races Congress. "What," asked he, "should be the attitude of one nation to another, or toward other peoples with which it has relations, in regard to diversity of customs, morals, and religion? The reply which presents itself immediately to us is not to attempt any change, and to respect the existing usages together with the sentiments which accompany them, because one runs the risk, from the resistance which is made to changing the manner of living, of disturbing good international relations, of inciting revolt, bloodshed, and war."

Those who hold this view usually apply it only to morals and religion. They deem trade and commerce quite legitimate intercourse, although the influence of these is enormous in its effect upon the life and thought of uncivilized peoples. What they resent is any effort to mould the religions of the other peoples. But a solution of the race problem such as this is ludicrous. The idea that ideals can be segregated, that races can be preserved from the moral and social influences of other races, is an utter delusion. The only effect of such a view is to expose the weaker races to the exploitation of the stronger without re-enforcing their moral powers or guiding them into a higher life.

A third answer is that of course the races must mingle and find their proper inter-relationships, but that these consist in the recognition of places of superiority and inferiority. There are the white peoples, and then beneath them "the lesser breeds" as constituting "the white man's burden," but because, being so heavy a burden they weary us, we climb up now and then to sit upon their shoulders and there to rest. Equality is the last word in the dictionary of this solution. The white races are to rule the earth, and the other races are to be happy in being ruled, and are to carry the wood and draw the water for their white masters wearied by the toil of ruling them properly.

A fourth solution is the dream of the great amalgam, the inter-mixture of all human breeds in one cosmopolite man. America is even now a blend of a dozen European races. England herself is the national offspring of a gigantic racial intermarriage. The Latin-American peoples include not a single nation of pure racial blood. So, men say, at last all the world will melt together into one harmonized racial unity. No man can say that it may not be so, but the dream offers no present solution of racial feeling. Such an end, if it ever comes, is centuries and millenniums ahead of us. And what we need is an answer to the race problem that will answer it now and show us how to live before we die.

Well, there is such a solution. "I have other sheep not of this fold," said our Lord. "Them also I must bring, and they shall hear my voice, and there shall be one flock and one shepherd." For Christ, said Paul, is our peace, who made all one, and broke down the walls of division, that He might reconcile all in one body. This is the one and only solution of the race problem. Humanity is a unity. It is one flock. The sheep may be of different strains. The hues of their wool may vary. But there is one Shepherd, and all the sheep are His sheep and one flock as they follow Him. Humanity is an organism with many members but one body. Each member is a race. All the members differ, but all are one. A common life pervades the whole. If one member suffers, all suffer with it. Each feeds the tissues of all the rest. There is no schism, no jealousy, no strife in the body. There dare be none in humanity. It is as irrational that Japan and the United States should be set in hostility as that a body should take its fingers and tear out its eyes.

Whatever strength any race possesses it possesses not for itself, but for all. If any nation is not so strong as others, and needs to be helped, it should be helped, in the spirit of the Chinese boy who was carrying a younger child on his back, when a stranger stopped him, and spoke pityingly of the heavy burden he was bearing. "That is not a burden," replied the lad; "that is my brother." And yet the weaker races have their work to do and their contributions to make to the full wealth and glory of humanity. In the light of the city whose lamp is the Lamb all the races are to walk, and men shall bring the honor of all the races into it; but nothing unclean shall be there, no race prejudice. nor the abomination of pride, nor the lie of race-exclusion that will not allow Slav or Teuton or Latin or Japanese its place in the flock of Christ and the sunlight of God.

This is Christ's view of the race problem. His solution was love and the brotherhood and the recognition by each race of its essential unity with all other races. The sheep. He said. were one flock. The color of their fleece made no difference.

The session closed with an impressive decision service conducted by Treasurer A. J. Shartle.

He began this service by quoting Romans 12:1: "I beseech you, therefore, brethren, by the mercies of God, that ye present your bodies a living sacrifice, holy, acceptable unto God, which is your reasonable service," and used it as a call of the Kingdom. He said:

I believe that God has a plan for every life, and when this plan is realized it brings with the experience to the believer the joy of service, the power of the Spirit, and the blessing of God. If there is one here tonight who has had a varied experience, hot today, and cold tomorrow; so close to the Master today that you may almost touch Him, and then so far away tomorrow that you question whether you have ever been saved, it is evidence of the fact that we have not permitted God to work out our plan for us, and there is yet much to be accomplished by His Holy Spirit.

Paul in testifying for the Master said: "I know whom I have believed. I know I have a building, a house of God, not made with hands. I know that all things work together for good to them that love God." When we know these things, our testimony is far too valuable to be suppressed. It is good to be here, and we have here gathered at the close of a memorable day in Christian Endeavor that we may get in still closer touch with God. Tomorrow we leave to go back to our societies. How shall we go? We came like empty vessels that we might be filled. Yes, filled with the practical and spiritual things necessary to the development of a real life of usefulness. But, have we been filled? It is a personal question. Have you caught the spirit of this Convention? Have you been in closer touch with God since coming here? Have you caught a vision of the greater need? Are you ready now to do some definite thing tonight that will be in accordance with God's plan? This is the moment, but something may be lacking.

The man who lies upon a bed of suffering in Northampton Hospital tonight, my associate, tells how when he was on the other side during the great war, and in a "Y" hut within shell range, they brought a lad belonging to a nearby regiment, and just seventeen years old, to the hut mortally wounded. Dr. Poling tells how he carried the mud and blood-bespattered lad in his arms, and then laid him down to give first aid. During the treatment the dying lad in the agony of soul placed his trembling hand upon Dr. Poling's shoulders; permitting it to fall to the wrist, he suddenly grasped it with all his dying strength and exclaimed: "Say, fellow, can you pray? Can you pray, fellow?" My associate dropped on his knees and prayed that the Master take the lad to His bosom, and while thus in prayer, the one who placed his life on the altar of his country, a willing sacrifice that a world might be safe for His people, passed beyond. He paid the supreme price.

May I turn the picture and ask the question that should be uppermost in our minds now. Say, Christian Endeavorers, can you pray? and you? and you? Say, you ministers of the gospel of Greater New York, and in the Convention, have you a message for the community in which you preach that will cause men to accept God and have them decide to set apart their lives to do some specific religious work?

This is the burning question. Christian Endeavor is the nucleus from which the world's kindred organizations have drawn for leadership. We organize, teach, train, and prepare that we may help others. For this Christian Endeavor lives,—others.

A few hours after the accident to Dr. Poling on July 4 I stood beside his cot in the hospital. While in great pain he took my hand and said, "It's all right Al, I have had a talk with God today. I'll come through."

Young people, have you had a talk with God today? Will *you* come through? Will *you* decide here, now, that at the opportune time in your life you will set apart your life to do some specific religious work as a life's work? No matter be it the ministry, the home or foreign mission field, the Y. M. C. A. or Y. W. C. A., the call for field secretaries of Christian Endeavor, or the larger work of the Sunday School. The need is great, the field is ripe, and the harvest plentiful. *Come,* will you accept the challenge? If there is anything in your life that should not be there tonight, say, "By the grace of God that thing dies tonight, that Christ's life may be magnified in mine." Then accept the challenge and come. Let souls be born anew here. Never refuse God. Will you stand,—*now!*

Then there were made in response to the call hundreds of decisions. To the right and left of the platform, the center aisle, the galleries, and the choir they stood, and at the request of Mr. Shartle they came forward in front of the platform and faced the audience, a line clear across the hall, three, four, five and six deep. A happy, joyous group two hundred and fifty-five strong, Life-Work Recruits in the making, and a stern rebuff to the critics that young people are not taking the religious life seriously.

Then Mr. Shartle challenged the great audience of ten thousand not standing to go back home and by the help of God make their home a better home, their church a better place, to do better Sunday School teaching, to do more efficient Christian Endeavor work, to be more loyal to the church, and to stand back of the program of the Kingdom. Would they accept the challenge? and the thousands stood up as one man. The challenge was accepted. They were willing to give their reasonable service.

While standing Dr. Clark made the closing prayer and pronounced the benediction.

Who will ever forget this evening?

CHAPTER XIX.

CHRISTIAN ENDEAVOR SERVING
FIELD SECRETARIES

ARMORY, MONDAY MORNING, JULY 11

Clarence C. Hamilton, Presiding

THE Convention crowds seemed to grow larger and larger as the days wore on, and Monday morning, the final day, the Armory was a perfect hive of activity. The conferences spilled over into the corridors, and a fine audience was in the main auditorium when Mr. Rodeheaver conducted one of his matchless and inspiring song services. Nothing is more enjoyed than these song services. How different they are from staid and sedate church.singing! What a mighty volume of song from fresh, clear, lilting voices rises from the audience of youth! No one that has attended a great Christian Endeavor convention can ever forget the soul-stirring effect of that singing. It suggests the music of heaven.

Snappy work characterized the innings of the field secretaries. They made a wondrously fine sight as they stood. these seventeen men and four women, in a semi-circle on the platform. Southwestern Secretary Breg introduced them one by one, and each one made his or her bow while delegations from the various States made manifest their approval by enthusiastic yells. There were present Reichel, of Pennsylvania; Brown, of California; Miss Bradt, of Minnesota; Miss Carter, of Kansas, Spafford and Miss Kyser, of Michigan; Lanning, of Missouri; Farrill, of Wisconsin; Evans, of the All-South; Little, Dendy and Wilson, of the All-South; Ernest Ligon, Minnesota's new secretary; Cecil, of Colorado; Freet, of Massachusetts; Williams, of Indiana; Hicks, of Connecticut; Huppertz, of Texas; Sherwood, of New York; and Steenson, of Manitoba. These are key men and women on whose consecration largely depends the immediate future of Christian Endeavor. A splendid lot!

Fresh-air work was the subject which Mr. John T. Sproull, for many years the honored president of the New Jersey union, presented in a most illuminating and eloquent way.

The Essex County Union is in the front rank in fresh-air camp work. The work was started years ago in a most modest way. It began in an old, broken-down cottage through which, in wet weather, the rain filtered badly. A young lady who had a vision of the children's need originated this work, giving up

120

CHRISTIAN ENDEAVOR FIELD SECRETARIES AT THE NEW YORK CONVENTION

Front Row, left to right: Evan Will iams, Field Secretary, Indiana Union. John Beady, Field Secretary, Alabama. John Gracca and South Carolina. W. Roy Brag, Southeastern Federation Secretary of the United Society of Christian Endeavor. J. C. Endeavor. Field Secretary of the United Society of Christian Endeavor. Harlan A. Marbel. Associate Secretary, Pennsylvania Union. Mrs. Frank L. Pace, Field Secretary. Ohio Union. Edwin M. Sherwood, Field Secretary, New York State Union. Mrs. W. F. Farrill, Field Secretary. Harold J. Orns, Field Manager, "The Christian En deavor World."

Second Row, left to right: Paul C. Brown, Field Secretary, Oklahoma Union and National Intermediate Superintendent. Harry L. Hergh, Field Secretary. West Virginia Union. Herbert W. Hicks, Field Secretary. Connecticut Union. Miss Margaret Key, assistant to the Field Secretary, Louisiana. Joseph M. Spalford, Field Secretary, Michigan Union. Miss Mary H. Mc Clanahan, Field Secretary, Iowa Union. Miss Madeline Carter, Field Secretary. Kansas Union. Miss Margaret Heath, Field Secretary, Wisconsin Union.

Rear Row, left to right: John Freel, Field Secretary, Colorado Union. E. P. Gates, Field Secretary, Kentucky Union and Tennessee Union. Legetant L. Stevenson, Field Secretary, Manitoba Union. J. V. Hagerty, Field Secretary. Texas Union. Frank O. Wilson, Field Secretary, North Carolina and Virginia Unions. Ernest Lagan, Field Secretary, Minnesota Union.

Present at the Convention but not in the picture: Charles F. Evans, Southern Secretary of the United Society of Christian Endeavor. A. J. Shartle, Treasurer and Publication Manager of the United Society. Stanley B. Vander sall, Alumni Superintendent, United So ciety. F. D. G. Walker, Field Secretary. Illinois Union. R. A. Walker, Manager of the United Society's Western Office. Carroll M. Wright, Field Secretary, Maryland.

to it her summer vacation. The work has grown until today the Essex County union owns property valued at more than $25,000. The workers who serve in this summer home do so at great personal sacrifice.

The aim of the home, of course, is to provide a two weeks' vacation for children of the slums. Last season 1,250 children were entertained at a cost of $12,000. This money is voluntarily subscribed, and it comes from the Endeavorers of New Jersey, especially Essex County, and their friends. The union in the course of its history has spent more than $77,000 for the health of little children of the poor.

Paul Brown's topic was institutional Christian Endeavor, and an eloquent plea he made for various forms of work. He began with prisons while two women held up placards telling of the great need. In San Quentin prison there are two hundred prisoners who are members of the Christian Endeavor Society, and the lives of a multitude of men have been changed by the message brought to them by Endeavorers. In a Reform School for Girls in California there are five societies that are doing excellent work. He touched upon work for army, navy and merchant marine, and told of two workers supported in San Pedro, Cal., by the Christian Endeavor union to look after sailors. In San Pedro the union owns property valued at more than $15,000. In the Los Angeles County Hospital there is a Christian Endeavor chaplain who is supported by the Endeavorers of the county, and whose work is marvellously blessed.

Miss Madilene Carter spoke on rural Endeavor, and told of the need of societies in districts where there are no church services. She told also how in many cases Endeavor societies in churches that have no pastor keep the church fires burning and carry on the only religious services that are held in the community. One rural society organized a county union, and at this organizing meeting a young man from a disorganized church received inspiration that sent him back to his home determined to try Christian Endeavor. The result was not only a new society, but a reborn church.

Southern Secretary Evans spoke about college Endeavor. A few years ago one might have said all that could be said about college Endeavor in a very short time, for there was very little of it. Now societies are found in many colleges. The Richmond Training School of the Southern Presbyterian Church uses "Expert Endeavor" as a text-book. · Two hundred and forty-six students of this college took the Expert-class course last year. Berea College has five societies with a membership of more than four hundred. Christian Endeavor work is emphasized in the college at Mt. Vernon, Ky. Davidson College recently entertained the district convention, and in this college Christian Endeavor is a part of the regular work. Thornwell College has a fine Christian Endeavor society, and the president of the colloge is a Christian Endeavor enthusiast. There are also societies in institutions for the deaf and dumb and blind, and Elon, Guilford, and other colleges recognize Christian Endeavor as a part of a young person's necessary training.

Floating Endeavor was the topic allotted to Haines A. Reichel, of Pennsylvania. Two Floating workers held, while he spoke, a banner giving facts and figures. At one side of the banner was a sample comfort-bag such as Endeavorers make in great numbers for sailors. These bags contain a great many articles that sailors need, and they are prized accordingly. The speaker urged unions to organize Floating committees and help to send Bibles and other gifts to sailors. A letter was read from a Brazilian Endeavorer on board the Brazilian battleship Minas Geraes, which was in the Brooklyn navy yard. This man stated that Christian Endeavor has conducted the best religious work done in the Brazilian navy under the guidance of the church at Caju.

Chaplain Ramsden, superintendent of the Christian Endeavor army and navy department of the United Society, spoke for the 225,000 men of the army who are away from home and church influences. The aim of the department is to have the State unions look after—through local Endeavorers—the men in forts within their borders. He pleaded for the men in uniform who come to our societies. They are clean, upright men, the pick of the soldiers, for they come to Christian Endeavor because they are interested in spiritual things. The other kind stays away. Societies may have army and navy committees. If a battleship has been named after a State the Endeavorers of that State may help the men on it by sending to the ship, or to Chaplain Ramsden, Bibles, books, magazines, song books, and so on. Such gifts are needed and appreciated.

Perhaps the most exciting period of the whole Convention was the close of this session, when W. Roy Breg and some of the other boys put on a *Christian Endeavor World* ballgame. The game was to secure subscriptions to *The Christian Endeavor World*. The hall was divided into two sections, and a group of workers was assigned to each section. One group or team was called the "Come-oners," the other the "Let's-goers." Every person in the audience was supplied with a subscription-blank, and had the privilege of signing up for the paper at a special rate.

When the whistle blew the game started. Captain Sherwood, of the "Come-oners," raced up and down the platform shouting instructions to the players on his side, who went among the audience and collected the signed papers and the cash. Captain Freet, of Massachusetts, did the megaphone work for the "Let's-goers." Ten subscriptions counted one home run. Paul Brown kept the score on a blackboard on the platform.

It was a most exciting game. At the close of the first inning, timed by Mr. Breg, the "Let's-goers" had four runs to four for the "Come-oners." In the second inning also the "Come-oners" came on and tied the score. In the third inning, however, the "Come-oners" made three runs to one for the "Let's-goers," and maintained this lead, with various exciting fluctuations, to the end. The score was 17 to 15 in favor of the "Come-oners," and Captain Sherwood was jumping up and down so joyously that he could hardly stop for an amicable handshake with Captain Freet.

The Field-Secretaries Confer

The Sandman, or, as the Scotch call him, "Wee Willie Winkie," had done most of his work by the time the field secretaries got together for a heart-to-heart conference Sunday night. The conference lasted till the "we sma' hours" of Monday morning, and, be it said, Wee Willie Winkie was denied admittance.

A good many subjects were discussed, but the principal result of the meeting, apart from its fellowship value, was a resolution which was passed to hold a five-day meeting of field secretaries and workers next winter at a place later to be determined.

This conference was really a meeting of the field workers' union, and consequently officers were elected for the new year. Haines A. Reichel, field secretary of Pennsylvania, was made president; Madilene Carter, executive secretary of Kansas, is secretary; and the treasurer is Field Secretary Spafford, of Michigan.

Chapter XX

THE JUNIOR CONVENTION

Marble Collegiate Church

Miss F. Lucy Hollings, Presiding

THE Juniors had their day in court—and what a magnificent day it was—on Friday afternoon in the beautiful old Marble Collegiate Church. Seldom have we heard anything so moving and so prophetic of the future as the cheering and the yells expressing the enthusiasm of the children. The church is not in danger with such young life as this growing up in its midst. For the church was packed to the doors, floor and gallery, and still they came, and still they came.

Miss F. Lucy Hollings presided and Mr. John Peters led the song service. Behind him on the platform was the Junior verse-motto, the chorus of one of the stirring Convention songs:

"We are happy Juniors,
    Proud of our C. E.;
To our Lord and Saviour
    True we'll ever be."

The first stanza, sung to "Onward, Christian Soldiers," with the fresh voices of childhood melted and thrilled the heart:

"We're a mighty army,
    Many thousand strong;
Jesus is our Leader,
    We to Him belong.

"Day by day we're growing,
    Trusting Him for strength;
He will always guide us,
    Victory give at length."

This was a real convention with all the characteristics of the older gathering, singing in sections and groups with far more than ordinary enthusiasm and intelligence. No exhortation to sing was needed. Youth is the time for song. There was not a soul in the crowd that did not use full lung-power in singing the chorus to the tune of "Brighten the corner"—"Training for service, J. C. E."

There was a period for simultaneous conferences on Junior methods. Miss Alice S. Fyfe was in charge. She confessed to having been a Junior herself in a Junior society in Edinburgh, Scotland, and her control of the meeting was proof enough that she knows the Junior heart.

Alexander Avenue Baptist Juniors presented and explained the Junior Training-Chart.

A clever general conference was conducted by Miss Agnes E. Baker. This took the form of a blackboard-talk. On the blackboard was drawn in simple outline an ordinary house, the parts of the house being compared to the Christian Endeavor society organization.

The stones of the foundation represented Jesus Christ. The front porch was compared to the lookout committee, not only "looking out" but "going out" for new members.

The reception room, next the porch, spoke of the preparatory members, who are received into the house or society. The living room was compared with active membership; the library, with good literature; the dining-room, with the Quiet Hour, for the soul must be fed; the kitchen, with the work of the social and other committees; the father's den, with the finances; and the bathroom, with the cleansing powers of Christian Endeavor.

Miss Baker used the roof as a type of God's loving protection. The nails in the building teach us of the promises of the pledge; when they grow rusty, or are broken, the stability of the house is endangered. The mother of the house was compared to the superintendent, who guides her children in the paths of peace.

"The Productive Life" was the topic of an interesting object-talk by Albert E. Meder. He showed four boards of equal size, on which were printed the words, Love, Light, Joy and Hope. He put them together to form a box, but they would not stay together until he slipped over them a band marked, "The band of faith," and then they held together. From this he drew the lesson that things cannot stand until they are supported by faith in God.

But the box is empty. So people say that there is nothing in Christianity, in the church, and in the society. But Mr. Meder took the box apart and from secret receptacles in the boards he brought forth a box of gold, speaking of the precious things of Christ; a box of silver, telling of His sterling value; a colored box speaking of all the virtues; a bouquet of flowers, that tell of deeds of kindness; and flags—flags that speak of loyalty and patriotism.

From the Junior Convention church the children went in parade to the Armory, singing as they marched to the hall. There they gave their demonstration, which has already been described.

CHAPTER XXI.

CHAPTER OF ADDRESSES

THE ENDEAVORER AND HIS READING
By Amos R. Wells

[As the speaker came to each division of his address he turned over a new page of his manuscript, thus displaying to the audience a long sheet of paper of the color under discussion. The first sheet was the longest and the rest progressively shorter, so that at the close the various colors appeared one above the other.]

IN Chicago and other cities the grain-elevators store up the real wealth of the nation. Those vast buildings, in spite of Wall Street's fancies, are the genuine banks of our country. There the shining harvest of uncounted acres is garnered. They are the close-packed reservoirs of health and strength for a continent. They are the substance of which our money is only the symbol.

Nothing in the material world is greater than a grain-elevator except a library. Every library is a grain-elevator of life. The shelves of every library have garnered the shining harvest of uncounted human experiences. Wise books are the deep and close-packed reservoirs of spiritual health and strength for the millions. Whoever owns a good library owns a bank infinitely richer than any in New York. He is the heir of all the ages, which is endlessly better, in the eternal reckoning, than being heir to a modern Croesus.

A young man, a student at Harvard, last year refused an inheritance of more than a million dollars on the ground that he had not earned it and therefore he did not believe it rightfully belonged to him. Whatever we may think of his reasoning, it is certain that few young men would follow his example. But our inheritance in books, worth infinitely more to us than millions of dollars, the majority of us are tossing heedlessly aside, or are well content with a mere pittance, with a dime a day when we might have our thousands of dollars a day. No wealth is so scorned, so contemptuously rejected, as our inherited wealth in books.

Some books, however, deserve to be scorned and rejected. Before I speak of the good books, a word about the bad books, the books whose appropriate symbol is black. Here in New York lived Anthony Comstock, that Christian hero who spent his life combating the evil of black books, that the youth of the land might be saved from pollution. If he had lived until today he would have seen much of this black literature masquerading in garments of light, and highly praised by the critics because of its admirable style. No book is well written that does not minister to well-being. No literary style is beautiful that panders to lust or fosters crime or argues infidelity or teaches treason. The fires of hell are kindled with the pages of such books. They take you by yourself. They whisper in secret shameful things that no company would tolerate if spoken openly. They offer themselves to your unguarded moments. They creep into the idle corners of your mind and fill them with poison. O Endeavorers, read no book that you would not read to your mother. Praise no book that your Master does not praise. Be as careful in choosing these friends of your mind, these most influential friends of your unfenced solitude, as you are in your choice of the friends that speak to the ear. And join with all true souls in driving to deserved oblivion these black printed progeny of the pit.

And now let me not waste further time in this address on these black books, even as I would not have you waste time on them in your lives. Let us turn to the books worth reading.

There are so many of these, tens of thousands of admirable new books published every year, to say nothing of the hundreds of thousands of splendid old books in our libraries. It is perplexing, it is even depressing: so much to read, so little time to read it in! Is there a guide through all this labyrinth?

Yes, there are many guides. I have a reading plan which has been useful to me, and may be useful to you. I compare the kinds of books that are worth reading to the colors of the rainbow or the spectrum. In every ray of white light there are seven colors. A wedge of glass will spit the ray into these seven colors. Now I find seven kinds of reading which correspond fairly well with the seven colors. I will speak of each, and they will be the seven heads of my library sermon.

Violet is the first color of the spectrum, of the rainbow. Violet is the royal color, the color of kings. It shall stand for the reading of history and biography, which are so largely the story of kings and of kingly men and queenly women. History and biography are the foundation of reading, as violet is the foundation of the spectrum and the rainbow. The violet is a most modest and shrinking flower, and in history and biography it often happens that the humble are crowned, that the last become the first. Rail-splitters and canalboat drivers become honored Presidents of the United States. A poor boy in Wales rises to be the prime minister of earth's mightiest empire at its greatest crisis. There is a twofold reason why violet is the color of history and biography.

Keep always at hand some notable history, such as those by Motley, Prescott, Parkman, McMaster, or Green, or read every day a chapter in some great biography, such as Holland's Lincoln, Irving's Washington, the autobiography of Franklin, or the lives of Henry Drummond, Frances E. Willard, Clara Barton, Florence Nightingale, or John Howard. Every such book doubles your experience. The Indian believed that he added to his own powers the strength of every enemy he killed. That was absurd, but it is true that you add to your own life the fine character of every hero or heroine whose biography you read. Who will continue lonely and ignoble when he can thus have for his friends the most resplendent personages of all time?

Indigo is the next color of the rainbow spectrum. It stands for essays, in my book color scheme. That is because indigo is to me the color of the evening, of thoughtful meditation. Also when I think of the friendly indigo plant beside the road, it becomes the color of cheerful and sociable thought, of chatty thought, which is just what the essay is.

Have you added indigo to your book spectrum? Do you know and love the essayists? Our English literature is especially rich in them, from the days of Bacon to those of Addison and Lamb, and down to the present days of Lowell and Emerson and Thoreau and Holmes, of Stevenson and Lucas and Lang, of John Burroughs and Bradford Torrey.

To love a good essayist is to have a winsome friend. He will not do your thinking for you, but will arouse you to do your own thinking. A good essay puts a tang into life like a stimulating conversation. It lifts you out of the mediocre, and into the land of noble thinking. Whatever his circumstances, the delighted reader of good essays is a gentleman.

What books shall the blue of our rainbow spectrum represent? Poetry, for that is the most ethereal of literature. Poetry is of the sky. Poetry lifts our spirits from the earth into a purer realm. Poetry may have to do with the most commonplace things, but it irradiates them with a heavenly light.

Sometimes you hear the boast, "I am too practical for poetry." The speaker shows how unpractical he is. Poetry has often moved the world. Often a few stanzas of poetry have accomplished what reams of prose have failed to bring about. If you leave poetry out of your life, you exile yourself from the greatest thoughts most nobly expressed.

But do not be content with inferior poetry, helpful as that often is. Seek to rise to the highest levels. Live in Shakespeare's world and you will be broad-minded, with wide human sympathies. Live in Milton's world, and you will think lofty and magnificent thoughts. Live in Dante's world, and you will become heroic and holy. An appreciation of the best poetry is as far beyond the ordinary mind as the blue of the sky is beyond the paving-stones of our streets. But there are airships of thought, and if we have ardor and perseverance we can learn to guide them.

Green stands for books on science, because green is the color of nature, of growing things, of the woods and the fields. No scheme of reading is complete that leaves out science. It is hard to understand the stupid indifference of many who are placed in the midst of this wonderful world, this marvellous universe, and are not eager to see the thronging evidences of God's wisdom, the beauties of His handiwork. Botany transforms every square yard of grass into a fairyland. Zoölogy fills every woodland with little friends in fur and feathers. Physics teaches us God's alphabet of power. Chemistry shows us His magic of transformation. Geology acquaints us with the vast reaches of God's time and astronomy with the immeasurable stretches of God's space. There is nothing like science to make one humble. Science fills the world with ceaseless interest and makes us at home in it. Science inspires in us the spirit of worship; we think some of God's great thoughts after Him. He is a poor reader that does not often master some work of science.

Now we come to yellow, the brightest of all the colors. Yellow is the harvest color, the hue of golden grain. For that reason it stands, in my library spectrum, for books on missions. These are the harvest books, the books of fruition, of ingathering. They are the rich books, the foodful, nourishing books. A wise Christian will always keep by him some missionary biography or some account of a mission field. There are no more statesmanlike books, no more stirring books of glorious adventure. A zealous reader of missions soon becomes a well-educated man. He gets travel of the finest, biography the most inspiring, history in the making. He reads living epics. There is no more profitable reading than missions. Read the life of one great missionary in each mission field, with an account of each great mission country, and you will immensely enlarge your mental horizon and elevate your plane of thought. You will imbibe the spirit of the world's chief enterprise, and it will not be long before you will be an active partner in it yourself.

The sixth color of the spectrum, orange, I assign to books of travel, partly because tropical countries, lands of the orange, are those we first think of in connection with travel, partly because the last letters of orange spell "range."

Some reading of travel must have a place in my scheme of reading. Travel today is cheap and easy as compared with past ages, but the reading of books of travel is still cheaper and easier. A reader of intelligence, imagination, and industry may sit in his easy-chair and become far more at home in distant lands than many a purse-proud globe-trotter whose eyes, but not his mind, have seen all corners of the world. Library journeys are free from danger and fatigue. Book-travel may be prolonged and repeated at will. There is no reason why you should not go to Europe this summer, to Africa in the fall, to Asia next winter, and to South America in the spring. If you read wisely you will gain the culture and experience that travel gives; and whoever

Rev. W. H. Foulkes, D.D.

Rev. P. A. Heilman, D.D.

Dr. Ira Landrith

Percy S. Foster

Rev. John Pollock, D.D.

talks with you will be sure, if you do not undeceive him, that you have circumnavigated the globe.

Only one color is left in our rainbow spectrum, and that is red. And only one category remains in our book survey, and that is fiction. Red, the hue of life and of the heart's blood, is surely the color of fiction. Here at the very end of our library survey we reach the only kind of books that the majority of readers really know.

Now great fiction is greatly worth reading, such stories as those of Scott, Dickens, Thackery, Hawthorne, Stevenson, Victor Hugo, De Morgan, Trollope, and Jane Austen. Lesser fiction also is worth reading if it is clean, elevating, and well written. Fiction fascinates the multitude partly because it ought to fascinate them, just as life fascinates them, and properly. But fiction is also enormously popular because it is the easiest reading, makes the least demands upon thought and attention, requires, indeed, no more brains usually than neighborhood gossip. Fiction is indispensable to a well-balanced scheme of reading, but most readers are wholly unbalanced by it. The rainbow proportion is right, one in seven. Out of every seven books you read let one, and only one, be a story-book. Then you will feed your mind in the right proportion. To give it more fiction is like feeding your body wholly upon ice cream soda water.

All seven colors, when put together, give us white again. That is what you want your reading to do—it must throw on your life and destiny the clear white light of God's truth. You do not want a world that is all red or green or blue or yellow, all orange or indigo or violet. You do not want to be color-blind, but to rejoice in all the colors of the rainbow. Then why acquiesce in mental color-blindness? Why not distribute your reading fairly among all the great classes of books? Each of them has its own message for you, its own work to do for you. Leave any one of them out of your life, and it will be unbalanced.

I have said nothing directly about the large division of reading in which I am practically interested, the reading of periodicals. But all I have said applies to that. White is my symbol for the ideal periodical, since it should bring together in one collection, weekly or monthly, all seven hues of the literary rainbow. The ideal periodical sets forth the period in which it is published. It sets it forth in all seven of the great ways we have been discussing. It furnishes accounts of the notable men and women now living before they get into books and libraries. It deals with current history, and with the history of the past as it is clearly related to current history. It pictures the rapidly unfolding marvels of science. It uses the essay, and poetry, and fiction. It takes its readers on journeys to other lands. It constantly reports the fundamentally significant movements of modern missions. That is my idea of an ideal periodical. Like Paul, it is to be all things to all men. Every issue is to be a little library, a contemporaneous library, a faithful cross-section of present-day living and thinking.

Thus far we have said nothing about religious reading, and yet everything that has been said applies to religious reading, because all seven kinds of books may be religious. That is why I represent religious reading by silver, which is a glorified white. There is religious poetry, such as Tennyson's "In Memoriam," and Whittier's "Our Master," and Lanier's "The Crystal." There are religious essays, such as Drummond's "The Greatest Thing in the World." There is religious biography, such as the lives of Spurgeon and Moody and Phillips Brooks. There is religious history, such as Farrar's "Early Days of Christianity." There is religious fiction, such as Sheldon's "In His Steps." There is religious travel, such as the travel-books of our own Dr. Clark. There is even religious science, such as Drummond's "Natural Law in the Spiritual World" or the works of Hugh Macmillan. And of course there are religious periodicals that cover all this ground in the religious spirit and with the religious purpose. The

Christian whose reading is all secular may get the white light of truth, but never the silvering splendor of the higher truth. This is why we Endeavorers emphasize the Quiet Hour, because we want to transform our white to silver.

But there is a glory greater than that of silver, the glory of gold. The crown of all books is the Bible. The summit of all talk about reading must ever be praise of this majestic and incomparable volume. Yellow, you will remember, stood for missions, and gold is glorified yellow. The Bible is the supreme missionary volume. And also the Bible contains the world's most glorious poetry, its fundamental science, its most inspiring biographies, the basis of all its history, its most interesting and momentous travels. No other essays yield so much wisdom as the Bible discourses and epistles; no other fiction comes so close to men's hearts as the parables of our Lord. The Bible is the Divine Library, the focus of inspiration, the supreme treasury of lofty thought. The Bible is the key to all other writings. In the light of the Bible all books are to be read, interpreted, and judged. The Bible is the guide-book of Christian Endeavor. We begin the day with it and end the day with it, that it may go with us all through the day. The Bible decides what other books we are to read, and the spirit in which we are to read them, and the results we are to carry from them. Be a reader, I would say to every Christian Endeavorer. Read widely. Read deeply. But above all, read loftily. And the summit of all reading is God's Holy Word.

THE HOUR OF OPPORTUNITY

By Daniel A. Poling

Associate President of the United Society of Christian Endeavor

The Sixth World's Christian Endeavor Convention is held in the United States of America and in New York, the imperial city of the land. The young people who gather here have come in delegations from every State of the Union, every Province of Canada, and in groups smaller, but no less representative, from more than a score of foreign countries. For ourselves, then, as Americans, and in order that our brothers from beyond the seven seas shall understand, we of the Christian church who bear allegiance to the Stars and Stripes frankly fling out the motto, "America First."

"America First!" but not in pride of station, not in selfish seeking, not in greed for gain. "America First," first in service and first in ministry for all. Let there be no misunderstanding; we have no false notions of an internationalism that supersedes love of country and fervor for one's native land. The deeds and lives of the more than two hundred thousand of our fellows, living and dead, in whose honor we gather this evening, will shout forever in our ears, "Patriotism begins at home."

"Patriotism begins at home"; but that it does not end there our graves "where poppies blow" and our covenants made in the days of disaster, when we brought our treasure and our sons to lay them in consecration upon the common altar of liberty, attest beyond all ravages of time, all denials of ambassadors, all gusts of partisan politics, all flames of racial hate. Patriotism begins at home, but it does not end there! for, if you would save America, you must serve the world. Beyond all power to change the order of things nations are bound together. There is no geography of distance; there are no separating seas. Economically, socially, politically, and religiously we are hopelessly one of another.

Strategically, the position of the United States is without parallel in the history of nations. From the world's blood-letting she alone comes rugged and unimpaired; she alone of all the countries has bread enough and to spare. Her coffers alone are full. The sore-pressed peoples turn to us as turns the morning flower to the sun; they wait in this crisis of the peace as they waited at the crisis of the war. One morning in March, 1918, I sat in the breakfast-room of the old Gillespie home in Edinburgh. When the war opened, there were two sons to add strength to the grace that two daughters brought to that fireside. Tom died in the rear-guard fighting from Mons to the Marne. Bey fell at the head of his men in a charge on the twenty-fifth of September, 1915. Tom's oars (he was the captain of the Oxford eight) hang in the hall, and his picture at the left of the mantel in the library. Bey, whose letters to his mother have been published as "Letters from Flanders," was the finest scholar turned out by Oxford in a generation. His picture hangs just across the mantel from that of his brother. The old Gillespie line runs out to the valley of the Somme, and ends beneath the flowers of Flanders.

In that quiet room I discussed with the mother of those two young heroes the mighty advance of the Central Powers, then at its height; the possibility of its reaching the Channel ports, capturing Paris, over-running France, separating the British and French armies. We dis-cussed the worst; and then she said, she who had laid so rich an offering upon the altar of Freedom, "Back against the shores of this island the British fleet will stand and hold while America brings up the reserves of civilization; 'they shall not pass; they shall not pass.' "

Today the impoverished and discouraged world waits for America, calls for America to bring up the last reserves; and America will not fail. The soul of America is sound. The heart of America has not changed. Hear America's answer:

"I am my brother's keeper; and no state has the moral right to exist free and strong and silent while other states are bound by chains of want and suffering they cannot break."

Delegates from other lands, carry this message back to all your countries. Tell it in the words that set the weeping villages of France to singing in another day when dark disaster stalked the keepers of the faith; tell it in those words, the words with which I heard the children shout the glad good news adown the streets of Toul, "The Americans come!"

The task of this Convention, perhaps the supreme opportunity of this Convention, is the revelation, the interpretation, the vocalization, of the spirit of internationalism. We have no demands to make upon our Government; we prefer to trust the administration in Washington, and we are glad to believe in those who represent us; but we will have no separate peace; we will have no repudiation of the honest efforts already made to achieve an association of the nations; and, while statesmen are perfecting the political plan, we will continue to build the structure of human hearts, the fellowship of free souls, the association of men and of women that must undergird any league that shall endure. This Convention is the first after-war convocation of the Christian Endeavor association of nations.

In 1911 at Atlantic City we gave to the world the slogan, "A Saloonless Nation by 1920"; tonight we lift again the motto, "A Saloon-less *World* by 1930." The problem of beverage alcohol looms large beyond our borders, and, indeed, our own land will not be free while elsewhere in the world the traffic has an open way. Our first and our great contribution to the crusade for world-wide prohibition is the effectual demonstration of prohibition at home.

Above the portals of the county building of Cleveland, O., appears this pregnant sentence: "Obedience to law is liberty"; and perhaps no hand has yet written a finer statement of what the purposes of the Government of the United States are with regard to the enforcement of the Eighteenth Amendment than the hand of President Warren G. Harding, who in October, 1920, addressed the following communication to the speaker: "This is a representative republican government, ruled by the majority as expressed at the polls or in the laws formulated by their elected representatives; and it is not within the right of any official of that government to lightly set aside the will of our people as so expressed. . . . I am opposed to the re-establishment of the traffic in intoxicating liquors, and will use whatever influence or power I possess to prevent such re-establishment."

President Harding believes that obedience to the law is liberty. This organization of more than four million young people stands for liberty under the law. We are for the Constitution of the United States. We pledge our unswerving loyalty to those public officials who at the risk of life and position are seriously regarding prohibition, and fearlessly supporting the legislation enacted for its enforcement. We challenge the good faith of individuals and of agencies that are today by open attack or by subterfuge seeking to nullify local, State, and national prohibition

The parade in this city on the Fourth of July was a stain upon the escutcheon of New York, an affront to patriotism, an open thrust against law and order, a threat against free government itself. It gave comfort to all who do their deeds in darkness. It weakened the hands of the brave men who stand between us and the enemies of society. It shouted encouragement not only to the rum-runner, but to the safe-cracker, the highwayman, the white slaver, and the Black Hand. It was the reddest parade that ever filled a New York avenue. The fact that there were decent people in it does not mitigate the evil. The man who strikes a blow against this law, who by his act or voice weakens it before the people, undermines every law that builds a wall of safety about his property and his children..

Laws are man's best effort to express and interpret law. Bad and mistaken laws must be repealed, but by the same orderly processes by which they were established. Violation of a law, whether by rich or poor, artist or mechanic, prince or pauper, official or thug, judge or jury, is repudiation of law itself. The habit of lawbreaking is contagious and progressive. All laws have enemies, and eventually lawbreakers do not discriminate. They shouted, "Personal liberty" as they marched. Personal liberty on the Fourth of July! Personal liberty on the day we celebrate in memory of our fathers who sacrificed personal liberty for public weal, who gave up all in order that a free government might be born. God pity the marchers, and God forgive them, for surely they know not what they did. Personal liberty! The liberty they marched for is the liberty of the man who breaks and enters, who murders in the dark alley, who steals the curly-headed lad to drown him in the river, who sows the seeds of desperate doing, who plants the bomb and fouls the home.

This Convention sounds a clear warning; the day is one of danger. The hour is heavy with menace. Those citizens who believe in democratic government after the plan of this republic dare no longer ignore the crisis. It is time for plain speaking as well as for clear thinking; it is the time for action. "Let the people be numbered." Who is for the Constitution? Who is for the flag? Who is for the United States of America? Congress has spoken. The legislature has spoken. The governor of New York has spoken. The President of the United States has spoken. Christian Endeavor has spoken; and tonight from the platform of her Sixth World's Convention she speaks again; solemnly as before God, passionately as beneath the flag for which her brothers died, she pledges her youth, her faith, her ballots, and her all to the completion of this work so well begun; that prohibition, now an amendment to the Constitution, shall everywhere become a fact by enforcement and the practice of the people.

One Sunday evening last winter I heard the closing words of an address delivered by a missionary before the Christian Endeavor society of the Marble Collegiate Church in this city. He told how for weeks he had lain in the fiery grip of the African fever; how on the evening of what he believed to be his last day on earth he called his native Christians together, and in complete resignation spoke to them of his passing, and gave them his departing blessing. With troubled faces his dark-skinned brothers turned away. For an hour they were in consultation and prayer. Then they returned; and standing in the doorway of their pastor's hut, they delivered their ultimatum; it was, "Sire, we do not consent!" And in the faith of his childlike people the missionary found hope and life.

Christian Endeavorers, this is the brave word for us tonight: *we do not consent.* To the doctrine of fatalism in international relations we do not consent! To the sneer with which some would replace our high motives in the Great War we do not consent! To forgetting that we made solemn covenants to end armed conflict, to overthrow secret diplomacy; to denying that we made these covenants with those who bear in their bodies and in their souls the deeper wounds, we do not consent! To a separate and stultifying peace we do not consent! To the repudiation of prohibition and to the violation of law we do not consent! To the spoliation of the Christian Sabbath by commercialism and desecration we do not consent! To the undermining of our free institutions, whether by the bomb-throwing anarchist or the equally vicious and more powerful criminal who violates civil liberties and prostitutes power in the interests of selfish gain, we do not consent! Not because we take pride from numbers, not because we gather enthusiasm from youth, but because God is in His heaven, Christ is on His throne, and "right the day must win," we do not consent with men to do evil.

"Go, preach! The Kingdom is at hand,
    The King is at the gate;
Go, tell the news in every land;
    He comes for whom ye wait.

"He comes! He comes with healing balm
    For all the hurts of men;
He comes! He comes with hope and calm
    Where all the wars have been.

"Sound, trumpets, sound, in golden flood,
    His reign that shall not cease;
He comes to make of all one blood,
    Triumphant Prince of Peace."

OVER THE BRIDGE OF FORTY YEARS

By Rev. James L. Hill, D.D.

I have traversed it both ways. It has taken me forty years to go and come. How different things look when we reverse our steps and face the other way! A river, a difficulty, the Dardanelles without a bridge, are very much aside from the usual order. Xerxes and Alexander made themselves early historic figures, being builders of bridges. What crown shall we bring to a bridge-builder that spans the yawning chasm between denominations and peoples with differing languages and customs and inherited forms of worship? The ancients used to canonize the builder of a great bridge. We have our own Pontifex Maximus, the master among the builders of bridges. He obviously started something. His greatest contribution to this extended work has been the gift of himself. Yonder stretches this gallery of the mind. As you walk, the heart is stirred. There are many well-remembered pictures. Each one suggests others. A bridge is the result of a useful, usable, active, worth-while idea. The soul of this great society of ours is right. Any one who repudiates the pledge has by that token shown that he has never felt a deep and true affection. Strong feeling of love seeks a pledge, and gives one.

The Man on the Fence

The soul, I say, of the society is right. It differentiates between those who are disciples and those who are not willing to be thus ranked. It aims directly to induce young people to pronounce themselves. It strives to secure self-committal, to draw a line, and then to cause persons to come across as an act of consecration. Of no other service that can be named or imagined does the church stand in such crying need today.

In going back over the bridge of forty years the place that best repays the visit, as a shrine, is not where you made a dollar, or consummated a good trade, or possessed yourself of various effects.

The Past Illumined by the Present

The occurrence that draws you most is the one that bred in you some sense of the value of unseen things, the spot where you felt the unmistakable pull of duty, where you were distinctly led to perform unselfish acts that illumine and transfigure life, and lift it up into fellowship with forces that are not of this world

The large number of believers that have so readily associated with us is a wonderful re-enforcement to our faith. I have presided at the altar when believers came forward for confession, who said that the great initial impression was made in our conventions by seeing large companies of young persons who had faith and feeling and resolution, while on their own part they felt their emptiness and their conscious need.

Full Steam Ahead

The efficiency of our beloved society depends on two things, having an approved and unmatched piece of machinery, and then upon working that machinery well. The organization, no matter how excellent, must be properly and adequately manned. Our highest wish is only for opportunities for a demonstration. Our whole history gives heart to a worker who is willing to do his best. In a closely contested baseball game in which I happened to be interested a man at the bat had two strikes called on him, and was becoming distrustful and disheartened. The man who was coaching came close to the home base, and confidently said to him, "You have the big one left." Here in our society you have an excellent organization, you have a fine field. The thing at stake is near to your heart. Now make your hit. You have the big one left.

THE ENDEAVORER AND HIS TOOLS

BY A. J. SHARTLE

Treasurer and Publication Manager, United Society of Christian Endeavor

Three of the essentials necessary for the building up of a Christian Endeavor society or a Christian Endeavor union are construction, instruction and inspiration. No matter be it in religious or secular work one cannot do successful work without having competent tools. If it is necessary, and it evidently is, to have tools wherewith to construct a house, it is likewise necessary to have tools in the form of intelligent helps such as books, booklets, leaflets and pamphlets to construct the up-to-date Christian Endeavor society of today in a manner sufficiently substantial to make that Christian Endeavor society the kind of an organization that will help to meet the larger requirements of the church. There are possibly thousands of Christian Endeavorers throughout the world who have never heard of our splendid Christian Endeavor literature, the kinds commonly called "Christian Endeavor tools" so necessary in building up a Christian Endeavor organization. No one will know how to organize a Christian Endeavor society unless by some manner he has learned the fundamental things pertaining to Christian Endeavor. Since Christian Endeavor is built upon four cardinal principles, namely, confession, service, loyalty and fellowship, tools necessarily need to be produced that will help stimulate the work along these lines. Therefore, the first great need in the construction of the society is constructive tools. It is easy to employ destructive tools embodying non-essentials that will when not promptly eliminated produce dire results. The kind of tools so necessary today are those produced by consecrated men and women whose hearts are afire for God, and who have the best interests of the youth of the church in mind in the production of these tools.

The second essential is instruction. To what extent will the best tools in all the world help a Christian Endeavor society unless the tools in hand are used in gleaning the information so necessary today? What we need in Christian Endeavor societies today, and also in many Christian Endeavor unions is a real Christian Endeavor library made up of the kinds of Christian Endeavor books, booklets and leaflets that can be used to instruct not only the officers of societies and unions, but also chairmen of committees and members of societies. No one can do anything worth while unless he knows how, and he surely will not know how unless first he has constructed his organization on a firm basis, and then used the tools at hand to instruct those who are supposed to take care of the structure as it is being built up day by day. What Christian Endeavor societies need today are classes of instruction for officers of the societies and chairmen of committees. There are today more than 35,000 Expert Endeavorers scattered throughout the United States, young men and women who have passed the examination for Expert Endeavor successfully, who have gained all the knowledge they can and put this knowledge into practice. and as a consequence Christian Endeavor in the communities where Expert Endeavorers reside has made steady progress.

The third essential is inspiration. The successful society of today is the inspired society, a unit made up of young people who have caught the inspiration for greater things, and have seen the need to inspire others in the building up of a world-wide Christian Endeavor movement. No one can arouse others who does not have enthusiasm himself, neither can he set others afire unless he has caught the inspiration of the "burning bush." We have many inspired Christian Endeavorers, Christian Endeavor societies and unions, but if this great movement is to continue going onward doing definite things for God, we need to carry the spirit of our own inspiration to the very heights of opportunity, there to scatter the methods of construction, instruction and inspiration in a manner that will attract those who are outside the pale of the church who have not caught the vision of this great young people's movement, and who are still inquiring as they did of the apostles on that memorable day of Pentecost when they asked, "What mean these things?"

The Publishing Department of the United Society of Christian Endeavor has during the past year produced many new tools, or books as they are generally known, that will be a great help not only to the constructive work of Christian Endeavor, but in the educational and inspirational work.

Frequently, after Life-Work Recruit meetings the question is asked, what can I do, what field is open for me? The best answer we have today is our new book entitled "Religious Vocations," by Frank Lowe, Jr. This book is the newest and most up-to-date of the kind on the market, and presents the matter of religious vocations in a manner such as no other book does, and is one that we can highly recommend.

Again, no Christian Endeavor society can be a successful society unless it is also a social society. By that I mean that Christian Endeavorers to be approachable Endeavorers must be good mixers, must be sociable, must know how to shake hands, how to greet people, make people feel at home. With this in mind we produced a new book entitled "Successful Socials," by Mrs. E. P. Gates, a wonderful book for societies desiring a wonderful time during social periods.

For many years Junior Superintendents have been wanting more Junior literature, more tools necessary to build up Junior societies, so we produced a "New Junior Manual," by Robert P. Anderson; another book entitled "Handwork for Juniors," by Mr. Anderson; still another, "On the Highway," by Mrs. Ella N. Wood; another, "Bible Auto-biographies," by Mrs. Francis E. Clark; four splendid up-to-date books that will make a kit of Christian Endeavor tools that should be found in the possession of every Junior worker, and in the library of every Junior society and Junior union.

There is another splendid book just published "Collected Poems," by Prof. Amos R. Wells. At the home office we call him "the in-exhaustible Wells" from which have sprung many Christian Endeavor books that have been of great help in the past as also in the present building up of the kind of Christian Endeavor we need today. When we think of the great need of these helps in the building up of Christian character, and the cry coming from tens of thousands of young people who are searching for the kind of tools that will give them the chance to do their best, we believe the best time in all the world to introduce these things and put them into practice is now. Today is the day when in this great Convention thousands here gathered resolve that beginning with the great New York 1921 Convention they will go back home determined to do their best and give their best for the up-building of the flower of American manhood and womanhood, the youth of the nation.

HOW SOME CHURCHES SOLVE COMMON PROBLEMS

BY MRS. WILLIAM V. MARTIN, ILLINOIS

"How Some Churches Solve Common Problems" was the subject of an enlightening address given by Mrs. William V. Martin of Illinois at the Saturday morning conference on Junior methods in the chapel of the Marble Collegiate Church. The securing of proper co-operation of parents, the determining of a suitable time for meeting, and proper and effective leadership are some of the problems which Mrs. Martin dis-cussed.

In her address she said:

Christian Endeavor is forty years old and has done wonderful things for the young people of the churches, but I believe that the majority of our churches and ministers have not even yet caught the vision of what it is possible to do for the Church of Christ. I hope the time will come when the average church of today has graded Sunday School work. Until that time comes and it is recognized that Christian En-deavor is not simply a little society in the church, but instead a vital working plan which is as necessary to the religious welfare of any church as is the Sunday School, we will continually meet the problem of how to give the society its proper place in the minds and hearts of our church people.

Some of our churches have already caught this vision. They begin with the cradle roll Juniors, putting on the list of possible members all the babies of the church and Sunday School. Next comes the Junior Society, with its Sunbeam Department of little folks up to eight years of age; then the regular Junior age, taking the boys and girls from eight to twelve or thirteen years of age. This is followed by the Intermediate Society of the "teen age" young people, and this in turn by the regular young people's society and, lastly, the Alumni Fellowship.

This plan provides very efficiently for the training of all ages and classes, and when our churches awake to the fact that this can be done it will be a big step forward in solving the problem of keeping the young people in the church, which we have to meet at this time. This plan can be more properly carried out by the creation of a Christian Endeavor Council composed of the officers of the Alumni Fellowship, of the Senior Endeavor Society, the superintendent and president of the Intermediate Society, and the superintendent and assistant superintendent of the Junior Society, to plan the work and see that all of them are working towards the one end of winning and training the religious life of our young people for service for Christ and the Church.

The next problem that occurs to me, as I think of the churches where there is no graded Christian Endeavor work, but where there are hosts of boys and girls in the Sunday School, is: "How shall we hold them in our churches and train them for the Master?" The Junior Endeavor Society offers the ideal place in which to accomplish this work. Many of us know this and believe it, but how shall we interest the adults in our churches and make them see the real need of a Junior Society in every church which has a Sunday School, and what it means to the future church of Christ to have the boys and girls trained to speak and to pray in public, trained to use the Bible, trained in missionary knowledge, and training service through the work of the officers and committees?

Some churches solve this problem by making Junior work a big thing in the church life and activity, allowing in the church budget a satisfactory amount of money for the furtherance and support of the Junior Society. Such a church believes that it is better to spend a little money in buying sasbes, attendance cards and other necessary equipment to make Junior Endeavor attractive and to give the Juniors a good time in the church rather than to have them lured away to the moving picture show and other questionable amusements. In such a society it is possible for the Junior superintendent to see to it that each Junior possesses a daily reading booklet to help him to remember to read his Bible every day, and his pledge card to help him remember his pledge. Junior Endeavor has helped many a thoughtless father or mother to think of the importance of daily Bible reading and prayer in the religious life of the boy and the girl.

Some churches emphasize the Junior work by having at least once a year a Sunday in which the Junior work is presented to the whole church, and a program given in which the Juniors take part, showing what they have done and what they have learned.

In Illinois we try to help these churches by sending out a special program once a year for what we call Illinois Junior Day. I believe this has helped many churches to see the importance and value of Junior Endeavor work.

Many superintendents find it hard to secure the co-operation of the parents in their work. Many parents who would not for a minute neglect their physical needs do not seem to realize that the boys and girls in the average Protestant home today receive only one hour a week of religious training to at least twenty-five of mental training. Providing attractive attendance cards on which are recorded not only the attendance, but also the behavior and the part the Junior takes in each meeting is a means used in some churches to interest the parents. These cards last for three months, are taken care of in the meeting by some member of the Junior committee or by the lookout or prayer meeting committee, who note on each card 'the part taken, using a "T" for testimony or talk, "V" for verse, and "P" for prayer. The Juniors enjoy having these attractive report cards to keep, and the parents usually ask some questions if Johnny or Mary have green or black stars for misbehavior. A mothers' society which meets once a month has solved this problem in some churches for the mothers get together and talk over the situation.

To find a suitable time for meeting is one of the hard problems of the work. Many societies think they can meet only on Sunday afternoon and many a society has disbanded because of that idea, coupled with the fact that it seemed impossible to get the children to attend on that afternoon. Some societies have overcome this by meeting on a week day after school.

TRAINING FOR LEADERSHIP

By R. A. Walker

There are three prime essentials to be considered in training for leadership. The first is *consecration*. A deep rooted conviction of the power of a life wholly devoted to the Glory of God. A definite personal knowledge of His saving Grace exemplified in the individual life.

In II. Cor. 8:5 we read, "but first gave their own selves to the Lord," and it is thus the leader today must do.

It is not how much we can get God to do for us, but how much we are willing to let Him do through us, that measures the depth of our Consecration.

The young aviator, Dinsmore Ely, expressed it in his (unknown to him) last letter home to his mother from the battlefields of France, in this way: "And I want to say in conclusion that if anything should happen to me let there be no mourning in spirit or dress, for a man's life like a Liberty Bond, is an investment, when given in defence of his country." Dare we let this young hero do more for his country than we would do for our Christ?

Why, if today the coming of His kingdom, the doing of His will, the hallowing of His name was your chief object in life, He could charter a million suns out of yonder clear sky and hitch to them your chariot, that the object he has for your life might be consummated.

The late D. L. Moody is reported to have once said, "The world has yet to see the power of a fully consecrated man at his best," and to this I would like to add there is no movement or organization in the world today, with the Spirit of Jesus Christ in it, that is so dead, but that *one* fully consecrated person can make it the livest corpse in existence, even though you have to sprinkle Choride of Lime on the remains to be able to get close enough to read the epitaph on its tombstone. Are *you* that *one?*

But as necessary as is consecration, "no amount of consecration can make up for the wastefulness of unplanned work." Hence the second essential is *preparation.*

In II. Timothy 2:15 we find our guide in preparation, "Study to show thyself approved unto God, a workman that needeth not to be ashamed, rightly dividing the word of truth."

The clarion call today is for hosts of young people to step out and prepare for a greater and more definite part in the ushering in of His kingdom. This is the greatest day this old world has ever seen since away back there 2,000 years ago when the shepherds looked into the face of that little Babe, on that first glad Christmas morning, and the wise men brought their gifts as a tribute to the young Child whose power the swaddling clothes could not hide. God is abroad in the land, not more than He has ever been but we are really beginning to realize the power of His great omnipotence, in our little affairs. These are great days of opportunities and the greater the opportunity the greater the responsibility.

In our preparation for leadership, a college education is by all means desirable, but not absolutely essential. Young people's conferences and Christian Endeavor conventions and like gatherings should be attended when possible.

Study people en masse and in the concrete, but above all things know the Book. We are salesmen for His cause, and the Book is our catalogue. We must know what it contains to be able to talk it convincingly to others. A soul knelt at the Master's feet to confess. "I have failed," he cried. "Thou hast done thy best," the Master said; "that is success."

No life can be a power for His cause without being familiar with the Bible, and, though other reading is essential, I venture to assert that really reading the old, old story is the most neglected of all reading, today. "Thy word have I hid in my heart that I might not sin," said the Psalmist long ago. Surely in this complex life of today, we need no less to have His word hid in our hearts to keep us from sinning.

In all your preparation, remember this one thing, that what this old world needs, yes, wants today more than any other one thing, is the plain old story of the life of Jesus Christ as told in the Gospels, as the only power that can save and keep to the uttermost. Any message delivered without this being manifest in it somewhere is a failure, regardless of how fine a piece of literature or oratory it may be.

The third essential is *determination*. O for a host of young people with the mental, moral, and spiritual ability to stay through to the finish! Anybody can start something but it takes a real man or woman to stay by and complete the task started. The world is full of starters, that stopped along the way, but both continents are calling for men and women who will stick to the job and *do it*.

In St. John, sixth chapter, we read the story of the feeding of the five thousand. There are three outstanding characters worthy of our attention. First, Philip, who counted the *cost*, 200 shillings, and *quit*. Andrew counted the *resources*, five loaves and two fishes, and said, *"What's the use?"* Jesus Christ first gave thanks for *what He had*, took it and blessed it, and God made it all sufficient for the need of the hour. The talent He has bestowed upon you, if used to His glory will be sufficient for all your need.

Marshal Foch, of France, said, "Of all sins only one is infamous— inaction." Whether we agree with the Marshal or not, one thing needed is men and women of action. Those who cannot stand the reproach upon themselves of good deeds left undone, who having seen a worthy end work toward that end, even though it be ten thousand miles away. Who see a way out or are out seeking a way, who when anything needs to be done says, "Come on, let's do it," and then go ahead and do it whether anybody else comes or not. Those who put ginger into all they do, yet leave out the mustard and the vinegar.

I would like to pass on to you for your challenge to the young people of today, the slogan of Great Britain, during the world war, "Your King and your country need you." Not a temporal king, but your King Jesus needs you to stay by until your job here is completed.

Then let us keep the star of Hope and Faith, burning just a little more brightly than ever before, for only when night shall have winged its way to the unnumbered days, and each of us ready or unready stand again at the dawn of a new day, may we if we will change our destinies. Not errors that have been, or our insufficient self, controls the hour, but the cloying drug of habit that makes cowards of us in the untried way. We need the blows that fall, and the storms and tides that set off shore are but measures for our greatest good if we but knew their meaning. For we are told, "All things work together for good to those who love God." What port of such delight as that which we have striven against greatest odds? What victory so dear as that which is bought with sacrifice? Then let us first conquer self and hand in hand urge on the mass to that far goal which never may we reach in this brief span here below, but which deep in our being, we know is there, as knows the wild bird in its flight, as points the needle to the pole, and we hold aloft for a little while God's banner that lights the way.

Truly has the poet said:

> God has His best things
>   For those who dare to stand the test.
> God has His second best
>   For those who will not have His best.
> There's scarcely one
>   But wants in some vague way to be blest.
> 'Tis not thy blessing Lord, I seek,
>   I want thy very best.
> I want in this brief life of mine
>   All that can be pressed
> Of service, both to Thee and man;
>   Help me to do my best.
> I want among that victor throng
>   To hear my name confessed,
> And hear at last those welcome words
>   Well done; you did your best.

CHRISTIAN ENDEAVOR IN THE WORLD CRISIS

By Rev. John Pollock

I'm from Ireland. I am from the most interesting city in the world, Belfast. I am delighted with my text because of its magnificent range; it gives me liberty to say anything I choose on any subject under the sun that is related to Christian Endeavor or the present crisis.

I want to say something tonight I should not like to say in Dublin, also some things I should be equally afraid to say in London. I can say them in New York, because, of course, the reporters won't take down anything I say. I don't mind whether I am reported or not. I am here to give you some information about Ireland. I am not an Irishman; I am a Glasgow man who keeps his eyes and ears open, and does not need information from the Irish about the situation. We perhaps know it better than the Irish themselves, just as those outside see how a game is going better than the players.

I believe the Irish problem is a problem that is soluble. I believe it will be solved, and I should be very sorry to utter a syllable tonight that might delay the solution of this problem, remembering the very earnest efforts now being made to reconcile the warring elements in that distressful land. Now Christian Endeavor is strong in the north of Ireland. It is practically unknown in the south and west. There are a few societies here and there among the Scotch and Protestant communities, but of course, there is no Christian Endeavor in large tracts of the south and west, which are solidly Roman Catholic; but Christian Endeavor in the north has, I believe, sweetened the relations between warring parties. I believe we have done something to bring reasonable and modern men together. I believe in the influence of Christian Endeavor, and I have strong evidence that this is not unknown and not altogether unappreciated even in the Roman Catholic Church.

Now, I believe that we are reaping today the harvest of the sowing of generations and centuries ago. Those who sowed the dragons' teeth are no longer among us. I stand here as a loyal Britisher, rejoicing that as a Scotsman I belong to a country, part of the United Kingdom, that had practically no responsibility for the state of matters that existed in Ireland centuries before the Scottish Union, when Ireland was misgoverned, cruelly misgoverned, terribly wronged, robbed and cheated. Since the Union there has been a very great improvement in the relations of the two peoples. What Ireland has suffered from is this: a perpetual alternation, and very often coercion without firmness, without sympathy. What we need today is a solution of the problem, and I believe Christian Endeavor is having a powerful and indirect influence in that direction. We want concession with firmness and coercion with sympathy. Two blunders have been committed, one by the Nationalist party (I use that term in the broadest sense), and the other by the Unionist party. The Nationalist party committed a blunder by insisting on living in the past, refusing to forget what had far better be forgotten. The Unionists committed the blunder of imagining that, when the knife is withdrawn, you have healed the wound. The wound is not healed. Perhaps it will heal now more speedily than our weak faith permits us to expect, and when Ireland shall sit in her right mind at the feet of Jesus. I come from Ireland, the land where the people don't know what they want, and won't be happy until they get it.

I said to an extremist on the other side not long ago, "Why do you wish to be cut off from the British Empire, to sever your connection with that great firm and open a little store on the corner?" He said the "Irish Union was dirty business"; but I said, "Not so dirty as the Scotch Union, opposing to the bitter end." When it was accomplished, they said, "If there is to be a British Empire, the sooner we are in London, the better." So he went south, and has lived in the British Empire ever since.

It is a very remarkable fact that the empire cannot apparently get on without the Scotch and the Irish and the Welsh; and yet you in your American ignorance talk about England as if we were all English. When I was a boy, I looked at England as your colonial fathers looked at England. England was the Germany of those days. Now we find our greatest strength and wealth in the imperial government. There was not a single Englishman at the great Peace Conference. There were Scotchmen and Welshmen and there were Irishmen; and yet we speak of the United Kingdom as English. I protest there is no such thing as the English flag or army; it is the British flag, the British army. We never shall be any more ready to permit Ireland to leave the empire than you were ready to relinquish your hold upon the South. We cannot afford to lose Ireland. I believe the time is near, if not already come, when the idea of separation from the great British commonwealth (I prefer that word to "empire," for we are one of the great republics of the day) will be inconceivable. I was delighted to hear the last speaker refer to the liberty of those even of another religion that are under British rule throughout the world. We cannot afford to permit Ireland to leave the empire. Ireland is an element of strength. I believe the idea of separation from the empire has been dropped; and, that being so, Ireland will receive the largest possible self-government. If you have a dog in Scotland, you have to pay a tax of six or seven pence; but, if you live in Ireland, you have nothing to pay. Much money has been wasted in this country to relieve the "misery and starvation in Ireland." The savings banks of Ireland were never so prosperous as they are now at the present moment, and wages never so high, not in the north merely, but in the south and west. I ask you to be sufficiently interested in Ireland to pray that God will have mercy on that distracted land, that He who turneth the hearts of men as the rivers of water are turned, that He who can still any storm that ever raged on any lake, by saying, "Peace be still," will say, "Peace" in Ireland.

Christian Endeavor and the present crisis. What is Christian Endeavor doing in Europe today? I look upon Christian Endeavor, and I speak from reliable information, I look upon Christian Endeavor as one of the great unifying forces of the continent of Europe today. In Germany Christian Endeavor has done much more, perhaps, than it has in the United Kingdom. I do not know how much it has done in Germany, but I do believe that Christian Endeavor more than any other organization and agency is doing much to sweeten the national sentiment towards the Allies since the war began. Christian Endeavor has progressed in Germany. There were larger increases in number of Christian Endeavor societies in Germany during the war than in Great Britain. I venture to say it was a larger proportion of increase than in the land of its birth. Christian Endeavor conventions in Germany are crowded with men and women coming from all parts of the state. We have only one secretary in Great Britain and Ireland; but Germany has several, and has increased the number of them during the war and since the war. The German national Christian Endeavor organization has a large paid staff, a printing press of its own, an organization such as we in Britain cannot boast of. Christian Endeavor in Germany—I speak from information that has come to me in letters I have received recently—Christian Endeavor is doing much today to restore peace in the hearts of the German people. I have a suspicion that if we (not including you; you may be of larger caliber)—if we had in Great Britain lost the war, and there had been a religious movement in Britain which had been more or less successful among us, which had its genesis in Germany, its president a speaker of the language of the enemy, I have a suspicion that our Christian Endeavor societies would not have increased as they have in Germany. Christian Endeavor in the present crisis has raised my estimate of the nobility of Christian German character. There is a Christian Germany, and there is an unchristian Germany, just as there is a Christian America and an unchristian America.

This is my fifth visit to this country, and on each occasion the friendliness towards Great Britain was among the Christian men and women more than elsewhere. If you found any antipathy to Great Britain, it was among those who are outside the influence of religion. That is the same in Germany today. The time is coming when Germany and we shall not only be one family at peace, but we shall trust and love each other as some of us did before the war. I remember having the honor as president of the European Christian Endeavor Union of presiding at the great European convention in Berlin. When I arose to address the audience, the Union Jack and the German imperial flag were crossed over my head. I hope that you will have that experience repeated. I have been invited officially to go in my official capacity to a convention meeting in Bremen.

There is a Spanish proverb which made a profound impression on me some time ago. It is, "The sword makes war; the heart, and the heart alone, can make peace."

THE SOCIAL TASK OF THE CHURCH

By REV. GEORGE W. RICHARDS, D.D.

The church has for its object the Christianizing of society of which it is a part. What is meant by social service? This is a phrase so popular and so often under suspicion. It means we bring basal institutions of society of every time and nation under the sun under the power of holy love; and, if you want to know what holy love is, go to Jesus. Follow Him in Palestine in His ministry, and behold Him on Calvary.

What are the basal institutions of society? The home, school, the world of industry, and the state. But these four in all of their relations and in all their transactions must be ruled by righteousness and love.

The city of New York in its council, and through its mayor must put into force righteousness and love as exemplified in Christ. The Senate of Pennsylvania through its Assembly must put into force in its legislation the principle of holy love. The council of the national government and the President of the United States in all relations must be controlled for the love of God, for humanity as manifest in Christ Jesus. Now, you will concede with me this is a great task. If it is a great task to evangelize the world, it is perhaps a greater task to Christianize the world. It may be comparatively easy to send evangelists over the world that every one may hear the gospel. It may not be so easy to apply the gospel of holy love in all the institutions of the social order.

Social service does not mean taking care of the wreckage of society, the blind, lame, poor, insane and defectives; that the church has always done. The Catholic Church has done it, also the Protestant. We must take a definite program, not in the name of democracy, not in the name of humanity, but in the name of Christ Jesus, so that a social order that has principles of love will prevail. What can the church do to perform so great a task? First of all, the church is not to take the part of the police and to go about and watch the vices of a city, and keep them under control. The church is not to dictate the policy of a corporation, how to run its business and how much wages to pay. The church is not to do the work of a labor union and care for it. The church is partisan to none, not to the rich, not to the poor; for it is the partisan of all in the name of Jesus Christ. The church has one thing greater to do. It is to sensitize the social conscience with the gospel of Jesus. If it was a great discovery to name the social meaning of the Kingdom, we have another great discovery in the twentieth century, and that is the social conscience. O, yes, men always had it. So the blood always circulated in the human body, but it was not until the seventeenth century that this fact was discovered. There was always a social conscience, but only recently men have been able to use it. Make this social conscience so sensitive to right and wrong that it would revolt against impurity, injustice and dishonor of every kind. Suppose we had in a community a cesspool out of which would come poisonous germs which would imperil the life of every boy and girl in the community, and the board of health, being notified, should refuse to remove the source of complaint. The social conscience of the community would be aroused, and in less than no time the cesspool would be removed and also the board of health. If we have a sensitized social conscience to that extent, we can sensitize it more. Only a few years ago there was a moral cesspool on nearly every street corner of New York, also San Francisco. Today those cesspools are closed, because in the course of fifty years and more the social conscience has been sensitized to the point where it will not tolerate the saloon. When we have sensitized the social conscience with the gospel of Jesus, it will do three things.

First, we will start social health. There must be playgrounds in every community of America for the child to develop his body, as there are schools to develop his brain. Playgrounds not simply in the name of humanity or efficiency, but playgrounds in the name of Him who said, "Suffer the little children to come unto me." We have closed thousands and tens of thousands of saloons, but that is only half of the task. For every door which prohibition has closed there should be wholesome places of amusement and recreation provided throughout the nation.

Secondly, we will have political patriotism. Politics and religion are inseparably united. We have one sacred heritage alongside of the gospel, the heritage of our ballot. If you will study the history of the ballot, you will find it comes to you dripping with blood. It has its martyrs on the field of battle. It is one of the sacred privileges of citizenship, and must be cast in the name of Jesus for political righteousness; and the whole nation will rise against any officer or representative that does not stand for justice to all, for freedom to every man, woman, and child in America. It is a great responsibility to be a Christian citizen.

We come to the last. We must have an industrial order that is Christlike. That perhaps is the most difficult task before us, and that of the corporations of America controlled by the principles of holy love; to think of the labor unions of America controlled by holy love; to think of our international relations between the nations of the world under the power of the spirit of the cross. Some time ago I read in a newspaper that America at last has one billionaire. My imagination was staggered. I cannot imagine how much that is. The average minister counts his money in three figures. America at last has a billionaire, and we confess that we should like to see how it would feel. We do not blame him; we admire him as a business man. He is one of the wonders of the modern world, and we admire him. What we want to work for is a social order that will make billionaires impossible. We do not believe in dictatorship of any kind, whether it be dictation of proletariat or Czar, union or capitalist. This word is hateful to the kingdom of God. We want a co-operative democracy, not a competitive democracy in which selfishness prevails.

I have outlined my conception of the practical working out of the kingdom of God. I have sympathy at times with that group which says that it is impossible. When I look at the task, I feel like throwing up my hands. The power for Christianizing the social order is not outside, nor in the life of man. That power is in God, in Jesus Christ, who overcame death and hell. I believe that the power is to be applied through us, not apart from us; through the church, not apart from the church; through history and in the kingdom of God; through Christians in the world; through the churches of the world to be slowly wrought out of the ends of the earth. That, I think, is the old goal of Christian Endeavor, a goal we see a little clearer than twenty-five years ago. We do not want to pray less, to read the Bible less, go to church less, or give less to the church; but we want to do more; we want to fix as our goal in advance the conversion of individuals, the transformation and Christianizing of society, school, and college. We cannot praise enough the boys who crossed the Atlantic to stand in the trenches, fighting and dying for democracy. We cannot praise enough the heroes who fought and died in the last war. There is just one thing greater, and that is to live in a community in America, and stand for Jesus Christ, stand for social health, political patriotism, and industrial justice. If you can so live, and so vote, and so act, you will understand just a little more clearly what Jesus meant when He said, "Take up the cross, and follow me."

THE CALL OF THE KINGDOM

By Dr. SAMUEL M. ZWEMER

There is no part of the world which has felt the effect of the war more deeply upon its institutions, its governmental ideals, and its hopes than the Moslem world. The earthquake shock has been felt from the centre to the very circumference. The Mohammedans in China, as well as the Mohammedans in Morocco, are talking about the results of this war on Islam. It is a world which is disappointed, distracted, disillusioned, sorrowing, expectant, but also defiant. It is a world that is disappointed and distracted because of divided counsels and unfulfilled hopes, centering on the one hand in the Caliph, and centering on the other hand in the success of Germany or the powers of Central Europe, which proved a failure.

Dr. Rufus W. Miller

Dr. Clarence A. Barbour

Dr. Samuel M. Zwemer

Mr. Winslow Russell

Mr. Polhemus Lyon

Hearts are disappointed, and public opinion among Mohammedans is distracted regarding the future. One has only to read the Moslem press—as far as we still have a Moslem press—to see what they are thinking and what they are saying.

It is also a sorrowing world. Entirely apart from the fact of their religion, the Moslem world stands for famine and pestilence and suffering and poverty and orphans and widows. Back of those two hundred millions are sorrows as deep as the sorrows of Belgium, or of northern France, or of the homes of England that still are looking for comfort. This Mohammedan world is a world that was never so responsive, never so expectant, as it now is. From every spot with which I have correspondence, from western China and Morroco and Algeria, from Egypt and Mesopotamia and even darkest Arabia, there come accounts of hospitals overcrowded, of schools packed with Moslem children eager for books of culture whose record sale is higher to Mohammedans than ever before the war. The Bible Society as a climax tells us that the circulation of the word of God was never so abundant, so free, so eager as it has been since August, 1914.

This great Moslem world, with all its needs, with all its disappointments, and with the terrible neglect of thirteen centuries, stands before us; and we may ask ourselves only one question, which is fundamental, What is the will of God for the Moslem world today? What is the will of God for you and me, face to face with the unfinished task outlined before us in these days? To a Christian man, to a Christian woman, that is the only thing that matters.

Considering those two hundred millions scattered over the great Eastern world, what is the will of God for the Mohammedans? It is not hard to answer that question if we take in our hands the New Testament and the Old Testament, the covenants of God's grace and love. We know God's will for the Mohammedans.

We know God's will, not only from His eternal purpose of redemption, but we know God's will very clearly from His commands. You cannot tear from the New Testament the great commission four times repeated; and whatever the great commission might mean for the South Sea Islands, or for North and South America, or undiscovered continents, the great commission was given in sight of the Near East. The great commission rang out from Jerusalem to Judaea, and to Samaria, and to the uttermost parts of the Roman Empire; and, whatever Jesus Christ intended, He never intended that the flag and the kingdom of a usurper should be supreme.

If God is the God of truth and we are disciples of truth, what eagerness there ought to be in our hearts to shrivel the falsehood from the souls of men by the patient, by the tactful, by the loving proclamation of God's eternal truth! Unless we are prepared to put foot-notes in our hymn-book, and crown Him Lord of all, *except* in the Mohammedan world, and put foot-notes in our New Testament, and say that Jesus Christ is supreme above all *except* Mohammed, we are in duty bound to proclaim the truth of the everlasting Christ among all nations, beginning in the Near East.

I think of workers on the borders of the Moslem world, on the far stretches of the great spiritual battlefields. Women are holding entire sections of the line; men unsupported are carrying on hospitals and churches; men and women are travelling vast distances, and opening out new areas, and planning new conquests, for Jesus Christ our Lord. The Armenian Church and the churches of the Near East are gazing for the rising dawn and hoping against hope, and at last the hour has struck for the triumph of the kingdom of our Lord. The Christians of Damascus, after Allenby's army entered, pointed to the old inscription engraven in the rock there: "Thy kingdom, O Christ, is an everlasting kingdom, and Thy dominion from generation to generation." Armenian nurses, nursing Turkish soldiers, wiped away their tears, saying: "How long, O God, how long? Thy kingdom come and Thy will be done in Armenia as it is in heaven."

What is your responsibility when you pray, "Thy kingdom come, Thy will be done in earth," in the Mohammedan world? What have you done to execute the will of God, as lightning does, and accomplish His purpose for these Mohammedan hearts? God is leading us into a great crusade of compassion for our Mohammedan brothers and our Mohammedan sisters, and any one of us today who will gird himself or herself for this great crusade of compassion will find, as Paul did when he said, "I beseech you that ye present your bodies a living sacrifice," will find, as Paul did, that once we put ourselves on the altar of service for this great, baffling task we shall find that God's will for us is good and acceptable and perfect.

The Mohammedan world is waiting not for big finance, but for big faith; the Mohammedan world is waiting today, not for spectacular reports of things that may be or might be, but for great sacrificial obedience. The Mohammedan world challenges us with God's mandate, and instead of discussing the mandate of our country, America's for Armenia, or Britain's for Mesopotamia, or France's for Palestine and Syria, let us turn the pages of God's book and look at that great mandate sealed with His blood, spoken by His loving voice, incarnated by His own passion, to watch the Near East, and, following that mandate of God, let us ask God what is His will for us now for the Mohammedan world.

PETER JOHNSON'S NEW FISHING EXPERIENCE

By S. D. Gordon

Peter was in trouble. It is our old friend Peter of the fishing-nets, called "son of Jonas." The Revised Version says "son of John"; so today we say, "Peter, son of John," or "John's son Peter," or "Peter Johnson." Now, I suppose we would call him Bishop Johnson.

Peter was in trouble. There was nothing unusual about that. It was a way Peter had, of getting into trouble; but this time the thing was serious. Jesus had died, and Peter had stood by as many as ten times and watched the crowd try to take Jesus, and had watched with staring eyes while He held them back. This time He allowed them to take Him. Peter has some bitter memories of the betrayal-night in the courtyard.

Then Jesus arose again, and Peter was keeled over with surprise and delight. Peter does not know where he is. He belongs to a large company of people who have lost their feet, or lost their heads. So Peter made a suggestion; he was always good at making suggestions, like a few Americans in that regard. Peter said, "I am going fishing." Any fisherman could see the sense of it. If your nerves are ragged, your program broken, it is a great thing to get off in the woods where nature is, and nature's God, all by yourself. They said, "We will go along"; there is always a crowd of people who will go along. Cheap leadership is very common still, outside of New York City.

But they caught nothing. Disheartened, never succeeding in anything they attempted to do, along towards morning you see them pulling in towards land, nets lying limp at the bottom of the boat.

As they come, a stranger is walking along the beach, nothing unusual about that. But this stranger puts his hands up to his mouth, and in a kindly way calls out, "Comrades, have you caught anything?" A question of that kind may be just a bit embarrassing. The kindly stranger is persistent. Again his hand goes up, and he said, "Cast your nets on the right side."

Who is this telling Peter how to fish? Peter has fished in these blue Gallilean waters all his life. Who is this to tell Peter how to fish? There is a something in the quiet voice of the stranger that takes hold of him. It is the touch of the Jesus man. The words may be simple words, but they throw their nets over into the water, and instantly their muscles grow tense, and they are put to it to handle the haul.

Then John who tells this story makes a discovery. Hate is keen; the war told us that; and hate is a stimulant which stimulates the brain, steadies the nerves, makes truer the aim; but hate cannot stand competition with love. Hate is keen; love is keener.

Fishing lost its attraction for Peter. He has a thing to talk over with the Master, and over the side of the boat he goes, quicker than any Irishman's "jiffy." Peter blundered so much like the rest of us, so much like the man I know best.

If you had some trouble about the fire in the courtyard on betrayal-night, it is a great thing just to drop things, and have a peaceful talk with Jesus. And so Peter and the Master had the thing out along the beach. I don't suppose Peter said everything. He didn't need to. I don't suppose he made a long confession of mistakes in his life. I don't suppose Jesus said very much. The look in Peter's eyes told the whole story, and the look in Jesus' eyes told the story of forgiveness. Peter found the knotted place in the palm of the Master's hand that tells the whole story of love, and love's death, and the result for himself. Peter was very practical, like our own Americans or Canadians. I suppose he was the original Christian Endeavorer on record. Peter turned to help land the haul of fish. Of course, they counted their fish. You will notice this time their nets did not break. Fishermen keep very careful tally for the folks at home.

After counting the fish, they turned their faces toward the shore, and saw a fire burning on the beach. They are chilled to the bone and wet to the skin. I suppose there is no irreverence in thinking of Jesus as making that fire, kneeling on the beach and preparing their supper of fish. Couldn't He have just spoken to the fire and made it burn? Of course, but God loves the natural. He can do the supernatural, but prefers the natural. I love to think of Christ gathering the kindling and making the fire. And then the supper; who could have cooked the fish to a better brown turn? Peter, turning from his fish said, "Even my wife couldn't have done the fish to a better brown turn."

Then there is a long walk along the beach with Jesus in the lead, and John always close by; and Peter, dear old Peter, has graduated. He used to follow afar off. He is close up now, and John on the other side. Jesus say, "Peter, do you love me?" Not. "Do you love?" But, "Do you love me?" I think I might name two or three names that cry out of this fishing-story, Peter Johnson, softly, Jesus was there. He was not recognized, but he was there, and when they were out on the water, failure in their fishing, wet, hungry, He was keeping tab, finger on the pulse-beat. Jesus was there.

Jesus is walking along your beach; maybe it is night-time. He didn't come. It doesn't say, "He came"; no; He was already there. He simply opened their eyes to it. He simply manifested Himself. He was there because they were there, and because men are a magnet, and He cannot resist us, and we cannot resist Him. He was there to do what they needed to have done. What was that? Did he give them a lecture on the resurrection? No; His presence was the best evidence of the resurrection, and it still is. His walking along the beach of your life is the finest evidence that He arose again. He was there to do what? To do what they needed to have done. They were cold; He built them a fire. They were hungry, and He cooked them a fish. They talked together, but He fed and warmed them first.

Gypsy Smith told a story of an incident in France. A woman was pouring coffee for the soldiers and singing, "Pack up your troubles, and sing, sing, sing." Mr. Smith came along with a Bible, and said to the woman; "Sister, let me get in a word for Jesus"; but, being a woman with a woman's wit, she kept on pouring coffee. Mr. Smith repeated, but the woman with woman's common sense, kept on pouring. A British soldier came out, and said, "She is putting Jesus into the coffee." He understood. Read the last chapter of John, this quiet talk heart to heart, getting this straight on the fishing-story. Let Him go with you; it will be better for your fishing if you do.

THE ENDEAVORER AND HIS MONEY

By Rev. W. A. MACTAGGART, B.A., Toronto, Canada

When Mr. Gates first asked me to speak on the question of money, perhaps if he had given me a choice, it would have been the last subject I would have chosen; but, when he linked money with Christian Endeavor, that was different. If I had been asked to speak to hard-headed Socialists, they might have said that money was out of date, that they wanted to do away with money. But I am to speak to Christian Endeavorers who use the world as we have it, and who place their belief and trust in Jesus Christ. Being a minister, I wanted a task, and I didn't have far to look in this great subject.

I suppose the collection-envelopes of every church have printed on them that verse from Corinthians 16:2, "Upon the first day of the week let every one of you lay by him in store as God hath prospered him, that there be no gatherings when I come." This was the first slogan campaign in the Christian church. This was a universal system, a systematic campaign, and they were laying by money regularly. It was a successful campaign, for the apostle added, "Let there be no gatherings when I come." This apostle had a difficult hill to climb. He was collecting money for the poor in Jerusalem, for people in his own Jerusalem. Those separated from his people in prejudice turned into bitter hatred, and they called them "dogs of the earth." But even without the help of these people he was able to put across a financial campaign and get all he wanted.

How did he strike the imagination so that when he came for the money they were ready? Go back to the chapter before it. Look to the closing part of the preceding chapter, "God which giveth us the victory through our Lord Jesus Christ," and, "Death, where is thy sting?" What homes it blights! what hearts are broken because death severs friends! but "death, where is thy sting; grave, where is thy victory?" That yawning chasm opens for all ages to receive all men and women; the one great certainty is the way we come into life, and the way we go out of it. Jesus came down from heaven, tasted death for every man, burst the gates of death, came forth on Easter morning. They sang the Hallelujah Chorus; they sang it in Ephesus, Corinth, Rome, and Jerusalem, and wherever the gospel is they will sing this chorus. Every Jew who sang this chorus was put out of his home, lost his job, made destitute. That bond of Christian fellowship said, "We cannot let our brother suffer; we must take up a collection; he is our brother, and we will help him." This was the first effort the church made to raise money, and it was to help the other fellow, and helping the woman who is in need. Ever since at the call of need from our brethren we have always been ready. When the call came from China, there was not a Christian church or congregation but was glad to raise hundreds of dollars for these people; and, if you will read the twenty-fifth of Matthew you will see what Jesus says about this giving; He will separate the left from the right. He will say, "I was sick and in prison and ye ministered unto me; I was thirsty, and ye gave me drink. Inasmuch as ye have done it unto the least of these, ye have done it unto me."

I was told a story of the Russian Tolstoy, who said a woman, very poor, living in an attic room, gathered her children about her, and told the story of Jesus, that He had not a place to lay His head; and she said, "Little as we have, we would make shift somehow to find a place for Him to lay His head." Just then a poor man rapped at the door, and asked for a night's lodging. The mother was about to refuse, when the little boy said, "Maybe Jesus could not come, and sent this fellow instead." The man was given a bed for the night. "Unto the least of these"; a new fraternity was born, and has swung down through the ages.

But philanthropy is only temporary. Armenia needs more today than a collection; Armenia needs a friend and big brother until she is able to help herself. China needs more than a collection; she needs a vision of the cross to make her able to administer the affairs of her country, and to make provision so there can never again be such a disastrous famine. God calls every one of us to go with the message for Him to China. If we are not willing to go and work for Him there, we are not fit to stay and work for Him here. He expects those who are able to go. You may go potentially through money.

Let us all join the Tenth Legion. We should not need the great Forward Movement; we could sweep the world and win the world for Jesus Christ if we gave one-tenth of what we are earning. If we give one-tenth to God for the extension of His kingdom, I plead with you Christian Endeavorers to administer not only the tenth for the extension of His kingdom, but be just as conscientious in your administration of the nine-tenths.

Our minds turn to economic problems. There is still a tremendous divergence between the economic conditions of the society of today and the economic conditions of the kingdom of God. We have a long way to go. Too much prestige is given to vested interests, and not enough to boys and girls and men and women. This must be in the new economy of the day that is to come, to take second place to humanity and the interests of society, the kingdom of God and Jesus Christ.

MESSAGES FROM MEN AND WOMEN WHO HAVE MADE CHRISTIAN ENDEAVOR HISTORY

BY REV. JOHN POLLOCK

I greet you from the great sister republic on the other side of the ocean. The difference between the Roman Empire and the British Empire is this: the Roman Empire was nominally a republic, really an autocracy; the British Empire is nominally a monarchy, really a republic. There is no intelligent Britisher who will seek to controvert such a statement as that. There is no freer country in the world than my country. If you don't believe that, I refer you to the governor of the State of Massachusetts, who made a statement to that effect not long ago. Under the British flag all are free. Under the British flag there is no oppression; not a single people, not a single nationality, suffers oppression under the British flag. Even that explains to some extent the welcome Britain gave to Christian Endeavor, the welcome we give to most things that come from the sister republic.

The difference between this republic and mine is that the president of your republic is elected; mine is hereditary. I don't expect you to agree with me; it wouldn't be right for you to; but I prefer a hereditary president for reasons Dr. Clark will not give me time to explain.

My president visited our city just before I left. He came to open the Ulster Parliament. He had more clothes on than your president has on at that occasion, and something on his head I shouldn't like to wear in this temperature. He calls himself—I don't mean to say in so many words—he rejoices to be the president of a free people.

Of course, we haven't always had presidents like that. There was a stupid, blundering royal fool; I feel in an awful rage at him tonight when I see this magnificent audience and city. O, I am angry at that man who lost us the American colonies. I believe Christian Endeavor is one of those things that are bringing the two great republics. the two empires by the sea, bringing them together in heart, and aim and ideal.

I represent more than the United Kingdom here tonight. I count it another honor to represent the European Union as president of the European Christian Endeavor Union.

I rejoice to stand on this platform immediately after a representative of one of the old "enemy countries," as we called them. God bless Hungary. God bless Germany. the new Germany, the Germany that is showing more than it ever did of the genuine Christian spirit. Germany was a noble nation, a peaceful nation. In one generation it was changed. It got into the hands of a parcel of scoundrels, cutthroats; and I believe it will take less than a generation for Germany to become again what it was before, a peaceful, industrious nation.

I visited Wales during the revival, and saw there that spiritual enthusiasm, such spiritual enthusiasm as I never saw elsewhere except in a Christian Endeavor convention. In a Christian Endeavor convention in Berlin I saw enthusiasm equal to that I saw at the Welsh revival. I pray those republics may be bound together in bonds of confidence and affection. God knows; it may be in His plan that the three great republics may yet be guarantors of the world peace. I salute the German flag. You may say "You wouldn't do it if you had lost a boy." I had two boys, one in the navy and one in the army. I never felt nervous about the boy in the army, but did about the boy in the navy, because according to the traditions of the navy a surgeon must stay with the patients below if the ship is flooded; but it was the boy in the army I lost. I know my boy gave his life for liberty and high ideals. I know he would say, "Go on, father; that is the stuff to give them."

I give you in closing the greeting with which I have been charged from the British Union; I was asked to represent also the Welsh and Irish unions; and, brethren, it is, "The grace of the Lord Jesus Christ, the love of God and the communion of the Holy Ghost be with you all."

"FISHERS OF MEN"

By Rev. John McNeill

John Ruskin said some years ago in speaking to English clergymen. "Remember, when it comes to preaching, you have only half an hour in which to raise the dead. Use as little pulpit frippery and embroidery as possible."

I have less than half an hour, but you are supposed to be living. Our Lord is the greatest example of the soul-winner, and He was always at it. One example of His soul-winning begins, "After these things Jesus went forth" and saw Levi. Matthew, and said, "Follow me." Matthew rose up, and followed Him; and it didn't take twenty minutes. "Rise up, and follow Me." Matthew left all, and followed Him. Jesus went forth; that was His business, seeking and saving. How about us? Is it a mere pastime, or is it meat to our souls? Jesus went forth. and saw Matthew, and saved him.

There is another point there. One would have said. "If you want to save Matthew, a public official. a tax-gatherer, times are very busy." We often wish they would slack up. You would have said, "This is zeal without discretion to go and tackle a man, in order to have him and bring him into Christ's fellowship and discipleship, when he is at work." The Lord spoke to him in the midst of the day's work and said, "It's time to follow me"; and Matthew said, "Is it? I think I'd better come." Jesus said, "Matthew, I want you"; and "Matthew said, "O, do you? Here I am." You know Isaiah said, "Here am I; send me." The modern revised version of this is. "Here am I, send him."

You would have thought it the wrong time and place and man; but you people who risk nothing lest you may be snapped at, lest somebody may growl at you, well, who are you that you should be growled at? Who do you think you are? Is everybody to pat you on the back and give you full credit for the most wonderful motive? Did the Master get that? Did Paul get that? Did any mighty soul-winner ever get that? No. they got rebuffs, and were told. "Your zeal outruns your discretion: and, if you are to save people, be prudent and cautious. so prudent that you say nothing so cautious that you never start." The church is first with it.

Prudence is a drug in the market, and it is hard for a Scotchman to say anything against prudence. I am half Irish; so I can claim the virtues of both countries without the faults of either. Sometimes the Irish gets the better of the Scotch, and I say things. There is a great lesson if you take the Master as a soul-winner. Jesus Christ saw this man at his work, and held him. Follow your Master; and, if some sinner looks down his nose as wise as an owl, refer him to Christ's example. Moody said, "I would rather have zeal without discretion than discretion without zeal." Paul said, "If you want to be wise, become a fool." He said, "I am a fool for Christ's sake." He that winneth souls is wise. If you put it the other way, he is wise that winneth souls; and Levi was a hard case. It was a case of living a noble life, or it was the love of money, and that is one of the most debasing traits. It sings its little hymns, and goes out glad Sunday is over and the money-making begun again.

When the Lord is with us, there is power. That face and two words, "Follow me," and he arose and followed Christ. Give us the power; give us Thyself, or we preach in vain; but give us Thy face, and the self-righteous shall loathe themselves, and the blind be healed, and the blood of the Lamb shall be exceeding fresh. Above all organizations and doctrines you must have what Matthew got, the face of Christ and the word of Christ, and it was successful. He rose us, and followed Him.

The rich young ruler got the same face and word, "Take up thy cross and follow me." The rich young ruler wasn't a blasphemer nor an adulterer; he was an officer in the church, but the face of God was wasted on him. The face of the world held him, and it is frightfully common today.

When John Wesley and Whitefield were in England, organized and established religion had become dead; and God sent power, and people were saved.. It was then they sang the hymns we can scarcely sing today, we are so cold-blooded. "Follow me." The voice of Jesus and the words of Jesus come to me now. No delays if you would ever be a soul-winner; be intelligent; be urgent; now is the accepted time, Matthew; today is the day to be saved, now, now There are two great words that should ever ring on the preacher's or evangelist's tongue, "Thou art the man; now, now." Try this, and see if God isn't with you. There is a glorious, appealing note in the gospel of Christ by the very drama. Don't weaken; but keep up the pitch, the pitch of the Master's voice, "Now, thou, follow Me."

Not doctrines, and I believe in doctrines; I believe in them, and I am a very definite Scotch Presbyterian. We are the creed-makers of the world, and haven't in these latter days given it up. I notice you do not cheer that, but you have a lot to learn. But, you are beginning young, and there is hope for you. Find a good, definite creed, and believe in the Bible as the word of God. It has doctrines, I believe in baptism and praise and prayer and preaching and the collection. But what did Jesus say? He said, "Follow Me." I will allow you, I was going to say, to be a little loose here and there as a soul-winner if you are sound on the person of Christ. Preach Christ. You will need all the doctrines to do it. They radiate from Him; but preach the person, "Follow Me."

You had Houdini here; he was handcuffed and tied up in every way; and then he went behind a screen, and presently a pair of handcuffs came over, and then the rope, and out came Houdini. That is nothing. It is a weak illustration of the glorious liberating power of the Son of man, the liberation of the soul from bondage. This is done through what Paul calls "the foolishness of preaching."

He saves them that believe. The Lord unloosed on Levi the great battery of His presence. Jesus is with us in greater power, the greater dynamo and redeeming grace. Don't hinder Him for your life. Men are dying; graves are opening; Christ is coming; be a soul-winner; you can always count on His presence and the power of that face. There is no other presence or power. Matthew left all, and followed Him. I think Levi looked at that ledger and the receipts and at the ill-gotten gains. I think he said, "This is the Gettysburg of my soul"; but, glory to God, the face won. "Follow Me." Hell was baffled; heaven rejoiced; another soul surrendered to the Christ to God.

Are you doing that today? What an opportunity! Can you be in New York an hour without saying, "What a city to win souls!" With nothing but that face and nothing but that word he was liberated from all the coils that tied him to sin and doom. Do you notice how it is put there? "He left all, rose up, and followed Him." It was put that way for Matthew, the thoroughbred Jew; before he moved off the stool he fought the battle, and without rising from his office stool, he fought the battle, and left all, rose up, and followed Him. There are too many people who seem to rise up on Sunday, take the sacrament, get behind a hymn-book; but the rest of the week their life shows their heart is in the world. When you are half convicted, the outward signs are sure to follow. Remember Lot's wife actually living in Sodom, but the doom of Sodom overtook her. She was a Sodomite down to the ground, and the doom of Sodom overtook her. You cannot cheat God; nobody can. Why should you want to cheat Him?

Be expert in handling the word of the Lord. Are we really set aloof, detached from the world; are we attached with an invisible wall? His heart and soul will find vent through us. He will justify His wisdom in season and out of season, for death is instant in season and out of season. Soul-winners save souls from death, "catch them alive," it says in another place. Jesus is the river of salvation that overflows all its bounds to carry out the boundless energy of Christ's redeeming power.

"EXPLORING FOR THE NEVER-NEVER COUNTRY"

BY REV. VAUGHAN DABNEY, D.D., BOSTON, MASS.

After listening to Dr. McNeill I am sure we feel there is nothing left to say, and we see the point of the story of the three men meeting together talking about their respective nationalities, a Frenchman, Englishman, and Scotch-Irish. The Englishman said to the Frenchman, "If you were not a Frenchman, what would you be?" and the Frenchman said, "I would be an Englishman," and said, "What would you be?" and the Englishman said, "I would be a Frenchman." They both turned to the Scotch Irishman, and said, "What would you be, if you were not Scotch-Irish?" and the Scotch-Irishman said, "I'd be ashamed of myself." I think if we were not Christian Endeavorers we should be ashamed of ourselves, and if we do not aspire to carry out into effectiveness the message of the former speaker we should be ashamed of ourselves.

We have come to the close of the greatest Christian Endeavor convention in the world's history. We are going back to our States, towns, and churches; and the further we go from New York, the smaller becomes our delegation. We have been on the Mount of Transfiguration. We have pierced the veil of the unseen and grasped the eternal realities of the spirit of Christ in our personal obligations to church, state, and to the world. But, when we get back home, the atmosphere is going to be entirely different. We shall not have this vast throng of Christian Endeavorers, or be led by men like these on the platform. We are going back to where things are different, difficult to carry out in reality. In these closing hours I would burn it into your hearts that we are personally obligated to carry out in our own lives what we have seen here.

Kipling's poem, "The Explorer," matches the temper of this Convention. When the Explorer came to the settler's house, the settler said, "There is no use in going further; this is the edge of civilization," but an everlasting whisper rang interminably day and night in the ear of the Explorer, "Something hidden behind the ranges; go." He packed his ponies, found the trail to the mountain-tops, found the pass; lost his pony, and, stumbling upon the country called in derision "the Never-Never Country," found a country rich in oils and minerals undreamed of. It reminds us of Columbus. This poem is a parable.

We have been led to the gospel of the realm of interdenominational co-operation, and that is a powerful feeling. With all respect to the doctrine of predestination, it cannot save the world; Baptists' water cannot save the world; Methodists' fire cannot save the world; but water and fire together make steam. A divided church can never save the world. It is only as Methodists, Baptists, Presbyterians. Congregationalists, and the rest unite their forces that the world can be saved; and Christian Endeavorers are going to do it. When you go back home and explore this "Never-Never Country," the interdenominational country, when one church sings, "Will there be any stars in my crown?" the other churches will sing, "Ten thousand times ten thousand." We are going to find in this "Never-Never Country" a co-operative spirit new in the realm of history.

One day I spoke from the top of a building to workmen in a shipyard. I spoke from the top of a building to get out of range of missiles they were throwing in my direction. One laborer in that ship-building plant said to me. "We will never get anywhere until the capitalists are driven off the map."

I had been to dinner with capitalists that day; and one said, "You know what the trouble is with the world today? We never can do anything unless we keep the laborers just two jumps ahead of starvation."

We have heard that our own Secretary of Labor has said that the only solution for the industrial unrest today is the church of the living God. We heard Mr. Babson say that the Golden Rule is needed in business, and the only thing that will save business is the application of the Golden Rule. Perhaps your father is an employer of labor with thousands under him; perhaps he is an employee in some plant; perhaps you hold some post of responsibility. In a regiment overseas were two sergeants who were full-blooded American Indians, also an Italian sergeant recently made American. He whispered to a comrade, "Those fellows make almost as good sergeants as we Americans." We can take the co-operative spirit between the classes; no color line has been drawn here, but the color line is drawn where you live, and you know the need of the hour. Remember the sacredness of this occasion and that there is neither Jew nor Gentile, bond or free, in Christ Jesus. If the city of Chicago had had one institutional church, the race riot between black and white would not have come. When we apply our Christian religion where we live and when we have learned to be explorers in the realm of patriotism, we shall know that no nation is great unless it is a serving nation, and the greatest thing for America to do is to lead the world in service. and do away with that slogan "America first." unless it means America first in world service. General Bliss said that the world is at the crossroads; either we are going on in the international race for armament, or we are going on into the era of international peace, when "they shall beat their swords into ploughshares." Unless the church mobilizes itself against armament we shall not gain peace; only the church can end world war.

I should like to make this suggestion: Instead of Dr. Clark's having to beg for a paltry million dollars turn over what we waste on one battleship, and we could save the world in one generation.

Finally, let us hold up the ideal of the face of Jesus Christ. It is easy to be religious when you are with religious people; but, when you are with the non-religious, it isn't. Here we have the contagion of the great crowd. There is a materialistic philosophy which throttles idealism so that one journal in this country said that Great Britain and America leading the world hand in hand is an idle dream. but let us hold to the ideal.

The people from Iowa will be interested to remember in that contest conducted by a Paris paper that during the war offered a prize for the best poem by a doughboy. A doughboy from Iowa won the prize. The burden of his poem was, "It is better for one great ecstatic day to strike a blow for glory and truth." They did not die to save their skins; they died for righteousness. We are expected to manifest that same spirit when we return home.

The key our badges refer to is more than the key of hospitality; Christianity is the key to liberty; let your light so shine. You hold in your life by the power of Christ the key to the kingdoms of this world, that they may become the kingdom of our Lord and Saviour Jesus Christ. May this be a consecration meeting. All we have heard in this Convention has focused on that key. to make the kingdoms of this world become the kingdom of our Lord and Saviour.

Endeavorers, carry on; fight the good fight in truth; believe in your mission; meet life with a cheer; that is why you are here. Carry on. May the world be better because of you. Let this be your cry, Carry on, my soul; carry on. God bless you.

CHRISTIANITY THE HOPE OF THE WORLD

By Mr. Fred B. Smith

Mr. Chairman and fellow-citizens:

I doubt if at any time in my life I have ever been introduced upon a great occasion with more mingled emotions than those that characterize my feelings at this moment.

First of all, I have been sitting here for an hour and a half or more which has stirred every emotion within me and carried me back in memory, back to the most precious incidents in my life. First, the pageant, the hope of the young people, the life of the young people that do not believe light is going out, still believe the best is yet to be.

Then the reason for this array, the message from all parts of the world, and only one country represented in which I have not travelled. I have just had a talk with Mr. Lyon, who penetrated Africa with us, and with our young and youthful friend Marsh, who went to Australia. You are very fortunate; I know him well. It is the first time in all his short life that he has ever finished in so short a time. He is just starting on his ministry today; he is just blossoming out into manhood. I have travelled in all this country, and I thank God for the cheer of this hour. I have seen the time when I have had to wait forty minutes past the time I was expected to speak. I have seen the time when I would have gotten nervous. If that could have gone on, I wouldn't have cared whether I was ever introduced or not.

Permit me to say first of all that I am very glad to stand on this platform at this wonderful Convention and add my testimony to the wonder and marvel of the leading of God in this Christian Endeavor society.

I had the privilege of being one of the charter members of the first Christian Endeavor society in South Dakota, and had the privilege of serving as president of that first Endeavor society in South Dakota. I think it is almost an accurate memory which tells me the first time I stood on my feet to give my personal testimony of Jesus Christ, I believe it was given in a Christian Endeavor society. I owe all in Christian training very much to those early years in Christian Endeavor. I think I must be entitled to be a member of the Christian Endeavor Alumni; I am not sure. I wish to say these have been good years, wonderful years; years that give us gratitude to God that this wonderful inspiration has been spread around the world; and I am glad to be in this Convention, which is a most solemn moment in Christian Endeavor work; for we are here to make a program which shall be worthy of the hour in which we are to live. Let us give due heed to the past, only that it may guide us in wise actions for the future. But never let us live in the past or dream of the past. Splendid as has been the past, more momentous will be the years to come.

Some one has given me the subject "Christianity the Hope of the World." I did not get up this topic. I have no address on this subject, never did have, do not expect I ever shall. I expect it was Dan Poling; it sounds like him. I suspect that even he did not understand, nor even Dr. Clark; they did not understand what kind of a setting this would have in the midst of an array that has marshalled nearly the whole world.

This topic raises the question, first, whether the world needs any new hope at this time. That is a serious thing. Is the world asking for a new hope? Never at any time in my life have I read such pessimistic things from men wiser than myself by far than I read in books like Stoddard's "The Rising Tide of Color." If one takes it seriously, the best days are past, and the sun is beginning to set on the present-day civilization. I should like to write him a letter and say he is a fool, and I should like to notify him of it. I am not going to write to him, as he would only say, "Very well then; you disapprove of some of the things I said in my book." I have been reading some of Madison Grant's books, "The Race Clash" and "Race Ambition." I have read Caine on "Economic Results of the Peace Treaty." I have read nearly everything by the great Mr. Wells. Also I have read pretty largely from Sir Philip Gibbs, and heard him lecture in this city. I come to you to say that these very wise men say that civilization is dying. There is a whole array of men who cannot be wiped out in a minute. The only answer I have is fundamentally, essentially that every one of these books, writings, or lectures has failed to recognize God, in the sense in which I recognize God; and yet this Christian Endeavor Convention has no right to run around a certain corner suddenly and wipe out those good men with what they say with some theological and ecclesiastical platitude.

This past week I have been with the two greatest minds in the United States, but it was significant to me that in this past week both said to me, "This present form of civilization is going to die, and something will eventually take its place." One of those men said, "This is the most solemn day since the feet of Jesus walked on the earth." In other words, from China to India, from Maine to California, the world is asking for some new work. This is a solemn hour in the history of the world, and the wisest hardly know the way out.

I want to ask here first of all the privilege of viewing things about the place of this country in this great hour. I wonder if I shall carry my subject too far if I say there is a feeling around the world that America is almost the hope of Christianity; and there are those who are saying that what this country is to do in the next ten or fifteen years will pretty nearly settle the destiny of the world for the next generation at least. I have just returned from Europe as far as Czecho-slovakia. Never in all the history of the world has all the world turned to any one nation for exactly the same purpose as that for which all the world now turns its face anxiously towards the United States. There have been times in the history of the world when some nation made the world afraid. Rome did. There was a time when England made all the world bow at her feet because of her economic power. I was not in London two hours when I was seated at a luncheon-table beside the great Lord Robert Cecil. He is one of the highest-minded Christian gentlemen I have ever met in my life. I should be glad to vote to make Lord Robert the president of the world, if possible. I had not been in London two hours when he leaned over and said, "What do you really think your country is going to do in this hour?" I went to France, Switzerland, Germany, Belgium. It seems to me that every man I talked with asked me that question. I came home with that feeling. Endeavorers, Endeavorers, we have a forum here the like of which exists nowhere. I came back home with this feeling: This nation of ours, in the terms of the kingdom of God, is standing at the crossroads.

One voice in terms of patriotism says: "Our duty in this hour is to look out for our own. The thing we should do now is to make ourselves secure while the going is good." A business man said: "I do not think it fair to inject too much humanitarianism; it may be our chance now; we'd better play the game as we hold the cards." I say this is paganism, not Christian. That voice sums itself up in the hysterical politician who gets somewhere, and shrieks, "America first; to hell with all the rest of the world." That voice is persistent.

I hear another voice calling America to service, sacrifice, to pour out herself for the good of the world, and somewhere, fellow delegates to this world movement somewhere between these two ideals, inside of twenty-four months we are going to feel our America's real heart. I appeal to every society in this country, in God's name have a kind of forum that will advocate that latter doctrine, that latter spirit, and announce that at least the Christian church stands solid for unselfish service for the good of the world. You and I may pause in this assembly today and view these two doctrines, one of service and generosity; one of greed and selfishness. I believe that service on the part of the United States demands that promptly, quickly, and with no longer foolish delay the United States take her place in some organization or guild for the work of peace for the world. I believe this is the Christian duty of this country.

When I say this, I am not a disappointed politician of 1920; so I have the right to say to you what I have said. I wouldn't want to give you a hint about my politics. I voted for Mr. Harding, and I worked very hard for his election; and, Dr. Clark, you remember a time when we sat a whole afternoon voting for Mr. Harding. You may have been right if you voted some other way. Let the facts be what they are, but as a man who voted that way I come back to my country now to find that he failed to make good the promise he made to me in his home in October, and wrote October 22, 1920, what he said in speeches on the platform, and in the White House in June reiterated it to me. I want Mr. Harding to say: "I am not among the seven million against the League of Nations. I did not vote that way." Do you see I have some right to say that those promises ought to be made good, and I am fully persuaded that it is intended to neutralize that thing until it vanishes into thin air? If they succeed, and isolation from other nations shall be the order of this nation, it will be the saddest hour in the history of the United States. For two reasons that promise should be made good, so we can finish the war we commenced in 1917. I hate to be called a "quitter," "sneak," or "yellow." We entered the war to do this: to make democracy safe for the world. Germany is more politically secure than the United States. Every other nation is living over a volcano. We entered the war to end war. Does any one think war is over? If so, go to Europe, and you will find the war is still on. I was in France in 1918 when the drive began. I watched the "Big Berthas" drop every twenty minutes. The German army was coming on, and every one thought they were going straight to Paris. That was in March, 1918. The only tidings were, "Speed up," no quitting then. If America quits in 1921, it will be just as cowardly as in 1918.

There is another reason we have to go into that League or some association. Paul Hymans said at one time: "We want America to come into some kind of an international instrument"; that was the word he used all the time. We must be in that grouping because it is about the best bit I know to prevent more wars. My friends, we are tuning the whole world up for another war, and anywhere you travel the stage is being set for more war; and I have come to this point: I will join anything with anybody that gives the best opportunity for preventing more war. Endeavorers, if some one would tell me today that Mohammedanism would make the world secure against more war more quickly than Christianity, I would be a Mohammedan. I would join anything that would make the world safe against war. I wish to say to you that newspapers and periodicals in a large degree are simply juggling with the possibility of more war. I have a proposal to make. I have a platform that will win. If we are to have another great war, every man in all the world on the day war is declared must sign an absolute statement of how much money he is worth. Then, when the war is over, let them all start at the same place. My friends, inject that in certain circles, and it will discourage war talk. I believe there is a group of people who are organized for the purpose of making war with Mexico to make money. If this is done, it will be the most rotten, damnable thing ever undertaken under the Stars and Stripes. No man shall make any young men go to war; just send men from forty-five to sixty-five, and keep the young men at home. We could take the older men to the battle-front; they would make just as good gun-fodder as the young. There will be a deal less enthusiasm for war on that basis, my friends.

Somewhere there might be a group of men sitting around a table where every grievance can be brought. This seems to be reasonable, and might prevent war. I have wandered over those sights which I cannot describe, three times; words fail to describe it. I do not believe there is any by-product of war. Do not say I am an extreme pacifist. If mere philosophy came riding down the road as it came in 1914, in the same way, and for the same purpose, nothing in God's heavens could we do but fight. But while there is peace, let's begin leavening the leaven that will not let the same philosophy start down the road again for the same purpose.

There is another link to this. This nation must have pressure brought upon it. I believe with all my heart that President Harding, Secretary Hughes, and I am sure Mr. Hoover, and Secretary Hays, those men mean that we shall take our place in that group. It is only the question of finding the better end.

Second, we have a kind of moral contribution that perhaps we can make in a way no other nation can make. Paul Hymans and Lord Robert said, "In God's name, in your name come with us in any kind of a way, leave out geography, reparations, or indemnities."

Paul Hymans said, "We need you because of your moral idealism." They have an idea that, if we start a task of that kind, we follow it through. Perhaps it is because just now we have nailed down prohibition so that only a fool talks about taking it down. If you doubt, get a photograph of the parade of the Fourth of July, which looked like an assemblage of the rag-tag civilization of the earth.

The world is crying today for a moral sanction that will hold and will bind and live; and you can sum that all up by saying, "That is a new appeal to the Christian church."

I was at luncheon with the new prime minister of New South Wales. He said he had heart disease, and was sent away, as he must not speak. I said that whatever heart disease he had, I wish to God I had it. He said, "A little while ago you came down and asked us to win a war for you; you said it was the 'last war.' Now, I have gone to Japan, and I have seen them building guns that will shoot seventy-five miles and hit you in either eye you choose. Now, we have one that will shoot two hundred and fifty miles. I come over here, and you Britishers do nothing but talk about war." Then said the prime minister, "Don't you come down to Australia and ask us to win the war for you." Then Story, that labor leader from Australia said, "I see only one hope. There is only one hope of stopping war, and it might be the Christian churches might be stirred up to stop it. That is the only hope in the world." A little later he said, "I am not pious, I don't go to church, and have not for twenty years; but we have tried Parliaments, newspapers, they can't stop it; and they know it. Let us try the church once." Tolstoy has been saying it: Sir Philip Gibbs says it; Wells says it, "Maybe the churches could be rallied in some world alliance to do it." It all sets back to what the churches are going to do.

You of a younger generation are now filling the places we occupied a little while ago. Young folks talk about a League of Nations, boards of arbitration. You who call yourselves Christians, in the name of God hold your heads high. It is no figure of speech today. Either the leaven of religion will take hold on this world, or we go back.

I said, religion, the church; but let's ask this question: Just what do you mean by religion? I am bound to say this: Religion must have the right kind of organization, and I am here to say that this segregated denominationalism will never leaven the world. Aren't you Presbyterians glad you are here? The Congregationalists are glad they are here; no discussion about Plymouth Rock; aren't you Baptists glad you are here, no debate on quantities? I wish every church that calls itself Christian had its young people in this group.

This movement, the world-leavening for peace, brotherhood, and order is going to be carried by the unit that represents us all, not by any conceited denomination that bids for itself. I do not believe in Christianity that meets in conventions to sing, "Will there be any stars in my crown?" I laugh when I think of it. The idea of thinking of that as religion! That is paganism. That is what their religion is for. If I ever get to heaven and saw a friend going around with one more star in his crown than I had, I'd start a row. Friends, don't you get conceited now about religion being a wonderful thing to save your soul, and then go to heaven to sing first tenor in the chorus choir. I have come to say this: Can this Christianity of ours evangelize the economic world? Every war had at its roots something wrong in economics; and, if we cannot evangelize the economic world so there will be no more riots, strikes, let's blow off. Some men wish to get profit as quickly as possible, and put a premium upon as little as they can do. There is another man at the other extreme, who says, "I have made some money, and I have a right to do anything I wish to with that money." He magnifies the money he uses as if it were his own. Unless our religion can teach this man the sacredness of production and private ownership, we have nothing. Can we evangelize the social and political world? Praise God for men who quietly think of the better interpretation of Jesus Christ. I hope for some man to bring us a definition of Christ. I believe we are only in the kindergarten of some doctrine that will evangelize relationships.

I was in Atlantic City when we passed the slogan, "A saloonless nation in 1920." You may be sure this doctrine has gone around the world. The British Isles are throbbing with that word. Everywhere that there is a saloon in the world there is some "Pussyfoot Johnson" who is going to arrive. Let me give you a new slogan. Give it to every society, in your forum advocate and nail at the masthead the slogan of "A warless world and universal brotherhood." This is big enough to challenge the whole world.

I congratulate you on the past, and bid you buckle on the armor, realizing the future ahead is vastly bigger than anything in the past. In the words you sing so well,

"In the beauty of the lilies Christ was born across the sea,
With a glory in His bosom that transfigures you and me;
As He died to make men holy, let us die to make men free."

Let us young folks die if need be to set this old world free.

CHRISTIAN ENDEAVOR IN PUBLIC LIFE

By Commissioner Frederick A. Wallis

I have just come from Ellis Island. I expected to be in this Convention all the morning, and then expected to conduct services in front of the Subtreasury on Wall Street. I was called to the island regarding matters which had to do with the comfort of six or seven thousand immigrants, a very congested hospital; and five great ships waiting for immigrants to be taken off. It seems to me a crime to keep them in the hot ships in the port of New York because we haven't adequate accommodations at Ellis Island for them, and we are doing what we can to expedite the passage of these people through the gateways of the nation.

I believe there is nothing, Christian Endeavorers, that so affects the commercial, industrial, social and economic conditions of this country as the foreigner, and there is no problem so great as that of the immigrant. I have said before in public audiences that the newspapers and magazines and many public speakers are all wrong when they say immigration is the problem of the nation; and I remember, when I was called to Washington, it was said to me, "If you go, you will undertake the greatest problem confronting Congress and the American people today," and I thought so, too; but now I know that not immigration, but the immigrant, is our problem. We can deal with immigration through legislation and reciprocity, but not with the immigrant. The immigrant is flesh and blood and spirit, and will have to be dealt with in that way. The day is gone when they are treated worse than cattle. I have said that it is possible to make an anarchist overnight at that island, or in a single day he can be started. It depends upon the way he is started on that island. We have looked at the immigrant in the wrong light; we got the wrong slant on him. There are great possibilities for good wrapped up in the life of the immigrant. Every man and woman in this audience has foreign blood in his veins. You are all immigrants unless you are North American Indians. We are all proud of it, that foreign blood. It may be ten generations back, but there it is. Our lines have fallen in pleasant places; we have been educated, and had opportunities for self-improvement. We think of the immigrant as only the day-laborer, the artisan, and do not remember that all have passed through this stratum of society. There is one of these who is a member of Congress, and today there sits in the Cabinet at Washington one who came to this country as an immigrant at five years of age; and, when he was at Ellis Island the other day, I took him out-of-doors to see the sky-line. There was a solid, radiant, blue summer sky, a wonderful inspiration. I said to the Secretary of Labor: "Isn't that a wonderful sky-line? Isn't that an inspiration to people? Look at the little red building, Castle Garden, the Aquarium, where we keep specimens of fish." He said, "When I was five years of age, my brother brought me through that little old round building. My mother brought two feather beds, and they were stolen"; and I said, "They are still fleecing them over on Manhattan." This man has progressed until he now occupies one of the most prominent places in this nation.

I believe that the fundamental, primary proposition in this immigrant proposition is, first, that the immigrant should be inspected on the other side of the ocean, long before he sets foot on the ship to come to this country. I do not know any crime or tragedy so great as to see these hundreds of thousands after they have landed. For then begins the process of separating the just from the unjust, the sheep from the goats, dross from the gold. All this should be done on the other side at the port of embarkation.

I said in a steamship conference this morning, "Gentlemen, it is wrong the way you bring people to this country. Last Sunday sixty

Dr Floyd W. Tomkins

Roger W. Babson

Dr. Vaughan Dabney

Chaplain W. Ramsden

per cent. of those on one steamship had to be set aside for inspection, not fit for American citizenship or domicile. This sifting should be done on the other side."

I could take you to Ellis Island and show you sights that would melt hearts of granite. Judgment-day on Ellis Island is every day. We are just cutting families in two every day, separating husband from wife, children from parents, grandparents from grandchildren, dividing the sheep from the goats, and sending them back to Europe, and to what? To starvation in many cases, chaos, to war, without work, food, clothes, or hope, literally sending these people back to a hell on earth. It is a great crime for these people to come to our doors, and then we say to them, "Depart to the devil and his angels." That's what it is to those from some sections of the world. We put 162 people out for deportation the other day. I could hear them crying, all the way back to the city. There were two women trying to throw their babies overboard, crazed with the idea of going back to Europe. Some jumped overboard. We had literally to carry them by force to the ships. I believe that inspection on the other side is ten thousand times better than rejection on this side. The time should come when the American nation will demand American doctors and inspectors to go to foreign ports and cull out the would-be immigrants. Perhaps you will say that other nations will not be willing for us to come and select the people we believe are worthy of domicile or citizenship of our country. Then, I say, "Let them all stay at home." I think I know whereof I speak.

I went into a room the other day where anarchists are held. I saw on the wall a great solid red flag, and I said, "No flag of that kind shall fly in this nation." I know that it is best for all concerned that only the Stars and Stripes should float in that great parade tomorrow.

I believe this of the foreigner who is coming to our shores today, there is very little difference between him and those men who came first whom we call the "Pilgrim Fathers" landing at Plymouth Rock. I see men every day in the fineness and fibre of civilization, men in uniform just out of the trenches on duty. I have said, "Would you go back and fight over again?" Every one said, "We will do it for America. We lived here before the war broke out, and we mean it."

These anarchists are ready to die for their cause. I said, "Tomorrow you leave this building. You go back to the other side."

They said, "We will never leave Ellis Island until we are free."

I said, "You don't believe in organized government, and every one of you men is going to leave this island tomorrow, if it takes a company of five soldiers to take you out of here."

A tall, black-eyed fellow said, "You can cut me into a thousand pieces before I leave this island." When we took them out the next day, we found that everything that could be destroyed had been destroyed. They left breathing out threatenings and slaughter against the American people. I say we have not standing-room for men with those ideas.

The day has come when we must distribute these immigrants. The cities are now overcongested. I can count on the fingers of my hands the cities where the majority of these immigrants go, New York City, Chicago, Philadelphia, San Francisco, and St. Louis. They are all overcongested, putting up prices of rents and foodstuffs, increasing disease, crime, levying excess taxes, jails, and courts. We should have some say as to where these people should go. The liberty we are enjoying in this house has cost this nation thirty-six hundred battles. Yet these people come to us, and in five years are electing the governor and president. We should have something like Canada, which determines to what provinces immigrants shall go. Here they go anywhere as long as they don't trespass on the life of the other fellow. I believe the time is coming when we shall have something to say of the character of the people brought to our doors, and where they shall be carried. This would build up a contented America.

I shall never forget the spirit I found on Ellis Island where six hundred men and women stood all day long, and women with babies in their arms. I said, "Why not open the door and let in fresh air?" A man who is in the public service and has no idea or conception of his public duties should have a rope around his neck and be pitched into the bay. Public service is no sinecure. I believe the church and public office are the last places for the lazy, for the greatest of these shall be servant of all. I went into another great room. I said to the restaurant man, "How many people did you serve last month?"

"Three hundred thousand meals last month, last Thursday over three thousand meals."

When I went to Ellis Island, there was not a drop of drinking-water. I called the head waiter. "Kaiser," I said, "what's the matter, no drinking-water?" Then I said to two other men, "Turn on the hydrant, if nothing else."

They said, "It would make the floor sloppy."

I said, "The whole island is sloppy; it might as well all be the same."

Everybody was opposed to turning the immigrants outdoors on hot days. I said, "Let them out, and see the great ships, and bask in the sunlight, and catch the inspiration of that great sky-line."

They said, "Immigrants don't like fresh air."

When night came, they couldn't get the people into the house.

The day came when I called "Kaiser" up, and said, "I want you to put sugar on the tables, and give these immigrants sugar Sunday morning for their coffee and charge the steamers."

These immigrants hadn't seen sugar for six years. Were you ever starving for candy or sugar? When those people saw the bowls of sugar, one man emptied a bowl into his pocket, and the women held up their skirts, and poured pails of sugar into them. Tables were knocked over and dishes broken. Those eight hundred people were all yelling, "Sugar" in a babel of tongues. When the "sugar riot" was over, several had to be sent to the hospital with broken ribs. It was all for sugar, the sweet things we all want, the sugar of life.

There are no better immigrants than those from Czecho-slovakia. I wish you women could see the way those Italian women dress. They try to see how many clothes they can put on, and wear from eight to ten skirts.

If Christian Endeavor preaches anything on this earth, it is the sweet things of life. What is sweeter than a smile? Nothing under God's heaven, whether on the face of some innocent baby or some old father or mother of Israel.

"Soon there will be miles and miles of smiles, and you will find it worth while to smile." Words fitly spoken are like apples of gold in pictures of silver, words of comfort and cheer to these people from foreign lands, broken in spirit and pocketbook, lost in the weary whirl. Let us remember the kind smile, the kind word, the kind deed. All these things we are trying to do at the gatewty of the nation, this great kindergarten of Americanization; and we are trying to let the light of heaven into that place so that it will function more effectively and humanely.

Christian Endeavorers, I believe these United States are moving towards social, political, educational, and religious ideals that are prophetic of a nobler day.

THE ENDEAVORER IN ACTION

By Rev. Clarence A. Barbour, D.D.

I am going to talk to you awhile this afternoon about the process of achievement, or the Endeavorer in action, and from long habit I am going to take a text. I am rather accustomed to taking texts when I speak. In fact, I am going to take two texts.

The first is taken from the great tercentenary this year. All of us observed that anniversary, I am sure. We followed the coming of the Pilgrims from their arrival on the bleak shores of this country; we followed them through that first hard winter when the graves multiplied on the hillside. All the time the Mayflower had been lying in the harbor, the Mayflower their only link with home. The ice broke up, and the captain said, "The Mayflower is going home; you can go if you want to, or stay here." The fifty-five left looked aronnd at their bleak environment, and at the forty-seven graves on the hillside, and at the ocean toward their old home, and again at their surroundings. The Mayflower set sail, and soon was below the horizon, leaving only the empty reaches of the sea. They turned to their work of making a nation. That was good stuff, wasn't it? I am glad the blood of the Pilgrims is in the blood of this country; and I am glad other blood is there, too, because a great cosmopolitan nation like this needs more than one factor in the blood in its veins and arteries.

I am glad the blood of the Pilgrims is there. When the Pilgrims came, they brought maps which gave them title-deed to certain parallels toward the Pacific. It took two hundred years before civilization actually crossed the continent, before we got possession of Louisiana, which now has been carved up into a great many of the Middle Western States; and still later the expedition under Lewis and Clark pushed to the Northwest, where are now the States of Oregon and Washington. Only a moment it took to draw those lines on the map, but over two hundred years it took to carry civilization across the continent.

My second text is from Kipling, in the "Explorer." "There is no sense in going further; it is the edge of cultivation." I followed with you this afternoon that principle through a few phases of life. It is the well-disciplined mind; it is the mind accustomed to over-come, that works swiftly and smoothly and powerfully. There is no other way to gain intellectual power save by treading the path between parallels of the farther sea. Give a boy a copy of Homer, Plato, Shakespeare. You say this will give him an opportunity to acquire a knowledge of Homer, Plato and Shakespeare; and there is no other way for him to acquire knowledge of these great writers save by the process of acquirement, threading his way out between the parallels to the outer sea.

I read the other day from Margot Asquith's autobiography. She was out one morning for an early morning ride, and found a tramp by the roadside just arising from a night's repose. She stopped to talk with him, and said: "My friend, I have often wondered about you tramps how you decide which way to start out in the morning. If I am correctly informed, it makes no particular difference to you which way you go." The tramp said: "Why, lady that's easy; every morning we start out with the wind at our back." I know a lot of young people who mentally determine which way they start according to that principle. They always start out with the wind at their back, reading the easiest books, putting out the least effort, always starting and going with the wind at their backs. I heard of a man who purchased a piano for his daughter, and procured a teacher. This man said to one of his neighbors, "Have you heard Mary practising?"

"I should say I had," replied the neighbor.

"What do you think of her execution?" said the father.

"I haven't heard of it, but I approve of it," replied the neighbor.

Apply this same principle to the knowledge of the Bible. How big is your Bible? Your Bible and my Bible is just as big as that part of the Bible which we have actually endeavored to possess. Some people have a Bible made up of Daniel and Revelation, and that is a very dangerous Bible. It always leads to a kind of abnormal development when your Bible consists of only the unfulfilled prophecies. It has been my business to teach the Bible for many years. What a terrible mistake some people make when they think of the Bible as all one level, one great, vast plain! The Bible is a diversified continent. There are mountains and valleys in the Bible. There are fertile and less fertile spaces; some stretches are dry and arid; and there are some stretches so rich they are a great harvest of richness and attractiveness. I have found by long observation that not always the people who are most vociferous in declaration of fidelity to the Bible are really the most loyal and loving toward the Bible. There is such a thing as substituting certain doctrines for real vital search into the mine where lies the incomparable treasure of the word of God.

Enter again upon the process of acquirement and achievement in this matter of knowledge of God's word. You can apply this principle also to the matters of world peace for which we are all praying. To listen to some people you would imagine peace was going to come about by the mere signing of a document, by mere entrance into an association of nations, or something of the kind. Those things might help, but they are not most vital things about the world's peace, after all. How long was this war in preparation? At least thirty or forty years had the German nation been sowing the seed. Bernhardi, Nietzsche, and the rest of their dastardly company were pouring poison into the veins of that friendly nation until practically the whole nation was poisoned, and the whole nation applauded when those German armies crossed the borders of a friendly nation. As long as was the process of inoculation, so long will be the process of elimination. You cannot get poison out of a body any faster than you put it into the body, and it will take a long time, no matter what documents are signed. It is going to take a long time for the peace we pray for to enter the hearts of the people of this world. It will be a process of achievement little by little.

Let me apply it to the matter of discovery of truth. I have a friend in Philadelphia whose name is William W. King. There is no name that stands higher in the realm of surgery in this country than his. He is eighty-four years old. I think we may well quote him at an Alumni meeting. On his eighty-fourth birthday he said, "Long since I gave up the opprobrious phrase 'old age,' and substituted 'accumulated years.' There is a certain joy in continued acquisition of adding one sparkling jewel of acquisition after another to a sparkling store. Don't stop; just keep right along; mix merry laughter with earnest labor; then you will never know ennui to kill time, which is murder in the first degree." Dr. King says that since he began practice these things had come into the knowledge of the world of medicine and surgery, anaesthesia, Pasteur's researches as to bacteriology, Pasteur's and Lister's discoveries leading to antiseptic surgery, the discovery that insects carry disease, the discovery of radio-activity, especially the X-ray—those all have come within the professional lifetime of a man still living. Do you suppose, my friends, that God is going to lead us into the discovery of new truth in the realm of medicine and surgery, and not going to lead us into similar discoveries in other realms, including the realm we call distinctively that of religious truth? I tell you, No. The man that has the same creed when he is twelve years old that he has when he is fifty, is going to come to the time when he is going to lay aside his creed as he laid aside his rocking-horse and drum. And don't be fooled. It is the old-time religion, but all the time God is leading us out into new methods of expressing the old religion. New occasions teach new duties.

The principle of the process of achievement holds in the realm of discovery of health, and also holds in the realm of worth-while living. Van Dyke has set forth in the following lines what worth-while living is:

> "Four things a man must learn to do
> If he would make his record true,
> To think without confusion, clearly,
> To love his fellow men sincerely,
> To act from honest motives purely,
> To trust in God and heaven securely."

There it is, clear thinking, love in our hearts for our fellow men, honest motives and conduct, and being in tune with the infinite, trying to direct our lives according to the divine demand. Do you suppose Christian character out of which a good life comes is built in a day? It is a long process, a long pilgrimage. It is going out and out between the parallels towards the farther seas. As an Alumnus with others of the Alumni around me here I bring you this message on the process of achievement for the Endeavorer in action. Some of us have made a considerable part of the journey. We are going west and west on the great adventure, over the Berkshires, the Alleghenies, over the Rockies, the Sierras, over the farther sea, and as Mr. Gordon said yesterday, there is some one by our side we can't see, and He goes with us on the pilgrimage.

I close with this. Fifty years after a certain class graduated from Harvard they met for a reunion. Oliver Wendell Holmes was a member of that class, and brought with him the poem we all know:

> "Has there any old fellow got mixed with the boys?
> If there has, take him out without making a noise."

Then he has these lines:

> "You hear that boy laughing? You think he's all fun;
> But the angels laugh, too, at the good he has done."

I will tell you what is like those lines. Jesus went about doing good; that is the greatest achievement for the Endeavorer young or old in action. Old and young, I give you the greeting of the Alumni today.

THE CHALLENGE OF THE TEEN AGE

By Rev. A. Ray Petty, D.D.

My topic is "The Challenge of the Teen Age," and I think there is a real challenge there. I was touring last year in an automobile through Oregon, and I soon discovered that Oregon was torn up, its roads being under the process of reconstruction, which meant that sometime Oregon would have splendid roads. We constantly came to signs directing us to "detour," or other signs reading, "Dangerous, but passable." The teen age of the boys and girls of America may be compared to these signs. Our boys and girls of the teen age are under construction to be the men and women of tomorrow. Let me hang this invisible sign around the neck of every boy and girl of the adolescent age.

There are three points in this challenge. First, a challenge to the church. We are not building effectively for the kingdom of God. We have been negligent all over the country. I know great financial campaigns have been inaugurated, but the young men and women of the church have been entirely forgotten, and coming up from the Sunday School their numbers are dissipated, and no one knows where they are. If we fail in that challenge, we fail in what good statesmanship demands. We must preserve that which we have and grip these youths for the kingdom of God.

What is the church going to do with this great industrial problem, with the great problem Commissioner Wallis brought to us, to make America safe? What is the church going to do in these days for world peace? What are we going to do with the promises made to the khaki lads who went across? We have only a short time in which to furnish this leadership. The challenge of the teen age is for the interpretation of Christianity that meets their particular problem. They are not interested in theology or theological doctrines. They tell us they want a hero; they want somebody who shall typify for them what is the best in life. Where shall we find a greater hero than Jesus Christ? I want them to understand that this boy and girl can be challenged by His life, challenged by His sacrifice, by the beauty of His service. Let me make Jesus a hero to the boy, and I will take chances on his theology when he becomes a man.

This other challenge is this: They challenge us to go far on a constructive program of action in the kingdom of God; a program of prohibition is very vital. Accept Jesus as their hero. Think of some heroic action He gave to us. I don't believe any red-blooded boy or girl is going to be normal if they can't enjoy prayer meetings. What they do enjoy is a program of action, where they can enlist their lives in service for others. Then we can make prayer meetings a means to an end, and we have a real challenge, and they are waiting for us to take the challenge. If you say, "Don't," "Don't" all the time, you lose your boy. A wonderful thing about these boys and girls is the spirit of making sacrifice. It was a little church boy down in the slums of the East Side who saw a little girl in an accident two blocks away from home. The little girl was taken to a hospital where it was decided an operation was necessary, but owing to loss of blood the surgeons said there must be a transfusion of blood first. Men who would sell their blood were brought in, but none was found to be of the right consistency. An interne came in and said a boy a brother of the little girl wanted to see her. White-faced, out of breath, great drops of water on his face, a lad of thirteen, a Jewish boy, came in. He was afraid as he saw the doctor, but he knew that somewhere in that hospital his sister was. The surgeon's face broke into a smile. They took the boy to the operating-room, and soon the boy's heart was pumping blood into his sister's veins. After the operation was over, and the boy had been bandaged, they noticed that he was very restless; and finally he said, "Doc, when do I croak?" Although he had thought that the operation meant his life, he had not asked a question. These teen-age boys and girls are willing to open up their veins to Almighty God in heroic service if we give them the chance. Give them the chance for discipline and service in sacrifice for the great kingdom of God.

TRAINING FOR LEADERSHIP

BY REV. C. E. HETZLER

Ordinarily, we would say that the subject of this address should be discussed before Intermediates and Intermediate workers, rather than in a Junior conference. A better vision of our opportunities and responsibilities, with relation to youth, and a closer study of the psychology of boy and girl nature, have revealed to us great possibilities in child-training, and a necessity of revision of our methods.

A continual disturbing and recasting of ways and means of dealing with young life is unwise, and unnecessary, while on the other hand traditional adherence to customs, established long ago, just because we always have done things in a certain way, is nothing short of ridiculous—yes, even sinful, when viewed in the light of our obligations and responsibilities to the rising manhood and womanhood of our time.

There are three facts which especially commend this subject for our consideration in a Junior conference: first, that time is fleeting, and ere we are aware, the boys and girls of today will be men and women of tomorrow; second, that more than we realize, the fundamental qualifications for leadership, are being developed in the child life, during the Junior years. The hackneyed phrases "Sot in his ways" and "As the twig is bent" lose none of their significance because they are commonplace; third, more than ever before is the age limit being removed as a qualification, or rather a determining factor, in choosing leadership, and more and more are conditions demanding young leadership—at least young in spirit, if not in years.

A sage has said, "The child is father to the man." It is not difficult, all contingent circumstances, and environment being normal, to predict with a remarkable degree of accuracy, just about what will be the tenor and fortunes of a child's life when once he has reached maturity. This is not denying the possibility of a great super-force coming in and recasting, in some particulars, the mis-molded life, but it does recognize the tendency to fixedness of character in the human life.

The speaker spent a summer vacation, working in a cement factory. It behooved the workers there to mold the mortar into whatever forms desired, within a certain limit of time, and any defect in workmanship of the molder was there to stay unless the material was reduced by crushing and pulverizing to its former state and then again treated with the original process. Even then, can you imagine the unnecessary waste of time and effort, in the remolding—unnecessary we say, because of inefficient workmanship? What actually happened, in almost all cases, was that the defective products were either consigned to the junk heap or put on the market, "reduced in price." It was found to be more profitable to let the imperfect output go for what it was worth and spend the time and effort on fresh, virgin, plastic material.

We may easily, and each one for himself, make the application of the thought, to the subject before us—"training for leadership." Consider the great waste of time and effort, in remolding a defectively formed life, occasioned by commissioned molders, pastors, Junior superintendents, Sunday School teachers, parents, public school teachers, and others being inefficient. Remember, also, that what actually happens, in a majority of cases is that the inefficiently trained leadership, is either "junked" or put on the market "reduced in price."

What has been said might well be a preface to remarks on any phase of Junior training. We relate it for the present purpose, to "training for leadership."

Not long since, we visited a former pastorate, where we found as president of the Senior society, a young lady who had been one of our sweetest and most interested Junior Endeavorers. It seemed, as we sat in that Christian Endeavor service, that it was but yesterday when as we gave those Juniors goodbye, we told them that we would be very much disappointed, if, when we passed that way, from time to time, we should not find them assuming their proper places in the leadership of that church, as Sunday School teachers, Christian Endeavor officers, stewards, trustees, etc., and even giving their lives in definite full-time service to the Lord.

In what particular ways will Junior training of today affect leadership of tomorrow?

If it be true—and we believe that generally speaking, it is—that things first learned are last forgotten; if it be true that childhood is the most receptive, and susceptible period of life; let us see that during these days and years of childhood, the things that make for the best leadership, shall have first hearing.

And what are some of these things which have a first claim on our attention?

First, *Service.*—We will not forget the words of the Master (Matt. 20:26-28) "Whosoever will be great among you, let him be your minister, and whosoever will be chief among you let him be your servant; even as the Son of Man came not to be ministered to, but to minister."

The world needs leadership today—not the leadership of bosses, but of servants.

Let us teach our boys and girls the principles of service, and let us also "clinch" our teachings by properly recognizing and rewarding service. Let us so plan the activities of our Juniors that they will find "joy in service."

Second, *Obedience.*—The Lord spoke through his prophet, Samuel, to one of the greatest leaders of his people, and said, "to obey is better than sacrifice" and Saul admitted that he had not obeyed the voice of the Lord and we know the sad story of the end of Saul's life.

But we will remember, also, the glorious crowning of the life of another man named Saul—Saul of Tarsus, better known as Paul—who, when on trial said, "I was not disobedient to the heavenly vision."

The world needs obedient leadership today—not grovellingly obedient to all demands, whether they be good or evil, which would result in disgusting vacillation, but obedient to the high and noble commands of Him whose we are, and whom we serve. Let us teach our boys and girls obedience to those in authority, whether it be God or man— obedience in the home, in the Junior meeting, in the Sunday School. Ofttimes, Junior superintendents feel that they have no right to demand obedience from boys and girls, not their own. In fact, they have no right to ask for the boys and girls, for the Junior meetings, unless they set for them, very worthy standards of obedience and respect for God's house, and insist on their "striving" to reach them.

Third, *Fairness.*—We have in mind, honesty, and would use that term, were we addressing ourselves to work for the Senior society. Honesty suggests uprightness in the exchange of tangible temporal values. Inasmuch as in the boy and girl at play, we see the man or woman at work, we use the word "fairness" for the sake of its connotation. The world is insisting on fair play, in its leadership, today. Show me the child that plays fair and I will show you an individual, that will in future years, be foursquare in his relations to his fellowmen.

In our Junior meetings—social meetings, especially—we have a wonderful opportunity to observe fair play, or lack of it, and wield a wonderful influence for good in the child's life, in this respect.

The evil effect of unfairness increases, in direct ratio with the increase of influence of the individual, hence we should, in our Junior work teach children to play fair, literally, in their play, that they may "play fair" when they come into positions of influence.

Fourth, *Trust and Dependence on God.*—We will bear in mind that in our Junior work, we are not training boys and girls for definite full-time religious service, alone. Innumerable are the testimonies to the benefits of Christian Endeavor training coming from men and women, engaged in secular work—political, medical, legal, etc. Many of these testimonies bear special reference to Junior training—more and more shall we hear testimonies in reterence to Junior training, as the Junior work is developed and more Junior societies are organized.

Were we pleading for training of religious leaders only, we could well take time to dilate on the necessity of trust and dependence in God, for how can they impart, as exponents of divine truths, and blessings, that which they do not even possess? And may we say it—we believe we as religious workers would see greater fruits come from our efforts, if our faith were but more simple and absolute.

But we emphasize this phase of Junior teaching and training, having in mind, especially, leaders in secular life. Does it mean anything to us to have a president of our nation who turns naturally, as he takes up the arduous duties of office, to Psalm twenty-five and reads "The troubles of my heart are enlarged; O bring thou me out of my distresses. Let integrity and uprightness preserve me, for I wait upon thee"? Are we not honored, that such a man as Frederick Wallis, who heads the New York committee of this great Convention, and who is a fullblooded Endeavorer, is Commissioner of Immigration at Ellis Island? Are we not delighted with the testimonies to their interest in Christian Endeavor and Civic Righteousness, coming from the governors of several of our states?

Multitudes, in constantly increasing numbers are demanding leaders "who trust in the Lord, and do good." (Ps. 37:3.)

Junior workers, who can tell what influence for good you may be exercising in your own church and denomination, in your community, in your city, state or nation—yes, the world—as you lead the boys and girls who naturally love and trust God, into a more fixed and abiding faith in God?

Fifth, *Administration.*—Not all of the benefits are included in the realm of the strictly spiritual. What a blessing it would be if the hundreds of folks who manifest embarrassment and awkwardness, when called upon to lead a mid-week prayer meeting, or speak in a missionary meeting, in the presence of a mere handful of folks, had had Junior training in the matter of public testimony, prayer, and supervision of a meeting. If this meeting were thrown open for testimony, many of you could name boys and girls who have developed wonderful executive ability, through the Junior offices and "the variety of committee work." It is a great advantage to have these positive habits formed by Junior training for church leadership, rather than some day to find ourselves fettered by negative habits in our church relations.

Sixth, *The Word.*—We have not pretended to list these six great factors in "Junior training for leadership" in the order of their importance—we leave that to you, as well as, to list, in your own minds, other phases of Junior training for which we have neither time nor space.

We cannot omit mention of Junior training in the Word, nor can we more than touch upon this great subject.

In harmony with the words of the Psalmist, who said, "Thy Word have I hid in my heart, that I might not sin against thee," we are sure that there is no more effective antidote to national and international, as well as individual sins, than the Word of God. God's Word is still true, and we read Ephesians 6:12 that we wrestle "not against flesh and blood, but against the principalities. against the powers, against the world-rulers of this darkness, against the spiritual hosts of wickedness in the heavenly places."

It may seem to be a long way to travel to our destination but nevertheless we are confident that the surest way to bring in the reign of our Lord, is to get His word, which, is truth, into the hearts of men and women, everywhere—especially our leaders in all walks of life.

If these promises be true, and we assume that they are, what greater service can Junior Christian Endeavor render in training leadership, than to promote training in God's Word?

In a few brief words of closing, may we suggest that some may fear that this is a rather heavy diet for Junior boys and girls. May we remember that all truth is a challenge to our finite minds, and the problem before us is to so present it that the child may grasp it. We should present these truths not in a childish way, but in a way adapted to children, and we may rest assured that with God's blessing, they shall be "as seed sown in good ground."

WORTH-WHILE MISSIONARY DEMONSTRATIONS

BY M. JOSEPHINE PETRIE

What makes a missionary demonstration "worth while"? What is the aim of a missionary demonstration? Certainly it is not to develop actors and actresses not to nurture the drama, but to make missions and missionary people vivid through reproducing the lives and environment of people of "the other world." Therefore of first importance is an object for the play and a demonstration which shall fit the object.

Settlement workers and teachers among foreign speaking peoples have found the pageant the most efficient form for teaching American history, laws, customs, etc. Child Welfare organizations found it expedient to teach sanitation, prevention of disease, etc., by this method.

There are various forms of missionary demonstration such as plays, pageants, tableaux, monologues, impersonations, questions and answers, conundrums, charades, etc. The missionary demonstration should instruct through impression, intensify the interest in missions of the persons taking part; make the people and the work so real that new members will be added to the society, create a desire to serve on the missionary committee and so interest the people of the church that they will always respond when an invitation is given to share in a program prepared by the C. E. Missionary Committee. Sometimes the aim of this demonstration will be to present the missionary budget for the year, sometimes to inspire the giving of money and of self, sometimes to help present the work of one special field or of one specific mission station.

The leader, or director of a missionary play must be carefully selected—one with tact to choose assistants who will enter heartily into the spirit of the parts they are to represent. He must be able to see things that may be far away and to make other people see them. He must have patience, perseverance and imagination. Scenery is not a necessity but it creates an atmosphere, a good or bad atmosphere according to how it harmonizes with the rest of the properties. Gestures of the body, facial expression and tones of voice are necessary. Costumes add to the effect and as a general thing amateur costumes leave a lasting impression. Flags always make effective drapery for the representatives of any country. The music should be in harmony with the theme of the demonstration.

The increased demand for missionary dramatics is of interest and the publication committees of the Mission Boards are constantly seeking help in the production of plays for the use of all departments of the church. The evolution of some of the older story leaflets is also interesting. For illustration, the story of the little mountain girl—"Cindy's Chance"—of which over 39,000 copies have been printed. At first it was a small folder, then increased for an impersonation, next enlarged as a dialogue, later made into a "play" for several characters and is now extended to an 18-page pamphlet.

A "worth while" demonstration for some societies is one which shows how the Board works. Several Boards publish demonstrations of this kind. Always consult the catalogues of your own denominational missionary Board in some of which will be found many pages of suggestions for long and short demonstrations—allegorical, musical, medical, historical, financial, stories of heroes and of pioneers, plays showing "how not to do it," Americanization and patriotic plays; splendid plays and pageants which weave together Home and Foreign Missions; plays showing "the evolution of the mite box" or the evolution of a box for the mission field. A beautiful play is tried out at summer conferences called "The Lifted Cross," another "The Church Victorious Through Love" is spectacular and one which will leave an indelible impression on the audience.

Always keep on file the latest catalogue of the missionary publications of your Board.

MESSAGES FROM CANADA

By LIEUT. W. STEENSON

It gives me great pleasure to bring to this, the Sixth World's Christian Endeavor Convention, a message of greetings from Western Canada that great Northwest country, with its many forests, fertilizing streams and vast industrial resources; where fifty years ago stretched wide unproductive plains over which roamed the Indian and the buffalo.

The prairies, "unshorn fields, boundless and beautiful," have undergone a marvellous transformation in these few short years. Still do they extend "boundless and beautiful" to a far horizon, but they are no longer the "unshorn fields," today vast wheat fields yellow to the golden harvest, and rich pasture lands stretch out to the golden West. Beautiful cities, and prosperous towns have sprung up as if by magic. Railroads and autos now follow the Indian trails, over which, groaning and squeaking, the Red River cart wended its way fifty years ago.

"Where once the silent red-man spurned the ground,
A land of peace and plenty now is found.
A land by nature destined to be great,
Where every man is lord of his estate."

To this great land peoples are coming from every country, and the church of Christ is confronted with the problems that are sure to arise in a new land. The Christian Endeavor Union of Manitoba, under the guidance of the great leaders of this world wide organization, is striving to do its part to carry out the great commission Christ gave to His disciples. We have these problems to face, let us consider the means to be employed for the advancemnt of our work, and the removal of the things that hinder the gospel of Christ in this new land. We need not expect God to do this work by a miracle. Human hands must roll away the stone, though the Lord of All is about to call the dead to life.

The bugle sounds reveille there's work for all to do, if we mean to keep the Christian Endeavor banner floating on the breeze. No, friends, until we as members of this great organization have done our duty in this respect we have no right to look to heaven for its blessing.

As the lovers of the well being of man, and of the souls of men, we who represent Western Canada, all combine to say—we shall see this thing through. We must not jog along in the old beaten track, nor sit in listless inactivity, and expect to have the benefit ot others' energy without any effort of our own. We are not to sit and sing ourselves away to everlasting bliss, while others fight to win the prize, and sail through troubled seas.

No man more highly esteems and honors the Canadian people than I do. I know their virtues and their valour; I know they can achieve anything but impossibilities; and I know that winning the world for Christ is not an impossibility; but we must all do our duty, and with the performance of duty will come wisdom, and with wisdom will come patience, because we shall learn to understand that what is gained easily too often passes quickly. God helps those who help themselves. That is what God gave us brains for, to use them, that is all there is in life—the use we make of it, as progression only in the cause of right and justice secures certain victory in the end.

"Wrong the right is hard assailing, all advances to defy;
Never mind, God's help availing, right will conquer wrongs entailing
Forward banners, never trailing, forward let us do or die."

We extend our greetings to this convention, wishing it every success; and our prayer is that Dr. Clark, our president, and all who are associated with him in this great and noble work, may have the peace of God that passeth all understanding, and may the Lord preserve them from all evil; preserve their going out, and their coming in from this time forth and for evermore. May they know that what they are sowing shall be reaped by them that come after us when bells in unbuilded spires, and voices of unborn choirs shall bless their name and the good work they have done; and may they be happy in knowing that the 'saplings they sent out, though perhaps they grew too slowly to give shade to us, will make the green and healthy everlasting bowers where our children's children's homes shall be.

Christian Endeavorers arise to the call,
Fling out the banner of Jesus our all.
Win for the Master the brightest and best.
Fair Manitoba, the Queen of the West.
Then will her prairies, so boundless and free. •
Offer their harvests, O Master to Thee,
Then lake and hillside their treasures will bring.
Glad dedications to Jesus our King.
God bless our Country with wisdom from Thee.
God bless our young men and maidens so free,
God bless our wheat fields waving with gold,
God bless our churches with treasures untold.

Manitoba, won for the Lord,
Manitoba, won for the Lord,
Then will she stand at the Saviour's right hand.
That will be glory for Manitoba.

CHRISTIAN ENDEAVOR IN BUSINESS

By Mr. Winslow Russell

Arthur F. Sheldon spells "business" with a "y." Wherever that word appears it reads as "busyness." Using his spelling, then, we would have our topic "Christian Endeavor in Busyness." These are days of tremendous import on the question of real "busyness"—morally, commercially and spiritually. One might be tempted to feel that there had been a breaking down in all three of these. While we should not be unduly pessimistic we must be careful not to get ourselves into excessive optimism. We must find a proper balance. We must seek facts on which to base reasonable optimism. Would these lines not accurately express the conditions as they exist?

"The country swarms with speculators who are searching all places, from the stores of the wealthy to the recesses of indigence for opportunities of making lucrative bargains. Not a tavern can we enter, but we meet crowds of these people who wear their character in their countenances. . . . . It is remarked by people very illiterate and circumscribed in their observation, that there is not now the same confidence between man and man which existed before the war. It is doubtless true; this distrust of individuals, a general corruption of manners, idleness, and all its train of fatal consequences, may be resolved into two causes—the sudden flood of money during the late war, and a constant fluctuation of the value of the currencies."

Strange as it may seem, this last paragraph is taken from the historian, Green, and the Essays of Noah Webster on the American Revolution. We, who are optimists, then, may feel that we are in a period of history repeating itself. If those who own the Nelson's loose-leaf encyclopedia will turn to the word "composite" you will find a full page picture of the composite of a thousand men's faces photographed into one picture. This composite photograph of a thousand men today will almost startle you with its close resemblance to the pictures of the Christ Himself. It is probably true that the composite of a thousand faces of men and women today is more nearly like the face of Christ than a similar composite of a thousand faces taken a hundred years ago would have been. If we do our duty today the composite of a thousand faces one hundred years from now will more nearly resemble the perfect face than would the composite picture of today.

Applying this illustration, then, to the present world situation, may it not be true that the composite of the American business conditions—morally, commercially and spiritually—show a distinct and marked advance over the composite cited in the paragraph quoted above from Revolutionary times? My belief is that there are easier and more far-reaching remedies for the ills in America today, which are so closely following similar ills following every great war, than there have ever been before. My real belief that there are better remedies for the ills of today than ever before is based upon my picture of the composite Christian Endeavorer in his "busyness."

Just previous to the opening of the World War a beautiful yacht lay in a harbor near one of the entrances to the Kiel canal. The name of that yacht was the "Hohenzollern." It was owned by William the Emperor. He was entertaining an American yachtsman at the races on this particular day. In the evening the American yachtsman was dined on this yacht by the emperor. Following the dinner a moralizing discussion took place. The substance of the discussion follows:

The American said, "The world seems determined to discuss emperors and czars and kings. Do you not think it possible that another hundred years will have seen the end of emperors and czars and kings?"

"Yes," replied the emperor of all the great German Empire, "that may be so."

"Assume," said the American, "that such changes should take place. In your opinion what form of government will take the place of our empires and kingdoms, and what nation will then be leading the thought of the world?"

After a few moments of deep thought the emperor replied: "I do not know what form of government will follow such changes as may take place, but your other question I think I can answer. The leading nation of the world a hundred years from now will be that nation which as a nation first gives up alcohol."

About that time a convention similar to this one was being held. A slogan was adopted. That slogan was: "A Saloonless Nation in

1920." It is likely that hundreds of thousands who read of that slogan thought it but an idle dream. How can Christian Endeavor in Business be better described? How can there be found a better illustration of undreamed of accomplishments with a vitalized force of people who mean "busyness" putting themselves into such an effort? There is enough potential power in this room at this time to revolutionize the world if it will but get busy and keep busy. The remedy for the ills of the moral and commercial and spiritual world today is an exceedingly simple one.

The story is told of Dr. Edward Everett Hale which has a bearing on this point. It is said that a considerable group of young men were seated at dinner with him one evening. One of them turned to him and said, "Dr. Hale, I just long to do something tremendously great thing in life—to accomplish a big thing. Tell me, please, from your experience, how can I begin to accomplish that great thing?" "It is very simple," said the great preacher, "I know of no better way for you to begin to do that great thing than by passing me the butter, if you please."

A great western concern has in its executive offices a motto which reads as follows: "Do unto others as though you were the others." Here is the essence of the solution of the whole world problem of today. A careful study reveals the fact that when this nation started a year ago last November into a period of business depression, largely surrounding, as it did, the automobile industry, during the period of inflation the users of automobile tires were overstocked in this country alone by seventeen million tires. The tire speculator in New York or the tire user who carried his unnecessarily large number of tires on hand didn't realize that the word "others" in this case extended to the rubber fields of the Island of Java. But the fact that America was overstocked by seventeen million unused tires is the reason why the Island of Java today is suffering with unemployment. The Golden Rule of a hundred years ago did not extend to the Island of Java in the rubber industry, but the American citizen today cannot contribute to the real "busyness" of American life without the knowledge that his act affects every part of this great world. It is a tremendous challenge to Christian Endeavor.

How can we let our light shine so that in some way we can bring back into the moral and commercial and business life of this world the simple remedy of those few words, "Do unto others as though you were the others"? Simply by keeping everlastingly at it.

A great writer has recently put these three words into a nationally circulated article as the three great needs of today in the world: "Work," "Tolerance," "Faith." Those of you who have not read the book, "The Day that Changed the World," by the man who was warned should buy it. It will tell you a story of tremendous possibilities, how unconsciously on a given day all the professing Christians of the city of London determined for one period of twenty-four hours to live exactly what they preached. A revolution in the way of service to the populace took place at once.

This country has had "National Thrift Weeks" and "National Gift Weeks" and national drives of all kinds. Why not at this great gathering start the wheel in motion for a great national drive to be known as "Golden Rule Week"? Let us put in the windows of our homes and our shops and our stores mottoes similar to the Red Cross and other insignia which might say, "This is Golden Rule Week. We pledge ourselves for seven full days to do unto others as though we were the others." This is truly applied Christian Endeavor in Business. We can do but little alone. With work and tolerance and faith we could carry out an actual revolution that would revitalize the morals, the business, and the religion of this whole earth of ours, and it is commended to this audience for thoughtful consideration as the great opportunity of the hour.

FLOATING CHRISTIAN ENDEAVOR

BY HAINES A. REICHEL

General Secretary, Pennsylvania Christian Endeavor Union

Mr. Chairman and Christian Endeavorers from all the World:

If you happen to be one of those who is unfamiliar with this department of Christian Endeavor work the subject assigned to me for a short discussion this morning may have misled you a bit because of your first impression on reading it. Christian Endeavor is by no means afloat, as my subject might suggest, it is anchored to the solid rock Christ Jesus, and has been for all these forty years of its splendid history.

The title rather refers to one of the very special departments of Christian Endeavor work and exemplifies in a very definite way Christian Endeavor as a real Christian service organization; a group of Christian young people banded together to serve others for the sake of "Christ and the Church," truly, as Dr. Clark said, "a Foursquare Organization" but many, many-sided in her activities.

You have heard this morning of "Fresh-Air," "Hospital." "Rural" and "College" Endeavor, and now what of "Floating" Christian Endeavor?

This department and its activities, like the other service departments of Christian Endeavor, takes Christian Endeavor to those who otherwise might not have the opportunities to enjoy its privileges. It particularly takes Christian Endeavor to the sailor boys on the Naval and Merchant Marine vessels that ply the great oceans, lakes and streams of the world and sends them out from port with a real uplifting thought of a true and all-powerful God who, through Christ His Son, can rule men's hearts today as Christ ruled the sea in days of old. What better companion for the seafaring man than the Ruler of wind and wave?

The work of the Floating Department is usually carried on through union activities in cities which are situated on or near navigable waters, and consists in the main of doing the following things:

1. Establishment of a Floating Department or committee in the local, State, provincial or National Christian Endeavor Union with a superintendent or chairman in charge of the work.

2. The organization by this Department or Committee of Christian Endeavor Societies on board the ships while the vessels are in port. The activities of this society are continued by the sailor members while the ships are afloat—thus the name "Floating Christian Endeavor."

3. The conducting of religious meetings for the seamen on board the ships while they are in port or in special meeting places on shore during the sailors' shore-leave. During such meetings the team which is working presents copies of the separate Gospels, the New Testament or a Bible to the men who will accept them and promise to read them.

4. The establishment of seamen's homes and recreation centers in cities where ships dock for the loading or unloading of cargoes.

5. The band of Endeavorers who comprise the party go to the meeting prepared to sing the songs of Zion and to offer prayers in the meetings and to speak about the Good News of Christ to these men who are away from their homes free from the restraint of parental oversight, out of the communities where they are known and consequently free from the surveillance of friends and others and because of all this subjected in a greater degree to all the temptations of a shore city. If it were not for the Floating Departments of many of our Christian Endeavor

Unions there would be no one to help these splendid fellows resist such temptations and while on shore help them to "go straight."

6. Our Floating Committees also frequently arrange special seamen's socials to which the ships' crews are invited and through these occasions an excellent opportunity is given for the committee to provide some forms of amusement as a substitute for the public dance halls, pool rooms, immoral picture shows, licensed liquor saloons and other recreations and so-called amusements which the fellows are tempted to hunt as soon as they land.

At such socials they are also invited to attend the local societies where they are made acquainted with the members and in every way possible are made to feel at home while they are on shore.

7. Another splendid service which Floating Endeavor renders is to minister to the sailors in times of sickness, by visiting them while in the hospitals, taking with them flowers, a message of cheer and Christ, and some good clean reading matter which is always very much appreciated especially during the convalescent period. Such ministrations in the name of Christ are rendered usually in the absence of the boys' loved ones and compensates in a measure for their absence.

8. Thousands of pieces of good literature in the form of tracts, magazines, religious stories and Scripture passages are distributed during a year's time and are highly prized by the boys as they have some spare time for reading while on the sea.

9. One of the most appreciated services that is rendered to the boys is the endeavor to make the special holidays joyful and happy for these young men who are away from home. To this end many of the unions arrange special meetings at these seasons of the year, they set up and decorate Christmas trees for the sailors, give each man some little Christmas gift as candy post-cards or a comfort bag.

These gifts which are presented are paid for, or are provided by the union of which the department is a part. The work done by the Pennsylvania Union is largely done through the Philadelphia County Union Floating Committee with the help of the State Union Department. Money to carry on this work at the Port of Philadelphia is provided by individuals and the various County Unions of Pennsylvania, from the State Union and many of the seamen who have been helped gladly and frequently send contributions to the Floating Department.

Some marvellous figures are presented to you in the parade on Saturday noon on the float representing this phase of Christian Endeavor work and what Philadelphia County has accomplished presents a challenge to other unions which may be so located as to make such work possible.

The State Floating Department and the Philadelphia Committee have the endorsement of the shipping companies and the good will of the ships' officers and hold passes issued by the Director of Wharves and Shipping which admit them without question on board any ship which comes in.

Among the gifts presented to the sailors, the sailor's comfort bag has probably been appreciated as much as any.

The comfort bag is a 10 by 1 inch, brightly colored cloth bag with a draw string at the top and is filled with useful articles which the sailor can use in keeping his clothes in proper repair, including needles, thread, emery, pins, darning cotton, wax, thimble, buttons and scissors. Also some first-aid material as vaseline, bandages, cotton, etc. A Testament or Bible and a personal letter from the one who filled the bag, written in the name of Christ and Christian Endeavor to our "Sailor Brother." These bags are filled at a cost of 75 cents.

The figures displayed on the chart in front of me show the remarkable work that has been done by the Philadelphia Floating Department with the help of the State Union during the past year.

AT THE HEAD OF THE PARADE

NEW YORK IN THE PARADE

The Chart

Meetings held	361
Ships visited	896
Barges	25
Song services	122
Requests for prayer	71
Conversions	-64
Socials held	26
Papers and magazines distributed	11,523
Comfort bags distributed	1,250
Christmas trees trimmed	13
Christian Endeavor helpers	3,197
Visits to sick sailors in hospitals	428
Total men reached	15,132
Women reached	70
Testaments distributed	737
Gospels distributed	674
Tracts distributed	14,970

The gentleman on my right is our State Floating Superintendent, Mr. O. M. Tressler, and the gentleman on the left is the Associate Superintendent, our former chief, Mr. Walter M. Lewis.

If your union is located near the water establish a Floating Department when you go home or if it is not do the best you can to support this work in some other section of your State, province or union.

For the good that can be done for the sailor boys, for the joy that you will derive from rendering a real Christian service, for the sake of Jesus Christ and what He can do for a needy soul I recommend to you the work of Floating Endeavor.

TRAINING FOR LEADERSHIP

S. W. DENDY

Field Secretary, South Carolina, Georgia, Florida and Alabama

From this Convention and from these conferences two facts have undoubtedly impressed us. First, today, as never before, the United States and the world feels very deeply the need of Christian leadership. And, second, we must begin the training for this Christian leadership among the boys and girls in the early teens and even younger.

We hear a great deal today, we young people do, about skilled surgeons and about skilled teachers and about skilled diplomats and engineers and attorneys-at-law, and we need them every one. But outside the church and inside the church you do not hear so very much about a skilled Christian. And even though we admire the man or the woman who can work skilfully and even though we know that the work of the world has been changed most and has progressed most by skilled men and women yet in our religious affairs we have too long neglected the sound counsel of Paul to his young friend Timothy, "Study to show thyself approved unto God, a workman needing not to be ashamed, rightly dividing the word of truth."

I heard a great southern educator say recently that if we place the scythe that was used in the time of Ruth by the side of a great 1921 McCormick reaper anyone could see the marvellous progress in machinery and science from the day of Ruth to the day of Mrs. McCormick. But, he said, if we draw a line, straight from the heart of Ruth to the hearts of men and women in the time of Mrs. McCormick, do we see such proportionate progress there? In other words, has the great heart of Christianity grown in proportion to the great heart of Commerce, and has the Gospel since Calvary been carried forward with as much enthusiasm as has the distribution of new machinery? Perhaps it has,

but if it has why is it that half the world today has no teacher; half
the world has no doctor; half the world has no Bible; and half the
world never has heard the name of Jesus Christ? It is not because
there is any fault in the gospel, but it is because men and women who
call themselves Christians have not tried to become skilled Christians,
have not studied to show themselves approved unto God, workmen needing not to be ashamed.

And how desperately we need skilled Christians! The great Interchurch World Movement tells us that there are three enormous armies
invading Christian United States today—one army of five and one-half
million illiterates above ten years of age; a second army of twenty-seven
million Protestant children not reached by any religious training school;
and a third army of fifty-six million people above ten years of age in
the United States not connected with any church, Catholic, Jewish or
Protestant. They tell us that these three armies, marching in double
file at the rate of twenty-five miles a day would need three and a half
years to pass in review before any given place. Contrast these three
great armies with the armies of preachers and officers in our churches
and the contrast is a little painful. Pick up any pamphlet dealing with
the matter and you will read that all our churches today are wofully
short of preachers. "But," you may say, "our preachers are not the
only faithful workers. We have a host of church members." And yet,
my friends, just a few weeks ago as I was riding along on a street car
in Atlanta, Georgia, I saw these words written on a sign across one
of the biggest churches in the city: "ninety-five per cent. of all Christian
people never have led another soul to Jesus Christ." Now I do not know
that that sign was accurate in the statement it made. I hope it was not.
But it was a terrible indictment.

To meet the great needs of this age our girls and boys must have
training to make of them skilled Christians, workmen needing not to
be ashamed.

Let us make happy Christians out of them. Let us show them that
Christian Endeavor's program develops the choicest kind of happiness,
that boys and girls can be the happiest kind of Christians and yet the
most sincere. I think that too many Christian people are like the old
darky who was always so morose and melancholy that a young lady
went to her on one occasion and said to her, "Aunt Mandy, why don't
you cheer up? You're always so blue." And Aunt Mandy replied,
"Well, Honey, I think that when the Lord sends me tribulation he specs
me to tribulate." Christian Endeavor believes in happiness, and we try
to provide for the social lives of our young people by the right kinds
of socials, and by training them for the right kind of service, service
that results in happiness. Skilled Christians should be the happiest
people on earth, and the long faced Christian makes the best leader in
mighty few instances.

Let us make consecrated Christians out of them. A skilled Christian
should not only be happy, but he should be consecrated. He should give
of his money, of his time, and of his life in this great cause in which
he is a champion. Do not let us forget to present to our Intermediate
boys and girls the Tenth Legion—consecration of money; Comrades of
the Quiet Hour—consecration of time; and Life Work Recruits—consecration of life itself. They are not too young and you can't make the
challenge too hard for them. I had the pleasure just two weeks ago of
being in a young people's conference in a little mountain school in north
Georgia, and at the close of that conference when Dr. Richard O. Flynn,
of the North Avenue Presbyterian Church of Atlanta put the challenge
of full-time service for Christ, thirty-four splendid young people came
forward, Intermediates, every one of them, and Dr. Flynn did not make
the call by telling them full-time Christian service is easy. Let us
train them to be happy Christians and let us train them to be consecrated Christians, workmen needing not to be ashamed, for the world is
calling for them, and it calls because it needs them, and we must help

them realize that "It's great to be in where the battle is strong, and to be where the heaviest troops belong, in the fight for man and God. Oh! it pinches the face, and it wearies the brain, and it brings us face to face with pain in the fight for man and God. But it's great to be in where the battle is strong, and to be where the heaviest troops belong in the fight for man and God."

And so first of all there is the need. This is so evident that it stares at us at every corner and it calls to us from every quarter. We have the young folks, we have the gospel in which and with which to train them, and we know quite well the qualifications essential to Christian leadership. What else then must we do? Three things.

As we leave this Convention, informed a little better, determined a little more, enthusiastic in a little broader way, let us decide to do these three things in regard to our Intermediate boys and girls back home. First, see the possibilities there; second, have a program to develop the possibilities; and third, use the power.

Some weeks ago I stood on a high place above the city of Sheffield, Alabama, and looked down upon the Tennessee River, in which there were several hundred men at work upon a piece of engineering that when completed will be the biggest thing of its kind in the world. An enormous dam is being thrown across the Tennessee at a point that will check the waters of that great river until the gigantic natural bowl extending miles up the river between the hills of Alabama will be filled with water. It is said that fifteen years ago a man saw the possibilities of a dam at Sheffield. He saw that if he could just get a dam across the river at that particular spot there could be gained almost unlimited power. For fifteen years that man has been talking that dam. He got others interested and others until finally the Congress of the United States felt justified in expending millions of dollars and years of work in the erection of that dam. There was possibility, then there was a program to develop that possibility, and the reward will be power— power sufficient to light every city in the south, if need be, from that one plant; power that will send scores of trollies speeding along their rails; power that will turn millions of spindles in the mills of a dozen states.

Forty years ago Dr. Clark saw the possibilities of his young people if they were trained, and he saw the possibilities of Christian Endeavor. Today Christian Endeavor is one of the world's biggest religious forces, a great organization of four million young people with the same four-fold purpose—confession of Christ, service for Christ, loyalty to Christ's church and fellowship with Christ's people.

A few years ago Mell Trotter by the grace of God saw the possibilities in his own life. When he was first touched by the power of the Spirit, Mell Trotter was one of the least of the earth. He was an outcast and a bum. He is today one of the big preachers of the country.

Possibility—your boys and girls back home are full of it; program— you must have that, and it must be a big one and a challenging one, leading them into training that will make of them skilled Christians; power—you will never know the power of one boy or one girl led right up to Christ and developed for Christian leadership.

JUNIOR CONFERENCE

By Mrs. H. W. Maier

We have for our theme this morning *instruction*. This theme applied to child-life involves a great many problems. Three things are included in our theme, first, there must be the instructor, second, there must be those to be instructed, and third, there must be teaching material which will be imparted by the instructor to those to be instructed. The instructor must know her material well enough to impart it, and she must know those to whom the instruction is to be given. The instructor must have the power to impart, and the ones to be instruced must be receptive to receive. The Junior superintendent is the chief instructor. I am wondering if we are really instructors, if we are really putting across the message. Do we know the thing we are trying to teach, do we know our material and do we know our boys and girls? If we will instruct, we must be whole-hearted, we must be happy, we must not go before our boys and girls tired and wearily; we must be fresh. We must improve our personality and appearance in any way that we can, so long as we do not destroy the natural. After we know our teaching material, we must know how to present it so that it will make the greatest impression upon the children to whom it is to be given. In presenting our teaching material let us remember that the child has several gate-ways through which messages are carried to the brain. Does most of your teaching go through the ear gate, the eye gate or the feeling gate? The eye gate is twenty-two times more powerful than the ear gate. The feeling gate is more powerful than the ear gate. Let us remember that in our teaching we are molding lives, and that if our personality is attractive, and if our message has been planned, the child-life will be impressed. What impressions are we making upon child-life. They are lasting impressions, but are they for good or for bad?

I. PSYCHOLOGY STUDY:
"The Child Learning"
It is natural for the normal child to learn. When the child is only a few weeks old, he begins to reach out for knowledge. So earnestly does he reach out for knowledge that his five gateways for receiving knowledge are called his hungry senses. A boy is by far a better student than a man. When a child begins to talk, the first thing he learns to say is a noun; after he has used nouns for a while, he begins to use verbs. Almost his very first sentence will be a question. When a little child asks a question, he is just reaching out for knowledge. When a child is a few months older, he wants to turn mother's sewing basket up-side-down, he pulls books down from the shelves; he is reaching out for knowledge. Boys when they get older want to tear a watch apart to see how it is made; some people call it destructiveness, but it is the child reaching out for knowledge. Some knowledge will be constructive to the child; some will be destructive. Some children would rather hear a good story than a bad, while others would rather hear the bad story. It is possible, during the tender years of childhood to instil in the little child the desire for the good and to repell the bad. We have an opportunity as Junior superintendents to instil in the lives of our Juniors an appreciation for the things that are high and holy and pure and good.

There are five gateways in the child; from each gateway there is a wire running to the brain; we call these sensory nerves. These sensory nerves carry every message to the brain which is received through the five gateways, and every message makes an impression upon the brain and becomes a part of life. Then everything that the child sees, hears, feels, tastes and smells is carried to the brain in the form of a message or impression. Let us think for a moment the relationship between these impressions and activity. There are motor nerves running from the brain to the tongue, hands, feet. After an impression is registered on the brain and becomes associated with other impressions already received, it travels along the motor nerves and finds an outlet through the tongue, hands and feet, and causes us to say and do the thing according to the impression. Good impressions produce good activity; activity and repeated activity becomes a tendency, a tendency soon becomes compulsion, and compulsion becomes a habit. Nine-tenths of all life, we learned Saturday, is lived in the mold of habit. Life then is dependent upon the impressions received. The Junior period is characterized by physical activity; he is stronger than is the younger child or the older child; as a rule, his health is good, but he needs good nourishment and plenty of sleep. His activity tends to find expression in constructiveness. In building a Junior program, we must keep this in mind. Give the Juniors big things to do. The Junior child has a growing sense of independency. The superintendent who would teach, must recognize this and always consult the wishes of the children when it comes to planning the work. The boys and girls are interested in reading; good reading material should be given them; tne boy is passing through the hero worship period, if we are really to build character through our teaching we must bring before him the lives of our modern and older heroes; he is passing through the habit-forming period, we must surround him with the right kind of impressions which leads to right activity which leads to right habits; he is passing through the golden memory period, we must give him the choice passages of scripture to memorize and the choice hymns to learn; his geographical and historical senses have their birth at this period, let us teach the child Bible geography and Bible history; it is the collecting age, let him collect the things to go in the mission boxes; his social instinct is developing, let us feed his social nature by surrounding him with all that is pure and wholesome.

II. JUNIOR METHODS:

1.—The Prayer Meeting

The Junior prayer meeting affords the chief opportunity for instruction; here the child learns the beautiful worshipful hymns which will remain with him all of his life, the psalms, some of the best Bible stories and others. The Junior superintendent builds character day by day as she carefully plans each Junior prayer meeting. Let us consider the elements that make up the service which we have chosen to call the prayer meeting:

1. *The Beginning*, or the pre-meeting activity, should begin just as soon as the Juniors enter the room. No Junior should be allowed to come thirty minutes early and then use the church which has been dedicated to God as a playground. Just as soon as the child arrives, some form of handwork should be given him. We will take up the forms of handwork later on this morning. Of course, the prayer meeting committee and the leader under adult supervision may well spend the five minutes before the meeting in a pre-prayer service. Or all of the Juniors can well spend fifteen minutes before the time for the opening of the meeting in handwork, then they can divide up into groups under adult leadership and have for five minutes their prayer group services. If either of the above methods are used, the problem of discipline has been solved. If the program is well planned, there will be no problem of discipline.

2. *Quiet Music.* The quiet music will simply be a hymn played softly on the piano. This will call the children to their places in the Junior room and prepare them for the worship service. Quiet music will do more to quiet noisy children than all the clapping of the hands, ringing of bells and loud voices.

3. *Worship.* I think we have not put enough of the worshipful element in our Junior programs. We have made our singing the rag-time type instead of teaching the boys and girls to worship the Heavenly Father in the soft quiet hymns when we can think the thing we are singing. There are four things included in worship as we learned Thursday, namely, praise, prayer, hearing of the word, and giving. Then our worship period of ten minutes must include praise or the singing of hymns in which we show our adoration, prayer, the prayer during the worship period should be by an adult member, hearing of the word, this may be read or repeated, giving, the giving service should be made an offering *service* and not merely a collection. During the praise part of our Junior worship service, we might use "Praise God from whom all Blessings Flow," or "Glory be to the Father," or "All Hail the Power of Jesus' Name." How do these compare with "Brighten the corner," or "If your heart keeps right"? During the prayer part of our

worship period the superintendent or one of her helpers might lead in the kind of prayer that will be comprehended by children, or she might explain to the children that there are three kinds of prayer, the prayer of thanksgiving, the prayer of petition, and the prayer of intercession; she might ask the children to think of one thing that we want to thank God for, and then one thing that we want to ask God for for ourselves, and then the thing that we want to ask God for other people; when the three things have been named, we will all bow our heads, the superintendent will form the sentence in dignified, yet simple, language and then the Juniors will repeat it after her. During the hearing of God's word, part of our program of worship, the scripture reading might be read responsively, a psalm might be repeated in unison or an adult member may read the verses. During the giving part of our worship, the offering must be lifted quietly and orderly, some giving verses to precede the lifting of the offering and an offering prayer to follow the lifting of the offering.

4. *Leader's Participation* will be the reading of the lesson, announcing the topic which may be done by having it written on the blackboard or having the children give it together, perhaps offering a short prayer, and giving a talk on the topic; the topic may be given in the form of a story, an object lesson or blackboard talk.

5. *Juniors' Participation.* Because this has been discussed, we will only mention it here as being one element of the Junior program.

6. *Superintendent's Part.* Her message might be given by blackboard, object, verbal story-telling, or illustrated story-telling.

7. *Memory Work* should be given place on every program; will be discussed later.

8. *Dramatization of Stories.* This may be offered for fifteen minutes just before the closing service.

9. *Closing Service,* hymn and prayer.

2—Stories and How to Tell Them

The story has been used in every age as an educational agency, the early Greeks used the stories of Homer, the Romans used the Plutarch lives, the Hebrews used the old testament stories. Jesus used the story in parable, and today, the story is one of our best educational opportunities. Everyone loves the story; it charms the little child and the older people alike. Good story-telling is the best intellectual qualification that a Junior superintendent can have. The stories of the gospel have done infinitely more to influence the lives of men than all the books of systematic theology; the stories of the saints used during the middle ages were not without their influence and power, in the midst of scholastic wrangling, they kept simple faith alive and stirred the longing with fellowship with God; the preachers of our own day who have had widespread popular influence have been those who have not scorned the story-teller's art. Jesus was a master story-teller; the most wonderful stories are the parables of Jesus. You may ask yourself the question, "What is a story?" A story is a narrative of true or imaginary events which form a vitally related whole so presented as to make its appeal to the emotions rather than to the intellect. There are four elements to the story that we must remember: first, the beginning which must be brief and which must, in an attractive way, introduce the characters or prepare the background for the story; second, the sequence of events which present the movement of the story toward the climax which gives meaning to the whole, the great essential is that it should be orderly, presenting the necessary facts step by step and preparing for the climax without revealing it in advance; third, the climax is that which makes the story, it is the point on which interest focuses, it is here that we make our moral and spiritual appeal; fourth, the end which should be very brief, but leave the mind at rest.

There are two kinds of stories, the idealistic and realistic. The idealistic are those which are recognized as imaginary in origin; the realistic stories are those which conform to facts. The idealistic stories are sometimes more forceful and make better story material than the realistic stories because they have been written for the purpose of telling while the realistic stories are true stories and in the true story, reward does not always follow right-doing and punishment wrong-doing as it does in the idealistic story. Then a realistic story must not only be true, but it must seem true to the child; while in the idealistic story the wildest extravagance may be used to teach a truth. However, some of our realistic stories form the greatest teaching material in the world, such as the Old Testament stories, the stories of Jesus and of Paul and of Peter. Jesus' parables are the idealistic stories and there is nothing better that we can use to feed the young mind upon. In the idealistic group, we have the fairy tale, the myth, the legends, the fables and the allegory; while in the realistic group, we have history, biography, personal reminiscences, and true stories of animals. Both the realistic and the idealistic are valuable in religious education. Let us now consider some of the things to remember in telling a story:

1. Select the story that will teach the truth which you wish to teach.

2. Adapt the story to meet your needs, eliminating all unnecessary material.

3. Study the story, the beginning, to see if your beginning is just as you want it; study the sequence of events, see if it is orderly and does not introduce parts that will detract from the climax; study the climax, how can you improve it? Does it make the appeal that you want it to make? Study the end, is there a moral tacked on? If so, take it off. Does it leave the mind at rest?

4. Read the story over about three times, then think upon the story for several days; make the story your own.

5. Plan to use as much direct discourse in your story as possible; also use repetition of certain words and phrases.

6. Plan to use simple language and short sentences and concreteness.

7. After you have studied and planned your story, just tell it. It will require a lot of practice to be a good story-teller, but anyone with the average intelligence who is willing to make the effort can be a good story-teller.

3—Bible Memory Work

During the years from nine to fifteen memory is in its most glorious period for storing away. In early life, a fact is retained chiefly through its impress on the soft brain cells, for the power of association is little developed. In later life, a fact is retained almost wholly through association with other facts, for the cells grow hard and an imprint is therefore faint. During the golden memory period, the fact has the double hold of impress and association, for the cells are plastic and the associative powers are undeveloped. It is important that we make use of the opportunity to give the children as much memory work as possible for the dual condition never occurs again. There are a number of memory work devices which are used in different Junior societies:

1. String of pearls.
2. Bible promised.
3. Bible gems.
4. Learning one psalm per month.
5. All "love verses" memorized and made into a book in the heart shape.
6. All verses on "strength" memorized and made into a book the shape of an oak leaf.
7. Bible alphabet, memorize one verse for each letter of alphabet.
8. Bible chains (demonstrated).
9. Memorize six or twelve of the standard hymns a year.

4.—The Pledge

It is a very serious thing to ask a child to make a pledge or as we term it to sign the pledge, and yet I believe that every child, after he is eight years old, if he wishes to become a member of the Junior Christian Endeavor society, should be requested to sign the Junior active pledge, but not until it has been analyzed and thoroughly explained to him. The pledge can be made one of the strongest influences in a child's life. I will mention a few illustrations which have come to my observation:

1. Robert, a boy in whose home I lived during my college days, was ready for bed; his mother had been upstairs to see that he had gotten ready for bed properly, and then went downstairs leaving the child in tears because he could not find his Bible. Robert refused to go to bed without reading his Bible. In another minute, there was a knock at my door, I went to the door and there a little white clad figure was before me, and with tears streaming down his face, Robert said, "Miss Smith, please may I use your Bible tonight." Robert's pledge was the standard for his everyday living.

2. Just a few days ago, I was talking with one of our college presidents, and he told me of his little daughter making ready for an operation. The doctors had come to take her to the operating room, but before she would allow them to place her on the operating table, she said, "Mother, will you please get my Bible so that I can read it and thus keep my pledge today; I won't be able to read it when I come back."

A child who takes the signing of the pledge as seriously as these two little friends, surely must have had the pledge presented to them in a very attractive way. I will give you a few of the methods I have used in presenting the pledge:

1. Keep the pledge hanging before the Juniors with the five promises underlined.

2. Draw a hand on the blackboard, letting one finger stand for each promise in the pledge.

3. Junior bridge (demonstrated).

4. Wheel, the spokes standing for the promises in the pledge, the hub, "I will," and the rim for "Trusting in the Lord Jesus Christ for strength, I promise Him."

5. Presenting a star, letting each point of the star stand for each promise in the pledge.

5.—Quiet Hour

The child's Quiet Hour means the giving of five minutes in the early morning, if possible, in meditation, reading of the word and prayer. I do not know of any other practice in which we can lead a child that will contribute more to his spiritual development than the practice of spending the early morning in the Quiet Hour. It has a tendency to make God very real to him, to teach him to depend upon God. If a child learns to take his childish problem to the Heavenly Father, it will be the natural thing for him to carry his problems to God when he grows older. Before a child is permitted to become a Comrade of the Quiet Hour, it must be explained to him and he must be taught how to spend those five minutes. Children after they are nine years old, can reason out a thing for themselves. I like to make my boys and girls feel a need for the thing that I think they ought to have, then the first thing I will do, I will try to make them feel a need for the Quiet Hour. I explain to them that they have a fourfold nature, physical, social, mental and spiritual; and I explain that food is necessary before there is physical growth and every child wants to grow to be a strong man or woman; that we must go to school and apply ourselves, if we grow mentally; that we must mingle with other boys and girls, if we will grow socially; then I ask the question, "What is necessary to make us grow spiritually?" They will immediately answer, "Bible reading and prayer." Then when can we pray best? Why, when we are alone, of course. This presents the reason for the Quiet Hour in the child's life. The next thing that we must do, is to plan a way to make it easy for the child to keep the Quiet Hour. First, get him to select a definite time and place where and when it will be held. Second, I like to get each child to make his own Quiet Hour book (demonstrated).

6.—Illustrated Stories
The illustrated stories are just another device to make teaching plain to the child. Most any Bible story or missionary story can be told by illustration. 1. You will want your material, all the poster patterns and cut-out patterns that you can get; these will be colored and kept in a box. The various stories can be filed into envelopes and used over and over again, year after year. The children can prepare much of this material. 2. You will want a burlap screen on which to pin the objects. 3. As the story develops, pin the figure on the screen. Each child can make his own figures if you like and he can illustrate the story as you tell it. Order poster patterns from Milton Bradley Co., Springfield, Mass., and from Smith and Lamar, Nashville, Tenn. Also order from Smith and Lamar, their Christmas story, their Easter story and the story of Rebecca at the well (demonstrated).

7.—Learning by Doing Handwork
The handwork period is the time just before the Junior meeting opens; its value is in that you can teach a truth one Sunday and then have the child to express the truth in some form of handwork the following Sunday. There are various forms of handwork, I will mention a few:
1. Twenty-third psalm printed so that credit is given to the child who memorizes the psalm; a picture illustrating each verse of the psalm is to be painted by the child.
2. Story of Good Samaritan, used in the same way as the Twenty-third psalm.
3. Creation Story, used as above. Each of these stories can be purchased for fifteen cents per set from Smith and Lamar, Nashville, Tenn.
4. Missionary handwork (demonstrated).
5. Picture pasting.
6. Paper cutting.
7. Making of maps.
8. Making of scrapbooks.

III. DEMONSTRATION OF METHODS:
1. Oriental models, encampment of the Children of Israel and tabernacle, scroll, oriental houses, temple furniture, etc.
2. Rainy day attendance devices, umbrella and chart.

IV. WORKER'S LIBRARY:
Stories to tell to children—
1. Index to short stories by Grace Salisbury and Marie Beckwick, Rowe Patterson and Co., Chicago, fifty cents. Stories are alphabetically indexed according to the subjects with reference to the books in which they are found.
2. A list of good stories to tell to children under twelve years of age, Carnegie Library, Pittsburgh, five cents.
3. Hurlbut's Bible stories.
4. Tell me a true story, Mary Stewart, one dollar and fifty cents.
5. Some great stories and how to tell them, Wyche, one dollar.
6. Mother stories and more mother stories, Maud Lindsay, one dollar.
7. The Golden Windows and the Silver Crown, Richards, one dollar.
8. Story Tell Lib, Slosson, fifty cents.

9. Parables from Nature, Gatty.
10. How to Tell Stories to Children, one dollar.
11. Stories to Tell to Children.
12. Why the Chimes Rang and Other Stories, two dollars.
13. Tell Me a Story I Never Heard Before, Stewart, one dollar and twenty-five cents.
14. Tell Me the Story of Jesus, Stewart, one dollar and twenty-five cents.
15. Tell Me a Hero Story, Stewart, one dollar and twenty-five cents.
16. The Little Hunchback Zia, Burnett, seventy-five cents.
17. Stories and Story-telling, St. John, fifty cents.
18. World Stories, retold, Sly, one dollar.
Sandtable—
1. The Sandtable, a manual for Sunday School Teachers, eighty-five cents.
Illustrated Talks and Object Lessons—
1. Three Years with the Children, Wells, one dollar.
2. The Soul of a Child, Hutchinson, one dollar and fifteen cents.
3. Object Lessons for Children, Tyndall, one dollar and twenty-five cents.
4. Missionary Story Sermons, Kerr, one dollar.
V. TAKE HOME THOUGHT:
"The Challenge of the Church to Its Children."

THE ENDEAVORER AND HIS BIBLE
BY REV. FLOYD W. TOMKINS

In the first place, every Endeavorer should have his own Bible. He should use it freely. Do not be afraid to mark your Bible, and do not be afraid to put into it anything that marks your religious life.

A minister divided the Bible's contents into two P's and four D's, persons, places, dates, doings, doctrines, and duties. There are three characteristic elements, history, poetry, and prophecy. Christians should know where to find any book of the Bible. There are some ministers even that do not know how to turn to the minor prophets readily.

Read your Bible; read it through; and read it through again continuously as you would read another book, only remembering that it is God's book. We should be so familiar with it as to be able to quote it readily.

Use the Bible as a means of spiritual growth. It is the inspired word of God. To me there is only one religion in the world, and that is the Christian.

Some get spiritual dyspepsia through not meditating enough and applying it. Go to the Bible in all the experiences of life. A Scripture calendar is an excellent thing to have. When I was a minister in New York, one day everything went wrong. I said, "What shall I do?" I looked at my calendar, and the text for the day was, "Whatsoever he saith unto you, do it." I grabbed my hat, went to see several persons that I knew wanted to see me; and, when I came back, everything was clear.

Be sure that every promise in the Bible is given to be fulfilled. Hold fast to them; study them; use them; and you will find in them that which will reveal them to you more and more every day.

MID-WEEK ACTIVITIES FOR INTERMEDIATES
BY NINA ROWLAND

Making religion real, intimately connected with the world's life and work and with one's own many-sided life, is one of the big tasks of Intermediate Christian Endeavor. How many of us, looking back to our 'teen age, remember that religion was viewed as a

Sunday matter connected with the church services, Sunday school, or mission band. But as for taking religion into our school work our play, or our social life, we never thought much about that.

Here is a fruitful field of discussion (and the 'teen age loves to discuss), "How can we bring religion to bear upon cleanness and honesty in sport, upon conscientious work, upon purposeful study, upon thoughtfulness and consideration in the home, upon learning to put first things first in social life?"

There is entirely too much "canned thinking" in America today. We have an address that agrees with out trend of thought or, that tickles our ears and we say, "That's just what I think!" and make it ours. We read a newspaper and we adopt what it says. We hear an address with a new idea and as soon as we gather what it is about we say, "I don't like this man!" and are prejudiced in our listening at once. 'Teen age, boys and girls, the future citizens of America, need to be taught to think a thing through, to discuss both sides of every question, to make a decision in the light of Jesus Christ, and then stand by that decision won by intelligent thinking. Try this out in your meetings.

Now demonstrate the principles that you have discussed by your mid-week activities. Provide the "gymnasium" where your boys and girls will try out these newly formed decisions.

The World of Sport

Let Intermediates have their basket-ball, baseball, tennis, or other athletic teams. Challenge other societies. These teams should be models for cleanness of play and of speech, absence of cigarettes, good losers, and modesty in victory. The Golden Rule might well be the motto. The team should be led to pray together before the game, not that they may beat the other fellow, but that they may fight fair and each man do his best.

In a certain boarding-school there were six teams of basket-ball that, at the end of every season, competed for a silver cup. The Spartans were an exceedingly strong team, and the cup had been in their possession for two years. They showed signs of being the winners the third year, covering up the tournament with an unbeaten record. The Reliance team, however, decided to challenge that record. The captain prayed about those games, and the finals found Reliance and the Spartans pitted against each other. Just before going into the big game, the captain prayed again, not that they might win, but that each girl should do her best. The game was on! Goal after goal the Reliance rolled up against the Spartans. Each girl played as though inspired. The cup was in the possession of Reliance. At the Victory feast the girls were talking over the game. Suddenly the centre said, "Do you know, girls, I prayed about that game." Up spoke one of the goal tossers, "Why, I did, too." Then the captain spoke, "And, girls, I did, too." Religion even in our sports makes us better players. What would have happened though, if the Spartans had also prayed about that game? Another fruitful field for discussion and a wonderful lesson on prayer for 'teen age boys and girls is opened up in that question.

There is a splendid chance for training in systematic setting aside of a proportion of income for the Lord, when boys and girls have work after school and in vacations. They may be encouraged to open an account with the Lord in a neat little book in which all expenditures are carefully kept. Such training is invaluable later in life.

For the girls, there may be special credits for bed-making, sweeping and dusting a room, making bread, or cake, or salad, and making one's own clothes. There is room here for sunshine work for folks in trouble or infirm or in need.   Good fairies will find an unexpected enjoyment in doing a work of kindness for somebody else.

How often the voice of the 'teen age is raised, "I don't see why I must study Latin or algebra." How many young people stumble upon their life work or never find it! Here is a chance to give Latin or history or algebra a new meaning, a vast importance, by relating it to the life work of the pupil. Let the Intermediate society help its boys and girls to find their place in life and if this cannot be decided definitely at this early stage, at least teach them that service to the world is the secret of success and that consecrating one's life to Jesus Christ is the first step toward finding one's life-work. Then every lesson prepares one for the call when it shall come.

Our homes would be very much happier if the members of the family would begin the day with listening to God through His word and talking to God in prayer. Every Intermediate boy and girl, then, the superintendent should ardently strive and desire to make a Comrade of the Quiet Hour. This is a matter of growth and habit. First stimulate daily Bible reading and prayer by a credit system, the spirit of emulation, by contests in the society or among neighboring societies. Through all this habit-forming should run the constant glorifying of the Bible, the discussion of prayer, its power, and what it has done for people who have developed the habit.

A healthy social life under the auspices of the church has a very definite place in filling the needs of the world of young people today. Out-of-doors there is the hike, the obstacle walk, the follow-the-leader walk. There are the campfire with its marshmallow and "doggie," corn and potato-roasting possibilities. There is no better place to tell stories with a message than around a camp-fire. There are parties so carefully planned and full of lively games that dancing falls in the background of interest. Watch "The Christian Endeavor World" for ideas for games and stunts. There is the dinner and the banquet with all its formalities of toasts and decorations, dearly loved by Intermediates. There are pageants and plays. Write to your Mission Board for suggestions. In all of these, prayer should be used as a means of bringing about a right spirit and finding true happiness.

In closing, I want to speak of the mission study class for the 'teen age, for it is perhaps the most difficult of mission-study problems. To boys and girls tired from school classes, the idea of going to another study is not often attractive. For that reason we make our mission-study classes real little parties, meeting at each others' houses and always closing with "eats" and some games and songs, if there is time. The lesson, which should come first, is half read, half told by the superintendent, who uses charts and pictures and printed mottoes to illustrate, and questions of conduct or application of principles are discussed.

At the end of the work the public is invited to a baseball game, girls vs. boys, in which the pitchers fire questions on the book just completed, to the batter. One question missed puts the batter out. If the man on base can answer first, he advances a base. Superintendents should not be discouraged if their study-class is not a brilliant success the first year. Like all good things it is a matter of growth. It may be necessary to continue on small lines for several years—but all Intermediate superintendents should remember that through prayer, personal consecration, and "pegging away," the kingdom of God may be brought into every activity of the 'teen age boys' and girls' lives.

FRATERNAL MEETING
The Sunday School
BY REV. FRANK L. BROWN

I believe the biggest business of the world is making character, and we believe that through the Sunday School this object can be fulfilled. This is a great business, headed by great business men, and one of the greatest counts the Sunday School as the beginning of his business success. He has brought me a message to read to this Convention:

"I regard the Society of Christian Endeavor as best of all that has grown out of the church, building the life of young people on the foundation of the Holy Scriptures as revealed to us, and it is the way of life, our life."

Men of big business are giving their time to this work. A broken world is waiting for our program. State and church are breaking apart in almost every land, in reaction from bloodshed and materialism. If China is to be regenerated as it must be, we can trust regeneration to the type we see in the Sunday School generation. I was in Shanghai, China, where there were ten thousand Sunday School members present. In the Philippines, five thousand Sunday School children gathered under the open sky to dedicate themselves to bigger and better schools. In Korea there has been a great evangelistic campaign for the Sunday School, and in Japan the Empress gave me a personal interview, and the Emperor sent a special message to the World's Sunday School Convention and fifty thousand yen towards the expenses of the Convention. If we can have the American Sunday School in Russia, it will mean a new Russia. Mr. Moody said, "If we can win one generation, we can put the devil out of business."

Boy Scouts

Dr. George J. Fisher spoke for the Boy Scouts, co-workers with us, equally interested in the youth of the land. Both Christian Endeavor and Boy Scouts believe that if social service is to be done it must be done by voluntary workers, and the greatest need of the boys of America is wise, consecrated, adult leadership; and this leadership must come, as it is now coming, from the church.

Y. W. C. A.
BY MRS. ROBERT E. SPEER

It is indeed a privilege to speak to this audience in behalf of the half-million of women members of the Y. W. C. A. Should I have only one word tonight as a message from these members from one Christian association to another association, it is that your generation may think in fresh terms that great word we esteem one of the greatest in the New Testament about our Jesus Christ as He is "the same yesterday and today and forever." What I ask of your generation is that you remember that, though He is always the same, our thinking about Him must never be the same from one day to the next. We must remember that each evening the sun sets in different terms from yesterday. He is always the same, but we must think of Him in new and larger ways through every day. It is only in this way that we grow nearer and nearer, and little conceptions drop away, and we see Him in the greatest largeness and glory that the world of young Christian men and women make of the future concepts which we can make of our Christ "the same yesterday and today and forever." This is the challenge of the younger generation, to think of Him without fear or shackles, always larger, greater, and more and more powerful than any conception we have had of Him, our Christ far greater and greater.

Y. M. C. A.

BY MR. COOPER

General Secretary, Washington, D. C.

I came to take the place of one of the representatives of our International Committee, and it is fitting the local secretary should fill this place because he is in constant and personal relationship with the Christian Endeavor Society. One of the first group assembled about you in Williston Church afterward became one of the distinguished leaders of the Y. M. C. A.; and from that day until the present time your movement has made a splendid contribution to both lay leadership and professional leadership of the Y. M. C. A. I bring personal appreciation and gratitude from the Association I represent. Standing behind my words tonight are nearly one million men of the continent, men on land and sea. We have the same purposes, ideals, and relationships; your programs are different somewhat, but in these particulars run parallel with our own. Like yourselves we rely on the word of God as a rule of faith and conduct. We approach that holy Word with reverent step and bowed head, and seek from it, as you also seek from it, guidance on the way of life.

Like yourselves we hold Christ supreme. To grow in stature and favor with God and man has always been held up as the ideal of the young manhood of the world. Jesus Christ is making His case with the young men and boys of the world. Now the day is just before us. May this Convention be the central powerhouse which will radiate new streams that will constantly honor Christ, His word, and His name.

Girl Scouts

BY MRS. SELDEN BACON

When I was young enough to be a real Christian Endeavorer and used to be at home, they used to sing, "I want to be an angel, and with the angels stand." This song was never popular, and I never knew why. But I know now why it didn't go down with me. In my childish mind I knew it should be, "You gotta be an angel, and with the angels stand."

The Girl Scouts bring you one great message of likeness which stands for voluntary organization. We understand yours is a government of young people, by young people, for the young people. In the olden days you had to go to school; but I don't believe any father says, "You will have to go to Christian Endeavor, or I will lift the skin off your back." In our childish days we were told, "You must wash the dishes;" but no one says, "You got to be a Girl Scout." We are in it because we want to be in it. If I address them, "Forward, march, wash dishes," they wash. This may not be sentimental, but it is awfully practical, and many are getting dishes washed by this simple method. Moreover, we give them a three-cent pocket badge if they do them well. If I ask them to wash a baby, and give the command, "Make ready, wash," you can't see them for dust. In one perfectly well-known town in New Jersey one long-suffering infant was given twenty-three baths in one afternoon.

We ought to be the best friends of all with you people, because our motto is, "Help other people all over the world whenever you can." The Founder of Christianity can do no more, and would do no less. We want to make this organization so fine and big that you big Christian Endeavorers will be glad to say "That girl is a good scout."

GREETINGS FROM BURMA

By Mr. SAN BA

It is a great privilege to come to this Convention and stand on this platform. I am a native of Burma, but not a regular delegate of Christian Endeavor to this country; but I am studying here, and also, being a Christian Endeavor Alumnus, am always interested in Christian Endeavor work. I have only these two things to say to you as a visitor here. This Christian Endeavor movement is to be found in every part of the world. Even in the smallest known country there are hundreds of Endeavorers. The Endeavor movement means a lot to the people, and is always a source of strength to the church. Personally, whatever spirit of leadership and initiative I have, I owe to the training I received in a Christian Endeavor society in a mission school in Burma. I started as an associate member, and was a stammering associate. I finally came through the different offices in that society. I am now a student in this country, and am about to finish my work; and I have determined that I will carry that spirit of the Endeavorer and try to carry Christian Endeavor ideals into my work. I also wish to tell you that the Endeavorers everywhere in the world are one with you in spirit and purpose. And so I am here to speak on behalf of those people, and to thank first of all Dr. Clark and those responsible for the origin and spirit of this movement. It is the spirit of fellowship that binds us together. We appreciate our fellowship with you, the people of the United States. By way of example I can say that we as Christians are still weak, and we still look to you for example and leadership. So I am not a regular representative of the people of Burma, but those people are interested in your work and in this meeting. They wish you great success, and so do I.

GREETINGS FROM CHINA

By Mr. EDGAR E. STROTHER

It is indeed a great privilege, dear friends, to bring to you this afternoon the greetings of twelve hundred Christian Endeavor societies and sixty thousand members. Thirty-five years ago Mr. Hubbard started the first society in Fuchau. Christian Endeavor has spread to every corner of that great land, so that now we have Christian Endeavor in every province of China and practically every mission of the different countries. Missionaries of different denominational missions are taking up Christian Endeavor very heartily, and we have scores of testimonies for Christian Endeavor as one of the greatest agencies for evangelistic work on the mission field.

There is only time for me to bring this word of greeting, and present to you these banners which have been sent to Dr. Clark. One is from China and one from Korea. Korean Christians in Shanghai have given a map of Korea and put the Korean flag and the Christian Endeavor flag across the top. They have sent these to you and Dr. Clark, and the nation which is broken and torn and bleeding beseeches your sympathy and prayers. They are looking forward to the time when they may have hundreds of thousands of Christian Endeavor societies. We ask your prayers in behalf of Korea.

The next flag was prepared by a Chinese field-secretary who has artistic ability. On the background is the flag of China, in the centre a map of China; and over the map is worked the Christian Endeavor monogram in flowers, because China is the Flowery Kingdom. Putting everything, all of your strength, doing with all your might. This is the meaning of Christian Endeavor to the Chinese. Across the bottom he has put the commission, the message of Christian Endeavor, "Go ye into all the world, and preach the gospel to every creature." At the top he has put the cross of Jesus Christ, which he believes to be the heart of Christian Endeavor in China, a message of sacrifice and service.

GREETINGS FROM CHINA

By Miss Emily Hartwell

This banner is presented by one thousand five hundred Juniors of the Christian Endeavor union of Fuchau, China. The characters mean Fuchau city and suburbs. I wish you could have been at the meeting when this was presented. About one thousand eight hundred children filled the church. Everything on the program was by a little Junior. This banner expresses to each of you the gratitude of the boys and girls of China, for you have sent to them Christian Endeavor.

We see these beautiful American flags, dear friends. Do you realize, do you know, that under this flag there are manufactured tons of morphia to be sent over to ruin China? This morphia has been sent over to China and distributed through Japanese and other foreign investors in China, over whom China has no control. China fought the opium war, but morphia is as much worse than opium, as opium is worse than cider. During 1916 to 1919 there were about ninety tons of morphia sent to China, and one ton equals 500,000,000 injections of morphia in the arm. Think of the ruin this means to China, and China is powerless to keep it out. Much of this morphia was manufactured in New York, and some in Philadelphia, some also in London. Now, Christian Endeavor stands for love and fellowship all over the world, and we are praying for peace. Good friends, we must remember the thousands and tens of thousands of widows and orphans made by the morphia manufactured under the American flag.

I am asking you to go home and ask others to help you to send petitions to President Harding and Congress to limit the manufacture of morphia, also to do everything in their power to urge Great Britain and Japan that they shall limit the planting of the poppy in India and Formosa more than is sufficient for medical uses.

As you look at this banner, it is an appeal to you to do your utmost, not only to save the boys and girls of China, but the boys and girls of Britain and America, for filtering back into the 'homelands the greatest ruin and greatest crimes of the nations are coming back upon the heads of the children of our homelands.

GREETINGS FROM CANADA

By Lieut. W. Steenson

It gives me great pleasure today to bear the greetings from Canada with its many forest-lined streams and the vast industrial resources of western Canada to eastern Canada with its ancient history of noble deeds in the great history of the past. Western Canada fifty years ago was uncultivated land to the Pacific. Its prairies, boundless and beautiful, have undergone a marvellous transformation. Today wide wheat-fields, yellow with the golden harvest, stretch out to the golden west. Cities, prosperous towns, sprung up as if by magic, and railroads now follow the Indian trails where groaning and squeaking carts wended their way years ago. Where was once the red man's land now is a land of peace and plenty, every man the lord of his estate.

People come from all parts of the world, and the church is sure to be confronted by problems. God never or seldom works by miracle; the human hand must move away the stone, although the Lord of all is about to raise the dead to life. The bugle's sound aroused us from slumbers. We wished to keep that blood-stained banner of the cross floating on the breeze.

ENDEAVORERS ON SATURDAY AFTERNOON IN CENTRAL PARK

ONE OF THE BOOK-STALLS IN THE CONVENTION HALL

The Christian Endeavor union of Canada under the leadership of this great world-wide organization is trying to do its part to carry out the commission Christ gave His disciples to evangelize the world for the well-being and souls of men. We are here today to say we shall see things through. I know they can achieve anything but impossibilities, and I know that the winning of Canada for Christ is not an impossibility. We must do our duty, and not sit listless in inactivity. When I think today of the millions north of the line who know nothing of the Christ, I think of the unions of Manitoba, Winnipeg, and other territories spreading the gospel of Christ throughout that land. We bring to you today our greetings and our prayer for Dr. Clark and his associates that the Lord may preserve their going out and their coming in from this time forth and forevermore.

GREETINGS FROM INDIA

BY MRS. F. H. GATES

From that sea-girt island of Ceylon with its palm groves, and the plains of India with their myriad population, from the far-off Himalayas, the roof of the world, we bring greetings from fifty thousand Endeavorers of India and Ceylon. You know of the diseases which invade India, but they are only samples of the influences which are a pestilence around the young people of India, and we wonder whether anything beautiful can come from them. From pools of stagnant water comes the lily. Sow seeds of the gospel in that soil, and human lilies may come out, and Christian Endeavor has done much to bring these lilies to the top. I think our Christian Endeavor societies could give you some pointers in this country. Our front seats are never vacant. Another point is that there are no long pauses while one waits for another Every one is ready to take his part and pray his simple prayer to God. The doors of the heathen nations have been torn down, never to be closed again. Are we going to let these people go back into infidelity? O you Christians in America, can't you come out to take hold of that work and tell those people about Christ? There is so much to be done. We want those who can love, those who can work.

Christian Endeavor is a sky-rocketing thing. There is always the star, the star of hope overhead, which brings joy and peace into our hearts. Boys, come over the top, and bring your best girl with you. We can give you all the work you want, twenty-four hours a day.

In greeting or parting we give necklaces of flowers; and, when I left for America, our Christian Endeavor society, our union, and some of the organizations of the church and private individuals brought up and put on my neck twenty-eight garlands. They said they wanted to give me something that would keep, and to "please take this to America, and don't forget us"; and I have asked Dr. Clark to accept this as coming from India and as a token of love and loyalty of our Christian Endeavor society.

GREETINGS FROM SOUTH AFRICA

BY POLHEMUS LYON

Mr. President and fellow-citizens of the world.—I bring to you greeting officially transmitted through me by the South African Christian Endeavor Union, of which I was a member for twenty years. Christian Endeavor was imported by American women who came there to teach. We have a large number of boarding schools, and American women as teachers. These teachers have imported Christian Endeavor into these schools, so that when the girls have graduated and return home, they start Christian Endeavor societies in their own churches and homes. There was no cohesion until in 1897 Dr. Clark came, and Dr. Andrew

Murray became our first president; since then we have progressed. In 1898 we had our first convention, and started a special train to Cape Town, the first train to go to a religious convention. When I was a Sunday School boy in New York, we used to sing, "I want to be an angel." The Christian Endeavorers of South Africa don't want to be angels, but wish to do their work for Christ and the church, and assist in building up the kingdom of God as a reasonable service. I have not time to give you details of the work in South Africa. These friends from the Orient have something much more interesting to say. We are doing the best we can in South Africa, and are loyal; but we have tremendous problems. Mohammedanism is growing, among the colored people especially. Let me assure you that a Christian must be optimistic in spite of all troubles and problems, because we are working with God as our leader. I have personally heard several able Christian ministers and laymen testify to what Christian Endeavor means to South Africa. Thank God for Christian Endeavor and our great leader, Dr. Clark.

GREETINGS FORM CZECHO-SLOVAKIA AND POLAND

By Rev. Bohumil Prochasna

In bringing you the hearty greetings from Czecho-slovakia I want to say that just about the time the Pilgrims came to these shores the Bohemian people lost its great leader in battle, November 8, 1620. Here darkness and falsehood celebrated victory. Through the ruin of Austria she received her freedom and independence, a nation which for three hundred years had been tormented and poisoned with lies and falsehood. The influence of this change upon the life of Czecho-slovakia is great, and the people are turning away from the ways in which they had been. About one million have left the Roman Catholic Church. I believe there is not another country at the present time which offers so great an opportunity for the spreading of the gospel of Christian Endeavor. The Christian Endeavorers of America can do a great piece of work by sending men to Czecho-slovakia who will help in organizing societies We would also be immensely happy to have the next Christian Endeavor Convention held in Prague. I would ask every member in this Convention to remember our Christian Endeavor in your prayers, and may God awaken in us the spirit of our great worker and reformer John Huss. May the whole nation become one great Christian Endeavor society.

GREETINGS FROM ARMENIA

By Lady Anne Azapetian

My good Christian friends.—I bring you greetings from the oldest, the first Christian nation on earth, Armenia; and with the greetings they want me to bring to you a little message. They want me to tell you that through two thousand years we have clung tenaciously to the belief in Jesus Christ in spite of massacre and every terrible thing. We gave 250,000 soldiers in the great war; and today our country is a country of widows and orphans, and we are standing on the brink of annihilation. The Turks threaten to rebuild with the skulls of Christian Armenians the mosques destroyed. At every convention I have addressed business men, rich people; and I come here to ask the Christian Endeavorers of the world to use their influence at Washington to protest against this slaughter of Christian people, and that you want your government to see to it that we are protected. We are of Armenia, that ancient land that is watered by the Tigris and Euphrates, where Ararat raises its magnificent head in what was once the Garden of Eden. The Turks have now made this garden into a slaughter-place for Christians. I feel sure you will do something quickly to protect us.

I bring you a message from Armenia. It was at the foot of Mt. Ararat that they gave me this message. On that day I saw five thousand little children whose fathers had died in your cause, and I saw two thousand refugees I had brought in and fed by American generosity. They said, "Go back to America and say this: 'We are assembled at the foot of Mt. Ararat because you in America haven't forgotten to send us the crust of bread. We of Armenia every hour of the day and every day of the week pray God to bless America. We pray God to bless and prosper America forever and ever more.' "

GREETINGS FROM AUSTRALIA

By Rev. W. T. Marsh

I remember when I went out some time ago to that far-distant land some one has named a "Yankee notion." Then another "Yankee notion" came, and another regarding churches, and that was Christian Endeavor, another "Yankee notion." Another "Yankee notion" has been brought before us, and by the grace of God we are going to have it in Australia, prohibition.

Australia is a large country, possibly larger than the United States without Alaska, with a population a little larger than New York. We have indeed had with us your president. He has not always left his face with us, but he has his identification printed on our hearts. Some years ago that awful war prevented you from coming to the South Convention we looked forward to in Sydney. I believe the invitation stands good.

When our boys returned from the war, they said, "We like those Yankees; they are just like us." When the Yankee boys came home, they said, "We like those Anzacs; they are just like us." In this spirit of Christian Endeavor we are all alike. We have heard a great deal about isms, Darwinism, etc., and I think Christian Endeavorers should recognize a divine power, the divine power of the Saviour, but what about the Holy Ghost? We hear in the pulpits of God our Father, God our Saviour, Redeemer of mankind; but how much do you hear about the power of consecration and the Holy Ghost? You cannot leave out the dispensation; we live at the present time in the dispensation of the Holy Ghost.

When I saw that pageant, I wished I had been in it. I would have liked to bring a kangaroo, and put my arm around its neck, because the Endeavorers of Australia don't run or walk; they jump. Consequently our work is going to jump.

"Stand fast and firm; be strong in the faith; quit ye like men; be strong."

GREETINGS FROM FINLAND

By Miss Esther Kokkinen

I want to bring the greetings of the Endeavorers of Finland. During this Convention people have said, "What are the Finnish Endeavorers; are they Experts?" We come from Finland, where national prohibition was voted years ago and women have had the vote since 1906 and where literacy is 96 per cent.

I wish I could put Finland on the map for Christian Endeavor. This small country has only three million people, and we owe it to Dr. Clark for putting it on the Christian Endeavor map through articles in *The Christian Endeavor World*. I represent not only Endeavorers of Finland, but of the Finnish in America, especially in New England. They wanted me to remember them to you, as all Endeavorers are one in Christ. As Paul said, "We are all one through Christ Jesus," we are all one through Christian Endeavor.

GREETINGS FROM THE UNITED BRETHREN IN CHRIST (OLD CONSTITUTION)

By A. B. Bowman

The Christian Endeavor work in our church is rapidly pushing ahead. We were a little slow in getting into line, but now the number of our societies is rapidly increasing. The past year we had a twenty-five per cent. increase in Senior societies, and a two hundred per cent. increase in Junior societies; while in membership we had a net increase of twenty per cent.

We had a general secretary in the field the past four years on full time; for the next four years we will have in addition to this a man in charge of all our Christian Endeavor editorial work. We have two pages per week devoted to Christian Endeavor in our church paper.

Our young people believe in the pledge and are reasonably faithful in keeping it. They believe in the Covenant of the Quiet Hour, and the Tenth Legion. We have many loyal members of the same. Our pastors are boosters for Christian Endeavor, and appreciate the help the young people are to their church.

Our Endeavorers are supporting a medical missionary in Africa, besides contributing to other missionary interests. All our foreign missionaires are true Endeavorers and received their training in the Christian Endeavor society.

GREETINGS FROM REV. JAMES KELLY, PRESIDENT OF THE CHRISTIAN ENDEAVOR UNION OF GREAT BRITAIN AND IRELAND

To the Delegates Assembled in Convention at New York, U. S. A.

My Dear Friends:

It was with very great pleasure that a little over a year ago I accepted the courtesy of an invitation from Dr. Clark to join your deliberations. For some time I have been looking forward with genuine pleasure to this Convention, and very deeply regret that owing to the unsatisfactory state of my health, and acting on the advice of my physician, I am unable to be with you on this occasion. Especially should I have esteemed it an honor to have conveyed to you in person the greetings of the British Christian Endeavor Union, and to join with you in thanksgiving to our Heavenly Father for His wonderful goodness to the Christian Endeavor movement during the past forty years.

I am, however, greatly pleased that my friend and colleague, the Rev. John Pollock of Belfast, the President of the European Christian Endeavor Union, has found it possible to be with you at this time, and will represent the British Endeavor in my stead. Mr. Pollock is already well known to you. He is one of our most trusted leaders on this side of the Atlantic, and dearly beloved by his brethren in all the Churches.

No serious-minded Endeavorer can study the world's life in these days without realizing that its evangelization, in the broad New Testament sense, is its most urgent need. I believe with all my heart in the application of New Testament principles to State affairs and to public life.

If Christian Endeavor is to meet the new need aright, first things must be put first. Christ must be made known in word and deed with passionate faith. Sin must be denounced, and its doom proclaimed with tenderness and conviction, and loving knowledge of the commandments of the Lord and obedience thereto must be the ever-deepening and ever-widening triumph of the Holy Ghost. Only the Divine Spirit can drive out the evil spirit of mammonism and militarism, of drunkenness and lust. Our program is a program of today as well as the redemption of the morrows. It is to establish the Kingdom of Righteousness here and now. It is both a program and an ideal, a policy and a prayer. I pray you carry on your battle against principalities and powers and spiritual wickedness in high places, and go forth determined to keep the soul of the world alive to God and the things eternal. Believe in the power of God to create something wholly new. Always believe that every command is a promise, every need a pledge of divine power to meet it, for those who are loyal to the call.

"The Grace of our Lord Jesus Christ, and the Love of God and the Communion of the Holy Ghost be with you all."

GREETINGS FROM INDIA

Dear Dr. Clark:

We, the officers of the India Christian Endeavor Union, wish to extend, through you, our heartiest greetings to the World Christian Endeavor Convention to be held in New York City in July of this year. According to our statistics for 1919 our union consists of 1,972 societies and 60,045 members. We are thus only a little more than one per cent. of the great host enrolled under the C. E. banner, but we feel that our position here in the Orient gives to our members a peculiar opportunity and responsibility. Christian Endeavor has thoroughly adapted itself to India; and the Associate societies in our village schools where most of the members are Hindoo children, and the societies composed of Christian Workers who come together only once a month, each from the village in which he or she is working, show how full of possibilities our movement is. We believe that Christian Endeavor was a God-given means for training the Christian youth of all lands and we pledge our loyalty to it in the days to come.

We have by no means as yet reached the zenith of our growth and influence. Great leaders we have had. Some of these have gone to their reward, some have retired from the work, but God is raising up others to carry on the work. The same spirit remains and will lead to greater victories. We need a National Secretary very much and trust he will soon come out. Certainly some man, thoroughly qualified, will offer himself at the Convention if he has not already been appointed.

We pray that the Holy Spirit Himself may be present in all the preparations for the Convention and that He may be the only speaker there, perhaps using many as His mouthpieces, but giving but the one message of Jesus and His love for all men. Would that all men might see His face and hear His voice for then they must accept Him as their Lord and Master.

Jos. J. BANNINGA, President.
B. DAS, Vice-President,
WILLIAM J. HATCH, Secretary.
J. M. BAKER, Treasurer.

SUNRISE CONSECRATION SERVICE

By Varick and Allen Chritian Endeavorers

On Sunday morning, July 10th, at six o'clock about thirty-five Allen Christian Endeavorers and Varick Christian Endeavorers met on the top of one of the highest hills overlooking the beautiful St. Nicholas Park at One Hundred and Thirty-fifth street and Eighth avenue. Although the weather was threatening, it did not stop the Endeavorers in their eagerness to have a quiet communion with their God. The singing was full of spirit. After an earnest prayer the principal message of the meeting was brought by the Rev. A. F. B. Horry, Allen Christian Endeavor superintendent of South Carolina Conference. Brief testimonies were given, followed by sentence prayers and Bible verses by the Endeavorers. The meeting was brought to a fitting close with consecration service led by Rev. M. E. Davis of Virginia. After the Mizpah benediction the entire company marched through the streets singing to Bethel African Methodist Episcopal Church, 60 West One Hundred and Thirty-second street, Rev. M. W. Thornton, pastor, where the services were continued, led by Mrs. Lucy Lewis, of Pittsburgh, Penna, field secretary of the Allen Christian Endeavor Leagues. The meeting was most enthusiastic, with testimonies and singing. At half past eight a fellowship breakfast was served to about seventy out-of-town delegates. After breakfast a short conference was called by the general secretary of the Allen Christian Endeavor society, Rev. S. S. Morris, to formulate plans for a Young People's Congress in Chicago, July, 1922, under the Allen Christian Endeavor Leagues. After the meeting the Endeavorers attended the morning services upstairs. In the afternoon at half past five the Varick Christian Endeavorers of Mother Zion African Methodist Episcopal Church, New York City, Rev. J. W. Brown, pastor, tendered an informal reception to the delegates, which was attended by about two hundred. A delicious repast was served, followed by speaking. Professor Aaron Brown, general secretary of the Varick Christian Endeavor society, was the principal speaker, with Mr R. A. Tucker of Washington, D. C., and many others.

CHAPTER XXII.

DENOMINATIONS AND STATES

ARMORY, MONDAY AFTERNOON, JULY 11

A. J. Shartle, Presiding

TREASURER SHARTLE presided in the Monday afternoon Armory session, and the opening prayer was made by Mr. Frank Goodman, the converted gambler, now a well-known evangelist. The beloved Scottish preacher, Rev. John McNeill, gave us a characteristically quaint and interesting talk, "Fishers of Men," full of humor, full of pith.

Ruskin once said to some preachers, "You have only half an hour in which to raise the dead." I have less than half an hour, but then you are supposed to be living.

Our Lord was the greatest example of soul-winning, and He was always at it. As Levi was sitting at the receipt of custom, Jesus passed by and said to him, "Follow me." And Levi, that is, Matthew, rose up and followed Him. And it did not take twenty minutes, no longer than the time I am taking to tell the story. If you met the Lord at any time of day you knew what He was after. He was seeking and saving the lost. *How about you?*

Jesus said, "Matthew, I want you." Matthew said, "Oh, do you? Well, here I am." You would have thought it was the wrong time, and the wrong place, and the wrong man. It proved to be just the right time and place and man. Now, you p-r-u-d-e-n-t people, that are afraid you will be growled at if you ask folks to come to Christ—who are you that you should not be growled at? Did the Master avoid that? Did Paul? No, they got jeers and rebuffs, even from fellow Christians. But you would be so prudent that you say nothing. You are so cautious that you never start.

Now prudence is a drug in the market; and it's hard for a Scotchman to say anything against prudence and caution. But, you see, I have a saving bit in me. I am half Irish, and I can claim the virtues of both countries without the faults of either. There's a great lesson, if you take the Master as an example of soul-winning. Matthew was a renegade, turncoat Jew. That's the man Jesus fastened upon to save him, and it was a week-day when he did it.

Follow your man. Moody said he would rather have zeal without discretion than discretion without zeal. Paul said, if you want to be wise, become a fool. I am afraid there is no great competition among us to be like Paul in this. He that winneth souls is wise, which we may turn around and say, Wise men will win souls.

Matthew's was not a case of drunkenness or lust or living a double life; it was a case of love of money, one of the most debasing and hardening lusts out of hell, and it is fearfully common. I have a passage of God's Word for that. If you don't know it, hunt it up. I haven't time to tell you everything in twenty minutes.

All Matthew got was a Face and a word. He lifted his eyes from the ledger, and he saw a Face. Angels veil their faces with their wings

199

from the insufferable glory and majesty of that Face today, but then the glory of God in the face of Jesus Christ was veiled; yet even then nothing could altogether veil the glory of the Son of God.

Very often today, before you get a man saved, you have to preach an hour to him, and then have a second meeting, and then somebody must deal with him for another hour, and even then he may go out as he came in. O Christ, give us the power to win souls. Give us the power, or we preach in vain.

Not always does even the Face win souls. The rich young ruler got the same Face that Levi got, and the same word that Levi heard, "Take up your cross and follow me," but it failed. The Face of Christ —God pity us!—was wasted on him. The face of the world held him, and this is fearfully common today—today.

But when Matthew saw that Face and heard that word, the tax-collecting and the riches it meant fell from him like dead flies in a moment. What a liberation! The voice of Jesus and the word of Jesus come to me now, saying, "No delay, if you would ever be a soul-winner." Be imperative. Be urgent. Now is the accepted time, Matthew. Today is the day to be saved. There are two great words that should always be on the lips of soul-winners, thou and now. There is a glorious imperial note in the gospel of Christ. Did you ever notice, dear Endeavorers, that all these gospel appeals are in the imperative mood? Do not weaken their urgency. Keep up the pitch—the pitch—the pitch of the Master's voice, "Now do thou follow me!"

Not doctrines—and I believe in the doctrines. I have a very definite doctrinal system, which is truly Biblical. We Scotch Presbyterians were the creed-makers for the world. I see you do not cheer that; you have a lot to learn. I believe in the Bible as the Word of God; but it is not the Book that saves, nor the church, nor baptism, nor the Lord's Supper, nor prayer, nor even the collection. I will allow you to be a little heathen in regard to some of these, I was going to say, if you are absolutely sound on the Person of Christ. Preach the Person of Christ! You will need all the doctrines to do that.

There was Houdini. We had him here in New York, the Handcuff King. He would let a man handcuff him, and tie him tight with ropes, and put him behind a screen. In a few minutes out stepped Houdini free. That's nothing. That's only a weak illustration of the glorious liberating power of God among the sons of men. Did you ever see it? If you ever saw it, you will never forget it. It is liberation into endless life, and the Matthew episode shows us how it is done.

I see Matthew on his office-stool. He took just a look at his ledger, just a glance at the private page on which he had summed up his ill-gotten gains. Then he shut up the ledger forever. Hell was baffled. Heaven rejoiced in another soul surrendered to the Christ of God. Glory to God! Are you doing that work today? What an opportunity!

Blücher, the German general, visited London, and when he saw its size and wealth he exclaimed, "Oh, what a city to loot!" Can you be in New York for twenty-four hours and not say, "What a city in which to be a soul-winner"?

With nothing but that Face and that word Matthew was liberated from all the coils that tied him to sin and doom. Did you notice how it is put there? He "left all," and then he "rose up and followed Him." It might have been put the other way, "He followed Him and then he left all." Without rising from the office-stool he fought his battle. He left all, then he rose up. We have too many people in all the churches that seem to rise up on Sunday, and sing the hymns and take the sacrament and listen to the sermon, but the rest of the week shows that they have not left all. Matthew left all. With the decision of his heart the rest was easy. But the act means nothing if the heart is not with Christ.

Remember Lot's wife. She looked back. Her heart was there in Sodom. She was a Sodomite down to the ground, though her body was elsewhere. You can't cheat God. Why do we want to cheat Him, if all our mind is naked and open to Him with whom we have to do?

Are we really detached from the world? Are we really detached from self and bound to Him with an indissoluble bond? Then His zeal to win souls will have its way with us. He will justify His way. We shall be instant in season and out of season, for Death is instant in season and out, and those who win souls from death should "catch men alive."

Following this unique address an honored Boston clergyman, Rev. Vaughan Dabney, D.D., spoke eloquently and earnestly on the unusual topic, "Exploring for the Never-Never Country." He based his thought on Kipling's poem of the explorers who were unsatisfied with the cultivated land though men urged them to stay there and insisted that there was nothing worth while beyond. But they constantly heard voices calling them beyong the ranges, into new lands and new blessings, "the Never-Never Country." "You'll never, never find anything there that is as good as this," the satisfied folks said; but the discoverers pressed on to richer fields and wealthier mines.

"Now," said Mr. Dabney, "you are going home from this great Convention full of the ideals that have inspired you here; and the people back home are going to discourage you, and tell you to settle down contented, for there is nothing better beyond. But press on, Endeavorers, in spite of all, into the Never-Never Country of your dreams."

The speaker unfolded the array of great ideals brought before the Convention—the ideal of co-operation that is to supplant our industrial strife and competition, the ideal of human brotherhood that is to take the place of race hatred, the ideal of international peace that is to abolish war, the ideal of love to Christ and to all Christ's children that is to drive away selfishness and cold indifference. Dr. Dabney urged us to be true to all these ideals on returning home, and in the face of any discouragement, press on into the Never-Never Country.

The denominational hour followed these two notable addresses. As Mr. Shartle called upon them, a large number of leaders in the various denominations, chiefly trustees of the United Society, told what Christian Endeavor has meant to their churches.

DR. RUFUS MILLER, *Representing the Reformed Church in U. S.*

Christian Endeavor was planted in the Reformed Church more than thirty-five years ago, and has been growing ever since in the regard and esteem of the ministry until last year the highest church body in our denomination permanently established a young people's work with a program of foursquare movement which stands for Christian Endeavor. Six young people's conferences are to be held this summer for the training of Christian Endeavorers. You can see what we have been doing when Shartle and Hamilton are products of what it can do. The Reformed Church always stands for co-operative Endeavor. It has stood for the great fundamentals which are incarnated in Christian Endeavor, liberty, loyalty, love. These are the tokens by which we must advance for Christianity to win the world.

REV. G. C. CARPENTER, *Representing United Brethren Church.*

In twenty years Christian Endeavor has had an increasingly larger place in the church. We are going to do our best to make this Convention help us reach those goals. We made plans to pass along as much as possible of this splendid inspiration we have received here to all our societies.

A. B. KENDALL, *Representing the Christian Church.*

I am sure that with all of you this has been indeed a great meeting and a great inspiration, and I wish I might be able to transmit all this blessing to all the members of our society. I have nothing but encouraging words to bring from the young people of our churches. The message is, "Endeavor is picking up; interest is increasing in our conferences." We have been putting on a strong program, and we are planning a 20 per cent. increase in Senior societies, 75 per cent. in Intermediate, and 75 per cent. in Junior. We are striving to put in an Alumni Fellowship where practicable. We have a movement for more active and progressive evangelism, a movement along the line of religious education, one for missions, and one for benevolences, consecration of the individual life in the line of Life-Work Recruits, and the giving of our substance. We are hoping for splendid results for the next three years ahead of us because we have been planning a four-year campaign. While we are not very large, we are proud of the fact that we are the people who put into the interdenominational side of Christian Endeavor the "inter." I believe outside of the church where it was organized the first society was in our church. We have always stood for the heartiest co-operation, and are looking forward with hope to the day when we may all be one.

REV. MR. PROUD, *Representing the Primitive Methodist Church.*

Twenty-seven years ago there were very few young people's societies in the Primitive Methodist Church in the United States. These were called Wesley Leagues, and had no affiliation with any other denomination. Christian Endeavor meets every need of the young people of our church. Under its broad and comprehensive constitution all requirements are met. No other organization of young people is necessary. God bless Christian Endeavor! Long live Christian Endeavor!

A. G. DICKINSON, *Representing the Methodist Protestant Church.*

For thirty-five years we have taken an active part with the other Christian Endeavorers of this country. We had a rally with thirteen States and the District of Columbia and Japan represented, and claim two of the field-workers of the United Society as our own. Our purpose is to work for Christian Endeavor shoulder to shoulder with you. God bless and lead us in our Christian Endeavor meetings.

REV. A. A. BROWN, *Representing the Zion A. M. E. Church.*

I am glad to bring you greetings adopted by the Christian Endeavor 1896 Conference held in Mobile, Ala. Today we have 2,600 Christian Endeavor societies reaching from Buffalo, N. Y., to Miami, Fla.; from Carolina to California. We have a large number of subscribers to *The Christian Endeavor World,* and it is our prayer to God that the great founder of this work may be spared many years to keep on with this great work.

REV. FRANK LOWE, JR., *Representing the Church of the Disciples of Christ.*

The Disciples of Christ love Dr. Francis E. Clark, the man behind Christian Endeavor. The Disciples of Christ love Mrs. Clark, the woman behind Dr. Francis E. Clark. The Disciples of Christ love something else which is behind Christian Endeavor; it is that old beloved, iron-clad pledge. Christian Endeavor stands or falls by the pledge, and the Disciples of Christ are going home from this Convention to emphasize that thing which Christian Endeavor best of all stands for; and that is the pledge of personal loyalty to Jesus Christ, and a daily program of worship and service for Him. As long as Christian Endeavorers are sufficiently Christian to take that pledge, and, having taken it, endeavor sufficiently to live up to it, Christian Endeavor can never die.

REV. S. S. MORRIS, *Representing the Allen C. E. League.*

I represent the African Methodist Episcopal Church. Since the great convention at Montreal we have had representatives at each and all of the conventions. I come to bring greetings from the Christian Endeavor Society of our church. We have something like 350,000 members in the Allen Christian Endeavor League of our church. We have any number of new societies organized this year. As I see it, the prospect for Christian Endeavor was never brighter in our church. We are asking for 25 per cent. net increase in our membership. We are laying special emphasis on the open Bible, which is back of our constitution, which is our Magna Charta. We are also emphasizing home worship. We are proud of Dr. Clark and Mrs. Clark, and stand by all the ideals of the Christian Endeavor Society. I wish you to pray in your Quiet Hour every morning for the young people of our church, that there may be fellowship in service whether East, West, North, or South. I greet you, salute you, in the name of our Lord.

REV. C. L. REGAN, *Representing the Friends' Church.*

I am sure that as a society of Friends we appreciate the helps and interest that Christian Endeavor has given us in the last third of a century. We believe in disarmament. We believe in interchurch work, and especially we are going to do all we can for the generation just younger than us.

MR. HYAM, *Baltimore, Md., Representing the Lutheran Church.*

The Lutheran Church like other great bodies in this country was divided into a number of separate bodies. Within the last three years six of these leading bodies have united into two bodies. The leading divisions of our church merged into one. It was recommended that our societies should be Luther Leagues, but they are Luther Leagues of Christian Endeavor. We stand loyal to the principles of Christian Endeavor, and the livest churches we have are those in which Christian Endeavor has a prominent part. They are working for Christ and the church, and we are trying our best to bring all into His kingdom.

MR. H. N. LATHROP, *Representing the Baptists.*

I have been an Endeavorer forty years and a Baptist fifty years. Baptists are especially long on water, and I don't know whether I am a better Baptist because I am a Christian Endeavorer, or a better Christian Endeavorer because I am a Baptist. I am satisfied with my earthly state, and think I shall be with my heavenly state.

This closed the denominational testimonies and Mr. Shartle passed without pause to the messages from the State presidents. He introduced President MacDonald from Maine as representing the original State.

Rev. J. Charles MacDonald, *President, Maine State C. E. Union.*

Long ago a call was sent from high heaven's battlements, which was answered promptly, and a man was born, the first Endeavorer. I am glad to represent the first State. Christian Endeavor is coming to the forefront in Maine, and we are looking forward to having a regular field-secretary, and to putting Christian Endeavor back again into the churches of Maine. There is a power to help us make Christian Endeavor a factor once more in the State of Maine, and that power is none other than that power given us by Jesus Christ.

A colonel was told to drive through some mountains and take the heights. He realized it would mean much destruction to his regiment. He said to the Duke of Wellington, "Do you mean for me to take those heights?" Then he said, "Give me but one grip of your conquering hand, and I will take those heights."

I want to take the grip of the conquering hand of Christ and make that State once more a centre of Christian Endeavor.

Bert Rudolph, *Pennsylvania.*

We have one of the greatest delegations present in this Convention. We feel confident that we have at least 2,000 delegates, and we feel glad to bring you the greetings of the great State of Pennsylvania.

I was told that, as the Pennsylvania delegation entered Central Park, there was born in the zoölogical department a leopard. They said that leopard will be called Pennsylvania. So we are leaving here a baby leopard named for the greatest State in the Union.

Rev. R. B. Fisher, *Iowa.*

I come with greetings from twenty thousand Christian Endeavorers of Iowa, the land where the tall corn grows. We have captured the Convention for 1923. We are supposed to go back and do some good work. As president of the State Christian Endeavor union, I propose we have some slogans to work for: make the movies moral; ballyhoos to the bottom; save the sacred Sabbath; put down the indecent dance and divorce; help restore the Scriptures to the school.

If we need anything, we need to teach our fellowship, teach citizenship to the foreigner, and loyalty to the laws of God.

Miss Lillian Dyer, *Oklahoma.*

I am very glad to greet you in the name of the Oklahoma Endeavorers. We are very proud of our delegation of the Southwest, proud that we are a part of that great organization that has done so much, Christian Endeavor; also we are proud of Roy Breg.

Oklahoma expects to go forward and take its place. We are glad of the new program, the program for the "foursquare Christian Endeavor"; and I assure you that Oklahoma's representatives are determined to put Christian Endeavor over for Oklahoma "foursquare" for Christ.

Fred Porter, *Texas.*

I come to bring you greetings from the largest State. We have done great things in Texas, but with the inspiration and knowledge we have gained here we believe we can go back to even greater things in that great State.

R. H. Singer, *Arizona.*

You haven't heard from the "baby" State. I count it a great privilege to bring you greetings from the Arizona Christian Endeavor union. We believe ever-working Christian Endeavor is a booster. We have set up for our slogan, "All workers, no shirkers." Christian Endeavor is going forward in Arizona in the coming years.

REV. G. H. L. BEEMAN, *West Virginia.*

I come from the little mountain State of West Virginia. Christian Endeavor as a State organization is not so old and experienced as some of the larger States, and we have mountains of difficulties to confront; but West Virginia is on the upgrade, and we expect to keep on up. We are increasing the interest along the line. The greatest difficulty is to get anywhere, speaking physically. Our railroads take very circuitous routes all around the valleys and hills. Our State convention in June was in Bluefield in the northern part of the State, and it took longer, ten hours longer, to get to Bluefield than to come to New York. We have to go all the way around the edge of the State to get anywhere, so that it is hard to have large conventions. Our *Mountain Bulletin* is increasing in circulation.

DR. W. C. SMOLENSKE, *Colorado.*

I am not here because I am from the greatest or largest State, but from God's country of Colorado, the "Playground of America." We have a new secretary, John Cecil, and in two months' time he organized twenty societies. We got him a car. We have had a terrible disaster in our State; but Christian Endeavor got behind Pueblo, and we are going to dig our way out to a greater and better Colorado Endeavor. We have a wonderful Christian governor. He helps us by his moral and financial support. One thousand great big dollars he gave us last year. He said, "There is no substitute for work"; and that is the motto we took. Before, we have had registrations of three hundred; a year ago we had one thousand eight hundred. We were supposed to have had a convention last week. Then another big bit of work we tried to do was to get that great State of Wyoming to come on down. We said, "We want to make you a part of Colorado." We are back of Dr. Clark, the United Society, and back of everything that stands for Christian Endeavor.

L. R. ROBINSON, *Oregon.*

I am very glad to bring the Endeavorers, the United Society officers, and Dr. Clark greetings from Oregon. We brought ten folks from Oregon, and we think this is a pretty good delegation for that distance. We have not had a field-secretary in the past, but we are placing one within the next two months. We are glad to enlarge the movement, and we are ready and willing to back the next Convention. We came with the hopes that we could get the 1923 Convention, but we fully realize it was best for the Christian Endeavor movement. We are coming back in 1923 for the 1925 Convention. We want your support.

MISS M. McARTHUR, *Utah.*

I am sure when people hear the word "Utah" it isn't connected with Christian Endeavor, but I want them to know Christian Endeavor is alive in Utah. Although small in numbers, we are great in spirit. The Endeavorers of Utah, "trusting in the Lord Jesus Christ for strength," are going to make Utah stand for Christian Endeavor more than it ever has before.

MISS E. CHRISTIANSEN, *Wyoming.*

Wyoming is the baby State in Christian Endeavor. The Wyoming Christian Endeavor union on the seventh of this month was two months old. We want Christian Endeavor to go forward, and, when we put before them this new program, something will happen. Every morning when we wake up we see the real sun, something I haven't seen in New York yet, coming up from 'those mountains; and we feel the warmth of God's love, and feel that God is guiding us. We want Christian Endeavor for Wyoming and Wyoming for Christian Endeavor. We are not here to go back.

JACK COLBURN, *Tennessee.*

I want to extend to you the greetings from the volunteer State that has always been first in everything. I want to say th^ I am glad I am here from Dixie. You saw a minute ago banner number one for meeting its quota first. Tennessee is the first State east of the Mississippi to reach her quota for registration for the Convention. Christian Endeavor is surely moving in Tennessee. We have better co-operation than we ever had before. The love for Christ in Tennessee is stronger than ever before. Then we have the prayers of all our State officers, one for the other, which helps out a lot. We have the prayers of our Endeavorers for the work in our State. I believe prayer is the main reason. Everybody is trying, and, after all, it is not what we really do that gets our reward in heaven; it is what we try to do.

REV. W. H. HARPER, *Kentucky.*

I think you should hear from the best State. In Kentucky people believe in the nation, the church, and the home. We believe Christian Endeavor is a God-appointed agency to train and send out into the land qualified leaders of God's type. We believe we need citizens who are really patriots. We need Christians who are really loyal to Christ. We need homes that are devout and worshipful. We are trying to provide this type of Christianity. Our State has given Mr. Wallis and Mr. Rodeheaver to Christian Endeavor, and we are going to try to give you some more like them.

DUNCAN C. CURRY, *Florida.*

Florida accepts Dr. Clark's challenge of the "foursquare" program, and we are aiming that our program shall be well balanced as to Juniors, Intermediates, and Alumni.

We had a letter from a man who would have liked to come to the Convention; but he said he was not a member, but his four grand-children were. We are very sorry his children won't let him come. We never grow too old in Florida to make Christian Endeavor worth while.

FRED BALL, *Ohio.*

Ohio today greets all the rest of the States in the Union, and all of the forty-eight that are greatest. We greet Canada, South America, Mexico, Asia and Europe. Practically all of these countries have contributed something towards Christian Endeavor. We are glad to greet you in this Christian Endeavor fellowship. We had two thousand six hundred delegates in Dayton. We promise our continued support in the "Foursquare Campaign."

FRED W. COLLINS, *New York.*

No matter what adjectives are used in regard to States, New York is the leading State. If you want to advance in Christian Endeavor, watch New York, follow on, and you may become next to the leaders.

We had a State convention during this great Convention. We elected a new State president, and I am giving him half of my time.

WILLIAM C. BROWN, *Rochester, N. Y.*

You know that New York stands already "foursquare" in Christian Endeavor, and I want to assure you that in accepting the program that this Convention suggests we will do our level best to put over the "foursquare" program.

GEORGE C. OTIS, *Vermont.*

Vermont is not the largest State, nor the smallest; but up there in those hills and valleys are people I am glad to represent today. The only message I have today is that whoever goes to Des Moines is going to represent just about twice that number.

Rev. Fred A. MacDonald, *Rhode Island.*

We may be little in Rhode Island, but they have some great things there just the same. It becomes my great privilege and happiness to bring greetings from the State that has given the largest conception of civil and religious liberty. We are proud of our past and of our future as far as Christian Endeavor is concerned. You know that some little things can cause a great deal of action. The boys in France found that out. We want to bring this to you, that "Little Rhody" is facing "foursquare" out on Long Island Sound and the Atlantic Ocean.

C. Walter Lotte, *New Jersey.*

We have five hundred Christian Endeavor societies in New Jersey, with fifteen thousand members, of whom one thousand five hundred are registered delegates at this Convention. I feel that you will agree with me that any State union that has 10 per cent. registered is not a dead State. For many years New Jersey has not been able to have a field-secretary, but it is with a great deal of pleasure to Dr. Clark and the Endeavorers that on September 1, 1921, the State of New Jersey will enter the ranks of great Christian Endeavor States with a full-time Christian Endeavor secretary.

Asa Burgess, *Massachusetts.*

We are the headquarters State, the live State, the dynamo State, the land where the Pilgrims came. If you have any good project you want to put over, send it down to Massachusetts. We are not very big, but by our red coats you saw we are full of fire.

We organized 163 new Christian Endeavor societies; we are 75 per cent. good in Alumni, a live State, the home of Dr. Clark.

T. T. Phillips, *Connecticut.*

Connecticut had the first local union and the first State union; but we are not living in the past; the best is yet to come.

Hugh Foster, *District of Columbia.*

Little Rhode Island has told you they are the smallest State, but we are smaller than Rhode Island. We try to entertain the Endeavorers when they come to us. We have had them come to Washington during the war. They are coming back now as the jobs are expiring. We hope they will bring back to you some of the good ideas of Christian Endeavor they have learned there. I don't suppose that every one knows that the District of Columbia has no voice in its government; we are not citizens; we do not vote.

Christian Endeavorers, by our petitions, by our trusting in Christ, we are going to make the District of Columbia a 75 per cent. organization at this time, and we are going to put this forward the next two years. We invite you to come to Washington in 1925. There is now a plan to have a great hall erected, and we hope to have it ready for the 1925 Convention and show you your nation's capital, and show you Washington, D. C.

Bert Jones, *North Carolina.*

I have been listening to all these things and wondering what kind of boasting they would have if they had a State like North Carolina, which has 416 Christian Endeavor societies, with a membership of sixteen thousand; one thousand three hundred Quiet Hour Comrades; organized last year 58 new societies, and put Christian Endeavor into the Episcopal Church. If you want to put a bid in for Christian Endeavor, just try to keep up with North Carolina.

Quoting Mr. Siler, *Missouri.*

The United Society gave us a quota of 100. We have 159 delegates at this Convention. We came by special train.

G. E. MILEY, *Virginia.*

I want to bring to you the greetings from the "mother" State as back of the United Society and the All-South for twenty-two years. For the last two years we have had many Life-Work Recruits. The outstanding feature of our last convention was that over half of our registered delegates were young men. We are going to uphold these young men in the next two years.

F. D. G. WALKER, *Illinois.*

I represent the greatest State in the Union, that furnished a general secretary for the United Society. We have organized 625 new Christian Endeavor societies, and we have scored over the top 312 mission-study classes, with 5,975 young people. The army knows not the meaning of "defeat" or "retreat." We can already say, "Come on" for we have already gone.

M. L. BRADFORD, *Arkansas.*

We are like the Chinaman in the following story: An American owned a store on one corner, with an Irishman on one side and a Chinaman on the other. They were talking about how long they kept their stores open. The American said his was open until twelve o'clock; the Irishman said his was open all night; the Chinaman said, "Me wakee too."

Mississippi.

We had 50 per cent. increase in membership during the past year. We are going to put strong emphasis on the Intermediates in Christian Endeavor.

South Carolina.

We have given two of the finest field-secretaries on this platform, Mr. W?—— and Mr. Denby?

PAUL BROWN, *California.*

I was born out in California, and do not know enough about it yet. We have made three thousand net gain in net membership, two thousand being Intermediates. We have finished our year out of debt, and with a new budget and resources that will give us $11,000 for the year. We had 3,465 delegates to our State convention and one day elapsed between that convention and this one. We brought thirty delegates along.

GEORGE J. RITTERBUSCH, *Maryland.*

I bring you greetings from Maryland. In 1919 we heard the challenge, and in 1920 in Baltimore we held a State convention. Our theme was, "Forward," and we come to this Convention pressing forward. In 1923 you will find our doors open for hospitality for the 1925 Convention in Maryland.

North Dakota.

The president of North Dakota's union, Mrs. W. E. Butler, pledged her Endeavors to the new program of Christian Endeavor.

This ended the cheering messages of the State presidents.

The Wall Street Evangelistic Meeting.
Rev. John Pollock, D.D., Belfast, Ireland, speaking

A Meeting in Chinatown

CHAPTER XXIII

WALL STREET EVANGELISTIC MEETINGS
(And at Many other Places, July 6-11)

REV. ARTHUR J. SMITH, *Chairman*

CHRISTIAN ENDEAVOR in action in evangelistic effort has long been an important element in conventions. The State delegations came to New York prepared to seize the opportunities offered. Sixty gospel teams had been organized. Thursday morning they met Rev. Arthur J. Smith, D.D., the chairman of the Convention Committee on Evangelism, to arrange details. Teams having few members were combined. Individuals were free to join teams.

At the morning sessions in the Armory members of the teams took seats in the rear, that they might easily leave promptly. At the proper time each leader of a team held up a large placard bearing its name and number, that the members might know where to gather; and a guide at once took the group to the place where they were to conduct a noon meeting at a dock, factory, square, or elsewhere. The police department of the city had granted unusual freedom in the use of the streets for the purpose. At the preparatory meeting, where an address was given on leadership for service, the Endeavorers were charged to avoid references to racial, political, or disputed religious points, and only to preach Jesus Christ and Him crucified.

On Friday noon a special service was held in Wall Street, the speaker standing on the steps of the Sub-treasury but a few feet from the tablet representing the Father of His Country in prayer. After selections by the Salvation Army band, Mr. Rodeheaver announced, "Everybody that is good-natured is going to sing 'America.'" Then came "Brighten the Corner Where You Are."

Dr. John Pollock told of the difference between being a Christian in the ideal sense and in the real sense. like the difference between a nominal and a true soldier, and appealed to all to become at once learners in Christ's school, soldiers in Christ's army.

"Onward, Christian Soldiers" rang out heartily from the throng, and Rev. John McNeill spoke on "Look unto me, and be saved." "If you do not believe that to be saved from sin is the greatest of all blessings," he said, "I may wonder why you are allowed. to go about loose." What could be easier than

209

looking as a way to be saved? The look that saves is a look at a person. Look as Barabbas may have looked at Jesus on the cross, saying: "You are there for me. But for you I should be lost and condemned and hopeless. There is life for a look at the crucified One."

Mr. Rodeheaver sang tenderly "Tell me the story of Jesus." Mr. John Mackay, who daily leads a service in Wall Street, asked, "How many in this crowd will say, 'From this day on, by the grace of God, I will lead a Christian life'?" Very many hands were raised in answer, and Mr. McNeill led in a closing prayer.

On Saturday afternoon among the swarming crowds at the Vanity Fair of Coney Island a service was held at which the life and liberty of the Christian were set forth by several speakers to a group not a few of whom probably had never heard the message in a church.

These are but samples of many gatherings where the gospel message was given to all classes of hearers. The results of the songs and testimony by the Christian Endeavorers at these services are beyond tabulation, but very many cases of changed lives will doubtless be made known when the workers have had a chance to tell their experiences more fully. The blessed influences of the Convention reached a vast number that did not go near the Armory.

CHAPTER XXIV.

CHAPTER OF REPORTS

ANNUAL REPORT OF THE PRESIDENT OF THE WORLD'S CHRISTIAN ENDEAVOR UNION

By Francis E. Clark, D.D., LL.D.
President, the World's Christian Endeavor Union

July 6, 1921.

To the Trustees of the World's Christian Endeavor Union,

Gentlemen:

Our latest world's convention was held in Chicago in 1915. If we do not count "Boston, '95," where the World's Union was organized, this present Convention is the Sixth World's gathering of the forces of Christian Endeavor. The previous conventions of this scope and character have been held in Washington, 1896, London, 1900, Geneva, 1906, Agra, 1909, Chicago, 1915.

The last world's convention was held near the beginning of the hideous war that has changed the face of our globe politically, socially, industrially. No such revolutionary years have been known perhaps in all history; no such enormous changes as these seventy-two short months have witnessed.

Has Christian Endeavor stood the strain? Has she moved from her foundations? I think we can honestly reply "Yes" to the first question, and "No" to the seond. Not in the slightest essential particular has Christian Endeavor removed from the great fundamental principles and practices which for forty years have been her sheet anchors. She still stands for the world-wide fellowship of all young people who love the Lord Jesus Christ, and are loyal to their own churches and denominational enterprises. She still stands for frequent confession of Christ and constant service for Christ. She still stands for the expression of the religious life through the prayer meeting, the consecration meeting, the committees, the Quiet Hour and the Tenth Legion, and multitudinous religious and social activities.

The number of the countries in which Christian Endeavor has found a home has been considerably augmented since 1915, including the new nations of Europe and several republics of South America. I said a few days ago that our societies were found in every nation on the face of the earth and every large dependency except the little republic of Paraguay. Since then I have been told that Paraguay has been added to the list.

Since our convention of 1915 I have been able to visit Hawaii, Japan, Korea, China, England, Scotland, France, Switzerland and Jugo-Slavia, and found much to encourage me in all these lands. In Germany there has been a great development in the number of societies of Christian Endeavor, from 500 in 1915 to nearly a thousand in 1921.

In the countries that have suffered most from war, Finland, Poland, Esthonia, Hungary, Serbia and others, the recovery and growth of our movement has been phenomenal, and can be ascribed only to the blessing of Almighty God and the inherent vitality of the principles for which we stand.

211

South America has made large advances in Christian Endeavor activity. She has representatives now in all the republics and is planning for a great continental convention in Brazil in 1922, the hundredth anniversary of the independence of Brazil.

Canada, South Africa, Australia, New Zealand, all hard hit by the war and its aftermath, like other countries, are recovering their pre-war status in Christian Endeavor, and we trust will far exceed it.

In Great Britain, the mother of so many nations, distinct evidences of Christian Endeavor revival are shown, and the last year has been the best of any in the last decade.

The greatest opportunity in many respects for the rapid growth of Christian Endeavor is found in the vast oriental nations, Japan, China, India and Burma. In these the four thousand societies might be multiplied by ten could we find the men and the money to adequately develop these fields.

I cannot at this time dwell more upon the encouragements, the opportunities, the needs of this vast field. Literally Christian Endeavor can adopt John Wesley's motto: "My field is the world." You alone, fellow Endeavorers, by your generosity or its lack, will open new doors or you may limit the World's Union in entering even those already standing wide open. God has shown Himself abundantly willing to bless our work, to fill our cups full to overflowing. Are we ready to provide Him more loving cups to fill?

The home expenses of the World's Union of Christian Endeavor are almost nothing. No salaries, no large office expenditures. Practically everything you give goes abroad. Will you not in these coming years allow us to send more of your money to these needy nations?

ANNUAL REPORT OF THE PRESIDENT OF THE UNITED SOCIETY OF CHRISTIAN ENDEAVOR

BY REV. FRANCIS E. CLARK, D D., LL.D.

July 6, 1921.

TO THE TRUSTEES OF THE UNITED SOCIETY OF CHRISTIAN ENDEAVOR,
Gentlemen:

Another year and another decade of Christian Endeavor's forty years of history have been recorded, and we have more reason to thank God for His abundant goodness to our cause than ever before. This decade has been more crowded with world-shaking events than any previous one for at least a hundred years. Our geographies have been remade, our histories have been. enormously enlarged, crowns and thrones have toppled, and democracy, though sometimes of a spurious kind, has captured large sections of the earth.

Yet Christian Endeavor has changed but little except by enlarging its borders. It has not been moved from its foundations by the shock of war. It has not been frightened by war's alarums, or led to believe that the world needs another gospel.

To be sure, the war affected our societies as it could not help doing. A world cataclysm that swept into its vortex 300,000 of our best young men to say nothing of hundreds of thousands of our young women in war and relief work of various kinds, could not help shaking our movement like every other to its base. But it did not move it from its foundations, for it is founded on the Rock of Ages, as its motto, "For Christ and the Church" has always proclaimed. As a giant elm is swayed by the hurricane and shivers in every branch and twig, yet is not uprooted, so Christian Endeavor, with its roots firmly planted in the Word of God, and in Christian Experience, bends, perhaps, in a storm, but does not break.

It must not be forgotten that the war bore especially hard upon young people's societies. Their young men were exactly of the enlistment age and of the age of the draft. Far more in proportion to their numbers went from these societies than from the Sunday Schools or the churches. So it is the more remarkable that in the good Providence of God our movement has recovered so quickly and is undoubtedly far stronger and more vigorous than in the peaceful early years of this decade.

The past year has been particularly a year of the "right hand of God." The State conventions as a rule have never been surpassed, in many cases they have never before been equalled. More field-secretaries have been employed than ever before. A multitude of new societies have been formed and many old ones which had been disorganized or halted in their progress by the war, have been revived and strengthened. New denominations have cordially added their quotas to the strength of the movement. Several countries, found only in the new geographies, and carved out of old lands by the bloody sword of war, are now listed among the 97 nations or large dependencies in which Christian Endeavor has found a home. As we think of our cause during this troublous war-racked decade, we can truly say, "The Lord is good and doeth good continually."

During the year I have been able personally to visit more States and local unions than for some years past, and have journeyed some 25,000 miles, including a visit to the coast, to the Southwest and to Mexico, having also returned from an interesting journey in Europe a few weeks before our last official Christian Endeavor year began.

The officers of the United Society of Christian Endeavor have had a year of harmonious and I believe successful service. Leaving the president out of the question, never has the society from the standpoint of the central office been administered more efficiently. The high praise for this year's unusually successful work is, under God, due to my colleagues in the central office, for their unwearied efforts. No eight hour law, five days in the week, has curtailed their efforts or their output.

We mourn the illness of our long-time general secretary, Dr. William Shaw, who for thirty-eight years in various capacities, from the humblest to the most important, has given himself to the advancement of Christian Endeavor. The story of Christian Endeavor can never be written with his vital and constant contributions to its progress, for nearly four decades, left out. We pray God for his early recovery, and for years more of his active presence and service in our midst. We are shocked and grieved inexpressibly by the terrible accident that has just befallen our associate president and his family. May God soon restore them all to complete health.

But I must not dwell longer upon the past. What of the future? I have been asked to serve still longer as your president. Ten long years ago I begged you to choose a younger and worthier man for that office, feeling in my then state of health that I could not longer carry the burden of responsibility, and desiring to resign before old age and failing powers made my work ineffective. Then you would not listen to my plea, and though very near to death on three different occasions since then, I have with God's blessing been able to give nearly if not quite as much time and strength to our work as ever in the past. As my day, my strength has been.

I had hoped that long before this my successor would be inaugurated. But conditions in that respect seem very much the same as they were ten years ago, and no one is yet in sight who can give his whole time to the cause, and no money is in the treasury to pay the salary of a president, which, from the beginning, I have been able to forego.

I see your difficulties and perplexities in choosing a new president and yet I do not see my way to accept the office again unless the responsibilities of the president of both the United Society and the World's Union are very considerably lightened. These burdens are in large part financial. We have not the money to extend our work either in this country or in foreign lands as we might. Twenty-five thousand dollars a year more than we are now able to raise, would, with the favor of the Almighty, enable us vastly to enlarge our work at home and abroad. It would enable us to send efficient secretaries to neglected parts of our own country and to Canada; to multiply ten-fold the number of our national secretaries in China, India and Japan, and to ensure the far more rapid progress of Christian Endeavor in many new countries in Europe.

After these many years of effort to raise necessary money for our work in all lands, I do not feel that I can continue in office unless larger funds are assured for our world-wide work. A trustee of the United Society of Christian Endeavor is not merely an honorary office. I am not complaining. It is largely my fault because I have not appealed to you oftener for help. Let me retrieve my mistake, and urge you to give us larger co-operation and furnish more substantial financial help. One or two hundred dollars a year, on the average contributed or raised from some source by each trustee of the United Society of Christian Endeavor, would largely help us to solve our financial problems.

A college always looks to its trustees for help in enlarging its plant and influence. No more than the Israelites of old can we make bricks without straw. Do not think I am finding fault with any individual. You have all been most kindly and considerate of me personally, some of you for many years, but unless I can have definite assurance from some source of larger resources, not for our office expenses (I do not ask for salary or travelling expenses), but for extension work in all the world, I cannot see my way to accept a re-election, though of course I shall always do all I can for the advancement of the cause to which my life has been devoted.

REPORT OF DANIEL A. POLING, LL.D.

Associate President and Citizenship Superintendent of the United Society of Christian Endeavor at the New York Convention

To the Trustees and Officers of the United Society of Christian Endeavor,

Gentlemen :

I shall make no effort to bring a detailed statement of my department for the past two years. From September, 1919, to September, 1920, I was officially absent from our organization on one year's leave of absence, and during this time served as associate general secretary of the Interchurch World Movement and director of the Laymen's Activities Department. The history of the Interchurch World Movement and the results of its various activities are more or less in your mind. Personally I have no reason to regret the year that I spent with the men and the women who dreamed so true and great a dream. My associations, particularly with the laymen, should be of value to us here in our future work. As vice-chairman of the commission which investigated the steel strike I have followed that grave industrial and economic controversy for nearly two years. The second volume of the report is now on the press. It is my conviction that this report will increasingly contribute to the information of those of whatever group or class who unselfishly labor to bring about better human relations. In general the report has been received favorably both in this country and abroad. In New York City, for instance, seven great daily papers carried indorsing editorials, while only one was unfavorable.

During the past year I have followed the fortunes of this Convention, giving as much time as possible during the week to the field. I have been able to attend eleven State conventions. These gatherings have all been exceptional in size and in program.

My Sunday services have been associated with the Marble Collegiate Church, of which our beloved and honored trustee, Dr. David James Burrell, is the minister. We as a board owe to the Marble Collegiate Church and to its staff far more than a vote of thanks. Without its tireless support under all the circumstances this Convention would have been impossible. The vice-chairman of the Convention Committee is director of religious activities in the church; the executive secretary of the Convention Committee is the president of its Christian Endeavor society. The headquarters of the parade committee have been in the church (and in the beginning the headquarters of the whole executive staff); the choir has practiced in the church auditorium; practically all sessions of the general committee have been held in the church parlors. The physical equipment of the church office has been for months congested with Convention materials and business. Without charge and without complaint this world-famous institution, which for thirty years has been a living testimony for Christian Endeavor itself, has stood behind and beside and before the Sixth World's Christian Endeavor Convention.

During the year we have continued our efforts to make contacts of value with allied agencies, and in May just past the United Society was formally accepted as one of the great educational groups recognized by the Council of Church Boards, the Federal Council of the Churches of Christ in America, the Religious Education Association, etc. We were accorded membership on the continuation committee appointed by the Garden City Conference, and shall have an equal voice in the setting up of the permanent council that has been authorized.

In other directions progress may be reported. Particularly happy have been our recent associations with such organizations as the Y. W. C. A., the Y. M. C. A., etc. It will be of very great importance for us in the future to maintain these associations and to create new ones.

I am glad to report progress in the matter of the presentation of our world-wide activities to Christian men and women of influence and means. While only a beginning has been made, it is a real beginning, and encourages us to expect large things. Within the past few weeks two pledges, one for $2,500 and one for $500, have been secured from friends previously uninterested in our work and unknown to us.

We are now in correspondence, under the direction of Dr. Clark, with certain of our overseas Christian Endeavor organizations, and perhaps several months of next year will be spent in Christian Endeavor work abroad.

I would respectfully suggest that there are some reasons for believing that our present name, "The United Society of Christian Endeavor," is not a name distinctive or distinguishing enough, that perhaps "The World's Christian Endeavor Union" should eventually be used to cover the activities of both of our international organizations. "United Society" does not express to the general public nor to many leaders of groups with which we are associated the international character of our organization. At this moment the Sunday School agencies are changing their names; we should not take the step alone. Objections arising, such as those that concern our copyrighted publications, should of course be fully weighed.

In connection with the citizenship conferences at this Convention plans previously considered and unanimously indorsed by our denominational representatives as well as our field-secretaries are being presented for the holding of citizenship institutes in selected Christian Endeavor centres of the country.

In conclusion we would respectfully testify that we are convinced that Christian Endeavor has not only an important message to deliver, an important program to support, but that in its relationships to the church and to youth it continues to be the strategic and prophetic training school of the Kingdom. It has yet greater things to do than it has done. We believe that it will secure the absolutely necessary, though modest, financial support to "carry on"; that this Convention will show us the way; and that from time to time leaders will stand forth in State and in nation throughout the world, called of God to lead us forward.

CHRISTIAN ENDEAVOR IS GROWING

REPORT OF EDWARD P. GATES

General Secretary of the United Society of Christian Endeavor, Given at the Sixth World's Christian Endeavor Convention, New York City, July 6, 1921

Christian Endeavor is growing.

Nine thousand two hundred and thirty-eight new Christian Endeavor societies have been organized in the past two years. Losses in societies and membership due to war conditions have been more than made up. There are more Christian Endeavor societies today throughout the world than ever before in the history of the movement. The total Christian Endeavor membership is larger. Christian Endeavor is represented in more denominations than ever before. More nations are included in our world-wide fellowship.

Three fundamental reasons have been largely the cause of this remarkable growth.

1.—Christian Endeavor is Adaptable

Christian Endeavor is adaptable in its pledge, its program, its prayer meeting topics, its committees, its membership requirements, its standards, and its service activities. No hard and fast program is laid down which every church must follow, but Christian Endeavor offers itself as the tool of the denomination, church, pastor, and community to be used as special needs require in winning and training young people for Jesus Christ.

Because Christian Endeavor is adaptable these two years have seen a large increase in the number of college Christian Endeavor societies, those in colleges or in churches ministering to college students. In an increasing number of institutions Christian Endeavor has been found to meet the needs of college young people for a co-educational society which gives training in exactly the type of Christian service for which they will be needed in the towns from which they come.

Equally encouraging has been the growth in rural Christian Endeavor. Hundreds of societies have been organized during the two years in small towns or open country communities. Because of its interdenominational character Christian Endeavor is especially adapted to the union church in the small town whose members include many denominations. It also serves as a union society in communities where there are several weak churches, each unable to maintain a separate young people's organization. Because Christian Endeavor requires neither elaborate equipment nor professional leadership, its meetings have been welcomed as practically the only religious service in scores of communities unable to maintain full-time preaching. The country is dotted with churches that have grown up around schoolhouse and family Christian Endeavor societies.

The possibilities for the extension of this rural work are almost unlimited. A careful survey of the field is being made, and our investigation has gone far enough to show that, if funds for organization were available, at least two thousand new rural Christian Endeavor societies could be formed.

Because Christian Endeavor is adaptable it has been found to meet the needs of the highly organized city church. An increasing number of pastors and directors of religious education are appreciating the value not merely of three societies, Junior, Intermediate, and Senior, but of Christian Endeavor societies corresponding to every important department of the Sunday school, with a definite effort on the part of the church to enlist every Sunday school scholar for the training which Christian Endeavor offers. A pamphlet giving the experiences of some of these churches in working out a program of thoroughly graded Christian Endeavor is now in preparation.

Because Christian Endeavor is adaptable it meets the needs of the small church as well as of the large church. The group of a dozen young people can use the Christian Endeavor plan as effectively as the group of two hundred. One pastor wishes to add to or subtract from the number of committees; another wishes to introduce special prayer-meeting topics; another desires a special form of membership pledge. Instead of changing to some entirely new and untried form of organization these leaders have discovered that Christian Endeavor is thoroughly responsive to their needs, and they are using it accordingly.

Because Christian Endeavor is adaptable its service program varies with different communities. It does the work it finds to do with the tools it finds at hand.

In Schenectady Christian Endeavor is rendering a splendid service for the foreign-born population through its Italian Community House.

In Brooklyn, in many counties of New Jersey, in Baltimore, and to an increasing extent all over the country, boys and girls from the congested sections of the cities receive summer vacations through Christian Endeavor fresh-air departments.

In Philadelphia a magnificent service is rendered to the men who come to the city in the great merchant vessels.

In Kentucky and North Carolina and California and a dozen other States Christian Endeavor is serving the men behind prison bars.

Christian Endeavor's service program is built from the bottom up rather than from the top down. Wherever there is a need for the volunteer effort of young people, Christian Endeavor stands ready to help.

Because Christian Endeavor is adaptable it has been able to keep pace with the modern demands for young people's work. Here are a few of the recent developments:

The Life-Work Recruit program has been strengthened by the publication of "Religious Vocations," a text-book on opportunities for Christian service by Mr. Frank Lowe, Jr.

A comprehensive program for citizenship and community service has been prepared under the direction of Associate President Daniel A. Poling.

A sane and constructive program for Christian Endeavor recreation has been prepared and published.

Leadership training courses, through which young people may prepare themselves for more effective volunteer service in the local church, have been prepared, and are being presented for the first time at this convention.

Under the leadership of Superintendent Stanley B. Vandersall the Christian Endeavor Alumni plan has made gratifying progress.

A complete revision of Christian Endeavor publications is being made under the direction of Mr. A. J. Shartle, our treasurer and publication manager. Many new books have been published, and all others are being brought strictly up to date as rapidly as new editions are printed. It is of interest to know that our publishing department reports this year the largest business in its history.

2.—Christian Endeavor is Loyal to the Church

Here is one organization whose responsibility is entirely to the church, pastor, and denomination. The United Society of Christian Endeavor exercises no authority over any local society. The national organization is merely a clearing house for Christian Endeavor information.

Incomplete reports indicate that more than one million dollars has been contributed to missionary enterprises by Christian Endeavor societies during the past two years. At least as much more has been given by the members of these societies directly through church channels.

Four thousand seven hundred and sixty-eight Christian Endeavorers have been enrolled as tithers. For the most part their gifts will go for the enterprises of their own churches and denominations.

Not fewer than half a million young people have been enrolled in classes for the study of missions, the Bible, or church history.

Eight hundred and fifty-five young people have been enrolled for full-time Christian service, and their names ha.e been reported to their own church leaders.

Thousands of vacant pews were filled and thousands of young people were won to Christ through the evangelistic and church attendance emphasis of the Loyalty Campaign.

While on some items, because of their very nature, it has been impossible to secure absolutely accurate reports, it is believed that every goal of the Loyalty Campaign has been more than attained.

At the Buffalo Conference in 1919 a resolution was adopted, placing the approval of future standards and programs for Christian Endeavor in the hands of a commission consisting of the officers of the United Society of Christian Endeavor and the denominational young people's representatives. More than ever the United Society has stood squarely on a platform of hearty co-operation with denominational agencies. We hold that Christian Endeavor is an instrument for carrying to the young people of the churches the program of the denomination to which they belong. Every item in the new program to be launched at this convention has been heartily approved by the denominational leaders.

3.—Christian Endeavor Emphasizes Spiritual Things

Christian Endeavor still believes in a young people's prayer meeting. Christian Endeavor still believes that young people must learn to testify for Christ. Christian Endeavor believes in the vital importance of daily Bible reading and prayer. Christian Endeavor believes in the power and need of personal soul-winning. Christian Endeavor has not been afraid to hold up for young people a standard of out-and-out consecration. And because the church today needs more than ever before these things for which Christian Endeavor stands Christian Endeavor is growing.

THE BEST YEAR IN FINANCE AND PUBLICATIONS

FINANCIAL STATEMENTS

For the Year Ending May 31, 1921, Presented at the World's Christian Endeavor Convention at New York City
July 6 to 11, 1921

BY A. J. SHARTLE
Treasurer and Publication Manager, United Society of Christian Endeavor

We have just closed the most wonderful year in the history of the United Society, wonderful from whatever angle we may view it. In making this sweeping statement we are not unmindful of the splendid record of the past with its magnificent achievements in finance, in membership, and in devotional spirit.

Executive Department

The year 1920-21 has been different in that the financial returns for the world's work were greater, the new publications of Christian Endeavor more numerous, the net sales of literature and supplies the largest in the history of the department, and the net results more definite in the aggregate than in any previous year. How mightily God is leading this organization!

We are here to give an account of our stewardship, an account relating to finance, embodying a presentation of numerical facts stripped of all embellishment. It is only thus a corporation may know, and since it is our privilege to serve, we take pleasure as treasurer of the United Society to report as follows:

Receipts from all sources for the year ending May 31, 1921, $66,119.19; Expenditures, $63,197.55; Balance, $4,499.65. The assets of the corporation as of May 31, 1921, are $455,383.45; liabilities, including annuities and mortgage, $222,840.41; net assets or surplus June 1, 1921, $232,543.04. This shows a gain of $21,190.22 in assets; an increase of $5,985.82 in liabilities, and a gain of $15,204.40 in net assets over the report made at Buffalo, August 6, 1919.

The four outstanding factors to which this increase may be credited are: the financial crusade of August-September, 1920, conducted so efficiently by Secretary Gates; the increase of business in the Publishing Department; the splendid showing of the Alumni Department under Mr. Vandersall; and the Real Estate Department with its steady return of 4½ per cent., net, on an investment of $220,000. This together with the hearty co-operation of World Wide Christian Endeavor and its friends make possible the religious training of the young in one of God's great units of power, Christian Endeavor.

Publishing Department

As Publication Manager, I would report a most successful year in the Publishing Department. It was the best year in the history of the department, best because of results achieved. It was a big year, big in production, big in sales, and big in opportunity. It was indeed a fruitful year, a year teeming with diversified activities characterized as successful Christian Endeavor. When we report of success, we present the actual net sales for the year as $85,000, a net increase of 22 per cent. in sales of Christian Endeavor literature and supplies over that of a year ago. This is the best indicator of the progressive, healthy, virile life of Christian Endeavor. Any organization the members of which will buy $85,000 worth of literature in a single year, that they may know and understand how to function in training the young for the larger work of the church, is surely not ready to sink its identity in a sea of religious uncertainty.

The cash receipts for the year are $93,284.41; the disbursements, $92,876.03; balance of cash, June 1, 1921, $1,707.63; gross sales. $84,938.15; gross profit, $40,097.85; gross expense, $34,234.12; net profit, $5,863.73; assets of the Publishing Department, as of May 31, 1921, $71,331.92, a gain in assets of $12,804.18 over that of a year ago. Our margin of net profit on all sales for the year ending May 31, 1921, is 7 per cent., or 2 per cent. less than for the preceding year. This is accounted for by the increased cost of production, salaries, and transportation, and our hesitancy to further increase the selling price during the period of readjustment. The attainment of a 7 per cent. net profit, when others may fall by the way, brings us within the realm of a perfect number, and outside the classification of a profiteer.

Our productions of Christian Endeavor literature during the year have been numerous. Much of it has been revised, and much is in the course of revision. Our new publications are: "On the Highway" by Ella N. Wood, "Bible Autobiographies" by Mrs. Francis E. Clark, "The New Junior Manual" by R. P. Anderson, "Hand-Work for Juniors" by R. P. Anderson, "Successful Socials" by Mrs. Edward P. Gates, and "Religious Vocations" by Frank Lowe, Jr. We have in the hands of the printer just now copy for the "Endeavorer's Daily Companion" for 1922, "Prayer-Meeting Topics and Daily Readings" and "Junior Prayer-Meeting Topics and Daily Portion," all for 1922 also, "Better Endeavor" by R. P. Anderson. Twenty-five thousand copies of the second edition of the 1921 price list have just been received, and are ready for distribution for the fall trade.

One of the features in the presentation of the report is the splendid result achieved in the Chicago office under the efficient management of our Mr. R. A. Walker. The sales for the year were charge sales, $8,175.45; cash sales, $15,460.49; total, $23,635.94, an increase of $3,614.62 over that of a year ago.

My work in the field during the year was in fourteen states and Canada, covering conventions, rallies, conferences, summer schools, colleges and Bible classes, miles traveled, 24,000.

Yes, this Christian Endeavor, born of God, cradled in the spirit of revival has had a wonderful year, and is a vital, living factor in the life of the church today. Led by a corps of efficient and consecrated men and women it is marching on in a spirit of unbounded enthusiasm, with the hope of youth in its heart, its face radiant with the flush of victory, ever pressing forward for the prize of the high calling of God in Christ Jesus. It is ever thus with youth, and the spirit of youth, the dominating factor in Christian Endeavor, the Christian Endeavor that will never die.

It is while in this spirit that I respectfully submit this report.

ANNUAL REPORT OF REV. ROBERT P. ANDERSON
Editorial Secretary of the United Society of Christian Endeavor

July 7, 1921.

The Board of Trustees of the United Society of Christian Endeavor,
Dear Brethren:

Apart from the work I have done in a general way for Christian Endeavor during the year, as associate editor of *The Christian Endeavor World*, my activities as editorial secretary of the United Society of Christian Endeavor fall into three groups; first, such work as reading and reporting on MSS. submitted for publication, preparing for the printer MSS. of books or pamphlets accepted for publication, reading proof of them and putting them through the press. Second, doing original work, such as writing leaflets, pamphlets and books. And third, giving time to conferences, meetings and rallies.

Dealing with the first class, I have read a number of manuscripts, including three books which were accepted: "Bible Autobiographies," by Mrs. Francis E. Clark; "Successful Socials," by Mrs. E. P. Gates; and "Religious Vocations," by Frank M. Lowe, Jr. All of these books are excellent and timely, and Mr. Lowe's work opens up a new field, that of religious vocations, and supplies for us and for the young people of the world much needed helps. These books were prepared on short notice, and owing to strikes in the printing trade we have raced against time to get them on the literature table of this Convention.

Last summer I read the proof of "The Endeavorer's Daily Companion," for 1921, and I also put through the press Ella N. Woods's fine book of Bible studies for Junior superintendents, "On the Highway."

I put through also a revision of Dr. Shaw's leaflet, "Essential Committees," and his pamphlet, "The Intermediate Handbook." "Junior Recitations," by Professor Wells, was also revised, and additional material was supplied by him for it.

At my request Alumni Superintendent Vandersall wrote an Alumni Day program for Christian Endeavor Week, and Miss Sylvia Tschantz kindly supplied a program for Junior Day of that week. In addition to this I was able to secure from Mrs. William V. Martin a Junior pageant, "Four Decades of Christian Endeavor," all of which helped to make the program for Christian Endeavor Week this year really worth while.

Turning, secondly, to original work done in the past year, I wrote the Christian Endeavor Day program for Christian Endeavor Week, and also the Decision Day program. I wrote a leaflet, "The Christian Endeavor Alumni Council," outlining a program of work which members of the council may take up. I wrote a four-page leaflet on tithing to take the place of one now out of print. I also wrote the Christian Endeavor Daily Readings for Senior societies for 1922, giving a selected Bible reading for every day in the year; and also "The Junior Daily Portion," a similar booklet of readings for the Juniors.

To meet the call for new memory work for Juniors, I prepared a series of Bible verses, "Bible Chimes," and another series dealing with practical Bible subjects. These two series supply memory work for about two years. Besides this, I have prepared and embodied in a new Junior Manual, which is just off the press, half a dozen other series, including a new Great-Word Bible Alphabet, a Bible Biography Alphabet, Bible drills, and a carefully selected series of longer Bible passages from Old and New Testaments which, I believe, every Junior ought to know.

Concerning original books proper, I compiled a book of plans for Junior societies, selecting the best plans from a series I had previously written. These are now in the hands of the publication manager.

I have completed and given to the publication department the MSS. of "The Endeavorer's Daily Companion" for 1922. I have written a booklet which will make between fifty and sixty pages, entitled "Better Endeavor," an analysis of the causes of weakness in some societies, with suggestions as to cures. This booklet was ready in ample time for the Convention, but printers' strikes have held it up and we have not been able to get it through.

Two other books, which I wrote, have, however, come through under great pressure. They are "Handwork for Juniors," and "The New Junior Manual." The former is a new departure and seeks to provide instruction for Junior superintendents in the application of handwork to the Junior topics. The second book is an attempt to place before superintendents the fundamental principles of the Junior society, with some helps toward child psychology and the conduct of the Junior meeting.

It may be of interest to note that the Daily Companion has been translated into Norwegian and is now used by societies in Norway.

Finally, during the year I have written a good many articles on Christian Endeavor for the secular press.

Thirdly, I have attended many meetings of the executive committee of the Board of Trustees of the United Society, and many other conferences. I was a member of the topics committee of the Young People's Interdenominational Commission and assisted in the preparation of the topics for 1922. Besides attending the regular meeting of this commission, I attended a meeting of Christian Endeavor denominational representatives at Cleveland to discuss the policy and plans of Christian Endeavor for the next two years. I also attended a meeting of a committee, appointed by this Cleveland body, to study the Efficiency Chart and possibly present a new scheme. For this committee meeting I prepared a new chart embodying a new principle, and this chart is now under consideration by the members of the committee.

I have attended many Christian Endeavor gatherings, rallies and conferences during the year, and it was my privilege to deliver two lectures on Christian Endeavor before the students of the Gordon Bible College, Boston.

SECOND ANNUAL REPORT OF ALUMNI DEPARTMENT
OF UNITED SOCIETY OF CHRISTIAN ENDEAVOR

July 6, 1921.

TO THE MEMBERS OF THE BOARD OF TRUSTEES,

Dear Brethren:

Two years ago the action was taken by the Board of Trustees that an Alumni Department should be added to the United Society, and a superintendent was called to the work. The actual accomplishment of the department began on September 1, 1919. Previous to that date Mr. Poling and other United Society officers had given large attention to the Alumni work, and had organized eighty-five Alumni Fellowships in various unions of the country.

The first few months were necessarily devoted to systematizing the records and revising the literature. Much work was also done in the field, and many new organizations started, so that last July we reported one hundred and seventy-two Alumni Fellowships. The number at the present time is two hundred and twenty-one, including nearly every one of the strong local unions of the country. We have likewise promoted the organization of the Alumni Councils in the local churches, and, while we have not attempted to keep definite record of these up to the present time, the reports of their usefulness in connection with local Christian Endeavor promotion are most encouraging.

During the past year the Alumni development has been steady and sure. We have, we believe, reached the point where the Alumni idea is accepted as a *definite, integral* part of our life, not a mere privilege or luxury to be the property of a few. Gradually we will train up a generation of Endeavorers who will naturally transfer from the Senior society to the Alumni Council and Fellowship; and that will be a happy experience, for it is much easier to hold a connection already established than to re-establish a severed connection.

With this in mind the department has as many as a dozen pieces of explanatory literature, all distributed without charge, and *The Alumni Journal* which has appeared each quarter since October, 1919. The Alumni idea has spread to other lands, with fine beginnings in Great Britain, South Africa and Australia.

While the sympathetic and social attainments of the Alumni Councils and Fellowships have been many, the direct returns to the United Society have been more clearly evidenced in the financial statements. The receipts by months from the Alumni Fellowships were as follows:

June, 1920	$2,886.33
July	1,702.13
August	352.51
September	795.80
October	2,973.50
November	1,614.20
December	1,309.74
January, 1921	1,047.77
February	688.45
March	976.90
April	405.20
May	664.36
Total receipts	$15,416.89

Of this amount $3,512.53 was paid to the State Unions, according to the agreement whereby the States receive 25 per cent. of all Alumni contributions from their respective jurisdictions, and $11,904.36 remained for the United Society to promote its large program. This amount, approximately one thousand dollars each month, has been of material assistance in the year's financial story. When it is considered that the budget expectation from the Alumni Department for the past fiscal year' was placed at $9,000, the total figure of $11,904.36 or 32 per cent. above expectations, is gratifying. With the ever-increasing number of Alumni contributors, this phase of our financial support should grow larger each year.

The superintendent has sought to be useful in other ways. Much time has been spent in the field, partly in the promotion of general Christian Endeavor work in addition to the Alumni interests. Tours have been conducted in Missouri, Pennsylvania, Oklahoma, Texas, Michigan and Kansas, with separate engagements in many other States. The duties of the treasurer of the World's Union have likewise been given attention.

With gratitude to my co-workers for all their assistance, and to God for all His goodness and blessings in the work.

STANLEY B. VANDERSALL.

LOYALTY DOUBLES INTERMEDIATE TOTALS

Intermediate Superintendent Paul C. Brown's Report for the Two Years of the Loyalty Campaign

During the past year I have travelled 25,153 miles in behalf of Intermediate work. This included trips to eight State conventions, the All-South Convention, the Oregon Summer Conference, the field-secretary meetings in Boston and Detroit, and visits in several other States en route. The trips took me out of my own State ninety-three days, nearly all of which time and expense was cared for by contributions from States and cities along the way. Twenty-two days of office time were put into this job, salary for which has been supplied by the United Society.

In connection with this work I have made 221 addresses during the year, participated in 168 conferences, and made 236 personal calls. I have also written 548 personal letters in promotion of the work.

During the early fall I prepared and distributed several thousand copies of "Special Efficiency Ratings" for Intermediate societies. These were used successfully by many societies throughout the country, first honors going to Immanuel Baptist Intermediates of Newton, Mass., with 720 points, and second place to First Baptist Intermediates of Berkeley, Cal., with 580 points.

During the winter, in connection with General Secretary Gates, the "Graded Christian Endeavor" leaflet was completed and over 16,000 copies were distributed.

State reports were called for the first of June. Nearly all the States having Intermediate superintendents responded. Those that did not are as follows: Alabama, Delaware, Illinois, Indiana, Maine, Missouri, Mississippi, Ohio, South Carolina, Tennessee and Washington. The reports received covered the entire two-year period of the Loyalty Campaign, but also gave statistics for the past year. The results are most encouraging. The States reporting show 1,154 new societies organized, and 30,431 new members received in the two years. Only two States failed to show a substantial net gain in societies, and all but one showed real gains in membership. The average State gain in societies was 60.3 per cent., and in membership actually 72.5 per cent. The comparative totals are as follows: two years ago, 1,179 societies; today, 1,890; two years ago, 25,085 members, and now 43,289. I am making no estimates herewith as to the totals in States that have not reported.

CHAPTER XXV.

BIRTHDAY CELEBRATION

ARMORY, MONDAY EVENING, JULY 11.

Rev. Francis E. Clark, D.D., LL.D., Presiding

AT the opening of the last meeting Percy Foster called on all to join in saying, "Long live world-wide Christian Endeavor." "When I came to New York to help in the convention in 1892," he said, "my firs' impression of the great convention was of the great Ira D. Sankey sitting at a reed-organ with thousands of people before him singing 'Bringing in the Sheaves'; and we are going to reminisce on twenty-nine years ago by singing that hymn now."

In the same way "There's a royal banner given for display" was sung in recollection of Boston, '95; Stebbins's "Saved by Grace," and Excell's "Count Your Blessings" as associated with Washington, '96, followed. "Brighten the Corner Where You Are" came next, each line being assigned to a different State. Then all under twenty-five were asked to sing the first line, those between twenty-five and thirty-five the second, those between thirty-five and forty-five the third, and any over forty-five the fourth. In memory of Peter Bilhorn "Sweet Peace, the Gift of God's Love" was tenderly sung.

"I'll Go Where You Want Me to Go" came next, and it was stated that Mr. Bryan while at the Convention had remarked that in his will he had asked to have that sung at his funeral.

Mr. Foster called on all to rise and sing one stanza of "America," waving flags, handkerchiefs, programs, in response to his signal. While still standing all joined in the Doxology.

Rev. Allen E. Cross, D.D., was introduced to read the hymn he wrote for the Convention, and he handed to Mr. Harvey Worthington Loomis the prize of one hundred dollars awarded for the best musical setting of the hymn, which was then sung with the composer accompanying at the piano. Words and music were in *The Christian Endeavor World* of June 30.

Dr. Clark read these telegrams from Mrs. Poling and from Dr. Poling himself:

"Dan's condition brighter this morning, due, we feel, to the prayers and thoughts of his many friends assembled the past few days. Dan's attitude has been of constant prayer for the success of the Convention. I want to convey to you our deep appreciation and thanks to all who have so graciously and unselfishly remembered us during these days. The boys and myself are doing well.

"MRS. D. A. POLING."

224

"This is my first direct message since the night of the accident, and I am dictating it to my father. I am here because of God, and Lillian would not let me go. She called me back when I lay crushed beneath the car. God gave her superhuman strength, and she moved the wheel a fraction of an inch that allowed me to escape. She had no thought for herself. For years I marched with you all towards New York, but Providence called me aside to mark time during the great event. The Convention, however, is part of my soul, and will live forever in my heart. My text for you is Ps. 91:15, 16. I will be ready for the great advance. The grace of the Lord Jesus Christ be with you all. Amen.   "D. A. POLING."

After the reading of the telegrams and a moment of silent prayer a brief prayer was offered by Mr. Carlton M. Sherwood, followed by an "Amen" from all.

Dr. Clark presented to Florida the Dixie banner, the winning State having attained a percentage of 74.5 in the competition among the Dixie States.

The Convention Committee was then introduced one by one by Mr. Harry A. Kinports, the associate chairman. Each received a hearty welcome, which was duplicated when Chairman Wallis presented Mr. Kinports himself as one that had borne the burden and heat of the day.

At this point Rev. W. H. Hopper, D.D., the president of the Kentucky union, in the name of the union handed to Commissioner Wallis a Christian Endeavor badge as a token of affection for him as a worthy son of the State. The Kentucky delegates joined in "My Old Kentucky Home."

In his acknowledgment of the gift Commissioner Wallis paid a tribute to the home training received from Christian parents, and said that whatever usefulness in the church he might have had he owed to Christian Endeavor.

At this birthday celebration gifts were naturally in order. While the Pennsylvania delegates stood, Mr. Rudolph, the State president, gave to Dr. Clark a hundred dollars to be used for himself.

Dr. Clark in his response said that during these forty years this was the first event of the kind that had come to him at a convention, and he felt selfish to keep the sum and as if he ought to drop it into the contribution box at once. He was somewhat in the position of the poor preacher who on finding a ten dollar bill in the contribution said his acquaintance with it was so slight that he could not call it Bill, but must call it William.

Percy Foster gave expression to the proposal that each delegate have an opportunity to show his regard for Dr. Poling by dropping a single cent into a collection on passing out, the money to be used for sending flowers either all at once or from day to day.

Secretary Gates, "the other Percy," as Mr. Foster termed him, came forward with a handful of beautiful roses, appearing in behalf of New Hampshire, a State too shy to speak for itself, but eager to express its loyalty and love to Dr. Clark, whose home was there during part of his boyhood and his college days.

The American young people surely showed no lack of power to give utterance to their enthusiasm, but Dr. Clark gave Mr. Marsh, the veteran from Australia, a chance to show how Australians do it, which he did by giving the famous cooey. The audience tried to respond, but stood in need of further instruction from Mr. Marsh. After that the cry was heard again and again during the evening until it had to be checked.

In the name of Massachusetts, the State of the Pilgrims, the president, Mr. Asa H. Burgess, of Plymouth, handed to Dr. Clark for the Christian Endeavor archives a bit of Plymouth Rock symbolizing the rock on which Christian Endeavor has been built.

Groves Kilbourn and William Gray, two Endeavorers studying for the ministry at Trinity University, one of them a cousin of Dr. Landrith, who had walked to the Convention from Waxahachie, Tex., getting only a few occasional rides on the way, were received with great enthusiasm.

Dr. Howard B. Grose had been in attendance at the Convention, but was not at the closing session. Rev. James L. Hill, D.D., the only one of the original trustees present besides Dr. Clark, and the contributor of the largest single gift toward the Headquarters Building, gave utterance to apt lessons from the years in an address that will appear in chapter twenty-one.

Mr. Hiram N. Lathrop, for thirty years officially connected with Christian Endeavor, referring to coming conventions, said that Boston would be the place for 1931 and that care would be taken to keep Dr. Clark alive for that fiftieth anniversary.

Commissioner Wallis interjected the remark that there would be one hundred thousand delegates.

"That means he is going to bring Ellis Island to Boston," commented Mr. Lathrop.

The series of messages from those that have been makers of Christian Endeavor history was succeeded by the introduction of a number of representatives of the work in other lands.

Mrs. Edgar E. Strother, one of the secretaries for China, told of the cheer that would go to that land from the Convention and especially the knowledge of the consecration of recruits for service like those volunteering at the service on Saturday evening, which means that workers are coming forward from all denominations. She told of the calls from Siam, the Philippines, Korea; of the large fields of opportunity; of the appeal symbolized by each stripe of the Chinese flag. She called for support of Dr. Clark by generous gifts for the work abroad. "If you cannot go, you can help."

A cheer came from Missouri, the Strothers' home State.

Dr. Amos R. Wells in recognition of Christian Endeavor's fortieth anniversary read the original poem that follows:

Do You Remember? *By Amos R. Wells.*

Do you remember—of course you remember—
When you first signed the Endeavorers' roll?
It may have been June or July or December,
But verily then it was spring in your soul.

Are you recalling—you must be recalling—
That first, faint, stammering prayer-meeting speech?
All of your senses were whirling and falling,
But the great Helper was still within reach.

Do you remember—I'm sure you remember—
Your first poor, hesitant, prayer-meeting prayer?
Only a glimmer of faith's kindling ember,
Just a beginning, but Jesus was there.

Have you forgotten—you can't have forgotten—
When you were leader the very first time?
Voice was of cobweb and tongue was of cotton,
Yet to the angels your words were sublime.

Are you reminded—no doubt you're reminded—
Of your first convention? So wondrous it seemed,
Your soul by its glory was dazzled and blinded,
You sung and you listened and thought that you dreamed.

Many a meeting since that far beginning,
Many a witnessing, many a song,
Many a service courageous and winning,
Many endeavors in Christ become strong.

Still our first ardor and wonder we cherish,
Still see a glory that never grows dim.
Never our first fond affection shall perish,
Love of our Saviour and service of Him.

Ever as duties grow easy and pleasant
New things and hard things arise to be done.
Ah, but our Helper is evermore present;
Who cannot work with the Masterful One?

Ceaselessly changing the sphere of endeavor,
Never a change in the Lord of it all.
On through all changes and onward forever,
Trusting His leading and swift to His call.

He to whose service we plighted our morning,
Bright in His service the noon of the day;
Sweet with His presence the evening adorning,
He shall go with us through all of the way!

Miss Cummings, the head of a Huguenot seminary in South Africa founded by Andrew Murray, brought greetings from the South African Christian Endeavor Union, and told of the many leaders that have been trained in the seminary and have gone forth for service throughout Africa. "The word that the Christian Endeavor union of South Africa passes on to you," she said, "is their motto, 'Greater things than these shall ye see.'"

Dr. Clark spoke of the noble work done in Macedonia by Miss Mary L. Matthews, who was asked to rise, that the Convention might see her.

Mr. W. Roy Breg, Dr. Clark's companion on the recent visit to Mexico, spoke an earnest word of commendation of progress there in Christian Endeavor, and pledged the help of the Southwest toward future advance.

An energetic Hungarian who came to this country seventeen years ago, one of seven children brought by his mother, who was also present at the Convention, is now a senior in Colgate University and pastor of a little Baptist church, having been won from the unbelief that followed his renunciation of Roman Catholicism. He made a telling plea for his countrymen, saying, "Hungary needs you; my people need you." His words were re-enforced by Dr. Clark's testimony about the work of Budapest Endeavorers.

As "the last of the foreigners" Dr. John Pollock caused a laugh by his opening words in addressing his hearers as "fellow republicans." He went on to make good his words by showing how the British empire is virtually a republic, and told of his conviction that Christian Endeavor is bringing the two great republics together in heart and aim and ideal. As president of the European Christian Endeavor Union, however, he represented more than one great nation. He could speak for lands lately enemy countries. "God bless Hungary. God bless Germany," he said as he went on to tell of the new Germany to be and of his prayer that the German republic and the two of which he had spoken might in future be bound together in bonds of affection and as guarantors of the world's peace. He could say this notwithstanding the fact that of his two sons in the war one laid down his life there, and could say it in confidence that his boy would encourage him to do so. Dr. Pollock, asked to bear the greetings of the Welsh and the Irish unions, closed with the greeting of the British union in the form of the apostolic benediction.

Dr. Landrith for the committee on resolutions presented a report whose ringing sentences were punctuated with frequent bursts of applause and were heartily ratified.

The evening that had been so rich in delightful surprises; in music and cheers; in merriment, pathos, sentiment and serious purpose; in fellowship; in reminiscences of the past and prophecies of the future, was summed up in Dr. Clark's closing words. At his suggestion the Convention expressed to its two devoted leaders in song, Mr. Foster and Mr. Rodeheaver, its heartfelt thanks, including also Mr. Sunday, who at much self-sacrifice had released Mr. Rodeheaver that he might be present in New York. With a hearty "Aye," the Convention commissioned Dr. Pollock to bear greetings to all the European lands.

"A warless world by 1923," a slogan proposed by Dr. Clark, was accepted by a rising vote. "Universal brotherhood" was a watchword naturally linked with it. "Never say 'No' to God" was impressed on the hearts of all at the end as it had been at the first session. A brief prayer followed.

Instead of a closing hymn Mr. Foster called for a single stanza from each of several hymns. First came "Blest be the tie that binds." Then in memory of Charles M. Alexander, one stanza of "The Glory Song." Finally, as all were standing clasping the hands of those nearest on each side, and raising and lowering the clasped hands as Mr. Foster led, all sang "God be with you till we meet again."

For the last time all voices joined in the Aaronic benediction followed by the Mizpah benediction; and the Sixth World's Convention of Christian Endeavor started from New York to go to the ends of the world.

NOTE.—For address by Dr. Hill, see chapter of addresses. For resolutions in full, see Chapter XXVI.

CHAPTER XXVI.

THE CONVENTION RESOLUTIONS

(Reported by Rev. Ira Landrith, D.D., LL.D., chairman. The other members of the committee were Rev. Howard B. Grose, D.D., and Prof. James Lewis Howe, Ph.D.)

"TRUSTING in the Lord Jesus Christ for strength," Christian Endeavor humbly accepts the greater duties of this greater day. Grateful for the welcome accorded it by all nations and nearly all denominations, and more thankful for the manifest favor of Him whose name our organization bears and whose will we are pledged to strive to do, and, as far as remembrance might be hindrance, forgetting the things of our first forty years that are behind, we promise that with Him we will go "forward."

Our Program of Loyalty

This Convention has been in many ways the greatest of them all, greatest certainly in the loyalty of its delegates to the business in hand; greatest in attendance upon the conferences of workers, where under the leadership of experts, among them the growing army of efficient field-secretaries, mighty things have been learned and done; and greatest in its militant note of fidelity to the fundamentals of faith and practice. This Convention's message to the Christian young people of the world is: "To the extent that 'the times are out of joint,' only the Great Physician can set them right and heal them, a tremendous truth upon which for the first time both the friends and foes of Christ are coming to agree; and, leaving doubtful disputations to those whose age, scholarship, and leisure may render them safe amid every kind of doctrine, we should be so much about the Master's business that we have time to cling only to the cardinal truths He taught." Rejoicing in the answered prayers of multitudes throughout the world, we acknowledge the almost unprecedented providence that has spared Dr. Francis E. Clark, the founder of Christian Endeavor, to its leadership for forty years of inestimably great fruitfulness. Humbly, teachably, never dogmatically, always democratically, he has gone many times over the world successfully offering, in the name of his Saviour, the instrumentality of the Christian Endeavor Society wherever it might be helpful in obeying the Great Commission. It is our hope that, while he should remain to the end of what we pray may be a very long life at the head of the Christian Endeavor movement, and that his wise counsels may always prevail in its policies, adequate provision can be made whereby he may be relieved of enough of the burdens of detail and exhausting travel to enable him to enjoy somewhat of the rest he has so richly earned, several times almost at the supreme sacrifice. In further testimony of our love for him and our faith in his Spirit-led judgment we hereby commit the whole Christian Endeavor movement to Christian Endeavor Foursquare as proposed in detail by our revered President Clark, whose annual message is by these resolutions adopted as our own platform for the next two years.

Similarly we accept and adopt the aggressive campaign plans graphically suggested by General Secretary E. P. Gates, whose labors, together with those of all the other United Society and World's Union officers, have been rich in blessing to us all. Their annual reports show that

230

Christian Endeavor has just closed its two greatest years. To God belongs all the glory; hence there is in this fact only encouragement to greater zeal and better service, and no occasion for pride of achievement.

Indorsements

The friend of every organization, movement, and individual whose aim is wise and unselfish, and whose work is for the welfare of the church, the child, the home, the school, and high character, we could not even name them all, of course; hence have had to limit indorsement to a few whose causes are most immediately imperative and whose work is intimately related to our own.

We commend to our societies everywhere the work of Near-East Relief, and hereby urge the Congress and President of the United States and the lawmaking authorities and executives of all the other countries we represent to seek the immediate and permanent relief and protection of the suffering peoples of Armenia and other oppressed Bible lands of the Near East. A Christian world cannot tolerate brutal injustice to its weaker members, and a democratic world will not endure it.

We sympathize with the movement for wholesome Federal censorship of moving pictures, which censorship decent film-makers should welcome, and to which the indecent ones must be compelled to submit.

The uncompromising friends of public morals and education we applaud pending Congressional measures for independent departments of Education and Public Welfare, each with a secretary in the cabinet of the President of the United States. Of the public schools we respectfully demand the universal teaching of public and private morality such as is proposed by the Moral-Hygiene Instruction movement; and such an attitude of sectarian neutrality as shall tolerate the presence of no teacher who sneers at Christianity or makes a jest of the Holy Bible.

The religion of Christ commits us to love and not to hate our fellow man, even though he be our enemy; and now as always Christian Endeavor accepts that divine committal. We therefore demand for all Americans equality of opportunity before the law; a fair chance and a square deal for native and foreign born; and freedom from racial and national hatred in government, education and religion. We deplore and denounce as un-American and unchristian such cowardly and unjustifiable mob murders and crimes of arson as lately have occurred South and North, and directly or indirectly because of race-prejudices born of sin and ignorance; and we consecrate ourselves to a spirit, not of antagonism, but of service, toward the alien races among us, whether crowded into the great cities of the East, or laboring in the mines of the interior, or working in the orchards of the Pacific slope. North America has no room for prejudice and hatred, racial, sectional, sectarian, class or partisan; and he is a public enemy who tries to create such strife or to fan the flame of so dangerous and destructive a fire.

Being the *Young People's* Society of Christian Endeavor, we pledge opposition to whatever weakens the moral, mental, or physical life of youth. We deprecate especially the carefully planned campaign of propaganda against the so-called "blue laws," the design of which campaign was to discredit the Lord's Day Alliance which we again indorse, and to make way for the commercializing of Sunday by the movies and money-making sports, encouraging contempt the while for prohibition and other such laws. We demand and pledge respect for the Christian Sabbath; indorse the aims of whatever helps young people to right living and decency and delicacy in conduct and dress, and that promotes happiness in homes and wholesomeness and health in the lives of young people. Naturally, therefore, we oppose the sale of cigarettes, particularly to boys and girls, and are against the unchaste dance and all else that tends to weaken character.

Of President Harding and others in authority we respectfully claim the enforcement of the Hague agreement for the suppression of the opium and morphine trade in China, a trade that just now seems to be carried on by conspiracy between citizens of certain self-styled Christian nations for the ruin of an unchristian Oriental republic that is doing its utmost to save itself from the unspeakable crime of Anglo-Saxon cupidity. We urge international agreement for limiting the cultivation of the opium-poppy to purely medical needs.

Our sympathies have been long aroused for the unmerited sufferings through which an alien government has forced the virile Christians of Korea to go; and as a condition of the continued friendliness of nations we urge that our own Government at Washington insist that Japanese officials in Korea shall interfere in no way with American missions and missionaries, and shall revoke all regulations by which mission schools are closed and devout Christians unjustly imprisoned; that the opium trade, ostensibly outlawed by the civilized world, shall no longer be forced upon the unwilling Koreans.

Peace

Since war hurts all that Christ died for, and helps all that He bade us hate, we urge upon our Government such conference and co-operation with the other nations of the world as shall tend to make them all love peace and pursue it. The pernicious doctrine, "In peace prepare for war," should be supplanted by the truth that the surest route to war is preparedness for war. Universal disarmament marks out the path of peace and restored international prosperity and happiness, and we earnestly ask President Harding to call an early conference for universal disarmament, thus making "America first" for the weal of the world. We also insist that as speedily as possible the United States be permitted to take its merited place of leadership in such a council, association, or league of nations as shall induce or compel all peoples to learn war no more, but brotherhood and the concern of every one for the real welfare of each. Since no nation can ever again live or die to itself, and since national neighborhood is geographically accomplished, let the United States see to it that her sons who died for world peace as well as for world freedom shall not have died in vain. Give us, Mr. President and the Congress of the United States, "disarmament, by agreement if possible; by example if necessary"; and give us no narrow partisanship at all in this black hour of a war-devastated world's Macedonian cry for our help amid the squalor and ashes of unspeakable ruin.

Loyalty to Law and Order

"A saloonless nation by 1920" was and is a fact. There is no saloon under the Stars and Stripes. The saloon was a licensed institution; an unlicensed so-called saloon is a bootleg joint, a traitorously criminal thing. Prohibition is no longer a debatable question; it is a part of the Constitution of the United States, and all loyal Americans must accept and obey it. The Supreme Court of this republic has decreed unanimously that prohibition is "as much a part of the Constitution as is any other portion of that instrument"; that "it binds all lawmaking bodies, courts, public officers and individuals"; and that Congress has no power to "weaken or thwart prohibition," but alone "to enforce it." Hence opposition to the enforcement of the Eighteenth Amendment on the part of individuals or organizations is essential Bolshevism and treason, and refusal on the part of any State to pass and execute laws to aid in its enforcement constitutes morally an act of rebellion and secession. "Unenforced law is the worst evil in any community" truly declared the late Theodore Roosevelt so long ago as his police commissionership of the City of New York; and Abraham Lincoln's prayer was that reverence for law become the political religion of the nation. Both voices should be heeded in this perilous hour. We pledge our support to President Harding in keeping to the letter his pre-election promise, "I shall use all my influence and power to prevent the return of the liquor traffic"; and we respectfully demand of our Congress at Washington that it speedily conclude the passage of pending bills for making more effective the enforcement of the provisions of the Eighteenth Amendment. Furthermore, we pledge ourselves individually to support at the ballot-box and after their election those officials, local, State and national, who observe their oaths of office and who do not perjure themselves by favoring violators of this or any other law of the land. The perjured official is our country's most dangerous traitor and most despicable enemy. True Americans obey the law whether they like it or not. Only anarchists refuse obedience to laws they do not like.

Thanks

The co-operating unions of New York, Brooklyn, and vicinity have won our gratitude for the way in which they have provided for the comfort and success of this Convention. Chairman Frederick A. Wallis and Assistant Chairman H. A. Kinports and their tireless associates have placed us individually and collectively under a great debt of appreciation, as has Executive Secretary Marc E. Jones, whose attention to duty both before and during the meeting has been of the most intelligent and result-producing kind. Further mention of individuals might seem invidious. Certainly a catalogue of all who merit such mention would be impossible. Big, blessed Convention choir, we thank you. The metropolitan press has been generous and sympathetic; and the people of Greater New York have been helpful and considerate. We thank you.

Conclusion

The only deep disappointment we have had during this Convention of Larger Things, which historically it should be called, has been the absence of Associate President Daniel A. Poling and former General Secretary William Shaw, the presence of whom would have added incalculably to what has been, even without their counsel and their call to larger campaigns, the most aggressive of all our national convocations. Our prayers for the speedy and complete recovery of both these beloved leaders will be unceasing; and our covenant with them is continuous loyalty to the cause for which both have been eager to live or willing to die.

Citizenship Resolutions

(Unanimously adopted by the Conference on Citizenship and Community Service, and reported by its leader, Rev. A. Ray Petty, D.D.)

The Sixth World's Christian Endeavor Convention meets in the year 1921 in a world that is floundering in the back washes of the war. The tides of idealism which kept hope in the hearts of the nations while they made their sacrifices have run out. Materialism, greed and licentiousness are rampant and aggressive.

But the great heart of humanity still hungers for brotherhood and longs for a leadership that can find a way to a better world. It is a supreme hour for the church of Jesus Christ, for we have dared to assert that we can supply that leadership.

It is a supreme hour, moreover, for the youth of the church. The young manhood of the great Christian nations of Europe lies buried on the eastern and the western fronts. Buried with them is the hope of aggressive European leadership for this hour. The youth of America, emerging unscathed from the war, must carry the cause of humanity in our generation. This challenge to youth is a ringing challenge to the Christian Endeavor movement to discover, to train, and to inspire leadership adequate for our task.

As a conference of this Convention for the study of citizenship and community service we submit to the Convention our belief in the necesssity for a forward-looking civic and social program for the coming year. Such a program is absolutely essential to release the enthusiasms for service engendered by the Convention and to answer the call of God to our organization.

As elements in such a program we submit the following:

1. That each Christian Endeavor society study the recreational facilities, public, private and commercial, in its community, and inaugurate constructive programs to replace what is discovered to be harmful to the youth of the community. No negative program will suffice.

2. That Christian Endeavor societies everywhere support actively all movements for the strict enforcement of the Eighteenth Amendment.

3. That Christian Endeavor societies seek to obtain declarations from candidates for municipal, State and national offices as to their attitudes on all moral questions that are before the voters, and that they work for the election of such candidates as stand openly and avowedly for Christian ideals in political life, regardless of party.

4. That Christian Endeavor societies seek first-hand contact with foreign-born peoples in their communities. That these contacts be made with open minds and with a willingness to learn as well as teach. That we strive to change the un-American and unchristian environments, social, political and economic, in which these potential Americans are now placed and in which they are learning everything but to love our country; and by such action to strengthen our evangelistic program. There must be better houses, less congestion, more human working-conditions, more adequate educational and recreational facilities, if we are to win them for Christ and America.

5. The problem of Christianizing industrial relationships is one of the most acute moral issues of our time. In many communities at the present moment open warfare or an armed truce exists between capital and labor. If the present situation continues, hatred and bitterness with their disastrous and unchristian consequences will become chronic in our industrial life. This situation in the realm of industry is of profound concern to the church and to all Christians. It is of vital importance to the youth of our organization, for they must live tomorrow in the world that is being made today. We would urge:

First, that Christian Endeavorers make an honest study of the situation as it now exists and of the application of the teachings of Jesus to it.

Second, that we insist on one day's rest in seven for all workers.

Third, that we urge upon the sympathetic consideration of our communities such principles as the eight-hour day in all machine industries; employees' representation in industry; collective bargaining between representatives of employers and employed; in the event of an outbreak in industrial strife after concilation has failed, the submission of controverted issues to arbitration, which even when imperfect is far more Christian than the methods of force.

6. The relationship of the races in many of our communities is a contradiction of the gospel and a menace to our national life. The crime of lynching in particular is a hideous barbarism. We urge the Christian Endeavorer to foster a spirit of brotherly understanding between racial groups and to foster the Christian spirit of a larger toleration in communities where racial antagonisms now exist.

7. Remembering the aspirations of the suffering nations during the war that this should be the last war, and remembering the promises of our Government that these hopes should not be frustrated, we urge that Christian Endeavor throw its united thought into a study of the causes of war, its result, and its prevention; that it lend its support to the rising movement for disarmament which shall ensure international peace, and that it furnish all the co-operation possible to the President of the United States in his purpose to form an association of nations which will serve to minimize the danger of future wars.

Chapter XXVII.

GLEANINGS

The Post's Contribution

THE daily Christian Endeavor editions of the *New York Evening Post*, four pages each day of up-to-date Convention news and Christian Endeavor pictures, were immense successes. The Endeavorers are very grateful to that noble newspaper, one of the few leading papers in the United States. It paid a fine compliment to our society with this Christian Endeavor daily, and materially added to the success of the Convention. Especial credit is due in this Convention to Marc Edmund Jones, the Convention publicity chairman, and to the members of the *Post* staff assigned to the Convention work.

Some lunch rooms displayed window signs, "Welcome, C. E." Was it selfish? No, it meant *service*.

It is a notable fact that Christian Endeavor is the first organization to give its members phonographic records of the voices and messages of its leaders, and there should be a large sale for the three records made by Dr. Clark, and the records made by Dr. Poling, Secretary Gates and Treasurer Shartle.

Two Misquotations

One of the penalties of fame is that men of the caliber of Dr. Clark are often thrust into the headlines of the newspapers and in as sensational a style as possible. One of the New York papers, for instance, heralded in its headlines an alleged statement by Dr. Clark to the effect that he could not find a shadow of Sodom in New York City. What he really said was that New York City was not Sodom or Gomorrah, for there are many high and noble influences working for good in the city.

Another newspaper story was to the effect that Christian Endeavor was not in favor of the enforcement of strict Sabbath laws and laws dealing with matters of public life. Christian Endeavor, of course, is not organized to push any special law or set of laws, but it stands squarely as a movement for law enforcement, and certainly it stands for the enactment and enforcement of laws that protect the sanctity of the Sabbath.

New York is Friendly

The sixteen thousand delegates to the Christian Endeavor Convention in the Seventy-first Regiment Armory find New York hospitable in every sense.

However this city may be famed abroad for the paganism of its inhabitants, which is more conspicuous than typical, the people of New York share the religious feeling of the nation generally. Indeed, in many respects New York is the religious headquarters of the country, just as it is the business or social headquarters. The Christian Endeavor Society itself is very strong here, very proud of its accomplishments, and very glad to meet and entertain its guests.

New York is accustomed to being courteous, notwithstanding the greatness of its crowds and the necessity of celerity in its movements. Against rudeness it frowns with more disapproval than any other city on the continent.

235

New York always welcomes with an open hand when it welcomes at all, and finds in cordiality a relaxation from business tension which makes the indulgence easy.

New York is the safest city in America and the most generous.

This gathering of Christian Endeavorers from all parts of the world, with its inspiration and value toward the perfection of Christian citizenship, is an event which New York welcomes from its heart.—*The New York Mail.*

Unchanged

In the Christian Endeavor conference a speaker commented on the Carpentier-Dempsey battle. "The prize-fight has not changed, but the people have changed," he says. It is true, the prize-fight hasn't changed. It is just about what it always was, except that it is decked with flowery description and advertised with consummate skill.—*The Brooklyn Times.*

Militant Christianity

The attention of the elderly pessimists who are constantly bewailing the degeneracy of the rising generation is respectfully directed to the assembling at New York of 15,000 delegates, representing 4,000,000 young people in all parts of the world who are engaged in some form of active Christian work. With the temperature soaring in the nineties and at a time when most persons who can get away from home and business duties are seeking coolness and pleasure at summer resorts, these thousands of young men and women are meeting to discuss plans for furthering the influence of their organization, the Young People's Society of Christian Endeavor. The United States naturally is most largely represented, but Canada has sent a delegation of 1,000; and there are delegates from Europe, Asia, Africa and Australia and the remotest republics of South America.

For forty years this world-wide organization has been at work raising the standards of young manhood and womanhood. If there were a general lessening of young people's enthusiasm for higher things, if in their opinion religion had "become a bore," as a blasé writer recently expressed it, we should expect to find this society declining in membership and influence. But reports show that it was never more flourishing, its membership being the largest in its history, over 9,000 branches having been established in the last two years. This growth is eloquent of the wholesome state, not of a single religious denomination, but of some eighty different communions which are associated, in this great society. An interesting feature of the Convention is the presence and active participation in the proceedings of the founder, of the society, the venerable Francis E. Clark. It has been his wonderful privilege to live to see the fruition of the seed planted so many years ago. No one can estimate the good that has been accomplished by that thought put into action, but it is typical of Dr. Clark's spirit of enterprise that, not satisfied to rest on past achievements, he hopes to lead the society to still greater attainments in the future.—*The Pittsburgh Chronicle-Telegraph.*

The Finer Side of Life

That the finer things of life have not been wholly lost sight of by young people in these days, amidst the mad pursuit of excitement and amusement, is indicated by the statement that more than four million active members of Christian Endeavor societies are represented by the delegates to the Convention now assembled in New York. And this is only one of several distinct organizations, with enormous membership and with the common purposes of applying the teachings of religion to the conduct of every-day affairs. Contemplation of this fact leads to the conclusion that, after all, the element in society whose dissipations attract so much attention are in no sense truly representative of the great majority of young people of today.—*The Boston Post.*

The Secret of Endeavor Success

If we were asked to tell the secret of Endeavor success, the answer would be that it has abolished the old passive Christianity where one sat and sang one's soul away in everlasting bliss, and substituted a practical and active Christianity. It has put the young to work for the church and the religión which it preaches, recognizing that faith without work is dead, and never more lethal than when it attempts to curb the youthful desire for action, for achievement, or even for evangelization. —*The Lowell* (Mass.) *Leader.*

It is to be hoped that Christian Endeavor's slogan of a "warless world by 1923" may become true. It is rather too good a wish to be realized, however.—*The Portland* (Me.) *Express and Advertiser.*

What One Minister Did

There are 15,000 delegates in New York today in attendance on the Sixth World's Christian Endeavor Convention, which opened last evening in the Seventy-first Regiment Armory. The organization they represent is a potent influence in the moral and social life of this country, with important branches in other lands; and its members have the privilege of seeing and knowing the man who made their strong association possible.

This individual is Francis E. Clark, who in Williston Church, Portland, Me., founded the Society of Christian Endeavor in February, 1881. Dr. Clark has been its president from the beginning, and since 1887 he has given all his time to its affairs.

The creation, extension and maintenance of such a society—its name sufficiently describes its purpose—require the exercise of imagination, great energy, and unusual executive ability. The man who possesses these qualities will go far in whatever activity engages his attention. Dr. Clark would have been a great merchant, a great politician, a great industrial operator.

It is asserted that young men nowadays refuse to go into the ministry because they feel it offers a restricted field. Men like Dr. Clark do not find the religious field restricted.—*The New York Herald.*

What C. E. Stands For

Men and women of all faiths and of no faith yet believe in the things for which Christian Endeavor stands, character and service. Because of that belief the Convention will have the good will of the town, expressed both officially and personally.—*The Brooklyn Eagle.*

The Christian Endeavor Convention in New York City has been a vivid reminder that young America is very far from losing its interest in the churches and in the world's work which they inspire.—*The Springfield* (Mass.) *Republican.*

The Christian Endeavorers at their Convention in New York gave a tremendous demonstration to an appeal for a "warless world." Would a riot have been started if some one had appealed for a mosquitoless world?—*The Troy* (N. Y.) *Record.*

The new slogan of the Christian Endeavor societies is, "A warless world by 1923." Which, if one may judge by present conditions in Europe, Asia and some of the Spanish-American countries, would be "going some," to say the least.—*The Springfield* (Mass.) *Union.*

New York's Goodness

Dr. Francis E. Clark, the honored head of the Society of Christian Endeavor, has shown again that he really believes in applied Christianity by not joining those who delight in bearing false witness concerning New York.

He finds that the great city, where is gathered the largest human population ever brought together, is no Sodom and Gomorrah. He is more interested in the sun than in its dark spots. He sees the better side as well as the worse. He has some appreciation, which many have not, of the mighty work carried on in the great metropolis for human betterment, and is acquainted with the fact that the average New Yorker lives a life which in its industry and morality answers the question of whether great aggregates of people can retain their virtue.

To help bring in the Kingdom here and elsewhere New York gives more per capita than any other community the sun shines on. It has more hospitals, more relief agencies, more institutions to lift up. Dr. Clark has found out these things, and deems it worth while to tell his co-workers so, that they may avoid joining those who have little respect for the Ninth Commandment.—*The New York Tribune.*

"A Warless World"

Just previous to the adjournment of the International Christian Endeavor Convention in New York it was decided that the slogan of the organization during the next two years will be, "A Warless World by 1923."

It is to be hoped that a lasting peace, such as the organization seeks, and such as all the world desires, will be attained within the time indicated. The influence of the Christian Endeavor societies in America and Europe will certainly be exerted along the lines indicated, but it is a great deal to expect within such a comparatively brief time limit.

A number of philosophers have declared that there will always be wars to settle great questions, but that is not so certain in view of the wonderful reforms which have been effected within the past quarter of a century.

Although peace must be effected, through negotiations by governments, powerful religious organizations like the Christian Endeavor Society can do a great deal in the way of influencing public opinion, which can exert powerful pressure upon heads of States, diplomats and legislative bodies, which can be compelled to act along the lines that all the world will approve.—*The Scranton* (Penn.) *Republican.*

The Christian Endeavorers' slogan of a "warless world" is timely and indicative of a splendid ideal. They can all rally for the campaign. —*The Barre* (Vt.) *Times.*

In Spite of the Heat

New York City in its entire history has seldom, if ever, seen a larger and more enthusiastic gathering of young people than that which attended the World's Christian Endeavor Convention last week. For six days—from July 6 to 11—16,000 delegates representing 4,000,000 Endeavorers in all parts of the world filled New York with the very spirit of joyous, untiring yet earnest and purposeful youth. The weather was not propitious, for New York offered to the Convention the hottest week of the present summer. But boys and girls, young men and young women from all States of the Union and Canada and many foreign countries, failed to be daunted by weather which even hardened New Yorkers found hard to bear, and their enthusiasm continued unabated.—*The Continent.*

Young People's Church Societies

Sixteen thousand Christian Endeavor delegates in Convention here offer visible evidence of a vast forest sprung in a generation from a single tiny seed. It is forty years since the Rev. Francis Clark at Williston Church in Portland, Me., established the first Christian Endeavor society, and this week he was again chosen head of the world's organization. From a few dozen members to four millions; from one society in a single religious denomination to many scores of thousands in a hundred denominations, and a growth in the last two years of more than nine thousand societies; from contributions of a few dollars for missionary work to more than a million—that is the record Dr.

Clark may feel something of the pride that Sir George Williams, founder of the Y. M. C. A. felt when the world celebrated its jubilee in Westminster Abbey; that General William Booth felt when he reviewed the Salvation Army in the far corners of the earth, and that General Baden-Powell may feel as he hears of the steady growth of the Boy Scout movement.

A German flag conspicuous in the Convention hall, and British delegates congratulating the Convention on the vigorous wartime advance of Christian Endeavor in Germany, evince the healthy world outlook of this young people's movement. Endeavor leaders boasted after the Boer War that the first cordial meeting of the Dutch and the British was at an Endeavor convention in Cape Town. International conventions have been held all over Europe, in Australia, in Hawaii, at Agra, at Kyoto, and at Fuchau.

The prominence of the spiritual element in this organization carries a lesson to those who wonder how the church can most effectively appeal to young people. Dr. Clark has confessed that its success amazed him. He had tried to reach young men and women by literary societies, musical guilds and social suppers; but eventually these experiments failed. In the Christian Endeavor society the young folk offered their prayers, gave their simple testimonies, and tried to bring their friends into the church. They did a good deal of practical work charitable and institutional; but the spiritual element has always been prominent. That is the root of the matter.—*The New York Post.*

Secretary Strother, of the China Christian Endeavor Union, went about during the Convention with a small silk flag of the Chinese Republic on his arm. The flag contained some Chinese characters, as follows, "Chong Hwa Ming Gwoh." This is the phonetic representation, as near as American ears could catch the sound, of words in the Mandarin dialect meaning, "China People's Country." The inscription on the flag testifies to the awakening of a national consciousness. The country is *theirs,* not their *rulers';* and they are going to run it, too.

Besides printing a special edition of eighteen thousand copies for distribution to the delegates, *The Christian Herald* extended an invitation to visit Mountlawn.

The great procession of Christian Endeavorers in New York City last Saturday was a most impressive object-lesson in loyalty to Christ and His church. Gathered from every State in the Union, and from many foreign lands, they were representative of the best and most promising elements in the world.—*Herald and Presbyter.*

The Two Parades

Two parades were held in New York last week. On Monday, Independence Day, the so-called wet parade was held. Fifteen thousand people marched in the parade. The marchers carried banners of a ribald nature, deriding the law of the land a part of the Constitution of the United States. On Saturday 16,000 people marched in a Christian citizenship parade. It was a part of the national Christian Endeavor conference being held in New York. The banners carried were an inspiration for Christian citizenship and service.

What a contrast between these two marching bodies! The one advocated a disregard for the laws; it quoted Scripture in a sacrilegious vein; it showed a supreme contempt for the highest courts of the land. The other advocated a better citizenship, a cleaner home life, a better place in which to live.

One was an inspiring spectacle of earnest Christian citizens, marching for the cause of righteousness. The other was a demonstration which had for its object the return of John Barleycorn and all his poor relations, such as crime, poverty, disease and vice.

One banner carried in the wet parade read: "The Eighteenth Amendment is unconstitutional. If this be treason, make the most of it."

Had a Socialist parade been organized, and one of the banners carried this motto, "The Fourteenth Amendment, which protects private property, is unconstitutional," the leaders would have been arrested and put in jail. Yet the wet parade denounced the same Constitution. But there is little to worry about. The wet parade laughed itself to death. The hundred thousand shrunk to a mere 15,000. No one took it seriously. —*The Watertown* (N. Y.) *Times.*

The Convention Badge

The New York committee gave the Endeavorers an exceedingly attractive and very original badge. The background was a blue and white ribbon, on which "July 6-11, 1921," was printed in red. The badge was a key resembling the key of a Yale lock, and bearing the motto, "Christianity the Key to Liberty," Liberty being represented by Bartholdi's famous statue, "Liberty Enlightening the World," beautifully reproduced in miniature. Surrounding this design was the motto, "Let your light so shine," with the Christian Endeavor monogram inside it. The shaft of the key bore the words, "New York." The bar from which the key was hung carried the words, "28th International Christian Endeavor Convention." Altogether, the badge was unique and pleasing.

"Post" Workers

The special Christian Endeavor edition of *The New York Post* was planned and arranged for by Marc Edmund Jones, executive secretary of the New York Convention Committee. Messrs. Willis Pratt and Daniel Sullivan were trained newspaper men, having special oversight of the edition. They were aided by the following: Harold W. Drown, president of the Boston Christian Endeavor Union and publicity director of the Massachusetts Christian Endeavor Union; Field-Secretary Freet, then of Massachusetts and now of Ohio; Stephen Von Euw, publicity director of the Boston Christian Endeavor Union; Field-Secretary Sherwood, of the New York State union; Elmer S. Schilling, publicity director of the Pennsylvania Christian Endeavor Union; Field-Secretary Cecil, of the Colorado union; and Mr. Clayton T. Coon, of New York City. No wonder that with this fine staff of zealous workers the Christian Endeavor edition of *The New York Post* was a conspicuous success.

Living By the Golden Rule

No phrase of but two words could carry deeper significance or be more full of spiritual stimulus than "Christian Endeavor." In it, for all its brevity, is comprehended a whole code of personal ethics and of wholesome community conduct.

For the essence of Christian Endeavor is the effort to have the mind which was also in Christ Jesus, to live after His example, and to render obedience to His precepts.

Is it an ideal impossible of attainment in the complicated state of human relations today? Who can assert it? Who can doubt that the ultimate ideal may be attained now and here by individuals who make of the Golden Rule their daily guide to conduct, and who walk in accord with the Lord's requirements—"to do justly, and to love mercy, and to walk humbly with thy God"?

Perhaps to the mass of mankind, entangled in the daily struggle for existence and preferment, unable to understand that what helps their neighbors helps them, and that the Golden Rule brings to those that practice it even more aid and comfort than it vouchsafes to those toward whom it is manifested, the true ideal is unattainable. But every striving toward it brings help and peace. In proportion as mankind makes the effort jealousies, hatreds, strife and suffering will be lessened, and society will progress toward true peace and harmony.

In the effort to advance this progress toward the ideal the members of the Christian Endeavor societies, now in convention in New York constitute perhaps the most effective organized force. In numbers, in world-wide distribution, in earnestness and sincerity of devotion to an ennobling cause, the members of this organization deserve the hearty welcome which New York extends to them.—*New York American*.

Behold, a group of painted, gum-chewing girls on Fifth Avenue during the parade. They were talking and joking about the parade when one of them suddenly broke out, "Well, say what you like, this is a different-looking bunch from the parade we saw last week!" That parade will go down into history as the Booze Parade, a sorry-looking collection of persons who marched in protest against the closing of the saloon.

Dr. John Pollock, president of the European Christian Endeavor Union, is ever ready with wit and wisdom to say something or other that is worth listening to. He is a Scot and is proud of the fact. He points out that his native land is the only country in the British Empire, perhaps in the world, that has two adjectives to describe it. They are Scottish and Scotch. There's a difference. According to Mr. Pollock, a man born of Scottish parents is Scottish. There are no qualifications. Either one is Scottish or not Scottish. One cannot be more or less Scottish. The word connotes nationality. But the adjective *Scotch* connotes idiosyncrasy, peculiarity. There are degrees in it. One man may be more Scotch than another. Mr. Pollock himself, one may say, is decidedly *Scotch*.

Not So Bad

Christian Endeavorers have been holding their Sixth World Convention in New York, and they are out for a "Warless World in 1923." That is a good sentiment and will have pretty general support. Dr. Murray Butler in Paris, speaking of President Harding's invitation to the disarmament conference, declared that the United States was determined that there should not be another world war. "It shall not happen again," he said. "It shall not happen to France. It shall not happen to Belgium. It shall not happen to Britain. It shall not happen to America. It shall not happen anywhere." He said that millions of American citizens felt that way about it, and that ninety-five per cent. of the intelligent people of the world agreed on the principles of disarmament and only differed about the methods.

Dr. Butler is not a gushing person whose emotions run away with him, and yet he spoke more strongly, if possible, than the Endeavorers about doing away with war. He has been quoted as saying that he had not come to Europe as President Harding's Colonel House, which is doubtless true, though it sounds almost over-modest.

The Endeavor policies on most things, as set forth in a list of resolutions, are not so bad. They want a federal censorship of the moving pictures, and oppose the sale of cigarettes to boys and girls, and are against unchaste dancing, and do not want the opium trade to be forced on Korea. They do not want Sunday commercialized, and some of them took a little exception to the current attire and deportment of women. They do not want the girls to paint their faces, and some of them think that skirts should be kept in the vicinity of shoe-tops. Paint on the face is bad style, and seldom well put on, but as for skirts, not in the memory of man have they been as near right as they are now. The best way to regulate the length of them is not to regulate it at all, but to leave that to the dressmakers and the wearers. Leave women to express themselves in their skirts. Those that have the best taste will get them nearest right and set the fashion.—*Editorial in Life*.

Dr. Foulkes had to rise at 4.30 A. M. on the Convention days in order that he might reach New York in time to conduct his Quiet Hour services.

The Great Christian Endeavor Movement

Greater New York, the organ of the Merchants' Association, which is composed of the majority of the business men of New York, devotes its issue of July 27 largely to the International Convention of the Christian Endeavor societies just held in that city, and dwells upon its importance.

Says this paper:

"Christian Endeavor is in a position to be one of the most potent influences in this disturbed world toward restoring order and understanding among the peoples. If the young people of all nations can be brought into a better understanding of each other and into a truer fellowship, they will be building a solid foundation for peace and justice among men."

This fine testimony paid to an organization that some think is only for "kids" and does not amount to much shows in what high esteem it is held by those who know what it means, and what it has done, and what it is still doing, and what its large possibilities are in the immediate future.—*The Sioux Falls* (S. D.) *Argus Leader.*

"A Warless World"

Practical politicians ordinarily pay scant attention to the lucubrations of clergymen and church leaders. But here is an organization which sends 15,000 delegates to its Convention, and which reaches into the heart of every community big enough to have a church. Its members are not commonly deeply interested in politics, taking their political views for the most part from the platforms and candidates of the parties to which they belong. But if this great body becomes interested in a political question for its moral value, as it has been interested in prohibition, it brings to bear upon that issue the pressure of some millions of voters who on most political questions will stand with the party to which they belong without hitching. "A warless world" is a good slogan, morally and politically. Its realization would help powerfully the good causes for which Christian Endeavor stands, and its adoption by a body of this size adds greatly to the demand for a guaranty of world peace.—*The Brooklyn Eagle.*

Christian Endeavor

Few gatherings of which New York has been the place merit more thoughtful attention than that which opens tonight. It will be attended by something like twenty thousand delegates from every State in this Union and from a majority of the countries of the world, and among its speakers will be some of the world's most eminent men.

It is known as the Sixth World's Convention of the Christian Endeavor Society. In fact, it is more than this. It is practically the fortieth anniversary commemoration of that organization, and thus brings to us an edifying reminder of a remarkable career. Forty years ago last February a young and comparatively unknown pastor of an inconspicuous church in a small New England city organized a society among the young people of his congregation for the promotion of Christian endeavor, or the practical application of Christian principles to every-day life. Today the organization has more than four million members, and its founder, Francis E. Clark, is one of the most widely known and most beloved of all contemporary spiritual leaders.

"Success succeeds." Such a record of growth is in itself sufficient vindication and commendation of this organization. Yet it will be profitable for others to consider the secrets of that marvellous success. These are, we should say, chiefly three. One is its practicality. It aims at making the essential principles of Christianity not a matter of preaching one day a week, but of living and acting seven days a week. Another is its catholicity. It is confined to no one church, denomination,

or creed. It does not seek to abolish denominational lines, but on a
basis which transcends them all it provides an agency through which
adherents òf all Christian creeds may harmoniously co-operate. The
third is its sincerity. Nobody has ever suspected it of any insidious
propaganda, of any ulterior purposes beyond those openly and frankly
avowed.

There has been much talk in recent years about the decline of
the churches, for which in some respects and in some directions there
is indeed some cause. Perhaps it may be profitable for those who are
seriously concerned about empty pews and powerless pulpits to review
the record of the Christian Endeavor Society and to consider whether
it might not be possible to solve the problem of the churches by the
application of its principles to them.—*The New York Tribune.*

The Voice of the People

The Christian Endeavorers in convention in New York City declare
that if America does not take its proper place among the nations of
the world for promotion of peace and the prohibition of war, it is
slacking in its duty.

For the United States to seek to stand by itself and play its own
game, regardless of the rest of the world, would be a "damnable thing,"
said one speaker who was cheered to the echo.

Our duty is not only before us, but it is a paramount duty. The
world has been looking to us for leadership, and in America they see
salvation from evils of the past. But we have been evading that duty
and playing domestic politics on the matter. As a result we stand
today pictured as the most selfish people in the world, giving the impression to all that we are in any game for what we can get out of it and
that we don't intend to be incumbered by alliances or league treaties.

Let a few conventions like the Endeavorers in New York assert
themselves in emphatic language, and a league of permanent peace will
be forthcoming.

The knowledge that ushers at the Armory were from the Church
Ushers' Association of New York led to inquiries about forming such
associations in other places.

Dr. Shaw's telegram to the New York Convention was received with
much pleasure, and a telegram was sent him in return, to which he made
the following interesting reply: "Grateful appreciation of loving greetings. My heart reciprocates. Rejoice in report of great opening session.
It is good medicine. I should like to play the bass drum and lead
parade Saturday. Let everybody get into line in Christian Endeavor's
answer to Monday's challenge. Blessings on Dan and you all."—*The
Lockport* (N. Y.) *Journal.*

A Great Event

The New York Christian Endeavor Convention was a great event.
Great in numbers, to be sure, but great in enthusiasm, in purpose, in
hope, in faith, in potential power. No one could be in the great
Armory without feeling the uplift of victory in the air. The volume of
song, the challenge of the mottoes on the walls, the buoyant good cheer
in the faces of the delegates, all betokened the optimism of youth.
The costumes of some of the Western delegates, notably those from
Iowa,—red waists with flannel trousers or skirts,—the cheers, the calls,
the songs and choruses, flags, banners, balloons, umbrellas, the bubbling
good humor everywhere, all produced an effect of youth and joy and
victory.

No one person is able to grasp the whole Convention and tell the
whole story. It was too vast, too detailed, too diverse. But it was
a very wonderful manifestation of the recovery of organized Christian
effort from the disorganization of the years of the war. No one could
be in the Armory without being convinced that Christian Endeavor was

still the most potent force in the life of millions of Christian young men and women. And the pledge the delegates made, which they will carry back to their unions and local societies, will be powerful factors in the development of the Kingdom in the coming years.

E. P. Gates, M.A. At the Convention Mr. Gates earned the degree of Master of Announcements.—*The Christian Intelligencer.*

The Influence of the Convention

The work of the Convention was not confined to the huge Armory in which the main sessions were held nor to the churches and other places which housed group gatherings. The spirit of the delegates was evangelistic, and daily outdoor services were held by scores of teams in various parts of the city, so that every resident had an opportunity to hear the gospel message presented with youthful enthusiasm. On Saturday there was a singing parade of 12,000 Endeavorers up Fifth Avenue, a good-citizenship demonstration which was a revelation to the many thousands of spectators in picturesqueness, color and interest.

But, after all, these were merely the more spectacular features of the Convention, which was termed the world's greatest religious gathering, and it is from the inspiration and enthusiasm which the delegates will carry to all quarters of the globe as the result of the addresses at the main sessions, the devotions of the Quiet Hour services, and the teachings of the leadership training courses, that the success of the Convention must be judged. And no man can attempt to judge how deep that influence will reach.—*The Christian Herald.*

Workers in the Vineyard

There have been few periods in the history of our country when so fruitful a field awaited action by the Christian Endeavorers as is the case today. Their Sixth World Congress is in session. Wherever they may glance, they will find a dire need for spiritual awakening, for moral betterment. It is not the voice of the few ravens among us that calls for a change. Sensible men everywhere are alive to the downward trend. The great religious and moral revival that was to follow the war did not materialize. The churches have admitted their inability to cope with the dangers that surround the grown, the growing, the third generation. Instead of treading the straight religious path, people have veered into by-ways only fitfully lighted by silly superstitions and sillier fads.

To be true to their ideals, the Endeavorers must not miss this rare opportunity. Of course, they must be careful not to ask too much; they must proceed cautiously against the common enemy—agnosticism that parades in various guises, but that always spells indifference to moral principles. They must guard against fads of their own; they must not permit themselves to condemn in a general, theoretical way, when they can do good in a particular, practical way.

The great world church movement fell to pieces because of its unhealthy financial background. There is no reason for the sort of schism that ruined these plans among the Endeavorers. Their cause is not new, it is not overpretentious. If they will make their appeal to those who have perceived the peril that lurks all around us, they will find recruits in the most unexpected quarters. Before long they may be able to lay claim to having consolidated the fine forces for good that are aching for real leadership.

Mrs. F. H. Gates, who presented to Dr. Clark a large necklace made of small looking-glasses connected by beads, inadvertently put Rev. John Pollock, president of the British union, into the shade, for his golden presidential chain was completely outshone by the gorgeous appearance and large size of Dr. Clark's new necklace.—*The Brooklyn Times.*

Still Father Endeavor

Not a few persons who had failed to notice that the Society of Christian Endeavor is holding its Sixth World's Convention at New York are reminded of it by the news that the Rev. Dr. Francis E. Clark has been re-elected international president. It is a reminder of many things in connection with the organization.

Forty years covers the long period of Dr. Clark's connection with Christian Endeavor. What that connection has been is sufficiently indicated by his title of "Father Endeavor Clark." The organization is his still growing child. Beginning in a little town in Maine, it has spread over all the earth. It does not enjoy, to be sure, the singular distinction of hold on the young people of the churches which it had in the eighties and nineties; but the multitude of organizations which have in a way come in competition with it should credit much of their inspiration, more than they do, to its influence. However, that it still embodies much of the virility and consecration and advance of youthful Christianity those who have been attending the gathering in New York will be able to testify when they come home. And not the least of the inspiration springs from the fact that the man who correctly conceived that the living germ of Christianity is the recognition of youth in the church, and the setting of that youth at work, still leads on. He is still "Father Endeavor Clark," the only man for its president.

Rev. John Pollock got off a new one on the Alumni. He said that since coming to this country he had not seen a single silk hat, popularly called in Scotland a "lum" hat. The "lum" in Scotland is a chimney. The Alumni have been jocularly called the Aluminum Fellowship. The "Lums" may yet become the popular designation.—*The New Haven* (Conn.) *Register.*

Show Them Your City

Last week some young people from Iowa came to New York to attend the Christian Endeavor Convention. Their uncle, who has lived in New York thirty-five years, agreed to show them the city. He took a day off. They returned home at eleven at night. The next day he said:

"Did I show them the town? No. They showed it to me. I never felt so infernally cheap and ignorant in my life. I could show them Broadway, some theatres, the place where some movie actress lived. They took me to the Metropolitan Museum, the Museum of Natural History, the old Jumel house, showed me where Hendryk Hudson anchored his ships, where Washington's soldiers drove the British up the Heights, insisted on seeing the Public Library, the warships in the Hudson, and a dozen other things I had to ask policemen or taxi-drivers to find.

"Those Iowa youngsters know more about the worth-while things in New York than we New Yorkers do. Hereafter I'm going to spend a lot of Sundays exploring this old town and learning the interesting things in it. Imagine a ten-year-old Iowa schoolgirl standing in Gramercy Park and telling me its history, while the best I could do to entertain her was to show her a restaurant where a man who deserted his wife for a moving-picture actress usually eats."

We talk of things and see things in which we are interested. Is it possible that people living outside of New York are interested in bigger, cleaner things than we city residents are?

There are more interesting and beautiful things and places to be seen in New York free of charge than there are to be seen by lavish spending of money.

St. Louis has foresight. A long banner announced to the New York Convention that the city wishes the Convention in 1931.—*The New York Mail.*

The Christian Endeavorers

The delegates to the Christian Endeavor Convention now assembled in New York are more moderate in their criticisms of the morals of New Yorkers than certain other visitors who feel moved to condemn the unfamiliar as dangerous and bad. The greater degree of moderation and tolerance which can be developed by persons who feel called upon to express their opinions upon existing conditions in so large and cosmopolitan a city, the more influential for good their remarks are apt to prove. Nobody desires to be impatient in such hot weather.

These well-disposed visitors are welcome as can be in a city big enough to shelter all shades of belief and mainly anxious to keep paraders and sightseers from being sunstruck in an extremely trying time of heat. These good people are not strangers in New York, save to such of our population as never knew New York until within ten years. Their purpose is of the highest, and among all their number probably not one will lay any extra burden upon the attention of the police, save of the sanitary squad. Their present visit may give a new idea to those New Yorkers who never heard of them before; may we all be the better for their presence, and may all live to come another day.

It was both inspiring and encouraging, just before nine on Friday morning of the New York Convention week, to see crowds of bright and happy young people flocking through the corridors of the Armory, looking for the halls in which the denominational rallies were to be held. Evidently denominational loyalty goes well with interdenominational fellowship, as it should, in the light of our Christian Endeavor pledge to be faithful to our churches.

When the doctor went to the aid of Dr. Poling's boy after the accident near Northampton, the boy, a real Endeavorer, said: "Never mind me. Go tend my daddy."

Dr. Clark, Sunday afternoon, asked Rev. John Pollock, of Belfast, to postpone his speech until Monday evening. "Can you hold it till tomorrow night?" he inquired. "If the audience is sufficiently grateful," came the ready response.—*The New York Sun.*

Work and Pray for It

The International Christian Endeavor Convention, which held its meeting in New York City, expressed the widely developed Christian spirit of the day by choosing as its slogan, upon adjournment, the words, "A Warless World by 1923." It will be remembered that the Convention of 1911 fell in with the determined Christian and moral sentiment of that day by choosing for its slogan, "A Saloonless Nation by 1920." As that hope was more than realized, so is it the expectation that in two years some plan may be agreed upon by civilized nations that will eliminate wars from their programs, and that will do away with armaments, on land and sea, save for policing the world against the lawless and uncivilized.

So let us all unite in working and praying for "A Warless World by 1923." Within two years a basis can be found and adopted by the sorely stricken and heavily burdened nations, and may God guide them to the adoption of a plan that He can bless.

Mien Li is what Christian Endeavor is called in Chinese, and the words mean "putting forth your strength," or "doing with all your might."—*The Herald and Presbyter.*

Goodness and Gladness

"Why should the devil have all the good tunes?" asked Rowland Hill nearly a century ago. And that one pertinent inquiry has made his name live in books of quotations and in the minds of the people. It was a good question to ask, and it set the church people to thinking, with the result that there was a refreshing livening up of church music later on. The once prevalent opinion that anything beautiful or delightfully pleasing must necessarily be sinful has been slipping ever since, until now the devil finds his one-time monopoly of pleasing things about played out.

It is interesting to note with what warmth and frequency the New York newspapers are still referring to the Christian Endeavor Convention and the Christian Endeavor parade held in New York week before last. Both were the largest and most interesting in the history of the society. The parade was an eye-opener to the blasé Gothamites, who are pretty well surfeited with such things. Doubtless they thought it would be a perfectly proper, well-conducted event, but hardly worth going many blocks out of one's way to witness.

As a matter of fact the papers report it to have been one of the most beautiful, colorful, snappy, extensive parades that city has seen. Its many thousands of virile young participants filled Fifth Avenue from end to end with life and beauty. The moving-picture takers exhausted their supply of film-ribbon, and clamored for more. The "features" were many and notable. The doings of the entire Convention were vibrant with new life and purpose.

All of which is significant. The churches of the land are going forward with a livelier step and a happier appreciation of their great mission. They are more noticeably registering the great fact that joy is their heritage and, in the very innate nature of things, the good tunes belong to them. Joyousness and goodness should be deemed synonymous terms. More than ever before the world is asking, "Why should a man, whose blood is warm within, sit like his grandsire cut in alabaster?"—*The Boston Traveler.*

Bryan on Christian Endeavor

Hon. William Jennings Bryan, speaking before the Indiana State School for the Deaf at Indianapolis, made the following pleasing reference to Dr. Clark and Christian Endeavor:

"Francis Clark, of Boston, is the founder of the Christian Endeavor Society, and more than five million boys and girls march under the banner of Christian Endeavor. We raised four million soldiers, and got them ready to go into the great war. Only two million went on to the battle-front, the other two million stayed in this country preparing, and yet the four million soldiers who are today our part of the war were one million less in number than the soldiers who marched under the banner of that great Christian Endeavor chief, Francis Clark. There is not a boy or girl here who may not render a service to the world beyond the power that man can calculate."

Only One Flag

None but American flags will be carried in the big Christian Endeavor parade in New York on Saturday, a decision to that effect having been reached yesterday after a lengthy discussion. The question was brought up when the Canadian delegates, who are the largest foreign contingent, asked whether they would be permitted to carry the Union Jack.

The decision was reached without prejudice to the Union Jack or any other national emblem, but because it was believed that the nationalist question might arouse prejudice in a city containing such a polyglot population as New York.

The question involved, however, goes further than the matter of carrying the flags of other nations in Saturday's parade. It is believed by many that there is altogether too much display of foreign flags in parades in this country; and, while the Canadian delegates were fully within their rights in asking about the carrying of their national emblem, for the reason that they are foreign subjects in this country as delegates to a Convention, the reason that sustained them should not hold good for ordinary occasions.

There is hardly a parade of any kind held in this country, such as those held on Decoration Day, Fourth of July, Labor Day and other holidays, where there are not seen the flags of many nations, carried by organizations made up of natives of other countries who have come here as immigrants. They are not the representatives of foreign nations here on a short visit, as is the case of the foreign delegations at the Christian Endeavor Convention, but are persons who have come here for the purpose of becoming American citizens, and as such the flag they should carry should be the Stars and Stripes, rather than the flag of the country they have left to come here.

There has been much discussion about Americanism in the press and the forum, and it is believed that one of the difficulties in Americanizing aliens lies in permitting the latter to identify themselves too much with their former country and its emblems and customs, rather than to impress upon them firmly and on every occasion that they are now either Americans or are about to become Americans, and that they have no longer any alliance or obligation to the country they sprang from.

The sooner the example of the leaders of the Christian Endeavor parade is followed generally in this country, the sooner may the spirit of Americanism find more fertile soil to grow in.—*The Paterson* (N. J.) *Call*.

Christian Endeavor Meeting

With the president and founder of the Young People's Society of Christian Endeavor presiding, the Sixth World's Convention of that organization was opened in New York last night. Forty years from the time of the founding of the society in Portland, Me., in 1881, by the Rev. Dr. Francis E. Clark finds it with a membership of 4,000,000 in thousands of separate societies in all parts of the world. The present Convention is the sixth world meeting,•the first of which was held in 1895. The New York assembly ranks among the world's greatest religious gatherings, and the result of its deliberations will be a great power for good in all parts of the universe.

The success of the Christian Endeavor Society, as it generally is called, is due to two facts, the first of which is that it provides a way for the employment of the activities of young people, to whom participation in church affairs aside from that of membership was closed prior to its formation. The second feature is that it is not confined to any one denomination. Had that been the case, it is likely that its membership now would be comparatively small, and it is not probable that a world's Convention would be under way at this time. Its founder is a Congregationalist minister, who was seeking a way to interest the boys and girls of his church in life's serious work and properly directed social activities. So he started weekly meetings of the young people of his congregation for prayer and consecration, with other religious work and social and literary features as part of the program. The success of his venture was so great that other churches took up the movement, and the Christian Endeavor Society grew from a local organization in Portland to such an extent that in a few years it represented the one unified entity of more than eighty separate religious denominations.

Although its head is a man well advanced in years and there is an occasional instance where other officers are not so young as they once were, the Christian Endeavor Society still is essentially a young people's organization. Its aim is the upbuilding of character during a period of life when it is most easily molded. It provides means for wholesome pleasure in the weekly meetings of the local societies, and in its larger scope it affords a training that cannot help but be beneficial to its members and tend to make them useful citizens and to develop them into a factor to restore to the home some of the religious life that it has fallen away from.—*The Pittsburgh Gazette-Times*.

Christianity Militant

In the vivid pageant presented last week on Fifth Avenue by the delegates to the Christian Endeavor Convention and in the picturesque session of children held in the Seventy-first Regiment Armory as an incident of the Convention lay the refutation of a good many misconceptions concerning religious life in the United States. The thousands of delegates to the Convention, representing the solid and enduring elements of American character, were drawn from every section of the nation, and their attitude toward things spiritual is of tremendous importance to the well-being of the country.

In the pose of the Christian Endeavorers there was nothing of the mollycoddle, nothing of apology, nothing of that defiance characteristic of the defenders of a weakening cause. They were as natural, as convinced, as confident in their belief as they were modern in their methods. If it please anybody to trace back to the mediaeval mystery plays, the parade with floats and costumed participants, it need only be said that in recent years such displays have become common demonstrations of community life and interest. Their historic background does not impair their up-to-dateness.

In the children's convention Biblical characters were cheered when their names were mentioned,—and with a fervor and sincerity which left nothing to be desired. At first this seems a strange manner in which to denote sentiment, yet cheers may be as reverential as any other form of recognition of greatness of character. That man must ever stand mute in his worship of God is not imposed by any creed; that praise and supplication shall always wear the garb of music and prayer need not be believed.

The echoes of those childish voices raised in cheers cannot have been rejected as frivolous or unworthy at the throne of heaven.—*The New York Herald.*

Pageant Juniors

The following list of Juniors who took part in the very pleasant Pageant of the Nations on Junior Day of the Convention, together with the character or country which each represented, is well worth printing:

America—Kenneth Reuss.
Christianity—Jean Scott.
Spirit of Christian Endeavor—Marjorie Siems.
Standard Bearers—
   Grace Graves. Gordon White. Lloyd Crockett.
Goddess of Liberty—Mary Shepperd.
American Indian—Conklin Kipp.
Philippine Islands—Dorothy Webber.
Cuba—William Wallace.
England—Warren Hyatt.
Scotland—J. J. Anmuller.
Canada—Dorothy Eadie.
India—Elizabeth Siems.
France—George Choping.
Holland—Margaret Gallaway.
Italy—Alethia Hanson.
Serbia—George Peters.
Rumania—Wendell Brandow.
Japan—Mary Webber.
China—Ruth Griffiths.
Korea—Winifred Scott.
Burma—Edith Brandow.
Siam—Lillian Kalm.
Armenia—Elizabeth Brandow.
Persia—Ernest Dennis.
Uganda—Beatrice Huff.
Portugal—Ruth Roth. ⁙
Norway—May Barbour.
Switzerland—Alvia Dewsbury.

Other nations were assigned, but the children did not appear.

Replies to the Peace Resolution of the World's Christian Endeavor Convention

Dr. Clark was instructed to send the resolutions in regard to national affairs passed by the World's Christian Endeavor Convention in New York, especially those relating to World Peace and International Good Will, to the President of the United States, to the Secretary of State, and to the chairmen of the committees on foreign affairs, both of the House and of the Senate.

He immediately forwarded them as requested, with a personal note, and has received the following replies:

The White House, Washington.

July 14, 1921.

"My Dear Dr. Clark—The President has read with deep appreciation your letter of July 12, and he asks me to tell you how very much gratified he is by your generous expressions. He also wishes me to say to you that he has noted the copy of resolutions with care and interest.

Sincerely yours,

GEORGE B. CHRISTIAN, JR.,
Secretary to the President."

The Secretary of State, Washington

July 14, 1921.

"My Dear Dr. Clark.—I have received your letter of July 13 with its enclosures, which I have been glad to examine. I am delighted to hear that the Convention was so splendidly successful.

"Thanking you for your kind words concerning my appointment, and with cordial regard, I am,   Very sincerely yours,

CHARLES E. HUGHES."

Committee on Foreign Affairs, House of Representatives, United States, Washington, D. C.

July 15, 1921.

Rev. Francis E. Clark, D.D., President, the World's Christian
    Endeavor Union, Boston.

"My Dear Sir—I thank you for your letter of the thirteenth instant with enclosure, and assure you that the same will have my careful attention and utmost consideration.

STEPHEN G. PORTER, *Chairman.*"

United States Senate, Committee on Foreign Relations

July 18, 1921.

"My Dear Sir—I am directed by the Chairman to acknowledge the receipt of your letter of the thirteenth, together with the resolutions you enclosed, which will be laid before the Committee for their consideration.   Very truly yours,

C. F. REDMOND, *Clerk.*"

Senator Henry Cabot Lodge is the chairman of this committee.

Good Cheer In These Greetings

One of the most interesting of all the greetings received at the World's Convention in New York came from a society at Andong, Korea. It was written in a beautiful native script, but fortunately an English translation was appended. It expressed joy at having established a society in Andong, and wished rich blessings upon the Convention.

Another welcome greeting was from the South American Christian Endeavor Union, which has about 130 societies with a membership of 5,000 in ten different countries. The heart of this greeting is significant, *"He is our peace, who hath made both one."* This union is planning for 1922 a Pan-American convention, to be held in Brazil in connection with the centenary of the independence of that country, and the greeting heartily invites Endeavorers from the United States to attend. The union is seeking to raise $5,000 for the expenses, and would be glad of help.

A letter from Rev. Edmond Gounelle, of Nimes, France, carries the greetings of the Endeavorers of that country.

Turning to the Balkan states, there is a greeting from Esthonia, one of the new countries carved out of Russia. "Separated far," this letter says, "we feel that we are united through Christ's love, and rejoice that we belong to the World Union of young converted Christians. . . . We have now in the union about twenty societies with eight hundred members."

A greeting from the Endeavorers of Germany through their general secretary, Rev. Friedrich Blecher, is a very cordial one. It tells of 1,020 societies—more than double the number in existence in 1914—with 32,000 members. There are twenty provincial unions, ten field secretaries, including two deaconesses for work among young women, while in the headquarters at Friedrichshagen there are twelve officers, one general secretary, and one director. Pastor Blecher reports an upward movement in all the provinces, good work done by the societies, and the consecration of many lives through Christian Endeavor.

Finally, here is a fine greeting from the National Council of the Congregational Churches of the United States, meeting in Los Angeles at the time the New York Convention was in session. It reads: "The National Council of the Congregational Churches of the United States, meeting in Los Angeles, sends greetings to Rev. Francis E. Clark, D.D., LL.D., upon the happy termination of forty years of magnificent service as founder and leader of the Christian Endeavor movement. The Council also sends its greetings to the thousands of young people now meeting in New York in the International Convention of Christian Endeavor. We rejoice in this child of the church, and hereby pledge our strength toward its future growth and usefulness.

"NATIONAL COUNCIL OF CONGREGATIONAL CHURCHES."

The Missionary Exhibit

The first object to catch the eye of one entering the room containing the missionary exhibit was a miniature lighthouse whose lantern proclaimed "Christ, the Light of the World." Set in the sides of the lighthouse were illuminated glass slides of scenes connected with the distribution of the Bible. Around the base were uniformly bound copies of Bibles in many tongues, issued by the American Bible Society.

Over the entrance was the Chinese flag with posters bearing Chinese inscriptions with large drawings giving graphic teaching about the way in which conjunctivitis is spread, how flies convey disease, and other practical object lessons on health.

Near by hung a map of the world showing the distribution of lepers over the world, two millions in all. Photographs and literature told the story of what the gospel is doing for this class of sufferers.

On one side of the room was a cardboard model of Jerusalem. Most of the rest of the space was given to exhibits representing denominational home and foreign missionary boards and all departments of their work. Two machines in corners were showing illuminated pictures, charts, statements, which constantly changed automatically. A series of screens contained on each panel the most telling facts and figures about such topics as the Southern mountaineers, the college girl and the gospel, Christian citizenship, evangelistic work, industrial education, agricultural training, educational missions, and the gospel of healing.

Photographs showed mission schools, hospitals, and methods of work. Samples of the handicraft taught in industrial departments were on display. The dress, customs, and worship of mission lands were represented by objects and small models that drew the attention of interested visitors. There was the cholera goddess carried from house to house in India when the cholera scourge is abroad. There were Chinese shoes of various styles and uses.

Abundant literature for sale and for free distribution was provided, and any missionary committeeman at the Convention could hardly fail to find numerous new ideas in return for even a few minutes spent in that room of suggestions.

This seems to be a Convention of rather big men. Yes, some of them have national reputations well worth while—but we are thinking of the big men physically. Chief among these are Landrith, Gates, Shartle, and Rodeheaver. The last named, familiarly known to practically every Endeavorer as "Rody," gave a wonderful exhibition of his gracefulness in his class in "song-leading" at yesterday's conference period. We can confidently expect an epidemic of graceful song leading all over the country as an aftermath of this gathering.—*The Outlook.*

New York's great international convention of 1892 was forcibly recalled in the opening session of the 1921 convention when Percy Foster of Washington, was introduced to lead one song. He was the leader of song in the 1892 convention and throughout all the years since has been a loyal follower and friend of Christian Endeavor.— *The Outlook.*

Many Simply Couldn't Wait For Convention to Open

Some indication of the interest and enthusiasm in the great gathering in the Armory was displayed Tuesday night when 1,855 delegates visited the building between 6.30 and 10.00 P. M., presented their credentials and received their badges for the first sessions of the convention yesterday.

While the first general session of the convention was not held until 7.30, members of all four divisions were eagerly expectant and, as one enthusiastic young member from Ohio remarked, "just couldn't wait until getting all set and ready for the big meetings."

Dr. Hill's "Iowa, Thank God," Brings Big Shout of Appreciation

Three of the original trustees of the United Society of Christian Endeavor have been present at the sessions of the New York meeting, Dr. Clark, the founder of the society; Howard B. Grose, the vice-president of the United Society, and the Rev. James L. Hill of Salem, Mass., who was present at the closing session and spoke. At the conclusion of his speech, Dr. Clark asked Mr. Hill where he came from, to which Dr. Hill responded promptly, "Iowa, thank God."

This response brought a shout of appreciation, for Dr. Hill's message had been, "Look to the future," and it had been decided that the next convention would be held in 1923 at Des Moines, Ia.

Hiked From Texas to Attend Convention—Two Endeavorers Spend 58 Cents on Transportation to New York

Groves Kilbourn of Waxahachie, Texas, and William Gray of Ferris, Texas, made the entire trip to New York by hiking. They were picked up from time to time by automobiles, but used no railway transportation. They left home exactly three weeks and an hour and a half before arriving in New York.

A Moving Scene

One of the most interesting scenes of the whole Convention took place, and was not photographed, at the door of the Convention hall. John Wanamaker had just driven up to the door in his car. Dr.

Clark happened to be there talking with. some friends. Mr. Wanamaker joined him and Bishop Fallows, of Chicago. At Mr. Wanamaker's left, unnoticed by him, stood Dr. William Patterson, for years pastor of Bethany Church in Philadelphia, Mr. Wanamaker's own church. Dr. Patterson now lives in Toronto. Suddenly Mr. Wanamaker turned and caught sight of Dr. Patterson. Instantly his arm shot out and·curled around the preacher's shoulder. The four men formed a close group, heads together, utterly oblivious .of onlookers.

Sunday Church Services

It is in a city like New York that one realizes the blessedness of the Sabbath. The roar of the city's life is hushed in great measure, and the streets that on business days are full of teeming life are quiet and comparatively empty. It is the day of the church. It is the hour of the spirit. It is true that many use Sunday for pleasure, but there are still many who find in it refreshment for the soul.

The Endeavorers had an opportunity to hear some of the great preachers of the metropolis. Each one chose for himself. Some went up-town to hear Dr. John McNeill, the great Scottish pastor and preacher, who now ministers to a congregation in New York. Others went to hear Dr. Albert Parker Fitch, of Amherst, who was in the famous Brick Presbyterian Church. Yet others took the opportunity to fare far up-town and hear Dr. W. H. Griffith Thomas, who was conducting tent evangelistic meetings. Others, again, went to hear Dr. Robert E. Speer, in the Fifth Avenue Presbyterian Church, while many listened with pleasure to Dr. David James Burrell, who discoursed in the Marble Collegiate Church on "Paul, the Endeavorer."

The Disciples Church, the Central Christian, made a great day of it. They invited their people attending the Convention to a sunrise prayer meeting. Then they provided breakfast for those that came. and a feast of good things in the church service at which Dr. Finis S. Idleman, Dr. D. W. Wilfley, and Dr. A. B. Philputt spoke.

Through Dr. Arthur J. Smith, chairman of the church service committee, many churches had invited Endeavorers to occupy their pulpits. Rev. John Pollock spoke in the Baptist Temple, Brooklyn. General Secretary Gates and Dr. Ira Landrith spoke in the Collegiate Church of St. Nicholas. Field Secretary Huppertz, of Texas, spoke in a Methodist Episcopal church on Broadway; Field Secretary Spafford, of Michigan, addressed the Home Presbyterian Church; Field Secretary Farrill, of Wisconsin, had the service in a Methodist Episcopal church on Sixtieth street; Field Secretary Hetzler, of West Virginia, was in an up-town Methodist Episcopal church; Field Secretary Little, of the South, was in the Second German Baptist Church; Field Secretary Freet, of Massachusetts, was in the Van Nest Presbyterian Church in the Bronx; Secretary Kendall, of the Christian Church. spoke in Olivet Memorial; Secretary Breg, of the Southwestern Federation, spoke in the Morningside Presbyterian Church, whose pastor is an old friend: Lieutenant Duncan B. Curry was in a Methodist Episcopal church in Brooklyn; Field Secretary Hicks, of Connecticut, spoke in the Anderson Memorial Reformed Church, and many other secretaries and ministers took the services in city churches.

Greetings From the First Seventh-Day Baptist Church

The young people of the Seventh-day Baptist bless the spirit and vision and courage of our beloved leader, Dr. Clark, who in projecting the Christian Endeavor movement has helped our young people to discover themselves, to develop themselves, to dedicate themselves, intelligently and enthusiastically, in and to the great moral, social, religious and spiritual interests to which' God has called all young people. We rejoice in the splendid spirit of fellowship and Christian co-operation.

HENRY N. JORDAN, *Representative.*

Between Sessions—By Raspberry

OUR STARS

Twinkle, twinkle, Percy Gates;
Wonder where he hibernates.
We just love his spacious grin;
No one gets beneath his skin.

Twinkle, twinkle, Alvin J.;
He has such a gentle way;
Al could sell a book on care
To a honeymooning pair.

Twinkle, twinkle, Amos Wells;
He's as cheerful as the bells
Ringing out on Sunday morn;
Not a chance to get forlorn.

Twinkle, twinkle, Vandersall,
He's a grace to any hall;
Lines 'em up when old and gray.
Talks 'em stiff and makes 'em pay

John Wanamaker Greets Delegates

John Wanamaker is one of the prominent men active in the religious and business life of the city who have extended a cordial greeting to the delegates to the Sixth World's Convention. Mr. Wanamaker earnestly urges a revival of general effort to rebuild the foundations of citizenship. In his message he says:

"A long continued intimacy with the vision of Dr. Francis E. Clark, who organized the first Christian Endeavor and the wonderful blessing that has rested upon it wherever faithfully officered and managed, is a challenge to the world to seek new strength, new devotion, new funds, and redoubled efforts in every direction for further extension of the work, for the revival of patriotism for our country, revival of religion for our churches, and a new awakening throughout the colleges for young men and women, public schools, and, above all, the Sunday schools, to unite with the Government at Washington to rebuild the foundations of citizenship, the future of which depends upon the mind and heart training of the young people."

Rev. Dr. David James Burrell

The Rev. Dr. David James Burrell, pastor of the Marble Collegiate Church, in welcoming the Endeavorers to New York, urged them all to bring their Bibles. In his message, which was received just before the so-called "wet" parade on July 4, he said:

"Everybody who lives in little old New York loves it but we are neither blind to its faults nor ungrateful to those who offer any contribution towards its betterment. For this reason we shall warmly welcome the invasion of the Endeavorers. We do not expect them to come with long faces, 'just as if their Maker, the Lord of glory, were an undertaker;' but we do expect them to bring with them what Dr. Maclaren called 'the glorious gospel of the happy God.' There are to be two processions in prospect. On July 4 the anti-prohibitionists are to march; and just a week later the Endeavorers are to follow in their train. This will give our people a chance to decide which they like best, the boozers or the Bible folk. Tell the delegates to bring with them their Bibles, their singing books, and their hearts full of the grace of God."

Rev. Charles E. Jefferson, D.D.

"As pastor of the oldest Congregational church in Greater New York, I want to extend to all Endeavorers from all parts of the world a most hearty welcome to the metropolis of America. New

York is built of brick and steel and granite, but New Yorkers have warm hearts. The city may seem to you preoccupied and indifferent to your presence, but that is because it is so big. A vast city cannot look or behave like a village. It has ways all its own. The people of New York are very human, full of the milk of human kindness; and the Christians of the city have to a high degree the mind of Christ. We are glad you have come. Your presence gives us cheer and strength. Do not forget that when within our gates you are among your friends."

Wherein Dishes Are Washed By Military Instructions

"It works—this Girl Scout training," declared Mrs. Selden Bacon in bringing to the Convention the greetings of the organization. In the pragmatic language of psychology, the Girl Scout training gets things done.

Say to a girl, "For the love of the mother who bore you and for fifteen years has toiled for you, please wash the dishes," perhaps the answer will be, "I'm sorry, but I haven't time." But if I take eight girls, put on them a $3.75 uniform, stand them up in line and say "Ready—Front—Wash Dishes," the dishes are washed. It works.

By An Observer

Solid, sane, unpretentious, always there and always dependable, "Al" Shartle, the bag bearer of Christian Endeavor, treasurer of the United Society, has a place in all hearts. Others speak oftener and as well, but nobody else is heard with greater satisfaction and profit.

Dr. Amos R. Wells, the "Caleb Cobweb" of the "Christian Endeavor World" of Boston, looks what he is, an encyclopedia without a dry page, a vast library without a dusty volume. Before his fountain pen the English—pure English—language bows down in respectful reverence and says, "Help yourself, Caleb!"

Edward P. Gates, general secretary, has certainly strengthened his hold on the affections of the vast audiences. When he speaks he says it well and right out loud and then quits; and he speaks only what and when and as long as he must

Two Greetings

"3 P. M. Spent a happy hour at the Convention Friday. John Wanamaker," was a message read by Dr. Landrith, followed by this one: "Dear Father Clark, in behalf of Williston Church and Christian Endeavorers I send heartiest greetings to you and to Christian Endeavorers of all the world. We rejoice with profound gratitude because of your aspiring leadership of Christian young people in all lands. We unite with you and Christian hosts in the sublime faith that Christ is the world's only sovereign. In the power of His cross let us conquer. The grace of our Lord Jesus Christ be with you all. Morris H. Turk, pastor of Williston Church, Portland, Me."

The Convention Boat Ride

After the hot Convention days it was a pleasure for about 3,500 delegates to spend a whole day on the historic Hudson River in a boat ride. The start was made in hazy weather, but soon the sun burst forth, dispelling the mists, and the unbroken journey to Newburgh and back was one long-drawn-out delight.

Of course, after the enthusiasm of the Convention, every one was in the right spirit for enjoyment. It was natural that groups from the same States should gather together, but there was a good deal of mixing around, and no doubt many friendships were formed during the trip. In after years many will meet at conventions and recall this day of fellowship and joy.

The trip was made under the management of Mr. Hiram N. Lathrop, of Boston, a master of excursions, who had made all possible provision for the comfort of the delegates.

Large staterooms were used in some instances for meetings of State delegations who wished to discuss their work, but most of the Endeavorers roamed around and enjoyed the exquisite panorama as the ship glided easily up the river past the Palisades, past what once was virgin wilderness, and past towns and villages nestling along the shores.

Some of the large delegations, such as Massachusetts and Pennsylvania, joined hands and marched around the ship, singing their songs. But the best entertainment of the day was furnished by a delegation of Negroes, perhaps thirty or more, who gathered at the stern and for two hours held a song service which was enjoyed by large numbers. There was a little speaking, but song was the main item, and it was such song as only Negroes can present, soft, delightful, and melodious.

The service of food taxed the capacity of the boat. Seldom has such a crowd been on board the Hendrick Hudson. Most of them were visitors to New York, and few of them had brought luncheons. This threw the burden of feeding the multitude on the ship's management, and for hours the dining room was a scene of ant-like activity. On the other hand, no crowd is better humored than an Endeavor crowd, and every one was patient in the face of a trying situation.

On so large a vessel, of course, no guide could point out for all the different places passed, but there were maps on board and one might follow the trip and read about the various places. Many were interested in seeing Sing Sing prison, famous the country over, that melancholy institution to which is carried the wreckage of civilization in the State.

And yet the contrast between this sad pile and the smiling countryside could not fail to suggest that after all failure is only a spot, a blot here and there.

The First New York Convention

There are many of us who remember the great convention in Madison Square Garden nearly thirty years ago and the delegates from the Christian Endeavor societies all over the world who came up for that great gathering. I think there have been few meetings as fruitful in their result as that convention. The seed that was sown then found good soil and sprang up and has borne harvest a hundredfold in every quarter of the globe. One cannot cherish a greater wish for this convention of 1921 than that it may be in its own measure and in its own day as fruitful for good as the convention of a generation ago.—Robert E. Speer, D.D., Secretary of the Board of Foreign Missions, Presbyterian Church in the U. S. A.

CHAPTER XXVIII.

PICK-UPS

DES MOINES GETS NEXT CONVENTION
Iowa City a Great Religious Centre—Christian Endeavor Strong There and Memorable Convention is Expected There

By A. J. Shartle

THE great Christian Endeavor convention now in session here was highly honored by having to consider as the place for holding the 1923 convention, the claims of Des Moines, Ia., and Portland, Ore. There was a spirit of friendly contest which culminated in the presentation of the advantages of both as convention cities before the board of trustees of the United Society of Christian Endeavor in the Seventy-first Regiment Armory.

The trustees voted by ballot, and the result was Des Moines, 31; Portland, Ore., 21. However, the predominant Western spirit, embodying the spirit of friendship, cordiality, and magnanimity, was manifest, and Portland, in all graciousness, made the vote unanimous and came before the large assemby of trustees and delegates wearing Des Moines buttons, and promising their heartiest co-operation in making the Des Moines convention of 1923 the best yet in the history of Christian Endeavor.

The selection of Des Moines as the next convention city for world-wide Christian Endeavor will tend to promote the widest spirit of Christian fellowship, and there is no doubt there are already groups forming Des Moines 1923 committees.

The great Des Moines Union of Christian Endeavor is one that has for a long time attracted nation-wide attention. It is this same union which, when Uncle Sam made the call for volunteers during the great war, gave up every male officer in order to help fight for a world-wide democracy. Their positions were taken by a group of consecrated, efficient women, who kept the fires burning on the altar of Christian Endeavor in the absence of the men officers, so that when the war was over those who had not paid the supreme price returned to Des Moines to find their union intact and upon a higher plane of efficiency and spirituality in the things necessary to the development of young people for the larger work of the church.

Centre of Religious Spirit

The spirit of the Iowa conventions of the past few years being a state-wide spirit, is but a counterpart of the spirit of Des Moines. possibly the State centre of religious activity in

257

so far as Christian Endeavor is concerned. We feel doubly sure that when in 1923, the great host of Christian Endeavorers from every corner of the globe turn towards the centre of the Middle West, Des Moines will be found in a position where every feature of a great world-wide convention will have been arranged, and every item provided for, so that the continuity of the Christian Endeavor host of successful conventions will not only be maintained but be placed on a still higher level.

The spirit of the Des Moines Christian Endeavor is a criterion of the spirit of Christian Endeavor in the Middle West, and not only will Des Moines rejoice because of its success in having the 1923 convention, but the Middle West will rally to the standard of Des Moines, and together they will prove that the selection of Des Moines for the 1923 convention on the part of the board of trustees was a most happy one.

It was Des Moines that came to Buffalo in August, 1919, with an invitation for the 1921 convention, just as did St. Louis and New York, with the result that the vote was Des Moines first, St. Louis second, with an invitation from Portland, Ore., but not voted upon at that time, and with New York 1921 in a position of honor. Because of our having been unable to hold the 1917 convention in New York, we came to New York for 1921.

And what a wonderful time we are having! Surely the spirit of Christian Endeavor was never more manifest than it is here, and when we take into consideration the fact that nearly 18,000 delegates are registered, attending dozens of conferences, rallies, and inspirational meetings in a sweltering heat, it simply goes to show that Christian Endeavor, born of God, is here to stay, and that with its unbounded enthusiasm neither heat nor cold, sunshine nor storm, nor conditions for which no one is responsible are sufficient to quench the everlasting spirit of this young people's movement ever pressing onward and upward to the glory of God and in His name.

We are having a wonderful convention, and a wonderful time in a wonderful city. Great is New York, and great is the New York 1921 convention! As we leave New York next Monday night facing towards the four points of the compass, I am very sure there will be fixed in the minds and hearts of thousands of young people present today just one thought: "Des Moines in 1923, the best yet!"

TRAINING IN CITIZENSHIP

The training-course on citizenship started with a consideration of the citizenship programs of allied organizations.

The plan of the Young Men's Christian Associations was presented by Mr. A. T. Gregg. It has in view particularly work with boys between the ages of twelve and eighteen. It centers around the character and work of Jesus Christ during

His early life when He was growing in wisdom and stature and in favor with God and man. The thought is that the boy should be swayed by the same Christian motive as the man, but finding expression in activities that appeal to the boy. The program embraces thirty-two standards of excellence, and at the end of each year the boy is brought face to face with a chart testing his progress. In all the program the group idea is made prominent.

The aim of the Federal Council of the Churches was set forth by Rev. F. Ernest Johnson. The conditions in different denominations do not allow a degree of standardization necessary for a detailed program for young people. The work must be essentially educational so far as concerns social service. Some denominations have programs of their own, but there has been little work even in the churches. Present conditions are shown by the difficulty the churches are finding in registering their will against war. The young people far more than the older ones, respond to the thought of the application of Christian principles to social questions, and a need is to supply them with literature to present guidance on this point.

The program of the Boy Scouts, according to their representative, Dr. George W. Fisher, is a course in the practice of patriotism, not the theory. We have been idealists about America. It came as a shock of disappointment when we found that very many in the country had not been touched by the influence. The boys of the country need some work to do. They are practising conservation now, while exploitation of resources has been the rule in the past. A fine thing for a Christian Endeavor society is to oversee a band of Scouts.

Questions and discussion of points suggested by the addresses followed. The importance of Christian leadership in work among the foreigners was emphasized alike by the lack of it and by the rich results of efforts along that line.

THE FOURSQUARE CAMPAIGN

A conference of union workers in the Marble Collegiate Church on Monday at noon gave an opportunity to General Secretary Gates to present to them the new Foursquare Campaign outlined for the next two years' work by Dr. Clark. This campaign will be distinguished from former campaigns by the fact that it puts its emphasis on education rather than on statistics.

1. The first goal or aim of the campaign is to work toward graded Endeavor. This means that we shall try wherever possible to organize in our churches Junior, Intermediate, and Senior societies.

2. The second aim is increased service to the pastor and church. Suggestions were given to unions to make a place in

their rally and convention programs for denominational representatives to present the work and the aims of the churches.

Mr. Gates urged that Endeavorers refrain from criticizing the pastor and refrain also from entering upon expensive enterprises. The gifts of Endeavorers should properly sweep through denominational channels. He warned against unions' permitting outside organizations, however good, to come before Christian Endeavor conventions to present their various special appeals. Christian Endeavor conventions are not places for this kind of thing. These organizations may appeal rather to the denominations.

Advertise Christian Endeavor. Underscore it. Talk it up in the conventions.

3. The third aim is religion in the home. We are not going to try to record the religious homes, but just emphasize the principle of the thing. Secretary Gates urged that the home be made more of a social centre than it is. An occasional "stay-at-home week" might be a good thing to try. And we should laso think about recreation in the home, and service, which is genuine religion.

4. The fourth aim of the campaign is personal stewardship —not only of money, but of time, personality, thought. Mr. Gates outlined definite leadership courses in order that young people may prepare themselves for service for Christ in their home communities. Not all can go abroad or give their whole time to the Lord's work, but all can prepare so that their voluntary service may be more efficient.

A leaflet entitled "Christian Endeavor Unions and the Foursquare Campaign" was distributed to all present. This leaflet clearly explains the relation of the unions to the campaign, and also gives many suggestions of work that unions may do. One section of this leaflet deals with promoting the campaign as a whole. This makes suggestions along lines of advertising material, newspaper publicity, convention and rally programs, and a whole union publicity program.

Although this campaign lays little weight on figures, some records will be kept and recognition of good work will be made. This will include an honor roll of churches, an honor roll of societies, an honor roll of unions, and the standing of the States will be carefully computed and shown month by month. This outline of promotion plans is full of good things. and union workers may secure copies free by applying to the United Society of Christian Endeavor.

The outline of plans also shows that in this campaign there is plenty of work to do for every department in the union.

Mr. Gates answered some questions from the floor in his gatling-gun fashion, and then turned the meeting over to Paul Brown and C. C. Hamilton to make further explanations.

This was one of the most practical meetings of the whole Convention. It was a conference of workers, and the problems dealt with were those that come up on the field. The conference was especially helpful in regard to plans and organization, vital points on which both the enthusiasm and the success of the whole campaign depend.

One point must not be overlooked, namely, that this Foursquare Campaign is the result of careful study not only by United Society officers, but also by trustees of the United Society and leaders of denominational young people's work. Thus there is behind the campaign the leaders of the denominations, the strength of the United Society, and the force of splendid field-workers in the various States.

INDEX

www.ingramcontent.com/pod-product-compliance
Lightning Source LLC
Chambersburg PA
CBHW051820040426
42447CB00006B/292